Monetary
Times

Monetary Policy in Our Times

Proceedings of the First International Conference held by the Institute for Monetary and Economic Studies of the Bank of Japan

edited by
Albert Ando
Hidekazu Eguchi
Roger Farmer
Yoshio Suzuki

The MIT Press
Cambridge, Massachusetts
London, England

This book was set in Apollo by Asco Trade Typesetting Ltd., Hong Kong, and printed and bound by Halliday Lithograph in the United States of America

Library of Congress Cataloging in Publication Data

Main entry under title:

Monetary policy in our times.

 Papers and discussions from an international conference sponsored by the Institute for Monetary and Economic Studies of the Bank of Japan, held June 22–24, 1983.
 Bibliography: p.
 Includes index.
 1. Monetary policy—Congresses.   I. Ando, Albert   II. Nihon Ginkō.   Kin'yū Kenkyūkyoku.
HG205 1983   332.4'6   84-19441
ISBN 0-262-01082-8

Contents

INTERNATIONAL ASPECTS OF MONETARY POLICY

POLICIES TO OVERCOME STAGFLATION

SUMMARIES

Foreword

This volume is the result of the first international conference sponsored by the Institute for Monetary and Economic Studies, which was established in October 1982 in commemoration of the centenary of the Bank of Japan. Sponsoring this conference, attended by a great number of prominent economists from our fellow central banks in Asia, Oceania, North America, and Europe, from international organizations, and from the academic communities at home and abroad, was a special honor to the Institute for Monetary and Economic Studies and also to the Bank as a whole.

For those engaged in monetary policy making, pragmatism remains a hard-and-fast rule. Most of them, I believe, like to consider themselves "practical men," and none of them, to be sure, like to become "the slaves of some defunct economist," as Keynes wrote in the concluding notes of his General Theory. However, central bankers cannot and should not be "exempt from intellectual influences." I was once told that an influential central bank governor in the interwar period had used to ask his staff economists to give him good reasons for his decisions only after he had taken them. This is certainly not the case now at any central bank. All of them have been making enormous efforts to strengthen research activities with the aim of contributing actively to more appropriate monetary policy making.

Despite these efforts made by all central banks, they have been frustrated by serious economic dislocations during most of the past decade. In particular, the combination of sharp price increases, slow growth, and high unemployment posed formidable challenges to policy makers in the 1970s. These phenomena contrasted strikingly with the earlier two decades, when we enjoyed rapid growth and high employment with relatively low inflation.

Indeed, most people now look back on the 1950s and 1960s as a Golden Age for the economies of industrialized countries, which was also beneficial to the world economy in general. By the mid 1960s many economists came to argue that they had finally learned how to apply modern economic theories to practical policy making, and that we could "fine-tune" the economy with short-run macroeconomic policy adjustment to achieve a certain mix of price performance on the one hand and output and employment on the other, depending on our social preference. At the beginning of the 1970s, economic aspirations of people, whether economists or not, were still generally high regarding growth and employment, with little concern about inflation. Why did events in the 1970s diverge so greatly from the general expectations?

In retrospect, we can say that a number of factors which had contributed to the remarkably good economic performance of industrialized countries in the 1950s and 1960s were not sustainable. Let me point out some of them. First, until the late 1960s we had benefited from the Bretton Woods system, which was supported by the dominant strength of the U.S. economy and generally stable U.S. domestic prices. Second, there had been the wave of movements toward free trade with associated benefits of international specialization. Third, a large-scale replacement of capital stock had occurred after World War II, and the shift of resources out of low-productivity sectors into high-productivity sectors with rapid technological progress had been fast and smooth. Fourth, there had been an ample supply of laborers who had maintained a strong positive attitude toward work. Fifth, real energy prices had followed the declining trend, and the supply of raw materials had been stable.

The industrial countries entered the 1970s without full recognition of the nonsustainability of these favorable factors and with a gradual buildup of inflationary pressures and expectations which reflected the generally expansionary posture of macroeconomic policy in the latter part of the 1960s. But it is certainly wrong to conclude that the stagflation of the 1970s was due solely to the weakening or reversal of these factors and the legacy of policy actions in the 1960s. There were also avoidable policy mistakes in the 1970s, such as excessive monetary expansion (notably before the 1973–74 oil-price increase), sharp increases in government spending and persistently large budget deficits, and continued preoccupation with fine tuning and consequent policy U-turns. In the highly interdependent world in which we live now, the undesirable influences of a policy mistake in a country can be quickly transmitted to the rest of the world. The floating-exchange-rate system has not satisfactorily shielded the domestic economy from external influences.

An important lesson we have learned from the unhappy experience of the 1970s is the need for closer international cooperation between policy makers under proper "intellectual influences." It is in full recognition of this need that the Institute for Monetary and Economic Studies organized the international conference on "Monetary Policy in Our Times" as one of its commemorative activities for the centenary of the Bank of Japan. The primary purpose of the Institute is to function as the Bank's center for basic studies such as theoretical and empirical research work on monetary and economic issues and the institutional and historical analysis of monetary and related matters in closer collaboration with the academic community, and organizing this conference was one of the ways in which the Institute has attempted to accomplish this purpose in an international context.

Haruo Mayekawa
Governor of the Bank of Japan

Monetary Policy in Our
Times

Introduction

Hidekazu Eguchi
Yoshio Suzuki

The International Conference on "Monetary Policy in Our Times," organized by the Institute for Monetary and Economic Studies[1] of the Bank of Japan, was held June 22–24, 1983. Participants included academic economists from Japan and abroad, economists from the central banks of countries in Asia, Oceania, Europe, and North America, and economists from international organizations.[2]

This conference was intended to tackle a wide range of issues in the theory and practice of monetary policy.

Both the Overseas Special Advisers and the Program Committee saw the importance of communication and dialogue among economists of different views, academic and central-bank economists, and economists from developed and developing countries. In inviting papers and formal comments on them, the Program Committee sought a balance among economists of different streams of thought.

The conference consisted of five sessions. Session 1 included the opening address of Governor Mayekawa of the Bank of Japan and the keynote speeches of Professors Friedman and Tobin. The keynote speeches evoked considerable discussion in subsequent sessions. Sessions 2 and 3 dealt with the domestic and international aspects of monetary policy, respectively. Session 4 addressed itself to anti-stagflation policies. The conference concluded with session 5, an overall exchange of views among participants.

In sessions 2–4, two academic economists delivered papers on each pre-assigned topic and made supplementary remarks. Four economists from central banks or international organizations commented on the two papers. The floor was then opened for general discussion.

The discussions are summarized in the following sections of this introduction. Here we offer three general conclusions.

First, as the keynote speeches by Friedman and Tobin illustrate, the views, diagnoses, and prescriptions of academic economists differ sharply—especially those of Keynesians and monetarists.

Second, the conference revealed large differences between theory-oriented academicians and pragmatic central-bank economists. The controversy over nominal-GNP targeting was a case in point; central bankers voiced opposition to this proposal on practical and political grounds. Yet each group learned from the other, and further dialogue between them would be productive.

Third, the conference offered economists from developed and developing countries a rare, precious opportunity to communicate. However, most of the papers and discussions at this conference related mainly to major industrial countries. A more intensive and balanced dialogue must await future occasions.

Main Points of Discussion

During the three days of the conference, monetary policy was examined from several perspectives. Many topics recurred repeatedly in different contexts and in different sessions. This summary will focus on the central topics: policies to overcome stagflation, nominal-GNP targeting, international aspects of monetary policy, and monetary policy in Japan.

Policies to Overcome Stagflation

Most of the papers presented at this conference were written with the U.S. economy in mind, and discussions naturally centered on recent U.S. monetary and fiscal policies. Of course, these discussions also have direct and indirect relevance to economic policies in other developed countries.

Appraisal of Recent U.S. Monetary Policy

In the course of the general discussion, Milton Friedman (Hoover Institution) elaborated some of his keynote remarks. As to the recent U.S. monetary policy, he argued that the money supply had expanded excessively since July 1982, that this expansion would inevitably result in an upsurge in inflation with a lag of a year and a half (that is, in 1984), and that such an abrupt change in the Federal Reserve's stance had brought additional uncertainty and instability to the economy. Moreover, Friedman expressed serious doubt about the Federal Reserve System's justification for above-target monetary expansion. The "Fed" claims that institutional changes and financial innovations rendered M1 statistics difficult to interpret and brought a sharp drop in M1 velocity in 1982. However, Friedman pointed out that major changes in the financial system (notably the introduction of Money Market Deposit and

Super NOW accounts) did not take place until the end of 1982. In any case, he said, a decline in velocity is not unusual during recession.

James Tobin (Yale University) criticized the behavior of the Federal Reserve System on quite different grounds. He questioned whether it was prudent for the Fed to stay with its restrictive, rigid monetary targets as long as it did, especially when financial innovation made the economic meaning of the money-supply statistics ambiguous and the velocity of money unstable. The Federal Reserve System was only facing up to reality in suspending its money-supply targets. According to him, the tide of monetarism is on the ebb. Furthermore, although the Federal Reserve System has averted further economic collapse by its change of policy, U.S. interest rates ramain too high. They are still a major obstacle to world economic recovery. He therefore stressed the need for further monetary easing.

In reply to the criticisms by Friedman and Tobin, Stephen H. Axilrod (U.S. Federal Reserve Board) and Frank E. Morris (Federal Reserve Bank of Boston) pointed out that under the current monetary policy the U.S. economy is enjoying recovery with hardly any sign of a new upsurge in inflation. As to Friedman's criticism, Axilrod argued that the recent rapid growth in M1 was partly influenced by precautionary demands in a period of economic uncertainty. But it probably reflected mainly a restoration of demand for M1 due to the lowered nominal interest rates accompanying a decline in the expected rate of inflation. This growth is likely to be a temporary phenomenon typical of a phase of disinflation and to have little impact on the future inflation rate. Furthermore, he opposed Tobin's call for further easing of U.S. monetary policy on the ground that it would endanger sustained noninflationary recovery.

The Transmission Mechanism of Monetary Policy

One major reason for economists' diverse outlooks on the future of the U.S. economy was the difference in the way they see the transmission mechanism of monetary policy.

Tobin, in his comment on money-supply targeting in the United States, questioned the existence of any direct and reliable relationship between money supply and inflation. He argued that money supplies affect prices via aggregate expenditure on goods and services, which are also influenced by other variables. The transmission process involves interest rates and other financial conditions, and the price and inflation outcomes depend on supply conditions in the economy.

Albert Ando (University of Pennsylvania) supported Tobin's argument by citing empirical findings based on his own macroeconometric model. On the other hand, Friedman stressed the impact of money-supply growth on inflation, while noting that the lag with which an increase in monetary aggregates translates itself into prices may vary from case to case. Thomas J. Sargent (University of Minnesota) added that the lag between monetary growth and inflation is getting shorter as private economic agents learn how to adjust their expectations to new information.

Fiscal Policy and Monetary Control

Sargent, in his paper and in the subsequent discussion, expressed his concern about the lack of coordination between fiscal and monetary policies in the United States. The Reagan administration has endorsed the policy of keeping money-supply growth constant. At the same time, its fiscal plans imply large government deficits over the indefinite future. These monetary and fiscal policies are incompatible in the long run; it is inevitable that one of the two must give way sooner or later. It is analogous to a game of "chicken." The future of the U.S. economy depends crucially on the outcome of this game between fiscal and monetary policies. The game injects new uncertainty into the economy; for this reason, the Reagan administration's attempt to revitalize the private sector has ended in failure.

Sargent thought that the lack of coordination between fiscal and monetary policy in the United States stemmed largely from the lack of centralization in policy responsibility under the U.S. system. But Peter Nicholl (Reserve Bank of New Zealand) commented that lack of coordination between fiscal and monetary policy had occurred and persisted even in a number of countries where the policy responsibility was much more centralized. There must therefore be some more fundamental reasons for this lack of coordination than an absence of centralized decision making—for example, conflicts within the government between the cabinet and officials of the treasury and the central bank.

Ando saw in the large government deficit in the United States a fundamental cause of high real interest rates there. He argued further that, since real interest rates on government securities are now higher than the sustainable growth rate of domestic output, the ratio of public debt to GNP is bound to become larger and larger. Deeply worried about this prospect, he suggested that the optimal policy mix is to reduce fiscal deficits while pursuing a more expansionary monetary policy.

Tobin agreed with Ando's point that stability of the debt/GNP ratio will require a different mix of fiscal and monetary policies. He stressed that this was as much a responsibility of the Federal Reserve as of the fiscal policy makers, the administration, and the Congress. Although he agreed that future deficits must be diminished, Tobin felt little concern about current fiscal deficits in the United States, which indeed are stimulating recovery. He said the future deficits in prospect result from noncyclical "primary" deficits on transactions other than debt service, accumulation of cyclical deficits into debt on which interest must be paid, and high interest rates.

In the ensuing discussion, most participants—including those from central banks, such as Richard G. Davis (Federal Reserve Bank of New York) and C. A. E. Goodhart (Bank of England)—agreed that there is no absolute limit to government debt absorption in the financial market. However, the consensus among central-bank economists seemed to be that the persistence of the fiscal deficits and the resulting accumulation of government debt is likely to increase both inflationary expectations and interest rates (thereby exerting negative impacts on private investment) and to complicate monetary policy aimed at price stabilization (since it is inevitable that high interest rates will put central banks under various political and social pressures). In this context, many participants expressed serious concern over the accumulation of fiscal deficits in the United States.

High U.S. Interest Rates and the World Economy

Cesare Caranza (Banca d'Italia), Alexandre Lamfalussy (Bank for International Settlements), and other economists from Europe stated that high U.S. interest rates and their influence on exchange rates had constrained economic policy in other countries. Hermann-Josef Dudler (Deutsche Bundesbank) and Sylvia Ostry (Organization for Economic Cooperation and Development) suggested that the deflationary impact of high interest rates may be greater in Europe than in the United States because of higher interest-rate elasticities of expenditures in Europe. Ostry and Goodhart added that, under the present U.S. tax system, after-tax interest rates are in fact substantially lower than pre-tax rates.

Friedman's view was quite different. He argued that high real interest rates are a transitory phenomenon peculiar to the disinflationary phase following hyperinflation and ought not to be of great concern. It is also not fair to hold the United States solely responsible for high real interest rates in the world. For one thing, there is a world capital market, so that, especially under the flexible-exchange-rate regime, real interest rates in different countries tend to be equalized. Insofar as large public deficits raise interest rates, many countries around the world, and not the Unites States alone, have large public deficits and thus contribute to high real interest rates.

Michael R. Darby (University of California, Los Angeles) and Axilrod argued that under the flexible-exchange-rate system individual countries are more or less capable of pursuing independent monetary policies. They could not really see why concern over the possible short-run effect on the exchange-rate movements should prevent countries from pursuing domestically desirable long-run policies, especially now that U.S. interest rates had seen some decline. Axilrod noted that if the dollar was considered to be unsustainably high on exchange markets—and there was reason to think so—then any short-run downward pressure on another country's exchange rate (if that country eased its monetary policy) would be transitory.

Microeconomic Policy to Overcome Stagflation

Ando identified an upward trend in the natural rate of unemployment during the 1970s and argued that the adjustment of economies to external shocks has become less smooth and more painful. To mitigate this friction, we should try to reduce the natural rate of unemployment through microeconomic structural policies. Robert Raymond (Banque de France) suggested that the natural rate of unemployment could not be precisely measured and doubted its practical usefulness in policy formulation; however, he shared Ando's emphasis on the importance of structural problems, arguing that the institutional rigidities in the goods, labor, and financial markets in his country have constrained the propagation of the effects of monetary policy. Kumiharu Shigehara (Bank of Japan) suggested that, while goods and labor markets remain rigid, deregulation and innovation in the financial markets have magnified the impact of financial disturbances on economic activity and hence made the conduct of macroeconomic policy more difficult. In this context, Ostry suggested that labor markets had now evolved so that wage formation in Europe had shown somewhat greater flexibility since the second oil crisis.

Nominal-GNP Targeting

Since the mid 1970s it has been a common practice among central banks in industrial countries to employ monetary aggregates as intermediate targets of monetary policy. Robert J. Gordon (Northwestern University) challenged this practice. His paper contained both a quantitative interpretation of macroeconomic behavior in the United States and a recommendation for the conduct of monetary policy. The quantitative interpretation concluded that the driving force of inflation is the excess of nominal-GNP growth over the growth in real economic capacity, and that inflation responds to changes in nominal-GNP growth with a long lag. The situation in the United States differs from that in some other countries because financial innovations and accompanying velocity instability have caused nominal-GNP growth to drift away from monetary growth for sustained periods (1975–1978 and 1981–1983) and because inflation-adjustment lags are longer, possibly reflecting the influence of three-year wage contracts.

On the basis of this quantitative interpretation, Gordon went on to propose that monetary policy be steered by a nominal-GNP-growth target or (preferably) a nominal-final-sales target. He claimed that a nominal-GNP-growth target is superior to a monetary target, because it is less sensitive to velocity instability. Thus, under money-stock targeting, the 1975–1978 upward velocity drift allowed the Fed to overstimulate the economy, whereas the 1981–1983 collapse of velocity was allowed to cause unprecedented unemployment. Under a nominal-GNP-targeting regime, the long lag of inflation adjustment would require that the desired path of nominal GNP be planned as long as 10 years in advance.

Once a path for nominal-GNP growth had been chosen to minimize oscillations of unemployment in the future, Gordon's procedure would require monetary policy to keep actual nominal GNP within a reasonable distance from that path. To avoid too-frequent corrections and to avoid overreaction to the past behavior of nominal GNP, monetary policy should limit adjustments in its short-run operating targets (interest rates, monetary base, and/or exchange rate) according to the difference between the target path and its own forecast of nominal-GNP growth over the subsequent four quarters.

Gordon's proposal about GNP targeting provoked a lively discussion. Tobin sympathized with Gordon's advocacy of nominal-GNP targeting; he had argued similarly in his keynote address. According to him, in specifying its targets the central bank should not limit its responsibility to nominal variables (prices, monetary aggregates) of the economy but should consider also its influence on real variables (output, unemployment, capital formation). He stressed the importance of discretion in economic policy and of responding to information and forecasts of the state of the economy. For example, a nominal-GNP-growth target should be somewhat higher in the early stages of economic recovery, as today, but should be lowered as full employment is approached.

Friedman, on the other hand, was skeptical about the idea of GNP targeting. In his view, Gordon's proposal would mean nothing but a return to the practice of monetary policy in the 1960s, when the central bank did not announce an intermediate target and manipulated financial variables on the basis of a wide range of indicators. To allow central banks to choose as a target a variable that it cannot affect directly would eliminate accountability for deviations from the target.

In general, the central-bank economists were negative toward nominal-GNP targeting, though on rather more eclectic or practical grounds. They shared concern for the problems with rigid monetary targeting in periods of fluctuating money demand. They advocated a "multi-scoped" approach that would attend to a wide range of information, including interest rates and the exchange rate. There was a strong feeling among them, however, that a long-term nominal-GNP target is neither feasible nor desirable in practice. Most central bankers envisioned no practical alternative to monetary aggregates as a nominal anchor by which monetary policy can be evaluated. The following specific difficulties were identified:

• The process of choosing a GNP-growth target may be too vulnerable to political influences. Once a public target for nominal-GNP growth is set, the central bank will inevitably be forced to split this target growth into real-GNP growth and price increase, and to make them public. It would be extremely difficult to keep political factors out at this stage; for example, in a practical horizon of 2 years, and given that lags between money and prices are longer than lags between money and real GNP, it would be difficult to make it understood that more real GNP over the short run is not always better than less (Axilrod).

• There is a historical tendency for official forecasts of nominal GNP to be biased upward. If central banks commit themselves to such biased forecasts, there is a great danger of triggering or accommodating inflation (Goodhart, Lamfalussy).

• The central bank can hardly achieve control of nominal-GNP targets with some precision using monetary policy only. Deviations of nominal GNP from the target path may jeopardize the credibility of the central bank (Axilrod, Dudler). In addition, there is a danger that the central bank may be put in the position of assuming exclusive responsibility for countercyclical policy, when in fact its influence is more limited and when the actual GNP is also influenced strongly by fiscal policy (Axilrod).

• Central banks, in pursuing their monetary policy, already take account of nominal GNP. Moreover, in many countries the government forecast of the nominal-GNP growth rate plays an important role in determining the target level. An explicit commitment to such GNP forecasting, however, would only make monetary policy more vulnerable to political pressures (Dudler).

• Even if the idea of GNP targeting is accepted, it would be meaningless to establish a long-term target path over 10 years, since the interest of the

Congress and the public does not really go beyond the first year or two of the covered period (Axilrod).

- For many developing countries, there are problems in GNP targeting. GNP data are usually available only on an annual basis and with a long time lag. Because of strong growth and rapid changes in the economic structure, a stable and predictable relationship among GNP, money, prices, and employment is hard to establish. In essence, such targeting as proposed has limited application (Lin See Yan, Bank Negara Malaysia).

International Aspects of Monetary Policy

Determination of Exchange Rate under Floating System

The discussants agreed that, although theories of exchange-rate determination had made remarkable progress in the last decade, they had proved themselves incapable of explaining the actual fluctuations or movements in the exchange rate. Charles Freedman (Bank of Canada) pointed out that exchange rates often do not adjust to inflation-rate differentials as smoothly as purchasing-power parity postulates (at least in the short run) and that real-interest-rate differentials or an unanticipated change in real interest rates may be playing an important role in the maladjustment of exchange rates to inflation differentials. Although central-bank economists agreed that interest-rate differentials are an important factor in the determination of exchange rates, Darby referred to recent findings that short-run fluctuations in exchange rates can be better approximated by a random walk than by any specific factors.

Increased Financial Interdependence between Countries

Akihiro Amano (Kobe University) reported on a simulation analysis using a macroeconomic model of Japan (Kyoto University's KYQ-Flex Model) and a world economic model (the EPA World Economic Model). He indicated that with floating exchange rates and increased capital mobility, the transmission of monetary disturbances has accelerated. Caranza and Lamfalussy noted that under the flexible-exchange-rate system, external disturbances, especially those originating from major countries' monetary policies, had become serious constraints on the conduct of domestic policy elsewhere.

With regard to the overshooting of real exchange rates under floating, Lamfalussy observed that it had tended to get more amplified and protracted and that it may exert an adverse influence on economic activity, particularly on fixed investment in exporting industries. He added that short-run fluctuations in nominal exchange rates had also become more erratic. Darby responded by expressing doubt whether short-run variability in exchange rates had indeed increased in recent years in comparison with the period immediately following the transition to general floating.

Exchange-Rate System

Alternatives to the present floating system were explored with regard to alleviating the adverse effects of international transmission of monetary disturbances. Referring to the recent performance of the European Monetary System, Lamfalussy expressed cautious optimism about the possibility of stabilizing exchange rates. Georg Rich (Swiss National Bank) argued for the independence the floating system allows for small open economies. Shigehara suggested that an economy's degree of "openness" ought to determine the relative importance of the exchange rate in policy formulation, but that in most countries the exchange rate should be used as at least one of the relevant indicators in the formulation of domestic monetary policy. In this context, Teh Kok Peng (Monetary Authority of Singapore) referred to the fact that Singapore, a typical example of a small open economy, had adopted the exchange rate rather than monetary aggregates as the object of monetary targeting.

International Policy Coordination

Amano argued that, in view of increased monetary interdependence under the floating system, international coordination of policies is desirable to circumvent the adverse effects of independent policy formulation by each individual country. The call for closer international coordination was supported by economists from central banks of medium-sized countries and international organizations. Rudolf R. Rhomberg (International Monetary Fund) observed that any policy coordination involving an arrangement on exchange rates, which in turn depend on domestic policy, must inevitably extend itself to the sphere of domestic policy formulation.

Friedman expressed opposition to proposals for policy coordination. He argued that coordination of domestic monetary policies between the United States, Germany, and Japan would hardly be practicable because of ambiguity in burden sharing between the monetary authorities. He suggested instead that each individual central bank pursue stabilization policy in the interest of its own country from the longer-run point of view.

Issues Related to Developing Countries

The high U.S. interest rates, it was pointed out, pose serious problems to the developing countries as well as the developed countries, though on rather different grounds. In his paper Ando made the observation that, with real U.S. dollar interest rates higher than the growth rates of developing countries, the external debts of these countries will grow without limit unless they manage to run an offsetting surplus on current account. Ahn Seung-Chul (Bank of Korea) and other participants pointed to the need for lower U.S. interest rates so as to reduce the burden of external debt servicing, which has imposed constraints on economic development.

On the other hand, there was a consensus among participants from developing countries that, as far as the conduct of domestic policy is concerned, the high U.S. interest rates have not proved to be as serious a constraint in developing countries as in the developed countries. The reasons for this, as cited by Lin and by Chaiyawat Wibulswasdi (Bank of Thailand), include widespread imperfections in the real and financial markets as well as in the distribution system, price control of essential goods, and an absence of market-oriented interest-rate determination. Monetary policy works mainly through regulatory or direct means on the availability of bank funds. On the whole, exchange rates are rather insensitive, in the short run, to changes in monetary policy.

Further, a majority of economists from developing countries stressed the need for stable recovery in the industrial countries to improve opportunities for exports. It was agreed that economic expansion in developed countries is an essential precondition for the development of developing countries. Lin added that the sustained expansion of world trade is equally important. The welfare of many developing countries depends on the continuing expansion of trade. However, the persistence of protectionism and the prolonged preoccupation with the global debt problem present obstacles to an early and stable recovery of world growth and employment. At the same time, warnings that inflation in developed countries would have adverse effects on the rest of the world were frequently noted. Ahn claimed that about 60 percent of the inflation in the 1970s in Korea was attributable to external factors. Wibulswasdi added that prices in Thailand are more sensitive to developments in international commodity markets than to changes in domestic monetary policy. Yu Guantao (People's Bank of China), Slangor (Bank Indonesia), Edgardo P. Zialcita (Central Bank of the Philippines), and others emphasized that for the developing countries it is of utmost importance that developed countries overcome stagflation as promptly as possible.

Monetary Policy in Japan

Koichi Hamada (University of Tokyo) and Fumio Hayashi (University of Tsukuba), in their joint paper, elaborated on the backgrounds of the relatively favorable macroeconomic performance of the Japanese economy. They identified as important factors the flexibility of real wages and the effectiveness of discretionary monetary policy. (Anticipated money does matter in Japan.) They then offered the following explanation for the success of Japanese monetary policy in recent years: First, the bitter lessons learned from the experience in the aftermath of the first oil shock have given the Bank of Japan back its *de facto* authority in pursuing its monetary policy. Second, the success of monetary management has been aided by the relatively modest pace of financial innovation, which in turn reflected stable prices. Third, the Bank of Japan has, without being distracted by erratic short-run fluctuations in narrow monetary aggregates, attached importance to the medium-run stability of a broader aggregate (M2 + CDs). In addition, the multi-scoped approach of policy formulation—which makes full use of various financial and economic indicators, including interest rates and exchange rates—has also contributed to the Japanese success in monetary management.

Most of the participants had no objections to this view. They agreed that monetary policy in Japan, especially since the second oil crisis, has responded to the difficult situation and has contributed favorably to the Japanese economy.

Friedman agreed that monetary policy in Japan has been successful. However, he claimed this was not a consequence of discretionary policy but rather one of keeping monetary growth stable. In comparison with the United States and the United Kingdom, the annual growth rate of the money supply in Japan displays little variability. In Friedman's words, the Bank of Japan is "less monetarist in rhetoric but far more monetarist in practice."

Marie-H. Lambert (National Bank of Belgium) and Goodhart questioned the viability of the Bank of Japan's direct control (window guidance) on bank loans in a more internationalized and diversified financial system. In response to this question, Yoshio Suzuki (Bank of Japan) made the following remarks: It is not that all interest rates have hitherto been regulated. There have existed a fairly wide range of markets, in which interest rates are determined by demand and supply, among which are the interbank money market, the Gensaki (RPs) market, the certificates of deposit (CDs) market, and the secondary market for government bonds. Window guidance is used as a supplementary or stopgap measure to speed up portfolio adjustment by banks. In Japan, monetary policy operates mainly through interest rates in these ways:

With a rise (or a decline) in market interest rates, banks adjust their portfolios so as to restrain (or expand) lendings bearing sticky interest rates. Interest regulations tend to widen differentials between regulated interest rates and freely moving market interest rates, causing disintermediation, which in turn affects bank lending. Changes in the overall interest-rate level affect economic activity.

Finally, Hamada, referring to the actual conduct of monetary policy, expressed the opinion that further monetary relaxation is desirable to promote economic recovery. Responding to this, Shigehara observed that, although domestic considerations may warrant some further reduction in interest rates, the unilateral reduction of interest rates by the Bank of Japan is—in this increasingly interdependent world—likely to induce depreciation in the yen rate, thereby intensifying trade frictions between Japan and its trading partners.

Notes

1. In October 1982 the Bank of Japan reorganized the Department of Monetary and Economic Studies into a new Institute for Monetary and Economic Studies in commemoration of its centennial. It was then decided that the Institute would arrange an international conference once every two years with a view to promoting mutual understanding between economists in the academic profession and those in central banks and international organizations while encouraging basic research at the Bank of Japan. In planning and organizing the present conference, which is the first in a series, we were proffered advice from many individuals. In particular, we would like to express our most sincere appreciation to Milton Friedman and James Tobin, Honorary Advisers of the Institute, for their valuable advice in the planning stage and for the active leadership they displayed in the course of discussion, and to Franco Modigliani for his numerous useful suggestions, though we could not secure his attendance at the conference. We are also grateful to Ryuichiro Tachi, Koichi Hamada, and Yoichi Shinkai, who acted as members of the Program Committee, and to all participants who presented discussion papers of high quality and/or made valuable oral contributions at the conference. Finally, we wish to express our gratitude to the members of the staff of the Bank of Japan, particularly those of the Institute, for their active involvement.

2. See list of participants at end of this volume.

1

Monetarism in Rhetoric and in Practice

Milton Friedman

To judge from the financial and popular press, monetarism has been tried in the past 10 years in the United States and Great Britain and has been found wanting. This judgment confuses monetarist theory with monetarist policy, and central-bank rhetoric with central-bank practice. Far from discrediting the implications of monetarist theory, the events of the past few years simply add another dollop of confirmation to the overwhelming mass of prior evidence. The rhetoric of the monetary authorities has indeed been monetarist, but their policies have not been—or, to be generous, have been only partly so. The deviations in practice from monetarist policies have had the adverse consequences predicted by monetarist theory. Far from weakening the case for a monetarist policy, these consequences reinforce the case. In developing these ideas, I shall summarize briefly what I take to be monetarist theory and monetarist policy, and then examine recent experience in the United States.

Monetarist Theory

I dislike the term *monetarist*. The theory that now goes by that label has a perfectly respectable ancient name, namely the quantity theory of money. However, the usage has become established, so I shall simply conform.

The essence of the quantity theory of money is the distinction between the nominal quantity of money and the real quantity of money. The theory, as elaborated by many theorists and as given content by many empirical studies, regards the nominal quantity of money as determined by conditions of supply and the real quantity of money as determined by conditions of demand. Though the variables affecting supply and the variables affecting demand are interrelated, they are also largely independent of one another. That is particularly true currently since the monetary authorities almost everywhere determine the nominal quantity of money.

The demand for money is best expressed as a demand for a given amount of purchasing power, that is for real money balances. The chief variables determining the quantity demanded are some measure of real wealth or real income as a scale variable, the costs of holding money (which include the returns on money and on alternative assets), and taste variables (one of which is specially relevant for our present purpose, namely the degree of instability anticipated in the economy).

The real return on the component of money that does not bear interest is the negative of the rate of change of prices. This is why inflation and inflationary expectations play such an important role in monetarist analysis.

Monetarist analysis goes on to say that any changes in the nominal quantity of money that are anticipated will be fully embedded in inflationary and other expectations, but that unanticipated changes in the quantity of money will not be so embedded. An unanticipated increase or decrease in the quantity of money tends to affect total nominal spending some 6–9 months later in the United States, Japan, and Great Britain. The initial effect is primarily on output rather than on prices. Prices tend to be affected only 18–24 months later. This does not mean that there is no further effect on real quantities. On the contrary, the delayed impact on prices means an overshooting of output (up or down, depending on the initial stimulus), which will then require an overshooting in the opposite direction to allow the price level to reach its appropriate level. As a result, the cyclical reaction pattern in both output and prices tends to last for a considerable period—years, not months. That is precisely why monetary instability is so destructive of economic stability.

These generalizations are for countries, such as the United States, Japan, and Great Britain, that have not experienced long periods of erratic and volatile inflation. For countries that have, including some of the South American countries and Israel, these lags are not relevant. In such countries, unanticipated changes in money tend to affect prices much more promptly, and the whole reaction process is much shortened. However, for the first set of countries, inflation tends to be rather inertial and to be determined by a fairly long-term average rate of monetary growth. As a result, short-term fluctuations in monetary growth are reflected primarily in real output.

The monetarist analysis also views the effect of changes in the nominal quantity of money on interest rates as complex, since it is first in one direction and then later in the opposite. An unanticipated acceleration in monetary growth tends at first to lower interest rates, through a liquidity effect. Subsequently, however, as the higher rate of monetary growth produces an increase in nominal spending, the demand for loans rises and interest rates reverse course, starting to rise. Later still, the actual and anticipated rates of inflation go up, at which point the Fisher price-anticipation effect comes into play and interest rates rise beyond their initial level.

Empirically, the liquidity effect (again for such countries as the United States, the United Kingdom, and Japan) has lasted about 6 months, and the subsequent income effect about 12 months, before the price-anticipation effect starts to be important and interest rates rise above their initial level. However, these lags are less well-documented, and I believe less consistent, than those between monetary growth and nominal-income growth and inflation. In the United States, from October 1979 to July 1982 the liquidity effect appears to have lasted only 2 or 3 months, after which interest rates moved in the same direction as monetary growth.

As to the Fisher price-anticipation effect, Anna Schwartz and I found no evidence that it was significant in either the United States or the United Kingdom before the 1960s. Before that time, interest rates behaved as if prices were expected to remain stable. Since then, inflation has had a very clear and very prompt impact on interest rates.[1]

Monetarist Policy

The policy implication that monetarists such as I have drawn from this analysis is that the primary task of the monetary authorities should be to avoid introducing uncertainty in the economy—that their primary task should be to produce a predictable pattern of monetary growth, preferably a steady one. The idea that monetary growth should be steady and predictable is the core of the monetarist policy view. All monetarists, I believe, favor steadiness. However, they differ considerably with respect to what monetary aggregate or aggregates should be targeted, what the numerical rate of growth of the selected aggregate or aggregates should be, and how it should be determined.

The desirable rate of growth depends on objectives. If the objective is to have zero inflation, that calls for a rate of monetary growth equal to the sum of the anticipated rate of real growth and the anticipated rate of change of velocity. The precise number will depend on the country and the circumstances. In the 1960s, when Japan was growing at an annual rate of close to 10 percent a year and when the money economy was still spreading so that velocity was declining, I estimated that an annual rate of monetary growth for an aggregate such as M2 of about 15 percent would be consistent with zero inflation. As the economic growth of Japan has decelerated and the economy has become increasingly monetized, the situation has changed. No doubt a decidedly slower rate of monetary growth is called for now. For the United States I have long believed that the appropriate annual rate of growth consistent with zero inflation is somewhere between about 2 and 5 percent for a definition of money conparable to the present M1. (That definition is closer to the concept I have typically used in my research, which the Federal Reserve earlier designated M2, than to the concept the Fed earlier designated M1.)

As these comments imply, steadiness and predictability do not necessarily mean constancy. I have favored constancy, partly because I believe we do not in fact know enough to specify a dependable and reproducible rule for varying the rate and partly because I believe it is easier to get public support and understanding for a constant rate than for a sophisticated rule for altering the rate. However, some monetarists favor varying the rate of growth in accordance with one or another rule. The common element is that all want to minimize the erratic and unpredictable element in monetary change.

Political considerations enter strongly into the choice of the particular rule for monetary growth, in two very different ways. First, it may be necessary to have legislation passed to change institutions or to institute or implement a specific rule. As economists, we should not be deterred by that necessity from considering what rule would be best. We are very poor predictors of political feasibility in that sense, and should stick to our last. Political considerations also enter in in a very different way that I believe we must take into account. Given the institutional structure and a particular rule, how will political pressures and public reactions affect how it performs? We have had a tendency to treat monetary policy as if it could and would be conducted by a pure and disinterested technical economist, completely isolated from political pressure and taking account only of technical knowledge and information about monetary arrangements. That is far from the fact. In practice, any rule will be operated in a political environment subject to pressures that experience tells us will produce results very different from those dictated by purely economic considerations. This consideration has become a major argument, in my mind, for a simple mechanical rule, such as steady growth in a specified aggregate. It must be mechanical in order to be predictable; it must be simple in order to have wide public backing and understanding.

In a situation in which policy has not conformed to a desirable policy, the further question arises of the transition to such a policy. In most cases that question has arisen when monetary growth has been abnormally high and inflation has been the major problem. Under those circumstances two different views have been held by people who are generally monetarist: that the desirable course of events is a shock treatment that reduces the rate of growth to the final level abruptly, and that the desirable course is a policy of gradual reduction. The shock policy has been supported by two groups. Believers in an extreme form of rational expectations have argued that a preannounced shock treatment would in fact lead to a rapid adjustment of prices with very little disturbance of real income. The second group has favored shock treatment for political reasons, believing that a government will not in fact be able to maintain a gradual policy.

The believers in a gradual approach, of whom I have always been one, have argued primarily on economic grounds that many arrangements have expectations of inflation built into them that, if suddenly disrupted, would cause serious economic disturbance. We have felt that it is best to move gradually in order to give people time to adjust to the new circumstances, to unwind the contracts that were entered into under earlier circumstances.

This issue has by no means been resolved. Experience clearly contradicts the more extreme rational-expectations models predicting extremely rapid adjustment to changes in monetary growth. Nonetheless, the balance of recent evidence, I must confess, is rather on the side of those who favor a shock treatment. The case of Japan in 1973 is a dramatic example. Annual monetary growth was brought down abruptly from around 25 percent to around 10–15 percent, held there, and reduced still further some years later. Inflation followed suit about 18 months later, along with a resumption of economic growth. Even more persuasive has been the failure of the United States to stick to a gradual program even though that is its announced policy.

Neither an abrupt nor a gradual reduction to a final level would be the ideal policy, in view of accurate information on money demand and both the technical and political possibility of fine-tuning a disinflationary process. If a reduction in monetary growth leads to a decline in inflation, and that decline is embedded in anticipated inflation, the resulting lower cost of holding money will produce an increase in the quantity of real balances demanded. Velocity, which rises because of the reverse effect when inflation accelerates and stabilizes when inflation stabilizes, will tend to decline when inflation declines. An ideal policy would therefore involve an initial decline in monetary growth, a subsequent rise when declining inflation reduces velocity, and a final decline to the desired long-run level when velocity stabilizes.[2]

Such a policy, though ideal in a world of perfect information and control, seems to me undesirable in actual practice. First, authorities never have the information required to approximate the correct pattern, except perhaps in cases of hyperinflation. Second, the authorities tend to be deceived by the decline in velocity when it comes, regarding it as more than a one-shot affair, and hence run the danger—which has been realized more than once—of reigniting inflation and having to start all over.

Monetarist Rhetoric

As inflation accelerated during the 1970s, it became increasingly clear that excessive monetary growth was a major culprit. In reaction, central bankers in country after country began to use monetarist rhetoric in describing their policy. Essentially every country in the world came to accept the announcement of targets for monetary growth as part of its standard procedure. The most dramatic episode occurred on October 6, 1979, when Paul Volcker, after pressure at an International Monetary Fund meeting in Belgrade, flew back to the United States and announced a major change in monetary policy. In commenting on this announcement at the time, I wrote the following.

The Fed's targets for monetary growth have become a laughingstock, as it has become clear that any relation between the targets and actual monetary growth is purely coincidental. For more than a decade there has been increasing pressure on the Fed—from academic students of money, the staffs of various regional reserve banks, the staff of the Board itself and, more recently, from Congress—to change the operating procedure by substituting the monetary base (currency plus deposits at Federal Reserve banks) for the Federal funds rate as the primary instrument for controlling monetary growth.
   Has the Fed finally gotten that message? The Fed's release sounds like it: "This action involves placing greater emphasis in day-to-day operations on the supply of bank reserves and less emphasis on confining short-term fluctuations in the Federal funds rate." However, those of us who have long favored such a change have repeatedly licked our wounds when we mistakenly interpreted earlier Fed statements as portending a change in operating procedures. I hope that this time will be different—but remain skeptical until performance matches pronouncements.[3]

Unfortunately, my skepticism was amply justified, as the following brief sketch of monetary policy in the United States from 1960 to date demonstrates. Incidentally, in judging what actually happened, it is not irrelevant that if asked "Are you now or have you ever been a monetarist?" not a single member of the Board of Governors of the Federal Reserve System would answer "Yes."

The United States

From 1960 to October 1979

Monetary restraint, encouraged by President Eisenhower's willingness to suffer two recessions within four years (1957–58 and 1960–61) in order to bring down inflation, eliminated inflation by 1960. The end of inflationary expectations laid the groundwork for a long sustained expansion from 1961 to 1966—the postwar "high tide" of the Federal Reserve System, which is comparable to the 1923–1928 period that Anna Schwartz and I designated the "high tide" of the Federal Reserve System in our *Monetary History*.[4] As in the 1920s, this proved to be a passing phase, though the immediate aftermath was inflation rather than depression. The rate of monetary growth roughly doubled after 1960. At first the effect was rapid economic growth, but then inflation started to gain ground, leading to a brief period of monetary restraint and a mini-recession from 1966 to 1967.

This episode was the beginning of a roller coaster of monetary growth, inflation, and unemployment that dominated the 1960s and the 1970s. Each increase in monetary growth was followed by a rise in inflation, which led the authorities to reduce monetary growth sharply, which in turn produced economic recession. The political pressures created by rising unemployment led the Fed to reverse course at the first sign that inflation was tapering off. The Fed took its foot off the brake and stepped on the gas.

After an interval of about 6 months, the acceleration in monetary growth was followed by economic recovery, then a decline in unemployment, and, after another year or so, by accelerated inflation. This roller coaster was superimposed on a rising trend. Each peak in monetary growth was higher than the preceding peak, each trough in monetary growth higher than the preceding trough. Each inflation peak was higher than the preceding peak, each inflation trough higher than the preceding trough. Similarly, at each peak in the economy unemployment was higher than at the preceding peak, and at each trough in the economy unemployment was higher than at the preceding trough.

Monetary growth during the 1960s, while high enough to rekindle inflation, was nonetheless relatively stable, which explains why there was only a mini-recession during that decade. But then it became decidedly more erratic, with sharp ups and downs. The result was a more erratic economy as well.

Rising concern about inflation and growing recognition of the role played by monetary growth in producing inflation led the Congress in 1975 to require the Federal Reserve to specify targets for monetary growth. However, the Federal Reserve, which had opposed the congressional action, succeeded in rendering the requirement largely meaningless by introducing a multiplicity of monetary aggregate measures, by specifying targets in terms of a range of growth rates rather than in dollar levels, and by shifting the base to which it applied its growth rates every quarter.

In practice, the Fed continued to target interest rates (specifically the Federal funds rate) rather than monetary aggregates, and continued to adjust its interest-rate targets only slowly and belatedly to changing market pressure. The result was that the monetary aggregates tended on the average to rise excessively, contributing to inflation. However, from time to time the Fed was too slow in lowering rather than raising the Federal funds rate. The result was a sharp deceleration in the monetary aggregates and an economic recession. The duration of these swings was relatively long—short gyrations lasting about 6 months, longer waves about 2–3 years up and one year or less down. Changes in rates of monetary growth were followed by changes in the same direction in both interest rates and economic activity after about 6 months and by changes in the same direction in inflation after about 2 years.

October 1979 to Summer 1982

By 1979 inflation and interest rates had both reached double digits, and a flight from the dollar, which had begun in 1978, accelerated. On October 6, 1979, the Federal Reserve announced a major change in monetary policy "to support the objective of containing growth in the monetary aggregates . . . by placing greater emphasis on the supply of bank reserves and less emphasis on confining short-term fluctuations in the Federal funds rate." The change was intended to produce lower and steadier monetary growth, at the cost, it was believed, of more variable short-term interest rates. Unfortunately, though the objective was excellent, the execution was not. The Fed tried to achieve its new objectives by modifying its earlier procedures without changing its regulations. In particular, lagged reserve requirements, which had hindered the achievement of the earlier objectives to a minor extent, proved an extremely serious hindrance for the new objectives. As a result, while average monetary growth was lower after the change than before (which accounts for the subsequent decline in inflation), monetary growth became much more variable after the change rather than steadier. The period of the gyrations also shortened. The short gyrations lasted about one quarter, the longer waves about a year or less.

Interest rates and economic activity followed suit, fluctuating more violently and over shorter periods than earlier. In addition, the lag between changes in monetary growth and subsequent changes in interest rates, economic activity, and inflation shortened from 6 months to about 3 months for interest rates and economic activity and from 2 years to a little more than a year for inflation.

Table 1.1, based on quarterly data, summarizes the experience since the change in monetary policy.

To the best of my knowledge, no earlier three-year period since the Fed was established shows such wide fluctuations in either monetary growth or economic activity.

Table 1.1
Impact of changes in monetary growth on nominal and real GNP and three-month Treasury bill rate.

		Annual rate of growth					
				GNP one quarter later			
Period monetary growth	No. of quarters	M1	M2	In current dollars	In 1972 dollars	Change in 3-Month T-bill rate	Period for GNP and T-bill rate
79:4–80:2	2	1.8	6.5	5.3	−4.1	−4.2	80:1–80:3
80:2–81:2	4	10.1	10.5	12.8	+3.2	+5.9	80:3–81:3
81:2–81:4	2	3.0	8.9	2.9	−5.2	−2.1	81:3–82:1
81:4–82:1	1	10.9	10.1	6.8	+2.1	−0.4	81:1–82:2
82:1–82:3	2	3.4	9.9	4.2	−0.2	−4.5	82:2–82:4
82:3–83:2	3	13.8	13.9	10.9	+5.4	+0.3	82:4–83:2
79:4–83:2	14	7.9	10.2	7.7	+0.4	−5.0	80:1–83:2

Since Summer 1982

Around July 1982, the Federal Reserve again appears to have made a major change in its operating procedures. To judge from its behavior, the Fed reverted to its pre–October 1979 policy of targeting interest rates and of delayed adjustment to market pressures affecting interest rates. The result, as earlier, was surrender of control over the monetary aggregates. In the 11 months from July 1982 to June 1983, M1 rose at close to 14 percent per year.

The shift to the earlier policy appears to have been accompanied by a return to the earlier relation between monetary growth and interest rates and economic activity.

Money growth accelerated in July 1982. On the 1979–1982 pattern, interest rates might have been expected to decline for about 1–3 months thereafter and then start rising. On the pre-1979 pattern, the lag was about 6 months. After money growth accelerated in July 1982, interest rates did decline sharply for about 2 months, but then they were relatively stable for some months and began to rise in late 1982 or early 1983.

Similarly, on the 1979–1982 pattern, the economy might have been expected to begin recovering about 3 months after money accelerated, or in October 1982; on the pre-1979 pattern, not until 6 months later, or in January 1983. The economy apparently reached its trough and started recovering in

November 1982, 4 months after the acceleration in monetary growth—
moving toward the earlier pattern, though closer to the later one.

The Fed has justified the monetary explosion since July 1982 on two main
grounds. At first, it asserted that institutional changes were rendering
changes in M1 difficult to interpret and hence made it necessary to depart
temporarily from putting major stress on M1. As the explosion continued, it
added the excuse that there had been unexpected and unusual shifts in the
demand for money—its standard excuse throughout the decades whenever it
has been subjected to criticism. The basis for the claim was the sharp drop in
M1 velocity from mid 1981 to early 1983, and especially in the fourth quarter
of 1982. This decline in velocity was entirely consistent with an unchanged
demand for money. It was in part the standard cyclical pattern of a decline in
velocity during recession; in part a reflection of the lag in the effect of
monetary change, so that contemporaneous velocity always tends to fall in the
early stages of a monetary explosion; in part a reaction to the sharp decline in
inflation, which lowered the cost of holding money; and in part a reaction to
the increased volatility of monetary growth, which also tends to increase the
quantity of money demanded.

As to the excuse in terms of institutional change, the major changes were
not introduced until December 1982 and January 1983 and hence cannot
explain the monetary explosion from July 1982 to December 1982. Both
excuses are, I believe, *ex post* rationalizations.

The money explosion puts the economy in a no-win position. Continued
monetary growth at anything like recent rates would mean an upsurge in
inflation in 1984 or 1985 at the very latest, and higher long-term interest rates
much sooner as more and more participants in the financial market come to
anticipate the rise in inflation. Already, the rapid monetary growth has
produced the early symptoms of an overheated economy.

A drastic reversal that would produce low or negative monetary growth—
something that the Fed has often done in the past—would produce a sharp
temporary increase in short-term interest rates, abort the economic expansion
now in process, and lead to a renewal of recession by early 1984.

Even the least harmful course—prompt reduction in monetary growth to
the Fed's own target limits (4–8 percent for M1)—will, unless we are very
lucky indeed, mean a rise in short-term rates, a slowdown in the expansion,
and a moderate increase in inflation.

Monetary Growth and Inflation in the United States

As noted earlier, inflation in the United States tends to be a fairly inertial
phenomenon that is affected long after the event by monetary growth. This

Table 1.2
Monetary growth and inflation (all growth rates, percent per year).

Monetary growth			Inflation		
Period	Monetary base	M1	Period	Consumer price index	Implicit price deflator
3/73–3/76	7.8	5.1	3/75–3/78	6.7	6.3
3/76–3/79	8.6	8.3	3/78–3/81	11.8	9.1
3/79–3/82	6.9	6.1	3/81–2/83	3.1	5.2

can be seen clearly in table 1.2, which shows monetary growth for successive 3-year periods beginning in the third quarter of 1973 and inflation in periods 2 years later, the first two periods being a full 3 years and the last period being until the first quarter of 1983, or $1\frac{1}{2}$ years.

Whether measured by the monetary base or by M1, the rate of monetary growth sped up significantly from the first period to the second period and then fell significantly in the third period. The movements in the consumer price index are much sharper than those in either the monetary base or in M1, both up and down (partly because the consumer price index as it was constructed during this period gave undue weight to housing costs and hence to the interest rate, which was particularly volatile during these years). From this point of view the implicit price deflator is a better measure. The rise in the rate of inflation as shown by the implicit price deflator from the first period to the second is roughly the same as in M1: a 3.2 percent increase in M1 and a 2.8-percentage-point increase in the rate of growth of the implicit price deflator. On the other hand, the tapering off of inflation is much sharper: a 2.2-percentage-point decline in M1 and a 3.9-percentage-point decrease in the rate of growth of the implicit price deflator. I believe that this difference is explained in considerable measure by the far higher volatility of both the monetary base and M1 in the third period than in either of the other periods. This is a point that I shall return to later. The main point is simply that the recent decline in inflation is to be attributed to the slower average rate of growth in money over the 3-year period from the third quarter of 1979 to the third quarter of 1982 than in the prior 3-year period.

Monetary Volatility

Average is one thing, variability is a very different thing. Table 1.3 measures the volatility of the monetary base and of M1 in the same 3-year periods used

Table 1.3
Variability of monetary and economic growth: standard deviations of quarter-to-quarter
annualized rates of change (continuously compounded).

Money			Economy			
Period	Monetary base	M1	Period	Nominal GNP	Real GNP	Implicit price deflator
3/73–3/76	1.3	1.5	1/74–1/77	3.8	5.6	2.7
3/76–3/79	0.9	1.3	1/77–1/80	3.7	3.2	1.6
3/79–3/82	2.3	4.7	1/80–1/83	5.7	4.8	2.5

in table 1.2. It measures the volatility of the nominal GNP, of the real GNP, and of the implicit price deflator in 3-year periods just 6 months rather than 2 years later than the periods for money, since changes in money tend to affect nominal income after a lag of about two quarters. The shortness of the lag between monetary change and nominal income change in comparison with that between monetary change and inflation is a major reason why monetary volatility is so disturbing for real income.

After declining somewhat from the first to the second period, monetary volatility rose drastically from the second to the third. The third period is the period of the so-called "monetarist" policy of the Federal Reserve. Nominal GNP shows precisely the same pattern. This is a relationship that Anna Schwartz and I investigated for a period of close to 100 years in an article published some two decades ago. I have subsequently extended that analysis. It demonstrates that so far as the United States is concerned there is a close relationship between the volatility of money and the volatility of nominal income and real income. The results for real GNP in table 1.3 may appear to contradict this conclusion, but they really do not. Real GNP is more volatile in the third period than in the second, but it is even more volatile in the first. The reason is that the first period reflects the aftermath of the price controls imposed by President Nixon in August 1971. Their release produced a rapid acceleration in recorded inflation, which was accompanied by a decline in real income. As a result, there is a negative correlation between the changes in real income and the changes in the implicit price deflator during the 3 years from the first quarter of 1974 to the first quarter of 1977, whereas for the other two periods there is a very mild positive correlation. That is why there is higher volatility for both real income and the implicit price deflator in the first period than in either of the others.

The third period shows the increase in volatility from the second that is already recorded in a different way in table 1.1.

Great Britain and Japan

I am not as knowledgeable about the details of monetary policy and performance in Great Britain and Japan. However, my impression is that Japan illustrates a policy that is less monetarist in rhetoric than the policies followed by the United States and Great Britain but far more monetarist in practice. In any event, since the change in policy in 1973, when inflation reached 25 percent and monetary growth was over 25 percent, Japan has followed a fairly consistent policy of holding down the rate of monetary growth and keeping it relatively steady. The rate of monetary growth has come down from the neighborhood of 12 or 13 percent at that time to something like 8 or 9 percent today. It has shown a good deal of variability from month to month but relatively little variability from year to year. It has been highly stable and highly dependable, and the result has been that Japan has been less affected by economic instability than the other two countries.

So far as Great Britain is concerned, my impression is that its experience was very similar to that of the United States: a very erratic monetary policy along with a decline in the average rate of growth. The result, I believe, has been again considerable economic instability along with a sharp decline in the rate of inflation.

Conclusion

The basic conclusion to be drawn from this survey is straightforward: Slower average monetary growth has tamed inflation in the United States and the United Kingdom. Under the best of circumstances, that would have involved a transitional period of recession and slow growth—perhaps 18 months in duration, to judge from Japan's experience. In practice, excessive volatility of monetary growth introduced severe instability in both countries and made the cost of taming inflation unnecessarily high. Moreover, it has left both countries (but perhaps the United States even more than Britain) without a credible, dependable monetary policy that can justify firm expectations that inflation will stay tamed.

A major cost of the volatile policy followed in the United States is the discrediting of a proper monetarist policy. As a result, we are back in a situation in which the monetary authorities are operating in a purely discretionary fashion, subject to no meaningful standards of accountability.

Their policy over the past few years would not have been different if they had deliberately set out to give monetarism a bad name.

Notes

1. See Milton Friedman and Anna J. Schwartz, *Monetary Trends in the United States and the United Kingdom* (University of Chicago Press, 1982), especially pp. 538–546.

2. I am deliberately oversimplifying by describing the "ideal policy" as a three-step policy. In principle, it would be far more complex.

3. "Has the Fed Changed Course?" *Newsweek*, October 22, 1979, p. 39.

4. The rates of growth of money in the successive 5-year periods (1950–1955, 1955–1960, and 1960–1965) were 3.2, 1.0, and 2.9 for M1; 4.0, 3.0, and 6.4 for the monetary aggregate we used in *Monetary History of the United States, 1867–1960* (Princeton University Press, 1963) and *Monetary Trends* (equivalent to the former Federal Reserve M2); and 5.2, 4.6, and 8.4 for the current Federal Reserve M2 [our M4 in our *Monetary Statistics of the United States* (Columbia University Press, 1970)]. It is interesting to compare these numbers with those in the earlier periods. The rates of growth of the monetary aggregate we used in *Monetary History* for 1918–1920, 1920–1922, and 1922–1927 were 14.1, −1.6, and 5.8. The periods preceding the "high tide" were shorter and more extreme, but the earlier "high tide" period itself had roughly the same growth rate as the later one.

2

Monetary Policy in an Uncertain World

James Tobin

Power attracts advice and criticism. These days central banks are the most powerful actors in the economic drama. Polls of American leaders rate Paul Volcker the second most powerful person in the United States. Outside military and diplomatic contexts, Chairman Volcker probably plays a more decisive role than the president himself. So if central bankers are receiving ever larger quantities of conflicting advice from citizens in general and economists in particular, that is testament to their recognized power. And if the counsels of the various critics cancel one another out, as may happen even at this conference and even in this session, then the central bankers can continue in good conscience to do what they would do anyway.

This conference is well timed, for several reasons. First, the world economy is just beginning to recover from its worst depression since the 1930s. A strong and sustained recovery is still not ensured. The monetary authorities of the leading economic powers, the United States, Japan, and the European Economic Community, bear proximate responsibility for the depression, which was the by-product of the severe counterinflationary measures they felt compelled to take at the end of the 1970s. The immediate practical question is what role monetary policies should play in accommodating or promoting recovery. Second, intellectual developments in macroeconomics converge with real-world events in raising just now some fundamental issues about the conduct of monetary policy. Monetarism, having won the hearts and minds of many economists and central bankers in the 1970s, may now be losing some adherents and influence—partly because of the depression, partly because regulatory, institutional, and technological changes have so clearly altered the meanings and velocities of monetary aggregates. In the summer and fall of 1982 Chairman Volcker and his colleagues suspended their monetarist targets, to nearly universal relief. But no coherent philosophy of monetary control, no systematic strategy, has yet replaced them. What responsibility central banks should assume for recovery in this decade is a specific instance of the general issue of how much weight real macroeconomic performance should have in monetary policy decisions. A currently influential view is that monetary policies can and should aim solely at nominal, not real, outcomes. Third, both recent experience and contemporary theory underscore the international dimensions of monetary policies. They will not be overlooked at a meeting here in Tokyo, with participants from several nations. Recent events in the United States played out with remarkable accuracy the textbook scenario for the effects of restrictive monetary policy in a world of floating exchange rates. High interest rates attracted funds to dollar assets and appreciated the home currency; deterioration of the U.S. trade balance was the major component of decline in final demand. Other countries have not welcomed the impacts on their interest rates, exchange rates, and prices. Rhetoric at the Versailles and Williamsburg summits recognized the interdependence of our economies and financial markets and the need for coordination of macroeconomic and monetary strategies. But very little concrete progress is evident. In consonance or dissonance, the major central banks together determine the international monetary environment and the general levels of interest rates throughout the world. None of the three "locomotives" can claim it is too small to influence the world economy. If in my discussion I fall into the old American habit of talking about one closed economy with one monetary authority, please interpret me as referring to the Organization for Economic Cooperation and Development as a whole and to the several leading central banks as a group.

My keynote remarks are divided into three parts. The first takes up the fundamental issue mentioned above: the place of real economic objectives in the making of monetary policy. I argue against the proposition that only nominal variables should concern the central bank. The second part discusses the hierarchy of ultimate objectives, intermediate targets, and instruments in relation to uncertainties monetary policy makers face over various horizons. The third part discusses some current issues of policy connected with recovery from the world depression.

Real and Nominal Variables as Objectives of Monetary Policy

Should monetary authorities consider the real economic performance of their countries in setting policies? Should their objectives include real outcomes of national and international importance (employment, trade, production, capital formation) as well as nominal variables (prices, nominal incomes, monetary aggregates)? Today many economists and central bankers answer No. Monetary authorities' capacities and responsibilities, they argue, cover only nominal variables. After all, they have only nominal instruments. Dedication of those instruments to real objectives has, they allege, not improved but if anything actually worsened real performance, while destabilizing prices and causing inflation. Chastened by the stagflation of the last 15 years, central banks should be content to provide a stable, credible, predictable, non-inflationary nominal path and to accept whatever real outcomes occur along that way. Devotees of the new classical macroeconomics assure us that those outcomes will be optimal. Knowing that the central bank will neither confuse them nor rescue them from the consequences of imprudent wage and price increases, private agents and free markets will achieve the natural equilibrium values of real variables, quantities and relative prices.

The issue is an old one, and the answer has oscillated over the history of central banking. The primacy of nominal objectives was well established before the Great Depression. Central banks and governments were expected to place defense of a fixed parity of their currency with gold or foreign currencies ahead of domestic economic performance. Today some economists, statesmen, and commentators, frustrated by exchange-rate instabilities these past 10 years, advocate restoration of an international gold standard. They believe that the discipline of gold convertibility will create and maintain anti-inflationary expectations and behaviors.

Monetarists concur with this objective but prefer the discipline of monetary rules to that of gold. They would commit central banks permanently and publicly to specific numerical rates of growth in monetary aggregates or nominal income. Some would impose such rules by legislative or constitutional mandate. The purpose and the effect are the same as those intended by advocates of the gold standard: Monetary operations will be, and will be seen to be, independent of actual economic performance, in particular independent of paths of real outcomes.

I believe that purely nominalist monetary strategies are neither feasible nor desirable, for two major reasons.

The first reason is political. The responsibility of the central government for real macroeconomic performance is strongly entrenched in the politics of democratic societies. This has been true at least since the Great Depression of the 1930s and especially after World War II. In the United States, the Employment Act of 1946 and the Full Employment and Balanced Growth Act of 1978 ("Humphrey-Hawkins") commit the federal government, including the Federal Reserve System, to the pursuit of real economic goals. More important in a realistic sense, employment, real growth, and related variables are significant factors in public opinion and in electoral campaigns. Central banks cannot stand aloof from objectives highly valued by the societies they serve. Central bankers and their constituencies frequently dismiss the priorities of elected officials (for example reduction of unemployment) as "political" and hence unworthy of respect. The legitimacy of such a value judgment is as doubtful as its welfare economics. A purely nominal stance of monetary policy, willfully blind to real developments, is not likely to be credible. Sooner or later the central bank of a democracy will rescue the economy from the worst unintended real by-products of a fixed nominalist line, just as Paul Volcker did in the summer of 1982. Expectation that this will happen is bound to undermine policies whose effectiveness depends on public belief that it never will happen.

The second reason is economic. The dichotomy between real and nominal policy operations, by which monetary instruments are classified as purely nominal, is not valid theoretically or empirically. Nominal price and wage paths are sluggish, and some are more sluggish than others. Prices and wages that are administered or negotiated change less rapidly and readily than the prices of financial assets and commodities traded in auction markets. Because of such inertia, fluctuations in aggregate nominal spending resulting from monetary operations have important real consequences over fairly long short runs. The 1980–1983 recession and depression confirm this obvious fact once again. Nor is it confined to downturns. Cyclical recoveries, stimulated or at least accommodated by monetary expansions, generate real as well as nominal gains. It is disingenuous, to say the least, for central bankers to pretend that their actions have no effects on real interest rates, unemployment rates, and other variables of concern to the populace. The claim that monetary policies (since they necessarily rely on nominal instruments) can have only nominal effects trades on an analogy between altering monetary stocks and changing the unit of account. Switching the unit of account from dollars to half-dollars would, everyone agrees, have no real consequence. Why shouldn't doubling the stock of dollars by other means be likewise neutral? The analogy is false. Actual central-bank operations do not change the public's stocks of all nominal assets in the same proportion, whereas changes of units do. Actual operations effect exchanges of some assets for others—usually obligations to pay currency on demand are exchanged for obligations to pay currency in the future. Since future currency is not a perfect substitute for present currency, these exchanges are not neutral. They generally affect real interest rates, real exchange rates, saving, investment, and other real variables. Price changes affect private wealth and its distribution. Changes in inflation rates and in the distribution of price expectations necessarily alter real rates of return on currency and other assets with fixed nominal interest, and therefore influence the whole structure of asset prices and returns. Some of these effects vanish in principle in long-run steady states, but others do not. Time will eliminate the inertia of price and wage adjustments. However, there are no long-run steady states whose properties are independent of the paths by which they are reached. For example, depressions and high real interest rates irreversibly interrupt the accumulation of physical and human capital.

History does not support the verdict that countercyclical monetary and fiscal policies failed. Today they are blamed for the inflation and stagflation of the 1970s and for the greater amplitude of business fluctuations in that decade. Against this currently fashionable interpretation of history I would make two points.

First, a somewhat longer historical perspective is desirable. Governments accepted responsibility for macroeconomic stabilization after the Great Depression and began practicing countercyclical monetary and fiscal policy after World War II. Compared with previous periods of comparable length, the last 35 years (and of course especially the period before 1970) look very good, both in their high trends of real growth and in the limited severity of cyclical fluctuations. Maybe there is no causal connection, but neither is there a *prima facie* empirical case for abandoning the policies on account of recent disappointments.

Second, we should be careful not to draw the wrong lessons from the 1970s. After 1965 there were three bursts of inflation, each followed by a recession deliberately provoked by anti-inflationary monetary policies. The first acceleration of inflation, associated with the Vietnam war, was a classic demand-pull episode. President Johnson, against the advice of his own economists, loaded his increased war spending onto an already fully employed economy without raising taxes, and the Federal Reserve was overaccommodative. The two bursts of inflation in the 1970s were associated with extraordinary supply and price shocks, the first (in 1973–74) due to the Yom Kippur war, the oil embargo, and OPEC's fourfold increase in the dollar price of oil and the second (in 1978–80) due to the Iranian revolution, the restriction of Middle East oil supplies, and a further tripling of the OPEC price. These events happened to occur in the late stages of cyclical recoveries, to which conscious stimulative and accommodative policies in the United States and other countries had contributed.

The lesson that pundits and policy makers commonly draw from these experiences is that recoveries are dangerous, especially if they are promoted by policy. Accordingly, central banks are most reluctant now to adopt expansionary policies, even when their economies are as severely depressed as they are today. But these are the wrong lessons if the frightening bursts of inflation were due not to recoveries *per se* or to policies that fostered them but to the extraordinary exogenous shocks. Vietnam, OPEC, and the Ayatollah Khomeini were not the endogenous consequences of normal policy-assisted business-cycle recoveries. Nor should governments and central banks be paralyzed and our economies kept chronically stagnant for fear of similar occurrences.

I have argued that monetary authorities should not and cannot escape responsibility for real macroeconomic outcomes. To avoid misunderstanding I stress that I certainly am not advocating that they disregard nominal outcomes, price levels, and inflation rates. Professor Friedman told us in his presidential address to the American Economics Association some 15 years ago that monetary policy could not peg real variables such as unemployment and real interest rates and should not try. If "peg" meant to seek a particular unchanging numerical value forever, I think no one wanted or wants to peg. Permanent pegging of unemployment is one thing; taking account of the state of the labor market is quite another. Trying to move unemployment down in some circumstances and up in others is not pegging.

Objectives, Targets, and Operating Rules

Central bankers cannot, I have just argued, hope for easy lives administering mechanical rules independent of actual and prospective economic conditions. In the end there is no substitute for stochastic dynamic models of the economy that link policy instruments to contemporaneous and future outcomes. Policy makers use, at least implicitly, their models of the way the world works. It is better to make these models explicit. They can and should regularly consider and evaluate various feasible deviations from a "current policies" reference path. New information about exogenous variables, stochastic disturbances, and structural equations is always flowing in. New observations tell whether current instrument settings are having their intended and expected effects. Periodically, policy makers must reconsider whether their policies are achieving to the degree possible the desired mixture of basic economic objectives.

Instrument settings and targets for intermediate variables are not locked in forever. It is important that their subordination to more fundamental objectives be generally understood. To simplify a complex decision process and to aid public understanding, the central bank could use a hierarchical structure. For example, the objective for several years ahead could be described as ranges of outcomes the bank seeks in paths of variables of basic concern: unemployment, real GNP, prices, capital formation. For a year ahead, an intermediate target such as nominal-GNP growth would indicate how the bank would allow price and productivity shocks to affect output and employment, while allowing complete freedom to offset velocity-of-money surprises with money supplies. For shorter periods, one month to two quarters ahead, the bank could indicate targets or operating rules relating to intermediate money stocks, bank reserves, and short-term interest rates. For each horizon, the target ranges or rules would remain constant for the period. The policy makers are thus deciding and announcing how, if at all, instruments will be changed in response to surprises that occur during the interval.

Obviously monetary and fiscal policies should be coordinated and should be consistent in their assumptions and their aims. It is likewise desirable to coordinate macroeconomic policies, or at least to exchange information about them, among the principal economic powers of the noncommunist world. I do not try here to say how these difficult tasks are to be achieved.

The policy makers' model will also tell how stochastic disturbances of various kinds that are not directly and immediately observed produce surprises in observed variables and displace the economy's path from its intended and expected course. Disturbances relevant to monetary policy take several forms: surprises in aggregate real demand (consumption, investment, net exports), portfolio shifts (especially those affecting demands for monetary base or bank reserves and the net demand for foreign currency assets), and supply price shocks (for example, unexpected movements in nominal wages, labor productivity, or import prices).

The structure of the economy combines with the rules that guide the policy instruments themselves to determine how those shocks are translated into observable macroeconomic outcomes—that is, into deviations of variables from their intended paths. The observed variables that absorb the shocks include real national product, employment, interest rates, foreign exchange rates, and monetary aggregates. An essential function of the model is to estimate these linkages and how they vary across different operating targets and rules.

Different structures and operating rules distribute the shocks quite differently among the macroeconomic variables. For example, as is well known from William Poole's "Optimal Choice of Monetary Policy Instruments in a Simple Stochastic Macro Model" [*Quarterly Journal of Economics* 84, no. 2 (1970): 197–256], pegging nominal interest rates converts real demand shocks into unexpected and presumably unwelcome deviations of output and/or price level, but prevents pure portfolio shifts from having such effects. Pegging unborrowed reserves, however, makes real output and prices quite vulnerable to portfolio shifts (velocity shocks) but relatively immune to real-demand disturbances, which will be mostly absorbed in interest and exchange rates. On these lines, monetarism could be characterized by the conviction that real-demand disturbances are much more likely than financial surprises. If so, an ultra-monetarist rule—*reducing* reserves or money supplies in response to positive interest-rate surprises—would logically be preferable to pegging those quantities, unless money demand is wholly insensitive to interest rates.

Of course the central bank need not peg anything for very long; our Federal Open Market Committee convenes monthly and knows how to telephone between meetings. As soon as the nature of a shock can be identified, the central bank will know how to alter any peg, whether for interest rates or for monetary quantities, to get back on track. Meanwhile the evidence may be ambiguous; nominal interest rates, net borrowed reserves, and monetary aggregates may rise or fall either because of real-demand shocks or because of purely financial shifts. During that ambiguous meanwhile, the appropriate operating rule depends on the probabilities of the different kinds of shocks. To use a formula relating reserve supplies to nominal interest rates, taking account of those probabilities, is generally better than to peg either of the two variables. The relationship might be positive ("leaning against the wind") or negative ("pushing the wind back," as in the ultra-monetarist case mentioned above). The interim rule should be the more accommodative the greater the probability that observed interest-rate deviations reflect portfolio shifts rather than real-demand shocks, but no such formula should be followed once the nature of the disturbance can be diagnosed.

Targeting of monetary aggregates amounts to a rule calling for restricting reserves when M1, let us say, exceeds the intended path and expanding them when M1 falls short. Like interest-rate deviations, M1 deviations sometimes reflect undesired strength or weakness in nominal income, and sometimes reflect innocuous shifts in money demand or in intermediation. In the first case they should be opposed; in the second case they should be accom- modated. It is hard to make a case for M1 constancy as the optimal interim rule. It is even harder to see why M1 targets should be maintained in the face of subsequent evidence on the nature of the disturbances. Interest rates carry much the same information sooner and more accurately. Indeed, considerable evidence on the sources of disturbances becomes available as soon as or even sooner than reliable M1 statistics. Monthly statistics on personal income, retail sales, industrial production, unemployment, and prices anticipate quarterly reports of real and nominal GNP. The central bank is in a position to know quite promptly a great deal about purely financial sources of M1 surprises. Decisions on how much to accommodate should rely on these kinds of information. What usefulness monetary aggregates have comes from their informational content, not from their semantic monetary character. Central banks should ask their research staffs to devote more effort to obtaining and utilizing alternative and supplementary information.

Those who follow the American financial press are only too familiar with the obligatory weekend news story about the latest, two-week old M figures. The reporter feels a professional obligation to explain to the innocent reader who wanders to that page of his newspaper why these numbers are so important. Nowadays the standard formula—maybe it's the Fed's own publicists who supply it—is that M1 "measures money readily available for spending." We economists know that is nonsense. M1 does not begin to measure the funds that could conceivably be mobilized and readily spent for goods and services. An increase in M1 may indicate or presage an increase in spending, or the contrary.

A target for nominal GNP or MV (money stock times its income velocity) makes much more sense over periods of several quarters, long enough for the central bank to detect and offset velocity surprises. This is what the Federal Reserve has been groping toward these last few years while it has been explaining its departures from monetary aggregate targets as corrections for identifiable changes in the "meaning" of the measures (i.e., their relation to nominal income). A nominal-GNP target implies for the duration of its tenure a one-for-one tradeoff between price and quantity. An upward supply-price shock will mean commensurately smaller real-GNP growth. These terms of trade may not accord with national priorities; separate ranges for price and quantity would allow an extra degree of freedom. But a nominal-GNP target range is simpler to understand. In any case it can be reset annually, taking into account price and wage developments, unemployment and excess capacity, estimates of sustainable rates of real growth, and other circumstances.

Adherence in recent years to money-growth targets, reinforced by the Federal Reserve's feeling that its credibility was at stake, has prevented the Fed from accommodating promptly and fully some changes in money demand that, on the Poolean principles sketched above, should have been accommodated as soon as the sources of the shocks were clear. I refer to increases in liquidity preference for precautionary motives bred by the depression, to shifts of lending transactions from open markets into financial intermediaries and thus into monetary aggregate statistics, and to deregulations that made deposits more attractive interest-bearing assets than before.

At the same time, structural changes are making the system less automatically accommodative than it used to be. Deregulation allowing payment of market interest rates on deposits makes velocities less sensitive to interest-rate levels than they were previously. In consequence, given the same monetarist policy rules, the economy is less vulnerable to real-demand and price shocks and more vulnerable to purely financial shocks. A related result is greater volatility of interest rates and exchange rates. It is also likely that the probability of financial shocks to the demand for moneys and reserves has been increased. These consequences were probably unintended; the reforms were made largely for standard microeconomic reasons. But the macroeconomic effects should be considered explicitly in a review of the hierarchy of goals, targets, and rules. Because of the structural changes, any operating rule that was optimal before is no longer optimal and should be replaced by a more accommodative rule.

Monetary Policies and Recovery from the World Slump

Not everybody thinks recovery is a good idea right now. Some believe it is premature because victory over inflation is not yet complete. They would would continue the relentless process of disinflation, at the cost of high unemployment and prolonged stagnation, until core inflation rates are dependably reduced to zero. That could take several more years. This is a coherent and candid position, whatever one may think of the cost-benefit calculations implicit in it.

It is not, I think, the prevailing sentiment, outside the United Kingdom anyway. Most governments and central bankers, most business managers and financiers, and certainly most of the general public would welcome recovery. The question is what, if anything, macroeconomic policy (particularly monetary policy) should do to bring recovery about. Many who would welcome a spontaneous-combustion recovery—one energized for example by a miraculous burst of business investment—are afraid of a recovery driven or even accommodated by monetary expansion. In their view, a recovery powered by a spurt of velocity would be fine but one generated by commensurate increase of money stocks would be dangerous.

The argument that recovery driven by monetary stimulus is more inflationary than recovery otherwise fueled but of the same shape and strength is not one that I understand. Standard macroeconomic theory says that, as a strong first approximation, price and output paths depend on the interaction of aggregate spending flows, nominal GNP (or MV), with the economy's capacity to produce goods and services. The division of demand impulses between prices and output, between wages and employment, depends on the ongoing inertial patterns of wage and price inflation, on the degree and composition of underutilized productive resources, and on the wage-setting and price-setting institutions of the society. The relevant demand variable is MV, regardless of its factorization between M and V. Prices do not depend directly on policy instruments, monetary or fiscal. Macro policy influences are indirect, channeled through the determinants enumerated, principally through aggregate demand. I am aware of some qualifications of this standard doctrine, but they are of second order.

What opponents of monetary stimulus generally have in mind, to the extent that they are not really objecting to recovery *per se*, is an expectational response to monetary expansion. Perception of expansionary policy will, they allege, lead the public to expect inflation. Expecting it, businesses and workers will raise prices and wages at once, and no improvement in output and employment will occur. The expectations will be self-fulfilling. No such inflationary expectations would block a recovery that started and rolled on its own steam, without monetary accommodation. In a spontaneous-combustion recovery, unemployment and excess capacity would discipline wages and prices; in a money-fueled recovery they would not. The scenario does not make sense. It certainly violates the canons of rational expectations, particularly if the standard model outlined above is correct. If the story had been true for monetary disinflation, similar self-fulfilling expectations would have unwound the inflation of 1979–80 quickly and costlessly.

A less extreme story focuses on the effects of inflationary expectations, generated by perceptions of expansionary monetary policy, on interest rates rather than on actual prices and wages. The "financial markets" will expect inflation in the future if not now. The resulting high long-term interest rates will hinder recovery. One source of such psychology is the monetarist habit of defining monetary policy by growth rates of aggregates. This leads to undiscriminating extrapolation of currently announced targets for one quarter or one year or of deviations from targets. In the United States, Chairman Volcker needs to convince his nervous financial constituency that the economy needs and can safely absorb a change in the *level* of money stock, and that this by no means signifies permanently higher rates of growth. The level change is needed for three reasons. First, recovery itself requires larger money stocks to make up for the restrictions of the past three years and to bring real interest rates down to levels consistent with recovery and sustained prosperity. Second, disinflation itself has made monetary assets more attractive. Third, as already noted, payment of market-determined interest rates on deposits has increased the demand for moneys. Events since the Fed adopted its more pragmatic stance in 1982 give cause for optimism. Money growth accelerated; however, contrary to repeated monetarist warnings, interest rates, long as well as short, moved down rather than up.

Lenders' expectations and fears do not set rates unilaterally; there are two sides to all markets, even bond markets. If long-term rates were to rise on expectations of inflation held by borrowers and lenders alike, real rates would not have risen and the high nominal rates would not be a deterrent to current investment and recovery. More likely, borrowers and lenders differ in their expectations and calculations of risk. Long rates high enough to compensate lenders for their fears of inflation would be high real rates for borrowers, certainly high relative to their current appraisals of earnings prospects. The effects of these asymmetries on term structure are ambiguous. The predictable result is that both sides will shift to short maturities or to long-term contracts carrying variable short-term rates. In short markets, central-bank supplies of base money, expanded by hypothesis, are decisive for interest rates. Neither banks nor other lenders will sit on idle cash.

Central banks should not be paralyzed in fright of bond-market psychology. Let them educate the public by words, deeds, and experience. World recovery, with real growth of production exceeding long-run sustainable rates for several years, is essential to bring unemployment down, to raise the utilization of industrial capacity, to generate the saving and capital formation needed for long-run progress, and (not least) to provide the Third World with the markets and the export earnings that alone can resolve their critical financial difficulties. High real interest rates, especially in the United States, are a major obstacle to world recovery. It is true that prospective structural budget deficits are part of the problem, though cyclical deficits now and in the fiscal years immediately ahead are not. But whatever contributions future fiscal corrections can make, interest rates cannot be lowered without substantial help from monetary policy. To bring them down will require a period of above-normal monetary growth in the United States and in the other locomotive economies. If monetary policy is to be made on the assumption that it cannot expand real economic activity even after monetary restriction has depressed it for several years, we are doomed to a downward ratchet or to a mix of fiscal and monetary policies unfavorable to capital formation.

Everyone agrees that in this recovery it is important to avert inflation accelerations such as occurred at the ends of the two previous recoveries in the 1970s. I have argued above that it is unduly conservative to frame policy on the assumption that the extraordinary supply-price shocks of those periods are bound to recur. There remains the serious question how much unemployment and general economic slack to maintain as insurance against another acceleration. In concluding, I wish to address this issue briefly as a problem of policy making under uncertainty.

According to a widely accepted model of inflation there exists at any time a minimum unemployment rate consistent with no acceleration of inflation.

This is called the natural rate of unemployment or, more neutrally, the non-accelerating-inflation rate of unemployment (NAIRU). Here the unemployment rate is serving as a barometer of general slack, of the overall pressure of aggregate demand on productive capacity. Unfortunately no one knows what the NAIRU is. Current estimates for the United States vary from 8 percent to 5 percent. For policy makers, this doubt is compounded by uncertainty about the translation of their instruments via aggregate demand into unemployment. The decision problem is to balance, given these uncertainties, the costs of unemployment and lost production against the risks and costs of accelerating inflation. Those costs and risks can be made commensurate by estimating the extra unemployment necessary to eliminate the bulge of accelerating inflation should it occur.

A conservative solution is to minimize expected unemployment subject to the constraint that the probability of trespassing the NAIRU threshold and aaccelerating inflation not exceed some ε, perhaps even zero. Thus, if there were any non-negligible probability that policies designed to bring expected unemployment down to (say) 9 percent would generate acceleration—either because the NAIRU may be at least that high or because the policies might actually bring a lower unemployment rate—then conservative policy makers would try to keep unemployment higher than 9 percent. This solution is the spirit of macroeconomic strategies prevailing today, and it is a recipe and rationale for stagnation.

An optimal solution would not apply so absolute a constraint. A marginal dose of stimulus is justified if, and only if, the expected gain from reduction in unemployment exceeds the expected loss due to inflation acceleration. The latter is the cost of the unemployment correction times the probability that such correction will be necessary, i.e., the probability that the NAIRU threshold will have been crossed. If, for example, the correction costs two unemployment points for every point by which the NAIRU threshold was crossed, then the median estimate of the NAIRU is the proper target of policy. A higher relative correction cost implies a higher unemployment target; a lower appraisal of the cost implies a more ambitious unemployment goal.

Permanently high unemployment and excess capacity are costly insurance, and quite possibly self-defeating in the long run as the same problems of reconciling price stability and prosperity recur at lower levels of output and employment. Incomes policies, for all their allocational inefficiencies, may be a much less costly mode of insurance. However, to discuss that nonmonetary alternative would take me beyond my subject and my time.

I have argued that the recoveries of the 1970s are not relevant models for the 1980s, insofar as they suggest that double-digit inflations are the inexorable outcome. Uncritically accepted, that reading of history could lock our economies in stagnation for another decade. A better analogy is to the 1961–1965 recovery. In 1961, as in 1983, fears of inflation persuaded many influential people in and out of government that the United States must settle permanently for higher unemployment and slower growth. At that time too a pair of back-to-back recessions had, at considerable social cost, diminished inflation and inflationary psychology. Building on that foundation, expansionary fiscal and monetary policies—assisted by an informal incomes policy in the shape of wage-price guideposts—successfully generated recovery. The unemployment target of the day, 4 percent, was achieved with negligible increase in inflation. There were even supply-side policies, notably the investment tax credit, designed to foster investment and long-run growth. Events belied and dissipated the initial pessimism, and the stock market soared.

DOMESTIC ASPECTS OF MONETARY POLICY

3   The Conduct of Domestic Monetary Policy

Robert J. Gordon

Monetary policy has traditionally shared with fiscal policy joint responsibility for attainment of the ultimate macroeconomic goals—full employment, price stability, and maximum feasible growth in per capita real income. In the decade after 1973, macroeconomic performance deteriorated in most major industrialized nations, with high unemployment and inflation rates and lower growth in per capita real income. The design of new procedures for the conduct of domestic monetary policy must start from an analysis of past performance. Assessments are required of the role (if any) that monetary policy played in contributing to worsened macroeconomic performance and of the implications of identifiable errors of policy and procedures.

A well-established view holds that real phenomena such as the unemployment rate and the growth of real per capita income are independent of monetary policy, which guides the evolution of nominal monetary aggregates, nominal bank reserves, and nominal interest rates. As stated by Milton Friedman (1968) and other traditional monetarists, this interpretation of monetary neutrality holds in the long run, whereas nominal monetary phenomena are capable of influencing real variables in the short run. A stronger version of monetary neutrality is maintained in the Lucas-Sargent Wallace (LSW) "policy ineffectiveness proposition," which holds that only unanticipated movements in nominal monetary aggregates can influence real output. (See especially Sargent and Wallace 1975.) Subsequent empirical work with quarterly data for the United States (Barro and Rush 1980) implies that monetary changes must be neutral for output over periods longer than one quarter.[1]

Since money is held in the monetarist and LSW views to be neutral for real variables over periods ranging from one quarter to a long run of perhaps 2–5 years, it might be concluded that monetary policy could not be held responsible for the poor performance of real variables after 1973. The same reasoning would hold monetary policy solely responsible for faster inflation. Indeed, a standard prescription for monetary policy has been to maintain tight control over the growth rate of monetary aggregates or of the monetary base along a steadily decelerating path to eliminate inflation.

This chapter develops an alternative view of the consequences of monetary policy. A long time is required for monetary policy to become neutral, that is, for its effect on real variables to vanish. Alternative scenarios for the nominal money supply can make the difference between smooth and oscillating paths for real variables over periods of a decade or more. Monetary policy operates within a set of basic constraints that limit the set of outcomes it can achieve. These include constraints on aggregate supply behavior that determine how a given path of nominal-income growth will be divided between inflation and output growth, as well as "velocity" constraints that influence the path of nominal-income growth that will result from any given monetary policy, whether that policy is stated in terms of the monetary base, monetary aggregates, or interest rates. The interaction of monetary policy decisions with shifts in the constraints helps to explain the sources of deteriorating macroeconomic performance. Explicit consideration of the constraints is required in the design of new procedures.

The presentation of a paper at an international conference on the assigned topic of domestic monetary policy poses a serious problem of delimiting scope. Ideally those aspects of domestic monetary policy should be isolated that are of such central importance as to be relevant in every country. The approach taken here is to develop a common theme that monetary policy operates in the face of constraints, and to regard the constraints as a dimension of difference across nations.

The constraints to be emphasized in this chapter fall into the two major categories of aggregate-supply constraints and velocity constraints. Among the aggregate-supply constraints faced by most nations are a short-run tradeoff between inflation and unemployment, "inertia" in the adjustment of inflation to nominal disturbances, the absence of a long-run tradeoff between inflation and unemployment, the exposure of the short-term tradeoff to the influence of supply shocks, and the influence on the tradeoff slope of the economy's degree of openness and its exchange-rate regime. For purposes of illustration, the chapter concentrates on the operation of these aggregate-supply constraints in the United States but refers to likely differences in other nations, particularly the lesser extent of inflation inertia and the greater degree of openness.

Among the determinants of monetary velocity that influence the path of nominal spending for a given path of the monetary base or a monetary aggregate are the level of fiscal deficits and the change in these deficits, shifts in the demand function for a given monetary aggregate as a result of changes in tastes or innovations in financial markets, and shifts in the expenditure function for private goods and services related to the cyclical dynamics of the demand for durable goods and to fluctuations in the foreign-trade surplus due to exchange-rate movements or exogenous foreign disturbances.

Again, the chapter concentrates on the consequences of velocity shifts in the United States, which in recent years have been particularly related to financial innovation and the appreciation of the dollar, which in turn has been partly caused by the anticipation of future fiscal deficits. Velocity shifts in other nations may have a different mix of sources but are still amenable to the same general policy prescription outlined below. The U.S. situation is also unique in the degree of independence of the central bank and the lack of coordination of monetary and fiscal policy, which makes fiscal policy more of a constraint than is the case elsewhere. In other nations it may be more fruitful to regard monetary and fiscal policy as part of a coordinated policy package, rather than regarding fiscal policy as imposing constraints on monetary policy.

Both the aggregate-supply factor and the velocity factor are treated as "constraints" because they limit the ability of the central bank to achieve its ultimate goals of price stability, full employment, and maximum real-income growth. What appears to be a constraint from the viewpoint of the central bank may be the result of maximizing behavior by individuals in the private economy or politicians influencing the government's fiscal decisions. For instance, the dilemma for anti-inflationary monetary policy posed by inflation inertia in the United States results indirectly from the American system of staggered three-year wage contracts, which in turn can be explained by a particular institutional history of unionization and labor strife in the early postwar years.[2]

The fact that central banks in different nations face a differing set of constraints does not, of course, fully explain differences in economic outcomes. For instance, some commentators point to domestic monetary-policy choices as the main explanation of "why West Germany and Japan coped with the oil crisis far better than the United States, or why they have been more successful during the past decade in avoiding high inflation than Britain or the United States" (Friedman 1983b). In my interpretation the central banks in West Germany, Britain, and Japan face a different set of constraints than in the United States, particularly a smaller degree of inflation inertia. Thus, maximizing subject to this constraint, it is optimal for the central banks of these three countries to react to an oil shock with less monetary accommodation than the U.S. central bank. The low-inflation outcomes in West Germany and Japan, then, resulted from the interaction of central banks' decisions and constraints, not from independent decisions taken by central banks operating in a vacuum. The wide choice set open to central banks implied by Friedman's comment is, I believe, well illustrated by the different outcome in Britain as compared with West Germany and Japan.

Examples developed in the chapter show how one can take aggregate-supply constraints explicitly into account in designing a path for nominal-GNP growth that aims to bring about stable future growth in output with a stable (but nonzero) rate of inflation. Much of the discussion in the second half of the chapter compares nominal-GNP targeting with the traditional dichotomy between money-supply targeting and interest-rate targeting. It shares with recent papers by Fellner (1982) and Bryant (1982, 1983) an emphasis on shifting the attention of the central bank from monetary variables to the ultimate targets of policy, while differing on the appropriate length of the horizon and the details of implementation.

Aggregate Supply Behavior

Basic Identities and Hypotheses

The term *aggregate supply behavior* refers to the set of factors that influence how the growth rate of nominal GNP is divided between inflation and real GNP. If the growth rate of nominal GNP is viewed as predetermined, depending on monetary growth and other factors determining velocity growth, then the three key macroeconomic growth rates of the nominal GNP (y), the real GNP (q), and the GNP deflator (p) can be determined with only two equations. (Here I adopt the notation that upper-case letters stand for levels and lower-case letters for proportional rates of change.)

One of these equations is the identity linking the three:

$$y_t \equiv p_t + q_t, \tag{1}$$

where the subscripts t designate the time period. This can be converted into a more useful form if we subtract from each side the growth rate of "natural" real GNP (q_t^N):[3]

$$y_t - q_t^N \equiv p_t + q_t - q_t^N. \tag{2}$$

Even though equation 2 is an identity, it contains an important kernel of truth about the underlying source of inflation. If real GNP tends to gravitate to its "natural" level in the long run, then in the long run actual and natural real-GNP growth must be equal ($q_t - q_t^N = 0$), and then inflation is simply the excess of nominal-GNP growth over the growth rate of natural real GNP

$(p_t = y_t - q_t^N)$. I call this concept of excess nominal GNP "adjusted nominal-GNP growth" $(y_t - q_t^N)$. Thus, the famous phrase "Inflation is always and everywhere a monetary phenomenon" (Friedman 1963) should really be replaced by "Inflation in the long run is always and everywhere an adjusted-nominal-GNP phenomenon."

Equation 2 identifies three reasons why inflation does not always and everywhere vary in proportion to movements in monetary growth. First, at least in the short run, inflation can fall below $y - q^N$ if real GNP grows faster than natural real GNP $(q - q^N)$, and vice versa. Second, inflation can speed up with constant nominal-GNP growth if there is a slowdown in the growth rate of natural real GNP (due, for instance, to the much-discussed worldwide post-1973 slowdown in productivity growth). Third, nominal-GNP growth by definition is equal to monetary growth plus velocity growth $(y = m + v)$, and there is no reason for velocity growth to be constant under every alternative monetary regime. For instance, the velocity of the M1 money supply in the United States (currency and demand deposits) exhibited a decade-long decline in the 1930s and a 36-year-long rise between 1945 and 1981. Between 1981 and 1983, the velocity once again declined.

One more implication of equation 2 provides an important link between inflation and unemployment, two of the basic goal variables of monetary policy. The difference between the unemployment rate and the natural rate of unemployment is closely related to the "output ratio," that is, the ratio of actual to natural real GNP. This relationship, usually called Okun's Law, has held up extremely well in the United States through the economic turmoil of the last decade.[4] This means that one can track movements in the unemployment rate accurately given knowledge of the current output ratio, for which we use the symbol $\hat{Q}_t \ (= Q_t/Q_t^N)$. Inflation and the output ratio are linked together by equation 2 once we take note of the fact that

$$\hat{Q}_t - \hat{Q}_{t-1} \cong q_t - q_t^N.$$

Thus, equation 2 becomes

$$y_t - q_t^N = p_t + \hat{Q}_t - \hat{Q}_{t-1}. \tag{3}$$

If we use some predetermined value of adjusted nominal-GNP growth $(y_t - q_t^N)$ and last period's output ratio $(\hat{Q}_{t-1})$, equation 3 contains the two unknown variables of central interest in macroeconomics: the inflation rate (p_t) and the output ratio $(\hat{Q}_t)$.

The additional equation needed to determine the value of both unknowns is a dynamic expectational Phillips tradeoff equation, which is sometimes, following Friedman (1970), called "the missing equation." In its simplest form this states that the inflation rate depends on the expected rate of inflation (p_t^e), the output ratio ($\hat{Q}_t$), and the influence of some proxy for the effect of supply shocks on inflation (z_t):

$$p_t \equiv p_t^e + b(\hat{Q}_t - 1) + cz_t, \tag{4}$$

where b and c are parameters.

The coefficient on the expected-inflation term is assumed to be unity, and therefore equation 4 incorporates the "natural-rate hypothesis." When supply shocks are absent ($z_t = 0$), inflation remains equal to the expected rate of inflation when the output ratio is unity ($\hat{Q}_t = 1$), that is, when the economy is operating at its "no shock" natural rate of output ($Q_t = Q_t^N$). Inflation tends to accelerate when the output ratio is above unity and to decelerate when the output ratio is below unity. If adverse supply shocks are present ($z_t > 0$), then inflation can accelerate even when the output ratio is below unity. Among the relevant adverse supply shocks in the United States have been increases in the relative prices of oil, food, and raw materials; a depreciation of the dollar; increases in indirect taxes; increases in the effective minimum wage; and the rebound of prices after various price-control programs. The post-1973 slowdown in productivity growth is taken into account in the measurement of natural real GNP (Q_t^N). Inflation-reducing supply shocks have been limited to the transitory effects of price-control programs and, more recently, the partial reversal of the oil shocks and the appreciation of the dollar.[5]

The relationship between inflation and adjusted nominal-GNP growth can be seen when the two basic equations are combined. Substituting equation 3 into equation 4, we obtain, after some rearrangement, the following:

$$p_t = \frac{1}{1+b}[p_t^e + b(y_t - q_t^N + \hat{Q}_{t-1} - 1) + cz_t]. \tag{5}$$

The economy is in long-run equilibrium when $p_t = p_t^e = y_t - q_t^N$ and $z_t = 0$. An acceleration of inflation relative to the expected rate can be caused by an acceleration in the growth of nominal GNP, a deceleration in the growth of natural real GNP, a lagged output ratio above unity, or any adverse supply shock.[6]

Nominal-GNP Growth, Inflation, and the Output Ratio in U.S. Postwar Business Cycles

This section provides an interpretation of the behavior of inflation and the output ratio in postwar business cycles. The following section summarizes the implications of recent econometric estimates of equation 5 for the effects on inflation and the output ratio of alternative paths for adjusted nominal-GNP growth that might be chosen by a central bank conducting domestic monetary policy.

Data for seven postwar business cycles are exhibited in table 3.1. The timing of each cycle is dictated by the choices of the National Bureau of Economic Research (NBER), which has established a chronology of U.S. business cycles extending back to 1837. The table shows each business cycle in a grouping of three lines, labeled *expansion, plateau,* and *recession.* The expansion begins in the calendar quarter designated by the NBER as the official cycle trough. The recession begins in the quarter designated as the official NBER peak. An intermediate stage is defined here that separates the period between trough and peak into two intervals, divided at the quarter when the output ratio reaches its peak. During the plateau phase, the economy exhibits positive real-GNP growth at a rate slower than the natural growth $(0 < q_t < q_t^N)$, so the output ratio declines.

The five growth rates in columns 3–7 of table 3.1 correspond to the famous quantity equation. Growth in money (m) plus growth in velocity (v) equals growth in nominal GNP (y), which also equals growth in the GNP deflator (p) plus growth in real GNP (q). These growth rates do not tell us much about extreme highs and lows experienced by the unemployment rate or the output ratio. Column 9 exhibits the official unemployment rate observed in the first quarter of each of the three cyclical phases. Column 8 exhibits my estimate of the output ratio; a detailed econometric study of equation 4 is used to derive the output ratio consistent with a constant rate of inflation in the absence of supply shocks.

Common features of the seven cycles are summarized in the bottom section of the table, which provides averages of the variables for each phase over all seven cycles, with each phase weighted by its length. Columns 3–5 show that nominal-GNP growth was highly volatile, with a 10.2 percent average growth rate during expansion phases and a 2.6 percent rate during recession phases for a difference of 7.6 percent. In contrast, M1 growth was much less volatile, with growth in expansion phases only 1.1 percent faster on average than growth in recession phases. As a result, fluctuations in monetary growth accounted on average for only 14 percent (1.1/7.6) of fluctuations in nominal-GNP growth. The remaining 86 percent is accounted for by fluctuations in the growth rate of velocity.

Two objections may be raised to the contrast between the roles of money and velocity growth in business cycles. First, some commentators have pointed out that the permanent income theory of money demand implies a large elasticity of velocity movements to transitory monetary changes. Yet an

Table 3.1
Basic characteristics of U.S. business cycles, 1949–1982.

Phase	Date phase begins (1)	Length of phase in years (2)	Four-quarter growth rates					Value at start of phase	
			Money supply (3)	Velocity of M1 (4)	Nominal GNP (5)	GNP deflator (6)	Real GNP (7)	Output ratio (8)	Unemployment rate (9)
Expansion	1949:Q4	3.50	4.3	6.5	10.8	3.3	7.5	93.5	7.0
Plateau		—	—	—	—	—	—	—	—
Recession	1953:Q2	1.00	0.8	-2.7	-1.9	1.4	-3.3	104.5	2.6
Expansion	1954:Q2	1.50	2.9	5.6	8.5	2.0	6.5	98.3	5.8
Plateau	1955:Q4	1.75	0.8	6.1	6.9	3.6	3.3	103.5	4.2
Recession	1957:Q4	0.75	0.6	-3.2	-2.6	1.0	-3.6	100.5	4.2
Expansion	1958:Q2	1.00	4.5	6.3	10.8	2.7	8.1	95.6	7.4
Plateau	1959:Q2	1.00	-0.6	3.8	3.2	1.5	1.7	100.6	5.1
Recession	1960:Q2	0.75	1.9	-1.4	0.5	0.6	-0.1	98.8	5.2
Expansion	1961:Q1	5.00	3.8	3.9	7.7	1.9	5.8	96.1	6.8
Plateau	1966:Q1	3.75	5.0	2.3	7.3	4.3	3.0	105.7	3.9
Recession	1969:Q4	1.00	5.0	-0.1	4.9	5.0	-0.1	102.3	3.6
Expansion	1970:Q4	2.25	7.7	3.5	11.2	4.6	6.6	98.1	5.9
Plateau	1973:Q1	0.75	4.8	4.7	9.5	7.3	2.2	103.7	4.9
Recession	1973:Q4	1.25	4.4	1.4	5.8	10.1	-4.3	102.6	4.8
Expansion	1975:Q1	3.75	7.1	4.7	11.8	6.5	5.3	94.3	8.2
Plateau	1978:Q4	1.25	7.4	2.7	10.1	8.5	1.6	100.9	5.8
Recession	1980:Q1	0.50	10.8	-5.5	5.3	9.5	-4.2	99.0	6.2
Expansion	1980:Q3	0.50	7.9	8.5	16.4	10.2	6.2	95.5	7.5
Plateau	1981:Q1	0.50	4.5	3.6	8.1	7.7	0.4	97.0	7.3
Recession	1981:Q3	1.50	6.1	-1.6	4.5	5.9	-1.4	95.5	7.4
Average, all cycles (weighted by length)									
Expansion		2.53	5.1	5.1	10.2	3.8	6.4	95.9	6.9
Plateau		1.28	3.9	3.5	7.4	4.9	2.5	101.9	5.2
Recession		0.98	4.0	-1.4	2.6	5.2	-2.6	100.5	4.9

Table 3.2

	Money	Velocity	Nominal GNP
1958–1961	1.9	3.3	5.2
1961–1970	4.4	2.7	7.1
1970–1975	6.2	3.1	9.3
1975–1980	7.5	3.3	10.8
1980–1982	6.1	1.5	7.6

inspection of the data reveals important episodes, such as 1967–68 and 1981–82, when money growth and velocity growth moved in opposite directions. The second and more legitimate objection is that the comparison in table 3.1 neglects lags. Since this reservation is legitimate, table 3.4 examines more sophisticated econometric evidence that takes account of lags in the impact of money on nominal GNP.

A prominent feature in table 3.1 is the steady acceleration of monetary growth in successive business cycles beginning in 1961. The weighted average growth rates of money, velocity, and nominal GNP in successive cycles were as shown in table 3.2 (in percent). Since velocity growth exhibited no significant change over these cycles, except for 1980–1982, the behavior of money can be blamed for the long-term increase in nominal-GNP growth and in the rate of inflation in the 1970s as compared with the 1950s and the early 1960s. Thus, a careful distinction must be made between the *small* role of money growth in contributing to the short-run timing of individual cycles and its *large* role in contributing to overheating in the decade 1964–1974 taken as a whole. This evaluation must be qualified to the extent that supply shocks contributed to the inflation of the 1970s. As pointed out later in this section, part of the 1975–1980 acceleration of money growth may have been a passive reaction to the 1973–74 supply shocks that forced the Fed to make an uncomfortable choice between lower output and higher inflation.

The behavior of the inflation rate in column 6 of table 3.1, averaged over all cycles, shows a striking countercyclical pattern, with average growth rates of 3.8 percent in expansions and 5.2 percent in recessions. An examination of the individual cycles, however, suggests that the seven-cycle average mixes up three quite different types of experience. The recessions between 1949 and 1961, as well as the 1980–1982 episode, display the expected procyclical movement due to the role of the output ratio in equation 4. The middle three cycles between 1961 and 1980, however, exhibit a strong countercyclical pattern that helps to demonstrate the effect of the other two variables in that equation. One of its key implications, when it is joined with an adaptive type of expectation formation, is that there will be a continuous upward adjustment of the inflation rate when the output ratio remains above unity. This gradual adjustment of inflation was most obvious in the long 1961–1970 cycle. Because inflation expectations adapted with substantial inertia to rapid nominal-GNP growth, the economy experienced a period between 1964 and 1969 when the output ratio substantially exceeded 100 percent and the actual unemployment rate fell substantially below the natural rate of unemployment. The gradual upward adjustment of inflation continued into the 1969–70 recession, which witnessed faster inflation than previous phases despite slower nominal-GNP growth. A complementary explanation is that the 1969–70 slowdown in nominal-GNP growth was the mildest of any of the postwar cycles, further inhibiting any deceleration of inflation.

Finally, the post-1970 period demonstrates the effect of the remaining variable in equation 4, the supply-shock proxy. The 1970–1975 and 1975–1980 business cycles both ended with recessions that were triggered by supply shocks and amplified by a slowdown in nominal-GNP growth. The relative price of energy increased by 25 percent between late 1972 and 1975, and again by more than 40 percent between late 1978 and late 1981. The relative price of food increased by about 10 percent between 1972 and 1974. Finally, the recession of 1973–1975 was aggravated by the extra inflation that occurred after the termination in May 1974 of the Nixon-era price-control program and by the 1971–1973 devaluation of the dollar. As a result, the inflation rate observed in the recession phase of these two cycles was substantially higher than that in the expansion phase. The marked difference between the countercyclical behavior of inflation in the 1973–1975 and 1980 recessions and its procyclical behavior in the 1981–82 recession provides a strong confirmation of the view that supply shocks matter and a refutation of those who focus narrowly on prior fluctuations in the growth rate of the money supply in explaining the inflation rate.

There was an additional consequence of supply shocks. Partly as a result of cost-of-living escalators in wage contracts, supply shocks had the effect of permanently raising the rate of inflation at any given output ratio. This forced policy makers to choose between a prolonged recession and an acceleration in monetary growth to ratify the upward ratchet of inflation caused by the supply shock. During the 1975–1978 expansion the choice was made to ratify the inflation rate. In this sense, the postwar peak in the growth rates of money and nominal GNP during the 1975–1980 cycle was not simply a perverse action by misinformed policy makers but rather an indirect consequence of the supply shocks themselves. This is a primary example of the influence of aggregate-supply constraints on the conduct of monetary policy.

Lessons from the Postwar U.S. Experience

This brief review of postwar U.S. business cycles suggests two lessons that should guide the development of any new approach to dampening business cycles:

• Because of inflation inertia, dampening cycles in real-GNP growth requires dampening cycles in nominal-GNP growth.

• Policy makers may be tempted to move the economy below the natural rate of unemployment to generate jobs or above that rate to stop inflation, but in doing either they only breed future instability. By allowing the economy to remain so far below the natural unemployment rate between 1964 and 1969, policy makers of the 1960s indirectly created future business cycles by forcing the policy makers of the 1970s and 1980s to implement restrictive anti-inflationary demand-management policies. By allowing the economy to remain so far above the natural unemployment rate in 1982–83, current policy makers are breeding future instability.

The Choice of the Nominal-GNP-Growth Path

The choice of a nominal-GNP-growth target for domestic monetary policy, as opposed to the traditional monetary-growth and interest-rate targets, has several advantages. Like money, nominal GNP is a nominal variable and therefore an appropriate object of concern for central banks. Like monetary growth, nominal-GNP growth places a lid on the inflation rate and thus just as effectively avoids the disadvantages of nominal-interest-rate targeting to which Friedman (1968) called attention. A focus on nominal-GNP growth rather than monetary growth centers the attention of the central bank on offsetting shifts in velocity growth, such as those that occurred between 1929 and 1939 and between 1981 and 1983. In a world of velocity shifts, both real output and inflation are more closely tied to nominal-GNP growth than to monetary growth, and thus nominal-GNP targeting allows the central bank to achieve more closely its ultimate goal variables. Since there are time lags between changes in the direct control instruments of central banks and subsequent effects on nominal-GNP growth, it would be futile for central banks to attempt to offset every monthly or quarterly wiggle in velocity. Rather, it is the historical fact that velocity exhibits serially correlated fluctuations of more than a year that justifies the concern with offsetting velocity movements over that longer-term horizon.

Aggregate-supply constraints make the choice of a nominal-GNP-growth path both difficult and fraught with long-term dynamic implications. Only if the economy is initially operating at its natural output level, the inflation rate is zero, and there are no supply shocks can the choice be issue-free. Then nominal-GNP growth is simply set to equal natural real-GNP growth, which ratifies the current regime of stable prices, i.e., $y = q^N$. Ironically, the United States was actually in this situation at the end of 1963, just before the famous Kennedy-Johnson 1964 tax cut, which was subsequently accommodated by an acceleration in monetary growth. An important lesson is suggested by the subsequent five-year period of overheating with an output ratio above unity: Economists were overly optimistic about the economy's sustainable output level in 1964, and they may be overly optimistic again. Only by evaluating and continuously updating the best available historical and statistical evidence can the central bank steer between the Scylla of overheating and the Charybdis of lost output. An additional lesson is that the central bank must act more cautiously when the economy is close to the estimated natural output level than when it is far below that level.

The next hypothetical situation to be considered is the same as that in the preceding paragraph, with output equal to its natural level and supply shocks absent, but now the inflation rate is some positive number. If this inflation rate is generally agreed to be above the optimum inflation rate, the central bank faces the traditional tradeoff. A reduction of adjusted nominal-GNP growth ($y - q^N$) below the rate of inflation will—in the presence of inflation inertia—lead to a temporary period of lower output and higher unemployment. Whether this sacrifice is worth making depends on the social cost of lost output and employment, on the social benefit of lower inflation, on the social rate of time preference used to discount the permanent benefit of lower inflation, and on the component of the lost output taking the form of lost investment (which endows society with a semipermanent loss that depends on the average lifetime of capital goods). This list of considerations is traditional. However, an extra nontraditional element is the problem of future cyclical instability and overshooting that results from a decision to push the economy away from its natural output level for the purpose of fighting inflation. A specific illustration of the problem, based on the initial conditions of the United States in early 1983, is provided below. The problem is realistic enough to warrant serious consideration of a policy that accepts ongoing inflation if the central bank finds itself lucky enough to be in an economy currently at the natural output level. Then the central bank would set its nominal-GNP target at the inflation rate that seems currently imbedded in expectations [Eckstein's (1980) "core inflation rate"] plus the growth rate of natural real GNP, that is, $y = p + q^N$. It may be more effective in the long run for the central bank to ratify an ongoing inflation and to lobby the legislature for reforms (such as indexed bonds and financial deregulation) that reduce the costs of inflation than for the bank to engage in a single-handed inflation-fighting restrictive policy.

The level of difficulty increases when the economy is exposed to adverse supply shocks, represented in equations 4 and 5 above by a positive realization of the z variable. This pushes up the inflation rate spontaneously without any required excess-demand pressure and, if nominal GNP growth is maintained constant, requires a corresponding percentage decline in the output ratio. The advantage of nominal-GNP targeting in the face of supply shocks is that it represents a compromise solution in between the extreme alternatives of targeting real output and inflation. To maintain constant real GNP would require monetary accommodation of any resulting inflation that might occur, which might be both substantial and permanent if there were to be widespread cost-of-living escalators in wage and price contracts and/or a permanent decline in productivity and in natural real GNP resulting from the supply shock. To maintain constant inflation requires that the central bank reduce the growth of nominal GNP sufficiently to cause a recession that fully offsets the inflationary effect of the supply shock. In the simple context of equation 5, it can be shown that the output ratio ($\hat{Q}$) must be allowed to decline by z_t/b if any acceleration of inflation is to be avoided, and this recession may be substantial if b is a relatively small fraction.

Estimates of the Tradeoff Equation and the Natural Rate of Unemployment

If the economy is initially operating at a significant distance from the natural level of real GNP, then the central bank must have some view as to the current value of that variable. Recall that this is defined as the level of real GNP that is compatible with steady inflation in the absence of supply shocks. Its estimation requires fitting a regression equation in the general form of equation 4. My own work (1982a) proceeds by estimating equation 4 with quarterly U.S. data in the following specification, which substitutes a demographically weighted unemployment rate (U_t^W) for the output ratio ($\hat{Q}_t$):

$$p_t = d_0 + a(L)p_{t-1} + b(L)U_t^W + c(L)z_t + e_t. \tag{6}$$

Here the estimated coefficients written in the form $a(L)$ are one-sided polynomials in the lag operator, and e_t is an error term. A distributed lag on past actual inflation is used as a proxy for the expected rate of inflation that appears in equation 4. Conveniently, the estimated a_i coefficients on the lagged inflation terms sum to unity over the 1954–1980 sample period, and so the estimated version of equation 6 embodies the natural-rate hypothesis.

Table 3.3

	Four quarters of 1981	Four quarters of 1982	Eight quarters of 1981–82
Actual inflation rate	8.5	4.9	6.7
Predicted inflation rate	7.5	5.1	6.3
Error (actual − predicted)	1.0	−0.2	0.4

Extensive tests reject the hypothesis that the constant term d_0 or the unemployment coefficients (b_i) have shifted over the sample period, and so the estimates imply that the "no shock" natural weighted unemployment rate is equal to $-d_0/\sum b_i$. The natural unemployment rate for the official unweighted concept has gradually shifted upward relative to the constant natural weighted unemployment rate due to demographic shifts; values for the official natural-rate concept climb gradually from 5 percent before 1963 to 6 percent after 1975.[7] Natural real GNP is then set equal to actual real GNP in periods when actual unemployment was at the natural rate, and is interpolated in between. This yields the outout-ratio series shown in table 3.1.

The central bank cannot accept such an estimate of the natural unemployment rate as carved in stone. In addition to estimation errors, unidentified factors can cause the natural rate to shift over time. Thus, an important step in planning future monetary policy must be to monitor recent errors in the forecasting ability of an equation such as 6 above. To allow such monitoring, I have been careful not to reestimate equation 6 since early 1981. To test whether errors have been systematic and significant since the end of the sample period in 1980, the estimated version of equation 6 can be used to forecast the inflation rate for 1981 and 1982, using actual values of the independent variables but generating its own values, quarter by quarter, for the lagged-inflation-rate terms. The result is the forecasting record shown in table 3.3.

Thus, the actual inflation rate has turned out to be slightly higher than predicted, indicating that, thus far in the prediction period, my 6.0 percent estimate for the natural unemployment rate may be a bit too optimistic. This prediction record also has another important implication: that the relatively rapid deceleration of inflation observed in 1982 is not "surprising" and does not suggest any important shift in the economy toward greater price flexibility as compared with the period 1954–1980. There is no evidence that any "rational expectations" or "credibility" effect caused inflation to decelerate faster than predicted by the inertia-prone history of 1954–1980.

Although the evidence suggests that the "no shock" natural unemployment rate might be 6.5 percent rather than 6.0 percent, the band of uncertainty surrounding this question is more important for policy making in future years than it is in 1983, when the unemployment rate is around 10 percent. Another mitigating factor that somewhat eases the Fed's task is the inertia of the inflation process itself. If policy errors do cause unemployment to slip half a point below the natural rate for 6 months or a year, no great disaster will occur. Five years with unemployment two percentage points below the natural rate in the 1960s were required to generate an acceleration of inflation from 1.5 percent in 1964 to 5 percent in 1969. More modest errors will have more modest consequences.

An Illustration of Alternative Nominal-GNP Paths

Managing the economy when the initial unemployment rate is far from the natural rate can be likened to bringing an airplane in for a smooth landing on a runway. Here altitude corresponds to the unemployment rate and the runway corresponds to the natural unemployment rate. The problem is to avoid crashing into the runway. The worst thing the Federal Reserve can do is choose a constant growth rate of nominal GNP and stick to it, for this guarantees a crash.[8] This point is illustrated in figure 3.1, which shows what happens beginning in early 1983 in a simulation with my econometric inflation equation (6) when the growth rate of nominal GNP is set at 8 percent forever. The economy's recovery is slow, inflation continues to decelerate in response to economic slack, and (by definition) real-GNP growth speeds up. It is as if the pilot had pointed the plane's nose toward the runway and then turned on the engines full throttle. The lower frame of figure 3.1 shows how the economy crashes through the assumed 6 percent natural rate of unemployment in the period 1987–88, and the upper frame shows how a companion airplane, the inflation rate, takes off at the same time.

The Fed's task is tougher than the pilot's, because there is no chart that shows the exact altitude of the runway. The band of possible outcomes in figure 3.1 exhibits only one of the possible sources of uncertainty: the likely future behavior of the main supply-shock variables (the relative prices of imports, food, and energy, as well as the exchange rate). The pessimistic path assumes a "full rebound" in which all of those variables return to their values at the end of 1980 (i.e., the value of the dollar falls by about one-third in 1983–1985 and the nominal price of oil rises to about $40 per barrel). The optimistic path assumes "no rebound" in these variables, in which they all remain at their values of late 1982.

The maneuver necessary for the pilot to make a soft landing is illustrated in

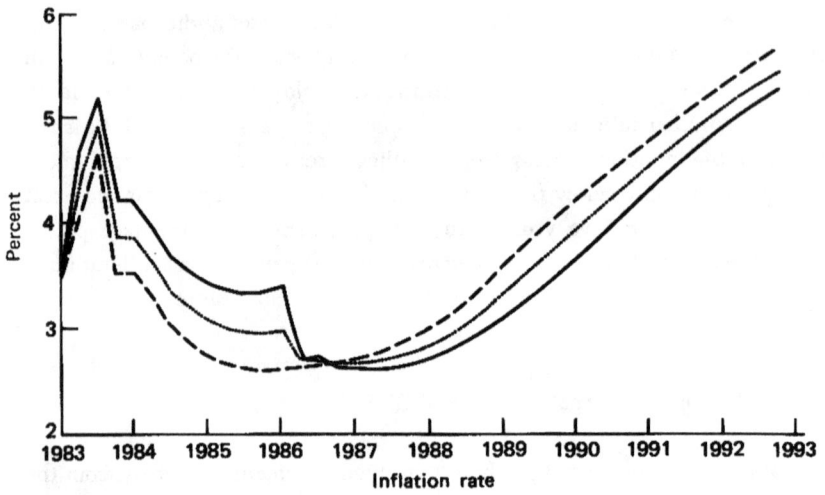

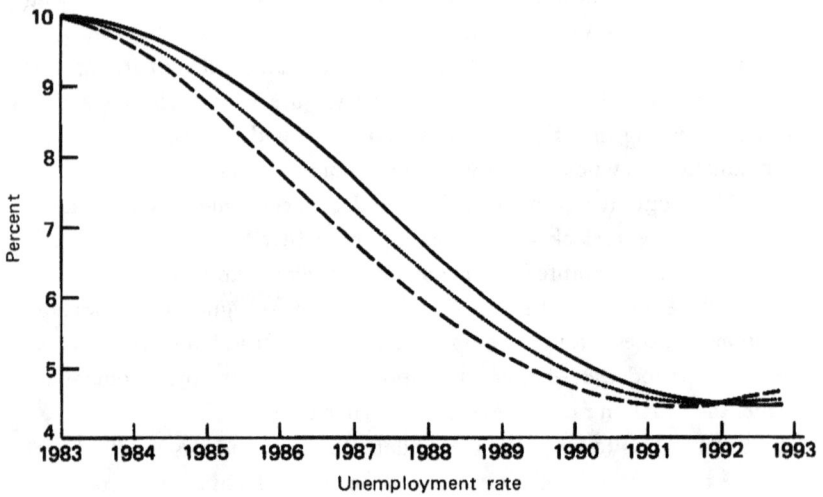

Figure 3.1
(− − −) No rebound; (· · ·) half rebound; (———) full rebound.

figure 3.2. Here the growth rate of nominal GNP starts out at 10.5 percent, but in late 1985 it is slowed suddenly to 8 percent. With either the optimistic or the pessimistic assumption about supply shocks, the unemployment rate glides smoothly in to the assumed 6 percent natural rate of unemployment. And, as shown in the top frame, the inflation rate (p) adjusts smoothly to the long-run 5 percent rate that is compatible with an 8 percent nominal-GNP growth rate (y) and a 3 percent growth rate of natural real GNP (q^N), since in the long run $p = y - q^N$.

The Fed must decelerate the growth rate of nominal GNP when the economy nears its natural rate of unemployment. That is the prerequisite for a soft landing. But a likely side effect of any attempt to achieve a sudden slowing of nominal-GNP growth is a sharp increase in interest rates and perhaps a recession during the transition period. To minimize the danger of inducing this type of instability, the Fed should plan to induce a rapid recovery when the economy is far from the natural rate and to gradually taper the growth rate of nominal GNP from then on. There is no compelling alternative. Rapid nominal-GNP growth maintained forever guarantees a crash landing. However, even moderate nominal-GNP growth maintained forever eventually leads to a crash landing, as is shown in figure 3.1.

Managing Monetary Policy in the Face of Unstable Velocity Growth

To this point most of the emphasis in this chapter has been on the influence of aggregate-supply constraints on the choice of target paths for nominal-GNP growth. Figures 3.1 and 3.2 showed that stable long-run growth of output without recurring oscillations requires a nominal-GNP path that is not constant but rather decelerates as the economy nears its natural rate of unemployment. If the rate of growth of M1 velocity were constant, then a policy of decelerating M1 growth at the desired pace of nominal-GNP deceleration would be adequate. If, in turn, the "money multiplier" (M1/monetary base) were constant, then a policy of decelerating the growth rate of the monetary base would be adequate. The latter policy has recently been recommended by prominent American monetarists, including Milton Friedman, Karl Brunner, Allan Meltzer, and William Poole.[9]

However, neither of the two required preconditions for targeting the monetary base—constant growth in M1 velocity and in the money multiplier—actually exists. M1 is flawed as a monetary target not only because M1 velocity has been unstable and unpredictable, but also because of multiplier instability. In this verdict we follow Bryant (1982, p. 599), who concludes that "the money stock cannot be an instrument of monetary policy:

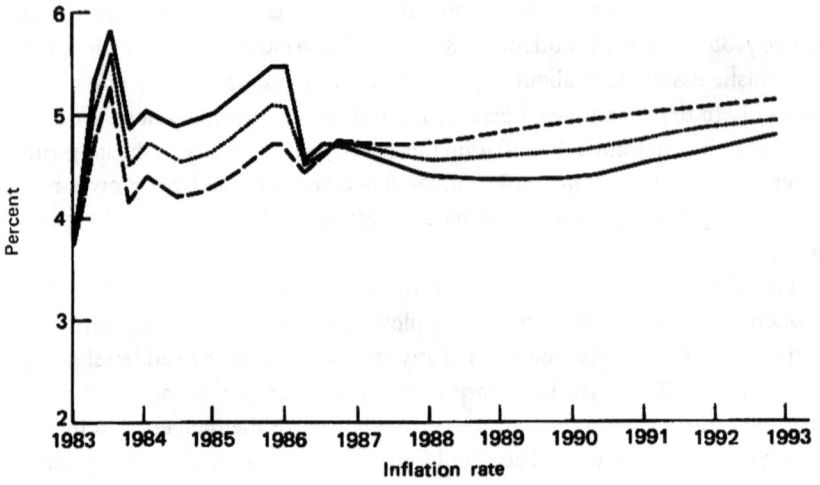

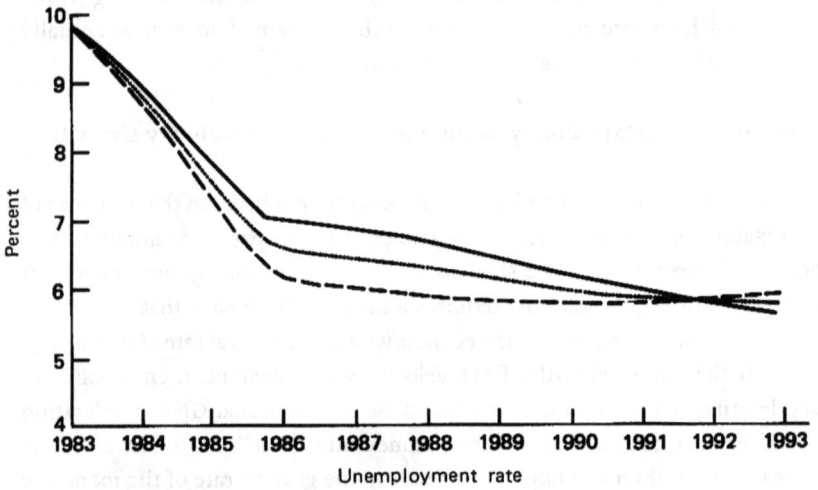

Figure 3.2
(– – –) No rebound; (· · ·) half rebound; (-   -) full rebound.

the Federal Reserve cannot control it precisely from one short-run period to the next." And growth in the base is flawed as a target for the same reason, because instability in velocity and the multiplier allows wide fluctuations in nominal-GNP growth to occur even in periods (such as 1971–1979) when base growth was remarkably stable.

The instability of velocity growth does create a significant problem for monetary policy, but it is important to avoid exaggerating the nature of the difficulty. Some short-term fluctuations of velocity growth are not only inevitable but impossible to forecast. The best forecasters have consistently missed the timing of cyclical peaks and troughs connected with inventory accumulation and decumulation. To avoid undue attention to nominal-GNP changes caused by the short-term inventory cycle, from this point on I exclude inventory changes from the concept of nominal GNP. In the American national accounting language, GNP less inventory change is called *final sales*.

The Historical Behavior of Final Sales, Velocity, and the Money Multiplier

Table 3.4 summarizes the historical U.S. behavior of the growth of nominal final sales, key monetary concepts, and the level of short-term interest rates over the period 1953–1982. Four subperiods are chosen, the first three divided into equal nine-year intervals through 1979 and the last subperiod chosen to begin in October 1979 at the time of the much-heralded change in Federal Reserve operating procedures. Section A of the table exhibits average percentage *growth rates* for nominal final sales and the monetary concepts and average percentage *levels* for the nominal and real Treasury bill rate.[10]

The most striking aspect of section A of table 3.4 is the common acceleration of all nominal growth rates in the first three subperiods, including nominal final sales, the monetary base, and M1. The nominal Treasury bill rate also increases over the same interval. Average growth in velocity was relatively stable over the first three subperiods, whereas growth in the money multiplier shifted from a small positive to a small negative number in the early 1960s. Notable features of the last subperiod, beginning in the last quarter of 1979, include the pronounced drop in velocity growth and the sharp increase in both the nominal and the real Treasury bill rate. There was almost no deceleration in M1 or base growth in comparison with the 1971–1979 average rate.

Section B of table 3.4 exhibits standard deviations of the same variables, calculated alternatively as one-quarter changes and four-quarter overlapping changes. The latter measure smooths out quarter-to-quarter noise in the data,

Table 3.4
Means and standard deviations of growth rates of nominal final sales and monetary variables
and nominal and real Treasury Bill rates for selected sample periods.

	1953:Q1 −1961:Q4	1962:Q1 −1970:Q4	1971:Q1 −1979:Q3	1979:Q3 −1982:Q4
A. Means				
1. Nominal final sales	4.6	7.0	10.1	8.3
2. Monetary base	1.3	5.3	7.6	7.2
3. M1 multiplier	0.4	−1.0	−1.0	−0.6
4. M1	1.7	4.3	6.6	6.0
5. Velocity (NFS/M1)	2.9	2.7	3.5	1.6
6. Nominal Treasury Bill rate	2.3	4.6	6.1	12.1
7. Real Treasury Bill rate	0.3	1.8	−0.1	3.8
B. Standard deviations (one-quarter/four-quarter)				
1. Nominal final sales	3.6/2.3	2.2/1/6	3.0/2.0	4.9/3.0
2. Monetary base	1.4/0.9	1.4/0.9	1.8/0.9	2.7/1.3
3. M1 multiplier	2.0/1.3	1.7/0.9	2.1/1.2	4.3/1.7
4. M1	2.0/1.4	2.3/1.6	2.0/1.3	4.7/1.5
5. Velocity (NFS/M1)	3.2/2.1	2.7/1.3	2.9/1.3	5.1/2.1
6. Nominal Treasury Bill rate	0.9	1.4	1.7	2.1
7. Real Treasury Bill rate	0.9	0.5	2.0	1.7

which the central bank can do little to control and which has little effect on economic well-being. The first three subperiods exhibit few interesting signs of change. The standard deviation of both nominal final-sales growth and velocity growth declined from the 1950s to the 1960s and 1970s. The variables showing the least variance were the growth rate of the monetary base, particularly by the four-quarter-change criterion, and the two interest-rate series. There was a substantial increase in the variance of interest rates, both nominal and real, from the first to the third subperiod.

The relatively stable behavior of growth in the monetary base requires more attention and comment, because growth in the base has often been suggested as the central operating target for monetary policy. The historical record suggests that the Fed has in fact maintained quite steady growth in the monetary base over long periods without preventing continuous large fluctuations in the growth of nominal final sales. For instance, between 1954 and 1961 the four-quarter rate of change of the monetary base never fell below 0.1 percent nor rose above 2.2 percent in any single quarter. The same narrow range was maintained between 1971 and 1979, when four-quarter base growth never fell below 6.6 percent nor rose above 8.9 percent. Yet, despite this steady pace of base growth, four-quarter growth in nominal final sales varied widely, from −0.3 percent to 7.8 percent between 1954 and 1961 and from 6.8 percent to 14.3 percent between 1971 and 1979. And, as Paulus (1982, p. 632) points out, "even though base growth has been essentially trendless over the decade, the core inflation rate moved from around 5 percent in the early seventies to almost 10 percent at the end of 1980." This examination of the historical record suggests that in fact past changes in the monetary base seem to have had little relation to changes in nominal final sales, except during the 1960s, when the economy made its transition from low to high growth rates of all nominal variables.

Much attention has been directed to the increased variance of monetary magnitudes after the change in Federal Reserve operating procedures in October 1979. Monetarists have claimed that the Federal Reserve did not, as often claimed, shift to "monetarist" operating procedures, because this would have required reducing the variance of monetary growth and increasing the variance of interest rates. Their claim seems validated by section B of table 3.4, which shows that there was no important change in the variance of interest rates (either nominal or real) after the third quarter of 1979 as compared with 1971–1979, but a huge increase in the standard deviation of one-quarter changes in the monetary base and in M1.[11] Changes in nominal final sales and in velocity also exhibit substantial increases in variance.

It is, however, also clear from table 3.4 that the monetarist claim results almost entirely from high-frequency quarter-to-quarter movements. The standard deviation of four-quarter changes in M1 after 1979 was virtually the same as that before 1979. There were larger increases in the standard deviation of four-quarter changes in the base and the multiplier, but these must have been offsetting since they did not make M1 more variable. The biggest shift after 1979 was actually in the standard deviation of changes in nominal final sales and in velocity. This implies that much of the instability in the economy after 1979 was due more to shifts in expenditure and money-demand behavior than to instability created by the Fed's control of M1.[12]

The Contribution of Monetary Variables to the Explanation of Growth in Nominal Final Sales

Thus far this chapter has contained two pieces of evidence that fluctuations in the growth rate of M1 or of the monetary base have not contributed much to the explanation of business cycles in nominal-final-sales growth (which in turn, because of inflation inertia, have caused business cycles in real output

Table 3.5
Contribution of alternative monetary variables to explanation of quarterly changes in nominal final sales for selected sample periods.

Percentage reduction in unexplained variance contributed by addition of four lagged values of	1953:Q1 −1961:Q4	1962:Q1 −1970:Q4	1971:Q1 −1979:Q3
1. **Nominal final sales**	23.8	24.8	1.0
2. **Alternative monetary variables**			
a. M1 changes (M1)	8.9	21.9	30.7
b. Base changes (MB)	5.6	18.6	3.5
c. Multiplier changes (MM)	6.6	17.8	28.5
d. Treasury Bill rate (i)	5.7	10.6	1.2
3. **Combinations of monetary variables**			
a. M1, i	10.9	25.7	34.1
b. MB, i	12.4	23.8	4.0
c. MM, i	9.2	22.3	31.0
d. MB, MM, i	26.3	34.8	48.3

and employment). The first was the observation based on table 3.1 that variations in M1 growth between expansion and recession phases of the business cycle accounted for only 14 percent of variations in nominal-GNP growth, and that velocity accounted for the remaining 86 percent. The second was the observation based on table 3.4 that smoothness of base growth in the 1950s and the 1970s relative to nominal-final-sales growth suggested a small causal role for the base in business cycles. This section examines these assertions more systematically.

Granger (1969) and Sims (1972) have popularized statistical tests to determine relations of exogeneity or temporal independence among time-series variables. One popular test is to regress a variable of interest (in the present case quarterly changes in nominal final sales) on its own lagged values and the lagged values of another variable of interest, such as changes in M1 or in the monetary base. The significance of the contribution of the monetary variable can be determined through the use of an F test that compares the complete equation with an alternative that excludes the monetary variable and thus includes only the lagged dependent variable and a constant term. A more general form of the test is to include several lagged monetary variables and test for their significance either individually or as a group.

Tables 3.5 and 3.6 carry out such tests for the first three subperiods studied in table 3.4. The period after October 1979 is excluded because there are not enough available observations for the test procedures to be used. Before we

Table 3.6
Significance level of contributions of quarterly changes of monetary base, Ml multiplier, and nominal final sales and of level of nominal Treasury Bill rate for selected sample periods

To explanation of	Significance level of contribution of			
	Base	Multiplier	T.B. rate	NFS
	(1)	(2)		(3)(4)
Base				
1953–1961	0.94	0.17	0.29	0.02*
1962–1970	0.95	0.16	0.92	0.19
1971–1979	0.44	0.13	0.11	0.15
Multiplier				
1953–1961	0.94	0.70	0.75	0.74
1962–1970	0.36	0.21	0.06*	0.69
1971–1979	0.77	0.95	0.08*	0.49
T.B. rate				
1953–1961	0.42	0.57	0.00*	0.92
1962–1970	0.13	0.03*	0.46	0.46
1971–1979	0.17	0.29	0.00*	0.13
NFS				
1953–1961	0.61	0.40	0.08*	0.30
1962–1970	0.64	0.44	0.48	0.11
1971–1979	0.17	0.04*	0.73	0.18

turn to measures of statistical significance in table 3.6, we calculate in table 3.5 the change in the percentage of nominal-final-sales-growth variance that is explained when alternative monetary variables are added to equations already containing the lagged dependent variable. In all cases the lagged dependent variable and the alternative monetary variables are included as four lagged one-quarter changes.

The first line in table 3.5 shows that serial correlation in the quarterly growth rate of nominal final sales (hereafter abbreviated NFS) explains about one-quarter of its variance in the 1950s and 1960s but virtually nothing in the 1970s. Line 2a shows that the addition of lagged changes in Ml to an equation already containing the lagged dependent variable explains 9 percent of the variation in the 1950s, 22 percent in the 1960s, and 31 percent in the 1970s. This compares to the contribution of 14 percent on average over cycle phases calculated in table 3.1. The next two lines contain an interesting result. Changes in the base contributed to explaining the variance of changes in NFS only in the 1960s, with virtually no contribution in the 1950s and 1970s. Almost all of the contribution of M1 in the 1970s (line 2a) can be traced to the behavior of the multiplier (line 2c). The small explanatory role of base growth in the 1950s and 1970s confirms the point made in the previous section that the Federal Reserve has really already experimented with maintenance of steady base growth without any success in dampening the cycle.

Line 2d indicates that the addition of the nominal Treasury bill rate by itself contributes little to the explanation of sales changes. Section 3 adds monetary variables in several combinations and confirms the results of section 2. The addition of the interest rate on lines 3a–3c adds little to the corresponding contributions on lines 2a–2c. The greatest contribution of the monetary variables is made when the base, the multiplier, and the interest rate are included together. The fact that the contribution on line 3d is greater than that on line 3a suggests that the base and multiplier components of M1 contribute to the explanation of sales growth with different coefficients, and so they are treated as separate variables.

Corresponding to this conclusion, table 3.6 exhibits the significance of each of four variables (changes in sales, the base, the multiplier, and the level of the nominal interest rate) in contributing to the explanation of each other's variance in the same subperiods. The four variables are estimated as a symmetric vector autoregressive model, with four lagged values of each variable entering each equation. The table lists significance levels rather than F ratios, and the variables that are significant at the level of 10 percent or better are indicated by asterisks.

Perhaps the most striking fact about table 3.6 is simply that there are very few asterisks. Another interesting result is that the three periods appear to exhibit quite different significance levels. Starting at the top of the table, the only variable making a significant contribution to growth in the monetary base is growth in NFS for the first period. This may imply that the Federal Reserve was sufficiently concerned about stabilizing interest rates to allow changes in the monetary base to respond to prior changes in NFS. In the 1970s the base was influenced at close-to-significance levels by all three other variables, the multiplier, the interest rate, and NFS. In the middle period the base appears to have been completely exogenous and thus a plausible candidate as the prime initiator of accelerating inflation. This response of the base may not actually have been exogenous, but rather may have been an accommodation of fiscal deficits (not included in the table) caused by the Kennedy-Johnson tax cuts and by spending on the Vietnam war.

Although the multiplier appears to have been exogenous in the 1950s, after 1961 its behavior reflects a significant influence of the Treasury bill rate. This may suggest a channel of causation by which changes in the interest rate alter portfolios, in turn shifting average reserve requirements and thus influencing the multiplier. The Treasury bill rate seems to have been influenced mainly by its own past values, but also by the multiplier in the 1960s. This interaction between the interest rate and the multiplier in the 1960s requires additional research to sort out the underlying causes.

The last section of table 3.6 comes to the variable that is of central interest: changes in NFS. Column 1 confirms the conclusions of the previous section that there was no significant causal role for the monetary base in the 1950s and 1970s. A new conclusion is that there was also no significant explanatory role for the base in the 1960s. This result seems hard to reconcile with the idea that acceleration in all nominal growth rates between the early and late 1960s was the source of the inflation of the 1970s. It is interesting to note, in fact, that in the 1960s the significance level of feedback from sales to the base (0.19) is greater than that from the base to sales (0.64).

The only monetary variables having significant explanatory power for sales growth are the Treasury bill rate in the 1950s and the multiplier in the 1970s. Since multiplier movements in the 1970s are significantly related to the Treasury bill rate, it thus appears that the latter plays a direct or indirect role in explaining sales growth in both the 1950s and the 1970s. Sales growth seems to live a life of its own in the 1960s, perhaps because of the omission of indicators of fiscal policy.

The results of this analysis differ substantially from those of a similar investigation carried out by Cagan (1982). Cagan's equations are in the same "Granger" format used in table 3.6 of this chapter, with the lagged dependent variable included (two lags for Cagan, four in table 3.6), but differ by including only one monetary variable at a time (and by explaining changes in nominal GNP rather than NFS). His results differ across two sample periods, 1953–1967 and 1968–1980. In the earlier period he finds that the checkable-deposits component of M1 is the only monetary variable that contains significant "advance information" about GNP movements, in the sense that the addition of five lagged changes in deposits adds to the fit at a high significance level. In the latter period M2 displays information not contained in checkable deposits or the monetary base. Cagan speculates that substitutions among M2 components have become larger, "reflecting no doubt the increase in level and variability of interest rates" (p. 683). In both periods, there is no significant advance information in the monetary base, reflecting what appears to be a contemporaneous correlation between GNP and currency demand and thus confirming my finding that the base contains no predictive power for NFS changes.

Cagan's finding that M1 contains advance information before 1968 and M2 after 1968 does not contradict my view that neither monetary aggregate is an appropriate operating target. My tests, which split M1 between the base and multiplier changes and which also include the level of the short-term interest rate, indicate that the main explanatory power of money comes from multiplier shifts that are associated with changes in the interest rate. These imply that control of base growth will not prevent fluctuations in the growth rate of monetary aggregates and NFS, and also that portfolio shifts make M1 unsuitable as an operating target. Although this chapter does not test M2 explicitly, recent shifts in M2 velocity also appear to render it unsuitable for monetary targeting. (See Kopcke 1983 and Tatom 1983.)

Implications of the Statistical Analysis

The most important conclusion is that changes in the monetary base appear to play no significant causal role in explaining changes in nominal final sales during the 1953–1979 period. Although estimated in a very different format, these results thus seem to confirm the negative results of Sims (1980) regarding the causal role of money. Unlike Sims's, my conclusion is not dependent on the inclusion of the interest rate. Also, there is more emphasis here on the lack of causal influence of base changes; multiplier changes seem to play a significant role, at least in the 1971–1979 subperiod. The major difference in the roles of the base and the multiplier confirms the results of King (1983), who deserves credit for directing my attention to the behavior of the two components of M1 growth. It also confirms the emphasis placed by Fellner (1982) and Bryant (1982) on multiplier instability as a major source of changes in M1.[13]

Implementing a Nominal-Final-Sales Target

The literature on domestic monetary policy can be viewed as drifting over a long period toward the conclusion that nominal spending should be the central medium-term target of the Federal Reserve Board. This conclusion has been reached by a "lesser of evils" process in which alternatives have been gradually omitted from consideration. First, Friedman (1968) demolished the case for targeting nominal interest rates by showing that this requires the central bank to accommodate any upward shift in spending and any downward shift in the demand for money, as well as any subsequent upward pressure on the nominal interest rate coming from an upward adjustment in the expected rate of inflation. Some interest-rate partisans have retreated from targeting the nominal rate to the real rate. Real interest rates are hard to target because they are not observable. Further, a real-interest-rate target leads to procyclical monetary fluctuations, as demonstrated in undergraduate macroeconomics texts. It has the additional perverse effect of requiring the Fed to institute a restrictive monetary policy in response to adverse supply shocks. For instance, in 1974 the Treasury bill rate increased from 7.0 percent to 7.9 percent while the inflation rate in the GNP deflator soared from 5.8 percent to 8.8 percent, reducing the real interest rate from 1.2 percent to −0.9 percent. A policy of stabilizing the real interest rate would have required the Fed to boost the nominal Treasury bill rate by 2 percentage points more than actually occurred, which in turn would have required that, instead of merely bringing M1 growth to a halt between April and October 1974, the Fed would have been required to achieve substantially *negative* M1 growth.

The only advantage of real-interest-rate targeting, as pointed out by Poole (1970), is in a situation when the demand for money is much more unstable than the demand for commodities. The period between early 1981 and mid 1983 in the United States, with unparalleled movements in velocity as financial deregulation caused portfolio shifts, is a good example of a situation in which the Poole analysis would call for interest-rate stabilization. But Poole reaches his conclusion in a theoretical model with fixed prices where the ultimate criterion is stabilization of real GNP, and with fixed prices this criterion is equivalent to stabilizing nominal GNP. Thus, even in a period of portfolio shifts and unstable money demand, a nominal-GNP or sales-growth criterion can do as well as a real-interest-rate criterion, without the need to identify whether or not money demand is unstable, without an undesirable tendency toward monetary accommodation in response to increases in commodity demand, and without procyclical movements in monetary growth that amplify the changes in real output caused by supply shocks.

The new element contained in this chapter, which builds on and confirms the work of Sims and King, is that both M1 and the monetary base are subject to severe limitations as possible operating targets for the central bank. Any causative role for M1 or the base is limited to the period of the 1960s, when all nominal variables accelerated together. The significance tests of table 3.6 find no evidence that the acceleration of the base preceded that in final sales. M1 had an important role only in the 1970s, because of changes in the multiplier rather than the base, and the Fed did not control the multiplier directly. In short, the famous monetarist recommendation of maintaining steady growth in either the monetary base or M1 has little potential as a remedy for business cycles. Because the targeting of interest rates must be ruled out as well, nominal GNP or sales emerges as the least objectionable target.[14]

Length of Horizon

Since 1979 the Federal Reserve has adopted the practice of targeting on "M1 growth cones," that is, ranges of the level of M1 that begin at a single point at the end of one year and then extend out to cover a considerable range by the end of the next year. The defect of this procedure is that years are considered one at a time, and no effort is made to correct for drift. Thus, if the range for year "1" were 4–8 percent, with a desired mean of 6, and if the actual outcome by the end of year 1 were a growth rate of 9 percent, then the growth cone for year 2 would begin 3 points (9 − 6) over the previous target.

This type of drift could be avoided by planning over a longer horizon, for example 10 years as in figures 3.1 and 3.2. The desired path for growth rates over the next decade is then translated into a desired path for the *level* of nominal final sales. Thus, any situation when the level of NFS exceeds the target path would call for monetary restriction, whether it occurs in the spring or the fall and whether it occurs this year or 3 years from now. There would be no jump to a new "growth cone" at an arbitrary date.

The entire growth path would be contingent on a continually updated estimate of the economy's ultimate long-run target: the natural rate of unemployment. If an inflation equation such as equation 6 above were to begin underpredicting the rate of inflation, this would imply that the natural rate of unemployment had begun to drift up, and that a lower NFS target path would be appropriate. The reverse could occur as well. The crucial distinction here is that the path would not be revised in light of "misses" in tracking the desired path during a particular year, but would be revised only if there were new information that the entire path should be revised from beginning to end. I share Fellner's belief (1982, p. 642) that the central bank should exhibit a "high degree of reluctance" to change the NFS path once it is set.

There is an overlap between this chapter and the papers of Fellner (1982) and Meltzer (1981). They would set a target for the average growth in nominal GNP over an entire business cycle but would not try to smooth fluctuations in nominal-GNP growth within the business cycle. Instead, Meltzer would calculate the desired trend path of the monetary base from historical trends in the multiplier and in velocity and require the Fed to maintain constant base growth as its prime objective. Fellner emphasizes the defects of base control, which arise from the instability of the M1 multiplier, and prefers M1 as the operating objective; this requires movements in the base to offset movements in the multiplier. The present discussion starts from the same place—the choice of a path for nominal GNP (or NFS) over the business cycle—but pays attention to the behavior of NFS growth *within* the cycle as well, on the grounds that historical trends in velocity have become a poor guide to the path of M1 required to achieve stable NFS growth.

The Use of Forecasts

Since quarterly changes in NFS tend to be erratic, a more appropriate focus for the central bank would be changes in a longer-term moving average, say four-quarter rates of change. This leads to the problem of the lags between changes in the control instruments of the central bank and the reaction of NFS growth. One possible solution would be to target forecasts for NFS growth over the subsequent four quarters. Imagine that the desired growth path for the United States in 1983 is 10.5 percent, as assumed in figure 3.2. As of July 1983, the "central tendency" in the forecasts of Federal Open Market Committee members was for nominal-GNP growth of 9.9 percent for 1982:Q4 to 1983:Q4 and 9.5 percent for 1983:Q4 to 1984:Q4.[15] In response to these forecasts, the Fed would have reacted by gradually allowing short-term interest rates to drift lower. It would have ignored rapid observed growth rates in the monetary base and in M1. It might also have encouraged a depreciation in the exchange rate, since the high value of the dollar appears to have been partly responsible for the slump in velocity growth since mid 1981.

The implication that in 1983 the Fed would have paid attention to interest rates in the short run and ignored base growth reflects both Poole's (1970) conclusion and the results of table 3.6. When the demand for money is unstable, controlling interest rates makes more sense than controlling the base. Further, since 1962 interest rates (working either directly or indirectly through the multiplier) appear to have had more influence on final sales than changes in the monetary base. Interest rates would be used only as a short-run indicator to help the Fed guide the economy to its desired NFS path, and not as a medium-term target. As the monetary stimulus is gradually reflected in an increase in the forecast growth of NFS, then interest rates could be allowed to rise.

There would be nothing novel in the Federal Reserve's using its own forecasts, since it does this already. In fact, the Fed is required by the Congress to publish twice a year its outlook for nominal-GNP growth and other variables. What would be new about NFS targeting would be a shift away from the Fed's tendency to "look at everything." Instead, the Fed would look at the natural unemployment rate in the long run, maintain the economy along an NFS path in the medium run, and guide the economy to that path in the short run by looking at the behavior of interest rates, the monetary base (in periods of more quiescent money-demand behavior), and the exchange rate. NFS growth would be transformed from a variable that the Fed forecasts, as at present, into a central objective of policy.

Some readers may feel, like Fellner, that it is impossible for the Fed to lean against velocity changes within the duration of the typical business cycle. The potential for the use of forecasts can be assessed with the evidence that has been compiled over the past 12 years by Stephen McNees. For every quarter since 1971:Q2 he has recorded the four-quarter-ahead forecast of nominal-GNP change (and other aggregate variables) for five leading commercial forecasting models. The value of these forecast changes in predicting actual four-quarter changes in nominal GNP can be assessed by running a regression in which the actual change is the dependent variable and the forecast made four quarters previous to that change is the right-hand variable (a constant term is also included). The coefficients and t ratios for such regression equations are shown here for three sample periods:

1972:Q1–1976:Q4   0.56   (2.42)
1977:Q1–1981:Q4   0.50   (2.56)
1977:Q1–1982:Q4   0.28   (0.80)

Thus, the forecast changes do help to predict the actual changes, with a coefficient of about 0.5. The comparison of the second and third sample periods indicates that forecasters made very serious errors in forecasting nominal-GNP growth in 1982, so that a central bank reacting to stabilize forecasts made in late 1981 for late 1982 would have been unable to counteract the decline in velocity growth that actually occurred in 1982. As the year 1982 proceeded, the level of nominal GNP (and NFS) and the year-ahead forecasts thereof drifted further and further below a stable growth path, and thus a central bank operating to control an NFS target would have moved earlier to reduce interest rates.

The 1982 forecasting failure does not detract from the value of forecasts that is evident in the record for 1972–1981. This record suggests that a central bank operating during 1976–1981 to maintain stable growth in NFS at, say, 10 percent per annum would have moved much earlier toward restrictive policy actions than actually occurred in the historical record, for the McNees series shows that nominal-GNP growth was forecast to exceed 10 percent for thir-teen successive four-quarter periods—those ending in 1976:Q1 through 1979:Q1. It is this serial correlation in the deviation of actual and forecast nominal-GNP changes from their mean value over the business cycle that supports an attempt by central banks to control NFS rather than a monetary aggregate.[16]

Objections to Nominal-GNP-Growth Targeting

A wide range of objections have been raised to the use of nominal-GNP growth as the central medium-term operating target of the central bank. Some of these are included in the July 1983 congressional testimony of Paul Volcker, the chairman of the Federal Reserve Board.[17] Critics do not all share the same objections; some feel, for instance, that nominal-GNP targeting would give the Fed too much discretion, and some feel that the Fed would be hamstrung with too little discretion.

Too Much or Too Little Discretion?

One view, currently advocated by Milton Friedman, is that a central bank cannot be trusted to engage in the discretionary actions (e.g., changes in reserve growth) that would be required under a system of nominal-GNP targeting. Central bank officials are viewed not as following the rational precepts of academic advisers, but rather as bureaucrats responding to short-run pressures from within and outside their organization. The Friedman solution, shared by some other monetarists, is to tie the hands of the irresponsible bureaucrats completely by limiting them to a simple rule, such as Friedman's recent proposal for the Fed to make "$X" hundred million of open-market purchases every Monday. The problem with this point of view, already documented above, is that stable growth in the monetary base has actually occurred in the past and has not prevented instability in the growth rates of monetary aggregates and nominal spending.

An opposite criticism is suggested by some Federal Reserve officials, including Chairman Volcker. The Fed should continue to "look at everything," or, in Volcker's words: "Decisions on monetary policy should take account of a variety of incoming information on GNP or its components. . . . This simply can't be incorporated into annual numerical objectives."[18] Yet the present approach of looking at everything has allowed the Fed in the past to allow nominal-GNP growth to drift upward, as in the late 1960s and late 1970s, or to fall far below anyone's objectives, as in 1982. Another response to this criticism is that the central bank has no control over the division of nominal-GNP growth between inflation and real-GNP growth, and that its proper business is to provide a "nominal anchor" for the economy.

The Fed Can't Control Nominal GNP

The linkages between the Fed's direct-control instruments (reserve growth and the discount rate) and nominal spending are loose, and the lags are long.

In Volcker's words: "the channels of influence from our actions ... to final spending totals are complex and indirect, and operate with lags, extending over years. The attempt to 'fine tune' over, say, a six-month or yearly period, toward a numerically specific, but necessarily arbitrary, short-term objective could well defeat the longer-term purpose." [19] However, a nominal-GNP-growth target like that in figure 3.2 is not "arbitrary" or "short term" but rather is designed to promote the Fed's basic long-term objective, which is achieving a soft landing that allows maintenance of steady real growth with moderate inflation. The length of lags has been exaggerated in some past research. Real activity responded within 6–9 months to shifts in Federal Reserve policy in numerous past episodes, including its tightening in 1966, 1969, 1974, and 1981 and its loosening in 1967, 1971–72, 1975–76, and 1982. By focusing on the best current four-quarter-ahead forecasts, the Fed could operate to counteract some of the extreme periods of excessive or insufficient nominal-GNP growth. There is no need for the Fed to lean against short-term within-year movements that cannot be forecast and that, if quickly reversed, would have no adverse consequences.

Coordination with Fiscal Policy

Ideally monetary and fiscal policy would take coordinated action to achieve economic objectives. In some countries governmental institutions make this possible, and there can be a single objective agreed upon by both monetary and fiscal policy makers. An important criticism of nominal-GNP targeting is that it allocates too much responsibility to the central bank. In the chaotic and uncoordinated policy setting of the United States, acceptance by the Federal Reserve of sole responsibility for sustaining an economic recovery would appear to remove the incentive for Congress to make difficult decisions on the budget. Unfortunately, the built-in limitations of the American constitutional system have already, for better or worse, handed responsibility for macroeconomic policy to the Federal Reserve.

Avoidance of Accountability

This criticism states that if the central bank has a nominal-GNP-growth objective and misses its target, it can avoid accountability by blaming other factors (fiscal policy, swings in consumer attitudes, and so on). Yet this problem already exists in the present system. The Fed failed to prevent either an undesired collapse of spending growth in 1982 or an explosion of double-digit money growth in 1982–83. It has already become expert at giving excuses—in this case, financial deregulation and portfolio shifts. There will always be an irreducible minimum variance in velocity that will prevent the Fed from achieving stable spending growth, no matter whether its proximate operating target is the monetary base, the money supply, or nominal spending itself.

Conclusion

Nominal spending cannot be controlled precisely. Forecasts are imperfect and will occasionally lead the government astray. The ultimate goal of guiding the economy smoothly to the natural unemployment rate and then maintaining that rate involves an unobservable variable that must be estimated, and any estimation procedure is open to controversy. Changes in institutions, for instance, can alter today's parameter values from those observed during earlier years of the sample period of estimation.

The empirical work in this chapter is limited to evidence for the postwar United States. A parallel research effort will be required to determine the procedures for the conduct of monetary policy that would be optimal in other nations. The merits of controlling growth in nominal GNP or in final sales rather than controlling the monetary base or the money supply depend partly on the historical record of the stability of velocity and the "advance knowledge" of nominal-GNP movements contributed by monetary aggregates. For instance, a target based on *forecasts* of nominal-final-sales growth rather than the actual outcome hinges on the availability of forecasts that actually make a positive contribution to the prediction of nominal-sales growth four quarters ahead. In the absence of good forecasts, a choice would have to be made between targeting a moving average of actual nominal sales changes, targeting a monetary aggregate, or targeting another concept such as liquid assets or aggregate credit.

Acknowledgments

This research was supported by the National Science Foundation, and is part of the National Bureau of Economic Research program in Economic Fluctuations. I am grateful to Stephen King and John Veitch for their help with the data, and to Stephen Axilrod, Hermann Dudler, Milton Friedman, Herschel Grossman, Jerry Jordan, Thomas Mayer, and Allen Sinai for their comments and criticisms.

Notes

1. The only variable with significant explanatory power in the equation used by Barro and Rush to proxy for the concept of "anticipated monetary changes" is a one-quarter lag on actual monetary change. Thus, it takes only a single quarter for a monetary change to become fully anticipated. The policy-ineffectiveness proposition is rejected in recent empirical papers by Mishkin (1982) and Gordon (1982b).

2. An explanation of the origins of three-year union contracts in the United States and the contrast with shorter-term contracts in the United Kingdom and Japan is contained in Gordon 1982c. The general idea of the central bank operating in the face of constraints in developed most fully in Gordon 1975, which builds on ideas contained in Reder 1948.

3. This is the growth rate of the amount of real GNP that the economy can achieve when operating at the "natural rate of unemployment," defined as the unemployment rate compatible with steady nonaccelerating inflation in the absence of supply shocks.

4. Estimates of the Okun's Law relationship between the U.S. unemployment rate and the output ratio are contained in Gordon 1982a (p. 94). The relationship between the demographically weighted unemployment rate and the output ratio remains completely stable over the 1954–1980 period. The natural aggregate unemployment rate drifts up relative to the constant weighted natural rate as a result of demographic shifts. The relationship has recently been studied for Japan by Hamada and Kurosaka (1983).

5. This list of supply shocks includes several factors, including the relative prices of oil, food, and raw materials, as well as the exchange rate, that also reflect the influence of monetary and fiscal policy. These are termed "supply shocks" solely for terminological convenience.

6. The concepts and equations in this section are explained in full, both graphically and algebraically, in chapters 8 and 9 of Gordon 1984.

7. The natural unemployment rate has risen far more in some other countries. The German evidence is assessed in this framework in Franz 1983.

8. Poole (1982, p. 592), in contrast, recommends a monetary airplane that requires no "pilot expertise" and instead runs in an "autopilot" or "hands off" mode.

9. See Friedman 1983a, Brunner 1981, Meltzer 1981, and Shadow Open Market Committee 1983. Poole (1982, p. 593) recommends a policy of "really stable growth in the nonborrowed monetary base."

10. The real interest rate is calculated as the nominal interest rate minus an eight-quarter moving average of the quarterly change in the personal-consumption deflator.

11. B. Friedman (1982) shows, however, that there was a marked increase in the variance of long-term interest rates after 1979.

12. In fact, Poole (1982) argues that the Fed did not change its operating procedures after 1979 in a fundamental way.

13. Fellner (1982) attributes most of the variance in the multiplier to shifts in the currency-deposit ratio.

14. A detailed consideration of other broader monetary aggregates, or a credit target, is outside the scope of this chapter. Targeting credit has all the disadvantages of targeting nominal sales without any of the advantages. Both credit and NFS are distant from the Fed's control instruments, but nominal final sales is a variable of central policy concern whereas no one cares directly about the level or growth rate of total credit.

15. See U.S. Federal Reserve Board 1983, p. 5.

16. In more detailed tests, Mayer (1983) also concludes that forecasts are sufficiently accurate to allow the Fed to achieve a modest dampening of the business cycle.

17. This testimony is included in U.S. Federal Reserve Board 1983.

18. U.S. Federal Reserve Board 1983, p. 15.

19. U.S. Federal Reserve Board 1983, p. 14.

References

Barro, Robert J., and Mark Rush. 1980. "Unanticipated Money and Economic Activity," in S. Fischer, ed., *Rational Expectations and Economic Policy* (University of Chicago Press), pp. 23–48.

Brunner, Karl. 1981. "The Case Against Monetary Activism. "*Lloyd's Bank Review*, no. 139, pp. 20–39.

Bryant, Ralph C. 1982. "Federal Reserve Control of the Money Stock." *Journal of Money, Credit, and Banking*, vol. 14, no. 4, pp. 597–625.

Bryant, Ralph C. 1983. *Controlling Money: The Federal Reserve and Its Critics* (Washington: Brookings Institution).

Cagan, Phillip. 1982. "The Choice among Monetary Aggregates as Targets and Guides for Monetary Policy." *Journal of Money, Credit and Banking*, vol. 14, no. 4, pp. 661–686.

Eckstein, Otto. 1980. *Core Inflation* (Englewood Cliffs, N.J.: Prentice-Hall).

Fellner, William. 1982. "Criteria for Useful Targeting: Money versus the Base and Other Variables." *Journal of Money, Credit and Banking*, vol. 14, no. 4, pp. 641–660.

Franz, Wolfgang. 1983. "The Past Decade's Natural Rate and the Dynamics of German Unemployment: A Case Against Demand-Policy." *European Economic Review*, vol. 21, no. 1/2, pp. 51–76.

Friedman, Benjamin M. 1982. "Federal Reserve Policy, Interest Rate Volatility, and the U.S. Capital Raising Mechanism." *Journal of Money, Credit and Banking*, vol. 14, no. 4, pp. 721–745.

Friedman, Milton. 1968. "The Role of Monetary Policy." *American Economic Review*, vol. 58, pp. 1–17.

Friedman, Milton. 1970. "A Theoretical Framework for Monetary Analysis." *Journal of Political Economy*, vol. 78, no. 2, pp. 221–222.

Friedman, Milton. 1983a. Monetary Policy and Economic Conditions. Unpublished memorandum, January 14.

Friedman, Milton. 1983b. "Is the Summit Worth the Climb?" *Newsweek*, May 30, p. 33.

Gordon, Robert J. 1975. "The Demand for and Supply of Inflation." *Journal of Law and Economics*, vol. 18, pp. 807–36.

Gordon, Robert J. 1982a. "Inflation, Flexible Exchange Rates, and the Natural Rate of Unemployment," in M. N. Baily, ed., *Workers, Jobs, and Inflation* (Washington: Brookings Institution), pp. 88–157.

Gordon, Robert J. 1982b. "Price Inertia and Policy Ineffectiveness in the United States." *Journal of Political Economy*. vol. 90, pp. 1087–1117.

Gordon, Robert J. 1982c. "Why U.S. Wage and Employment Behavior Differs from that in Britain and Japan." *Economic Journal*, vol. 92, no. 365, pp. 13–44.

Gordon, Robert J. 1984. *Macroeconomics*, third edition (Boston: Little, Brown).

Granger, Clive W. J. 1969. "Investigating Causal Relations by Econometric Models and Cross-Spectral Methods." *Econometrica*, vol. 37 (July), pp. 424–438.

Hamada, Koichi, and Hoshio Kurosaka. 1983. The Relationship between Production and Unemployment in Japan: Okun's Law in a Comparative Perspective. Presented at International Seminar on Macroeconomics, Paris.

King, Stephen R. 1983. Interest Rates and the Influence of Money on Output and Prices. Presented at NBER Conference on Macroeconomics, Cambridge, Mass.

Kopcke, Richard W. 1983. "Must the Ideal 'Money Stock' Be Controllable?" *New England Economic Review*, March–April, pp. 6–10.

Mayer, Thomas. 1983. Forecast Errors and the Efficacy of Countercyclical Policy. Working paper 2, Research Program in Applied Macroeconomics and Macro Policy, University of California, Davis.

Meltzer, Allan H. 1981. Consequences of the Federal Reserve's Reattachment to Free Reserves. Presented at Western Economic Association meetings.

Mishkin, Frederick. 1982. "Does Anticipated Monetary Policy Matter: An Econometric Investigation." *Journal of Political Economy*, vol. 90, no. 1, pp. 22–51.

Paulus, John D. 1982. "Comment on 'Federal Reserve Control of the Money Stock,' by Ralph C. Bryant." *Journal of Money, Credit and Banking*, vol. 14, no. 4, pp. 626–631.

Poole, William. 1970. "Optimal Choice of Monetary Policy Instruments in a Simple Stochastic Macro Model." *Quarterly Journal of Economics*, vol. 83, pp. 197–216.

Poole, William. 1982. "Federal Reserve Operating Procedures." *Journal of Money, Credit and Banking*, vol. 14, no. 4, pp. 575–596.

Reder, Melvin W. 1948. "The Theoretical Problems of a National Wage-Price Policy." *Canadian Journal of Economics and Political Science*, February, pp. 46–61.

Sargent, Thomas J., and Neil Wallace. 1975. "Rational Expectations, the Optimal Monetary Instrument, and the Optimal Money Supply Rule." *Journal of Political Economy*, vol. 83, pp. 241–257.

Shadow Open Market Committee. 1983. Policy Statement and Position Papers." Working paper, University of Rochester Graduate School of Management.

Sims, Christopher A. 1972. "Money, Income and Causality." *American Economic Review*, vol. 62 (September), pp. 540–552.

Sims, Christopher A. 1980. "Comparison of Interwar and Postwar Business Cycles: Monetarism Reconsidered." *American Economic Review*, vol. 70, no. 2, pp. 250–257.

Tatom, John A. 1983. "Money Market Deposit Accounts, Super-NOWs and Monetary Policy." *Federal Reserve Bank of St. Louis Review*, vol. 65, no. 3, pp. 5–16.

U.S. Federal Reserve Board. 1983. *Monetary Policy Objectives for 1983.*

4 Monetary Policy in Postwar Japan

Koichi Hamada
Fumio Hayashi

When we look back over the past hundred years, we cannot help feeling that the Bank of Japan is now at its zenith as far as the autonomy of monetary policy is concerned. In the past, there were many occasions of forced funding of government expenditures, particularly the wartime expenditures that led to nationwide inflation. The current situation is different. There is room for minor disagreements over the way monetary policy should be handled now. In particular, one could argue that a slightly more expansionary monetary policy should be adopted. Broadly, however, Japan's monetary management after the second oil crisis can be regarded as one of the most successful such experiences in any industrialized country.

Now the Japanese economy is indeed in recession. However, the unemployment rate is much lower than in most Western countries. The price level is more stable, and the instantaneous rate of inflation is almost zero. The monetary policy of the Bank of Japan has contributed to the relatively successful macro performance of the Japanese economy after the second oil crisis, because the Bank learned much from the stagflation that followed the first oil crisis. The Bank of Japan was able to gain *de facto* autonomy of monetary policy,[1] because the government and the public learned how costly it is to use monetary policy for objectives other than price stability and the maintenance of an adequate level of aggregate demand.

It is also true, however, that the scope of monetary policy in Japan at present is quite limited because of the worldwide recession. Radical experiments in demand-management policy are being tried in industralized countries, notably by the Reagan administration in the United States. Never in postwar history have such large-scale contractionary policies and such an extreme combination of fiscal deficits and tight monetary policy been practiced in major industrialized countries. One could appreciate them as a monumental attempt to cut down inflationary expectations among the public and to revive flexibility in wages and prices. Alternatively, one could regard them as a weapon to realize a magnified political business cycle by weakening the influence of labor unions, or as a political maneuver to redistribute income from recipients of social-welfare expenditures to upper-middle-class taxpayers.

In any case, the extreme policy mix of tight money and (forecasted) large budget deficits in the United States and other countries has contributed to the high levels of real interest rates throughout the world, which might work against economic growth. The flexible-exchange-rate regime may block the link among nominal rates of interest, but it does not block the link among real rates of interest across countries. Policies that are oriented to lower growth can easily transmit themselves across national borders. This situation imposes a quite restrictive constraint on the range in which the Japanese economic policies can be conducted, as easier monetary policy may cause further depreciation of the yen. We prefer the combination of a more flexible budget and easier money for present-day Japan. However, one of the reasons the Japanese macroeconomic policy looks too timid is the presence of this international constraint.

Ideally, we should attempt a comparative study of monetary policies in our times among many industrialized countries. However, in the presence of distinguished economists from the central banks of many countries, we do not find it to be our comparative advantage to accomplish that task. It seems more appropriate for us to give a general description of Japan's monetary experience, and to summarize and supplement macroeconomic research done there. We shall also attempt to provide a brief institutional background for an understanding of the monetary mechanism of the Japanese economy and for an assessment of the performance of monetary policy.

The Japanese Financial Structure in Transition

It would take another complete chapter to explain fully how the Japanese financial system works.[2] We shall confine ourselves to a brief description of its traditional characteristics and some of the gradual but steady institutional changes to which it is subject. We shall start from the characteristics of the flow of funds in Japan.

Japanese households exhibit a saving ratio that is higher than that in almost any other industrialized country—a ratio matched, perhaps, only by Italy and some newly industrialized countries. The ratio of saving to disposable income is around 20 percent. (See table 4.1 for an international comparison.) This very high saving rate is a driving force of Japan's economic growth, and at the same time remains one of the great puzzles of the Japanese economy.

Table 4.1
Savings ratios (percentages).

	Japan	United States	United Kingdom	West Germany	France	Italy	Canada
1970	18.2	8.2	6.6	17.9	12.6	19.2	6.1
1971	17.9	8.3	4.8	17.0	13.5	20.8	6.5
1972	18.2	6.7	7.1	15.5	13.7	21.9	7.7
1973	20.9	8.9	8.3	14.0	14.2	21.7	9.5
1974	23.7	8.7	8.4	14.8	14.1	20.7	10.8
1975	22.1	8.8	8.7	15.2	15.3	22.8	11.1
1976	22.4	7.1	8.0	13.4	12.9	22.5	10.3
1977	21.0	5.8	7.2	13.4	13.2	22.1	10.1
1978	20.6	5.4	9.7	13.3	14.2	23.5	10.7
1979	18.7	5.4	11.3	13.8	12.5	22.0	10.9
1980	19.4	5.7	12.4	12.8	10.6	19.0	—
1981	—	5.5	—	—	—	—	—

Source: Bank of Japan, *Kokusai Hikaku Tokei* [International Comparison of Statistics].

Historically, most of these savings have been channeled into the business sector through the commercial banking sector.

A basic change in the flow of funds occurred around 1975. The Japanese government emerged as a big spending unit. Thus, recently a large part of the savings from the household sector has been channeled to the government sector as well. In 1978, 82 percent of the surplus of funds in the individual (noncorporate) sector was absorbed by the government sector to finance the budget deficit, while only 9 percent was absorbed by the private corporate sector. This tendency has changed a little (see table 4.2), but the government sector remains the largest user of funds. Why large government deficits seem to have less of an effect on the Japanese economy than on the American economy is yet to be explained.

As a result of substantial deficit spending by the Japanese government since 1975, a large amount of government debt has accumulated in the portfolio of the public. At the end of March 1983, the outstanding national debt was 96.4 trillion (i.e., 96.4×10^{12}) yen, more than 36 percent of the projected GNP of fiscal 1982 (which ended in March 1983). This creates a difficult problem of debt management and future debt refunding for the Japanese monetary authorities. Also, it implies that, as maturities of government bonds shorten, a large amount of short-term assets will be available to asset holders in the financial market and will compete with the currently

Table 4.2
Ratio (percentage) of financial surplus or deficit to GNP, by sector and calendar year.

Sector	1965	1966	1967	1968	1969	1970	1971
Corporate business	−4.38	−4.58	−7.15	−6.53	−6.62	−6.92	−6.23
Personal	7.71	8.75	9.26	8.88	8.38	7.90	9.40
Public	−2.82	−3.87	−3.07	−2.65	−1.58	−0.91	−1.90
Central government	0.30	−0.73	−0.69	0.12	0.58	1.30	0.89
Public corporations & local authorities	−3.12	−3.15	−2.38	−2.77	−2.16	−2.21	−2.79
Financial institutions	0.51	0.89	0.80	1.01	1.05	0.90	1.21
Rest of the world	−1.03	−1.19	0.15	−0.72	−1.23	−0.97	−2.49

dominating saving instruments, such as savings deposits. Thus, these changes in the flow of funds bring about important changes in portfolio behavior that may trigger fundamental innovations in Japan's financial market.

A second characteristic of Japan's financial structure has been the dominance of the banking sector in its role of channeling funds from the noncorporate sector to other sectors, particularly to the corporate business sector. Households hold their ample saving in the form of "ordinary" and saving deposits.[3] Corporate business firms rely heavily on borrowings from the banking sector rather than raising funds through equity or bond issues. Because of the importance of bank loans to the business sector, the Japanese financial market has often been described as dominated by a *tête-à-tête* or customer relationship between lenders and borrowers rather than by an open market for securities (Royama 1982). The dominance of the banking sector as a financial intermediary gave rise to an idea similar to the "credit paradigm." The Bank of Japan still retains its control over the amount of lending by commercial banks through moral persuasion, called "window guidance" or "window control" (*Madoguchi Shido* or *Madoguchi Kisei*). It is often considered crucial for the central bank to control the amount of bank lending in order to control the money supply. Recently, however, because of the changes in the flow of funds mentioned above and because of ongoing financial innovations, disintermediation has been taking place. Table 4.3 shows that the relative importance of the banking sector as a financial intermediary has been declining. This implies that the Bank of Japan cannot control overall liquidity by controlling bank lending alone.

A third characteristic of the Japanese financial system is the dual structure of interest rates. There is a coexistence of rigid, regulated rates of interest and

1972	1973	1974	1975	1976	1977	1978	1979	1980	1981
−7.98	−7.63	−8.60	−4.15	−3.97	−2.60	−1.02	−3.07	−3.54	−3.11
11.55	8.89	10.34	10.59	11.47	11.16	11.14	9.20	8.34	11.20
−2.68	−2.89	−3.74	−7.37	−7.49	−7.29	−9.13	−7.97	−6.85	−7.45
0.65	1.08	0.73	−2.73	−3.31	−3.98	−5.39	−4.51	−3.24	−3.84
−3.33	−3.97	−4.46	−4.65	−4.17	−3.31	−3.74	−3.47	−3.61	−3.61
1.32	1.59	1.00	0.79	0.64	0.27	0.73	0.94	0.95	−0.19
−2.21	0.03	0.99	0.14	−0.65	−1.54	−1.72	0.90	1.10	−0.46

market-determined rates of interest. As in many other countries, the interest rate at the discount window of the Bank of Japan is naturally determined by the monetary authorities (the Policy Board of the Bank of Japan). Also, as is not unusual in many countries, the rates of interest on "ordinary" and savings deposits are regulated by law. [The Temporary Interest Rates Adjustment Law (*Rinji kinri Chōsei Hō*) of 1947 is similar to Regulation Q in the United States.] The ceiling on interest rates is determined by a special committee, the *Kinri Chōsei Shingikai*.[4] In addition, rates on newly issued national bonds are determined by the Minister of Finance. In practice, the conditions and yields of new issues are negotiated between the Ministry of Finance and underwriters' syndicates composed of major banks and security dealers. The levels of interest rates on newly issued bonds are often set slightly lower than the prevailing market rate in the secondary market, however. New issues are rationed to the members of the syndicate.[5]

In accordance with these partly regulated and partly negotiated interest rates, other interest rates are also under subtle guidance. In particular, the prime (long-term) rate for lending by investment bankers to most-preferred borrowers is set to move together, with an almost fixed difference, with the rates on newly issued government bonds. These practices are reflected in the idea of the "system" of interest rates rather than the structure of interest rates. In other words, interest rates are often conceived to move according to a natural law (A. Kuroda 1982). That is, short-term interest rates should always be lower than long-term interest rates regardless of expected movements in interest rates; interest rates on government bonds should always be lower than those on private bonds. Also, the regulated structure or system of interest rates is usually determined in such a way as to secure normal profits for every

Table 4.3
Channels of Finance (percentage, by fiscal year).

	1972	1973	1974	1975	1976	1977	1978	1979	1980	1981
Financial institutions	92.1	93.4	91.9	91.4	90.4	89.0	88.7	85.0	85.0	88.9
Banks	43.7	33.1	36.0	36.8	33.9	31.4	33.7	26.5	23.4	34.6
Financial insts. for small business	16.5	17.7	13.3	15.8	14.7	12.1	13.5	14.5	10.5	12.3
Financial insts. for agriculture, forestry, fishery	5.7	9.3	6.4	5.0	5.6	5.3	5.1	7.3	5.5	3.3
Public financial institutions	14.2	21.1	23.9	21.9	24.7	29.4	27.2	24.2	32.1	26.6
Securities market	6.4	6.9	4.1	7.7	7.9	9.4	8.3	10.3	9.9	9.5
Foreign capital market	1.5	−0.3	4.0	0.9	1.7	1.6	3.0	4.7	5.1	1.6

Source: Bank of Japan.

financial intermediary.[6] Figure 4.1 shows in a simple scheme the idea of the "system" of interest rates.

On the other hand, there have been steady developments of homogeneous open markets where interest rates function well to clear the market for funds. The Call market for reserves, whose participants are financial institutions, helped for a long time to channel funds from banks with surplus funds to banks with deficits in funds. As indicated by Suzuki (1966), this market was considered as the principal short-term market in which the price mechanism worked well. The part of the Call market that deals with funds with maturity longer than a month was separated in 1972 as the *Tegata* (Bills Discount) market, that is, a discount market of bankers' bills. Some interest rates in the Tegata market were under the guidance of the Bank of Japan until 1979, but since then all the interest rates in the Tegata market as well as the Call market have been freely determined.

The *Gensaki* (RPs) market, that is, bond trading with repurchase agreements, developed quite rapidly after 1970. This market, accesible also to nonfinancial institutions, is essentially a short-term market with public and private bonds as collateral. Moreover, commercial banks began to issue certificates of deposit (CDs) in 1979. Even though there are restrictions on the amount of CDs issued by each financial institution, and even though there is a minimum denomination of 500 million yen, the rate of interest on CDs is beyond the control of the Temporary Interest Adjustment Law.

These developments in open markets for standardized securities are a

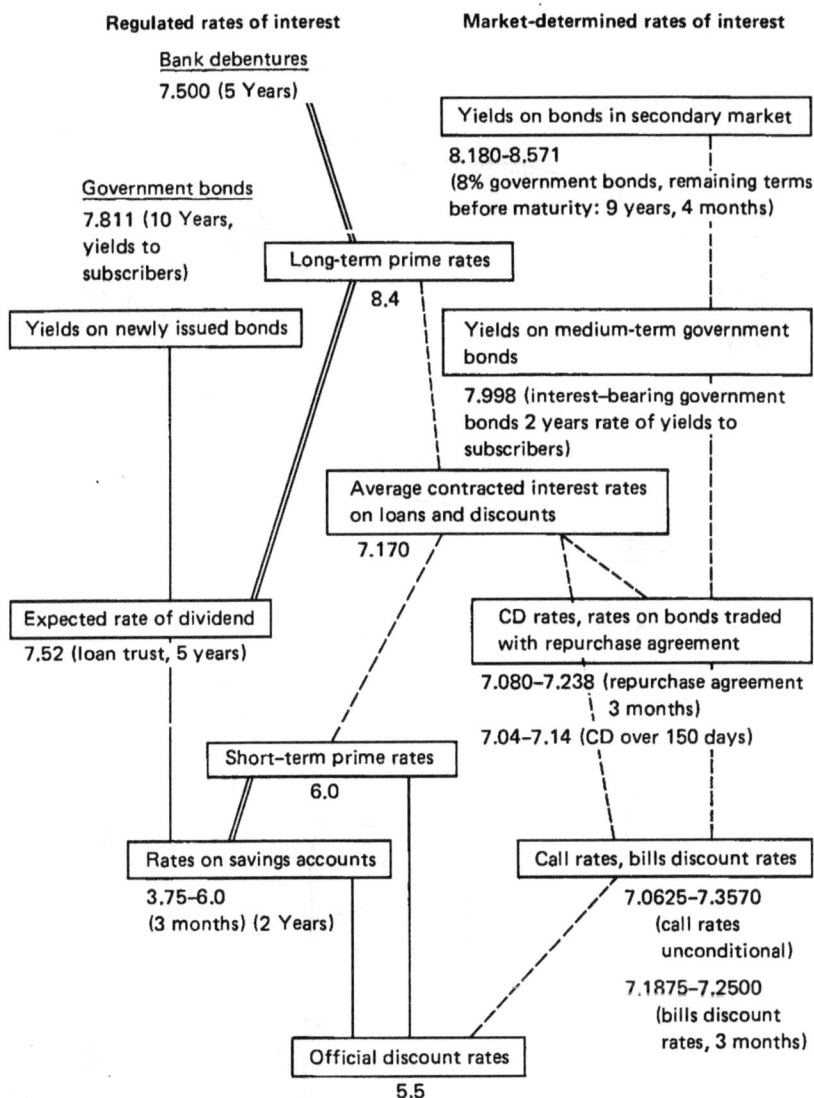

Regulated rates of interest   Market-determined rates of interest

Bank debentures
7.500 (5 Years)

Yields on bonds in secondary market

8.180-8.571
(8% government bonds, remaining terms
before maturity: 9 years, 4 months)

Government bonds
7.811 (10 Years,
yields to
subscribers)

Long-term prime rates

8.4

Yields on newly issued bonds

Yields on medium-term government
bonds

7.998 (interest–bearing government
bonds 2 years rate of yields to
subscribers)

Average contracted interest rates
on loans and discounts

7.170

Expected rate of dividend

7.52 (loan trust, 5 years)

CD rates, rates on bonds traded
with repurchase agreement

7.080–7.238 (repurchase agreement
3 months)
7.04-7.14 (CD over 150 days)

Short–term prime rates

6.0

Rates on savings accounts

3.75-6.0
(3 months) (2 Years)

Call rates, bills discount rates

7.0625–7.3570
(call rates
unconditional)

7.1875–7.2500
(bills discount
rates, 3 months)

Official discount rates

5.5

Figure 4.1
The dual structure of interest rates. Percentages are given for June 1982. (- -) Arbitration
of interest rates; (———) institutionally consorted movements of interest rates; (====)
assurance of profit margin of financial institution. Adapted from Suzuki 1983.

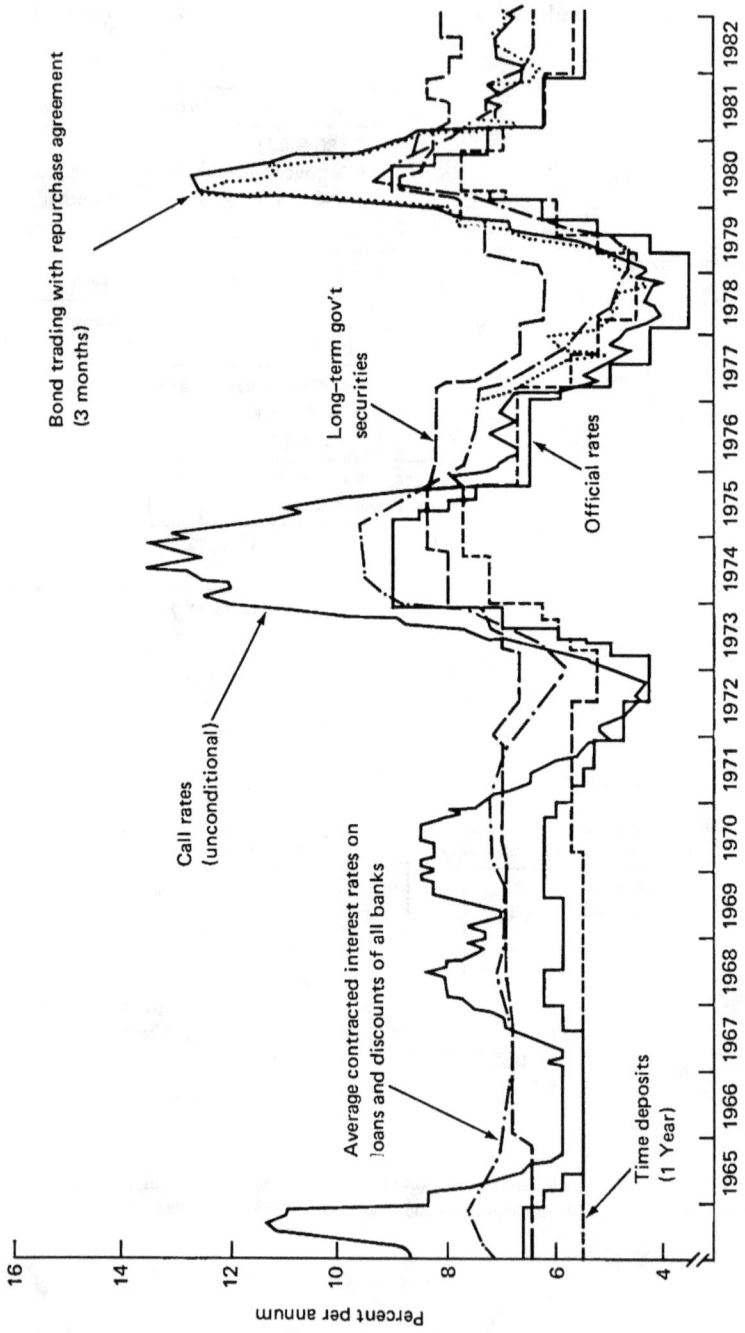

Figure 4.2
Changes in interest rates. Source: Bank of Japan.

recent phenomenon, but they seem to be here to stay. The Japanese financial system has begun to reach a stage of qualitative maturity in which the price mechanism is more pervasive. Thus, along with the rigid structure of the interest-rate-regulation system, the price mechanism (through the development of a system of flexible rate markets) has crept in and now prevails. Figure 4.2 shows time series of regulated and market-determined interest rates.

The market for short-term lending by commercial banks lies in a gray zone between the two extremes of regulated and market-determined interest rates. Controversy exists as to whether the market for lending by commercial banks to firms is competitive or characterized by rationing. There is a practice of setting the prime rate for short-term lending by some implicit agreements among banks. The prime rate is usually set rather mechanically as a fixed percentage (e.g., 0.5 or 0.25 percent) above the discount rate. This leads to the view that in the commercial loan market interest rates do not necessarily equate supply with demand. That is to say, there should be quantity adjustments in the form of "dynamic credit rationing" as defined by Jaffée and Modigliani (1969), Kaizuka and Onodera (1974), and Iwata and Hamada (1980). But there is an alternative view that, because of compensating balances and other conditions that accompany loan agreements, there is an "effective" interest rate that clears the loan market. (See I. Kuroda 1979.) There are several empirical analyses that look into the degree of competitiveness in the loan market. Ito and Ueda (1982) find some degree of interest-rate rigidity that is absent in the American capital market. It may be conjectured that the Japanese commercial loan market is becoming more and more competitive. However, empirical evidence is not yet available to support this view (Tsutsui 1982). In any case, the presence of quantitative controls or guidances on the amount of lending by commercial banks through moral persuasion by the Bank of Japan (*Madoguchi Shido* or *Madoguchi Kisei*) implies that the amount of credit extended by banks is considered a policy instrument (Eguchi and Hamada 1977).

These characteristics of the Japanese financial system have several implications for the transmission of monetary policy.

First, let us consider factors that affect the asset-holding behavior of households and, accordingly, the demand for money. For a long time Japanese households have put a major part of their savings into ordinary and time (savings) deposits at the commercial banks. Recently, however, because of the increased availability to the general public of information about interest-rate differentials, Japanese households started to divert their saving from bank deposits to other savings instruments. Also, the expected different tax treatment of interest income from bank deposits and that from deposits at the

Postal Saving System has created, and is likely to create at any time in the future, a shift between these two types of deposits. New saving instruments are now allowed to attract savings. The new loan trust with compounded interest called "Big," the new bank debentures with compounded interest called "Wide," and the new unit bonds trust called "Jumbo" were introduced in 1981. As a defensive measure to prevent the flight of funds to postal savings deposits, commercial banks introduced a new type of deposit called *Kijitsu Shitei Teiki*, whose maturity can be designated by depositors. In addition, long-term government bonds will be close substitutes for bank deposits as their maturity shortens.

Although Japan has not experienced and probably will not experience a period of very high and volatile nominal interest rates comparable to the one observed the United States in the past few years, the new development of saving instruments and the large stock of government debt may cause sudden shifts in the public's portfolio. The dual structure of interest rates itself leaves room for further disintermediation. These observations will give an institutional basis for understanding the reasons for shifts in the demand for money.

The second consequence of these characteristics is related to the money-supply process. The predominance of the banking sector as the main intermediary and the high degree of indebtedness on the side of the private business sector lead to an idea similar to the "credit paradigm." The idea is that the amount of credit extended by commercial banks determines the amount of investment, and that the control of the amount of credit extended is most crucial to the control of money supply. The Bank of Japan used to focus on lending by commercial banks as an important indicator of liquidity conditions. Quantitative regulations on the amount of bank lending were considered to be among the most important means of monetary control.

The importance of the banking sector as an intermediary, the exogeneity of banking credit, and the effectiveness of credit control are all familiar ingredients of the credit paradigm that is being popularized by Modigliani and Papademos (1980) and Benjamin Friedman (1980). A similar idea has been preached for a long time by Bank of Japan economists, while most academic economists who have discussed the money-supply process have relied on the traditional asset or money paradigm which asserts high-powered money is multiplied into M_2 and M_3 by the money multiplier. Among many propositions derived from the "credit paradigm," we shall focus our attention on the particular proposition that the availability of credit is an important exogenous policy variable. (See Ueda 1982.)

The availability of credit strongly affects firms' investment behavior and

Table 4.4
Test of Granger causality.

Sample period	Hypothesis 1	Hypothesis 2	Hypothesis 3
June 1967 – December 1982	$\chi^2(8) = 14.0$	$\chi^2(8) = 22.1^b$	$\chi^2(16) = 13.3$
June 1967 – December 1973	$\chi^2(8) = 15.8^a$	$\chi^2(8) = 30.4^b$	$\chi^2(16) = 6.5$
January 1974 – December 1982	$\chi^2(8) = 7.7$	$\chi^2(8) = 6.3$	$\chi^2(16) = 4.3$

Hypothesis 1: High-powered money does not cause M2.
Hypothesis 2: Loan does not cause M2.
Hypothesis 3: Neither high-powered money nor M2 causes loan.
a. Significant at 5 percent.
b. Significant at 1 percent.
Numbers in parentheses are degrees of freedom.

households' consumption behavior if bank credit is the only principal way to finance spending. In the 1950s and the 1960s, when the Japanese economy was growing very rapidly, the business sector was a large borrower and interest rates were relatively rigid, so that the conditions for the effectiveness of credit control were more or less satisfied. However, since 1970 these conditions have not been satisfied. Moreover, a large surplus in the current account gave room for the money supply to expand without further extensions of bank credit.

Many economists at the Bank of Japan thought they could control the money supply through the control of bank loans. In other words, it was thought that bank loans are determined first, that deposits are created as a result, and that high-powered money is then supplied to help commercial banks secure required reserves. To see if this story is supported by data, we undertook a Granger causality test using vector autoregression (VAR) with three variables: H (high-powered money), M2, and $LOAN$ (bank loans). The fact that monthly time-series data on high-powered money are not readily available for dates before September 1966 led us to choose a sample period from September 1966 to December 1982. We took first differences of the logs of the raw data in order to obtain three stationary series. The data have been adjusted seasonally by Census X11. The lag length was taken to be 8 months, although we found that variations in this specification did not affect the test results strongly. We tested three hypotheses using a likelihood-ratio test: that H does not cause M2, that $LOAN$ does not cause M2, and that neither H nor M2 causes $LOAN$ (i.e., $LOAN$ is exogenous in the three-variable system). Table 4.4 reports relevant χ^2 statistics for these tests for the entire sample and for the two subperiods. The exogeneity of $LOAN$ is strongly supported by the data. As for the effect on M2, $LOAN$ is much more statistically significant than H, except for the subperiod from January 1974 to December 1982. The estimate of contemporaneous correlation in the error term in the VAR system indicates that *LOAN* is more strongly correlated with M2 than *H* is with M2. Furthermore, the quantitative effect of *H* on M2 is minute in comparison with that of *LOAN*; the estimated lag coefficient for *H* in the M2 equation is about one-tenth that for *LOAN*. Thus, the results are favorable to the credit paradigm, particularly when the sample period ends before 1974. For the sample period January 1974–December 1982, we cannot reject the hypothesis that M2 is exogenous, which is consistent neither with the credit paradigm nor with the money paradigm that emphasizes the role of high-powered money in the money-supply process.

Let us now turn to the money-supply multiplier in Japan. The familiar decomposition of the money multiplier can be expressed as

$$\frac{M}{H} = \frac{C+D}{C+R} = \frac{C/D+1}{C/D+R/D},$$

where *M* is the monetary aggregate (M1 or M2), *H* is high-powered money, *C* is currency, *R* is reserves, and *D* is deposits (demand deposits if *M* is M1 and demand and savings deposits if *M* is M2). *R* is decomposed into required reserves $\bar{R}$ in the form of deposits at the Bank of Japan and vault cash *V* in the banking sector; that is,

$$R = \bar{R} + V,$$

or

$$\frac{M}{H} = \frac{C/D+1}{C/D + \bar{R}/D + V/D}.$$

Studies by Horiuchi (1980) and by Bank of Japan economists [for example, Narikawa (1981)] indicate that in Japan the value of the money multiplier is affected mostly by changes in the legal reserve requirement $\bar{R}/D$ and by changes in the cash-deposit ratio C/D for the public. Economic theory would suggest that the money multiplier should be related to the interest rate; that is, a higher interest rate should cause agents to economize on their use of non-interest-bearing liquid assets. With legal reserve requirements, a higher rate of interest would mean smaller values of V/D and C/D and, accordingly, a higher value of the money multiplier. However, Horiuchi and Narikawa found that C/D moves procyclically rather than countercyclically. One can see the movements of various components of the multiplier in figure 4.3. When economic activity is high, the public holds more cash relative to deposits, and this effect has outweighed the interest-rate effect over our sample period. Therefore, the

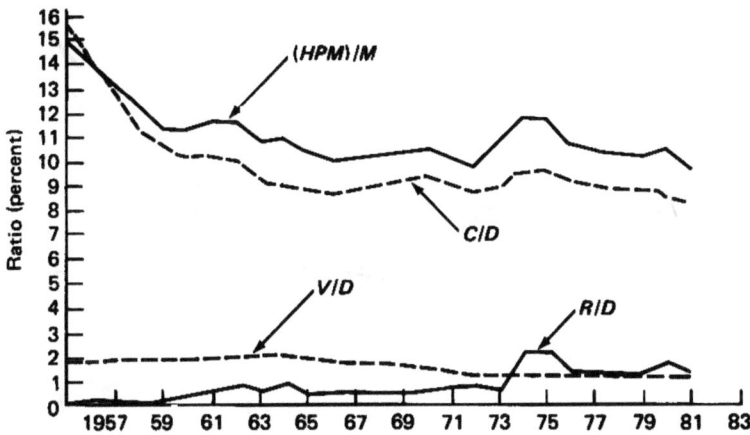

Figure 4.3
Reciprocal of money multiplier (HPM/M) and related ratios. M = M2 + CD.

money multiplier is smaller rather than larger during the period of tight money. This effect, sometimes referred to as the Mitchel-Hawtrey effect (Cagan 1965), is more important than the liquidity-preference effect.

In spite of the timing or chain of causality (or lack thereof) between high-powered money and various monetary aggregates, and in spite of the variable money multiplier, the Bank of Japan has sufficient policy instruments to control the money supply. Until recently the existence of inertia or rigidity in some rates of interest did not offer significant obstacles to effective control of the money supply. Indeed, it could be argued that quantitative measures together with moral persuasion made monetary control easier than it otherwise would have been. Recently, however, the rigidity in interest rates has given rise to a conflict with the flexible execution of monetary policy. The rigid rates on banking deposits (particularly those on postal savings deposits, which are determined by a slow negotiation process) have begun to work against flexible monetary policy. When the interest structure is rigid, money management might lead to disintermediation. Thus, the caution against possible disorder in the financial markets is a potential constraint on Japanese monetary policy.

Stances of Monetary Policy during the Postwar Period

In describing the motivation and the effectiveness of monetary policy in Japan, we may divide the postwar period into two periods: the period under the fixed exchange parity (1947–71) and the period since Japan left the fixed

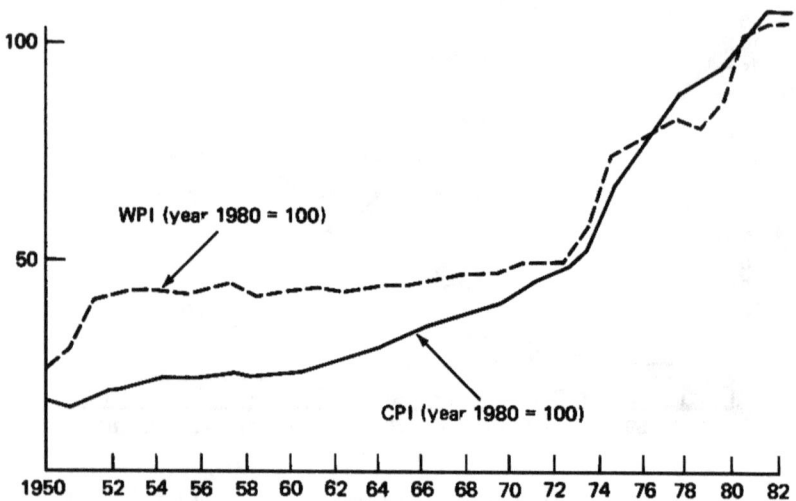

Figure 4.4
Movements of the domestic price level.

exchange parity. Until 1971 it was almost a categorical imperative for Japanese policy makers to keep the parity of $1 = 360$ yen, which was established in 1949 during the American occupation. As was found by Kaizuka (1967), monetary policy thus reacted sensitively to the current account. As soon as the current account went into deficit (surplus), contractionary (expansionary) monetary policy was followed. Until the late 1960s no chronic surplus developed in the balance of payments. This stop-and-go policy enabled the price level in Japan to follow a rather stable path.

As is shown in figure 4.4, the wholesale-price index showed only a very mild upward trend until 1972. This is because the wholesale-price index was closely linked to the international price level of tradables. Fortunately, during the first period the monetary policies of major industrialized countries, particularly the United States, successfully contained the price level within a range of a low rate of inflation. Because of the difference in the rate of productivity increase between the manufactured-goods sector and the consumer-goods sector including foodstuffs and services, we can observe a scissors-like phenomenon in which the consumer-price index showed a mild upward trend while the wholesale-price index remained almost stable. This period can be regarded as one with a desirable international policy assignment, as proposed by Mundell (1971), in the sense that the United States, as a paternalistic leader, kept in mind domestic price stability, while Europe and

Japan followed a stop-and-go policy, reacting to the current-account surplus or deficit under the fixed-exchange-rate regime.

After around 1968, however, partly because of the active expenditure policy of the Johnson administration, the U.S. economy was led into a period of substantial price increases. Similar upward trends in prices occurred in Europe. Japan should have appreciated the yen in order to keep her domestic price level stable. With no changes in the exchange-rate parity, Japan started showing a substantial trade surplus after 1968. If the exchange rate was to be kept constant, the choice was between the policy of keeping a stable price level with an accumulated large surplus in the balance of payments and the policy of inflating the economy in pace with the world inflation. The first alternative was taken until President Nixon's New Economic Policy began, in 1971. After the interlude of the Smithsonian realignment of exchange rates, the Japanese government chose the second alternative and turned to an inflationary policy to keep the value of the yen from appreciating further. Policy makers were excessively worried about the possible deflationary effect of the appreciation of the yen and its adverse effects on exports.

This policy, aided by Prime Minister Tanaka's ambitious plan of remodeling Japan, created excessive liquidity before the severe supply shock hit the Japanese economy. Here, perhaps, the fact that the central bankers' thinking was close to the credit paradigm might have helped the policy makers to neglect the inflationary effect of a large money supply, because the source of the money supply was the inflow of foreign reserves and not bank loans. Certainly some people at the Bank of Japan must have been worried about the rapid growth of money. However, the political environment did not allow the Bank of Japan to resist the pressure from the government and the ruling party for an inflationary policy to prevent the appreciation of the yen.

The first oil crisis hit Japan precisely when there was already ample inflationary pressure at home (Komiya 1976). This created a panic; for example, many consumers ran into grocery stores to buy bathroom tissue out of the fear of shortages of paper products. From this bitter experience the Bank of Japan learned a great deal. The Bank also learned the danger of sacrificing the objective of stable prices for other objectives, such as the stable parity of the yen. The labor-union leaders, who won a double-digit wage increase in the 1974 *Shunto* (spring offensive), learned that it could be quite costly in terms of potential loss of jobs to demand excessive wages increases. It took a long time—two or three years after 1974—for the economy to return to a normal rate of unemployment.

After 1973 Japan adopted flexible exchange rates, along with other industrialized countries. Thus, monetary policy gained more autonomy and the

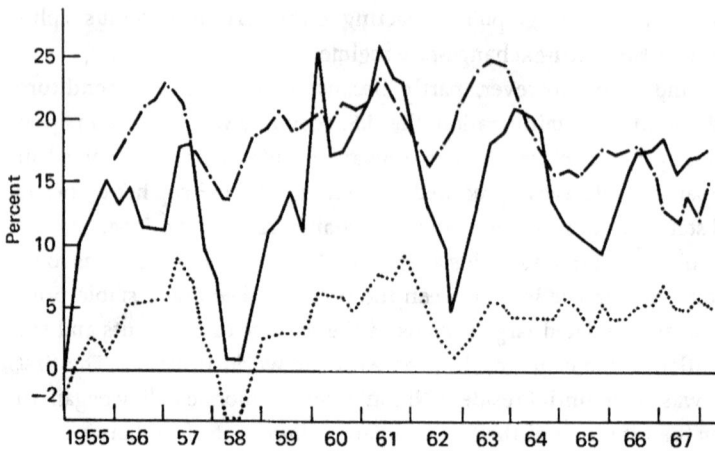

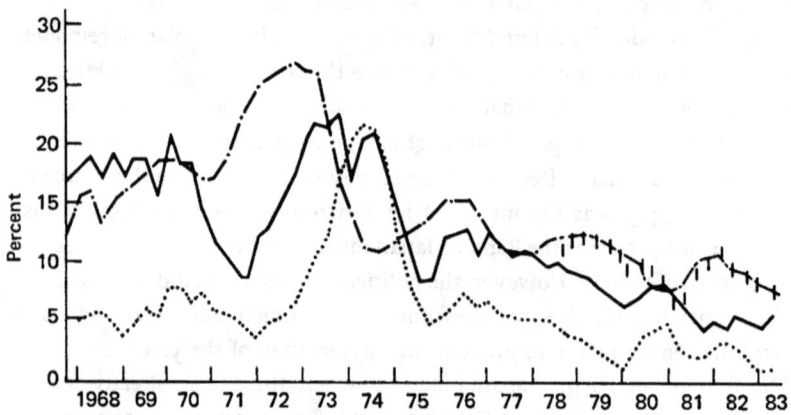

Figure 4.5
Growth rate of the money supply. (—·—) Rate of change of M2 + CD; (———) rate of
change of nominal GNP; (·····) rate of change of GNP deflator; (|) Bank of Japan's forecast
of M2.

Bank of Japan began to focus on the control of the money supply. As is shown in figure 4.5, the growth rate of money, particularly M2, has been controlled rather smoothly. In 1978 the Bank of Japan started announcing the forecast of M2 for the subsequent quarter, as depicted in figure 4.5.

There are several reasons why money management in Japan has been conducted quite smoothly in recent years. First, as mentioned earlier, the Central Bank regained *de facto* autonomy because of the lessons of the first oil crisis. Second, even though we can trace signs of financial innovations, they are taking place quite slowly thanks to stable prices in the past 6 or 7 years. Third, the Bank of Japan aims at not immediate but medium-run control of M2, without paying too much attention to M1, which can often exhibit erratic movements. Needless to say, the Bank pays sufficient attention to other indicators rather than a single monetary aggregate. The Bank watches levels of interest rates, particularly the Call market rate, price indices, liquidity conditions of firms, the retail-sales index, the general business outlook, and, recently in particular, the value of yen exchange rates. It is perhaps appropriate to say that monetary policy in Japan has been successful because the perspective of the Bank is multi-scoped rather than single-scoped on a single monetary aggregate.[7]

The Demand for Money

We now turn to the other side of the money market, the demand side, and review the current empirical facts concerning the money demand function. This section, therefore, updates the parameter estimates of Tsutsui and Hatanaka (1982), whose sample period ends in 1978:IV. The narrow money stock, M1, includes currency held by the public plus demand and ordinary deposits. A broader measure of money, M2, adds time, saving, and other deposits to M1. In this chapter, for the sake of convenience, we use M2 to mean the sum of M2 defined above plus certificates of deposit (CDs). Yet another broader measure is M3, which is M2 plus nonbank deposits (including deposits in the Postal Savings System, the interest payments on which are largely tax-free). It is worth noting that M2 (and M3) are major components of the portfolio held by the public. At the end of 1980, the gross financial asset holdings of Japanese households were about 340 trillion yen (with equity holdings valued at market prices), and M2 held by households represented about 65 percent of this. The comparable figure for the United States was well below 40 percent.

The money demand function to be estimated is the standard one:

Table 4.5
Money demand function.

Line	Dependent variable	Sample period	Point estimates with t values				R^2	D.W. or ρ
			b_1	b_2	b_3	b_4		
1	logM1	1965:II–1982:IV	0.893 (24.5)	0.104 (2.49)	−0.0434 (−2.98)	0.0236 (0.709)	0.998	D.W. = 1.34
	logM2	1965:II–1982:IV	0.875 (28.7)	0.143 (3.74)	−0.0440 (−4.99)	0.0391 (2.01)	0.999	D.W. = 0.95
2	logM1	1965:II–1973:IV	0.831 (14.2)	0.215 (3.18)	−0.0710 (−2.90)	−0.0132 (−0.099)	0.997	D.W. = 1.66
	logM2	1965:II–1973:IV	0.807 (21.7)	0.222 (5.25)	−0.0704 (−5.88)	0.0168 (0.265)	0.999	D.W. = 1.71
3	logM1	1974:I–1982:IV	0.733 (7.41)	0.186 (2.52)	−0.0191 (−1.06)	−0.0248 (−0.627)	0.978	D.W. = 1.56
	logM2	1974:I–1982:IV	0.757 (8.45)	0.370 (2.95)	−0.0283 (−2.32)	0.0376 (1.50)	0.997	D.W. = 1.20
4	logM1	1974:I–1982:IV	0.665 (5.78)	0.235 (2.75)	−0.0137 (−0.631)	−0.0394 (−0.833)	0.999	$\rho = 0.240$
	logM2	1974:I–1982:IV	0.749 (7.40)	0.380 (2.69)	−0.0241 (−1.49)	0.0245 (0.735)	0.9999	$\rho = 0.400$
5	logM1	1974:I–1980:I	0.537 (3.34)	0.467 (2.79)	−0.00691 (−0.329)	0.00647 (0.136)	0.999	$\rho = 0.177$
	logM2	1974:I–1980:I	0.684 (5.83)	0.515 (3.26)	−0.0208 (−1.34)	0.0510 (1.43)	0.9999	$\rho = 0.360$

R^2 in lines 4 and 5 is calculated from equations transformed with ρ. ρ is the first-order autocorrelation coefficient in the error term.

$$\log m = b_0 + b_1 \log m_{-1} + b_2 \log y$$
$$+ b_3 \log RCALL + b_4 \log RTD,$$

where m is a quarterly average of monthly data on the money stock deflated by the GNP deflator, y is real GNP, $RCALL$ is the Call rate (the Japanese equivalent of the Federal Funds Rate in the United States), and RTD is the interest rate on one-year time deposits.[8] All data except interest rates are seasonally adjusted by Census X11. Table 4.5 displys parameter estimates for the two money-stock measures, M1 and M2, and for various sample periods. For the entire sample period of 1965:II–1982:IV, the parameter estimates by the OLS (ordinary least-squares) method, shown in line 1, seem reasonable. Except for the RTD coefficient in the M1 equation, all coefficients have the "right" signs. However, estimates of the speed of adjustment $(1 - b_1)$ of around 10 percent seem to be on the low side. The long-run income elasticity, $b_2/(1 - b_1)$, is very close to unity for both M1 and M2. To test the stability of the money demand function, the sample was split at the end of 1973, the time of the first oil shock. Lines 2 and 3 of table 4.5 show parameter estimates for the two subsamples. They look very different; the speed of adjustment is higher and the long-run income elasticity diverges from 1 for the latter sample period of 1974:I–1982:IV. In fact, the F statistic for the usual Chow test is 4.1 for M1 and 6.8 for M2, both of which are highly significant.[9]

Correction for serial correlation with a first-order autoregressive process in the error term yields the results in line 4 of table 4.5 for the sample period 1974:I–1982:IV.[10] The actual and predicted values of the log of real M1 are depicted in figure 4.6. For several quarters, starting in 1980:II, there was a sharp drop in real M1 (this did not happen for M2), and the estimated money demand equation keeps track of it very well. To see if this high in-sample predictive performance carries over to an out-of-sample movements in the log of real M1, we estimated the money demand function for M1 for the shorter sample period 1974:I–1980:I with the same method of correcting for serial correlation. The resulting parameter estimates are given in line 5 of table 4.5. The results of "dynamic" simulation, where the lagged values of the dependent variable that are fed into the equation are not the historical values but those that are generated by the equation itself, are reported in table 4.6. Clearly we have a case of missing M1.[11]

The reason for the missing M1 is not clear. Undoubtedly there was a large-scale shift from demand deposits to other kinds of deposits, since M2 and M3 do not exhibit noticeable dips during the period of missing M1. No drastic financial innovation seems to have taken place during the period. One explanation that is commonly mentioned is the "green card" episode. The "green

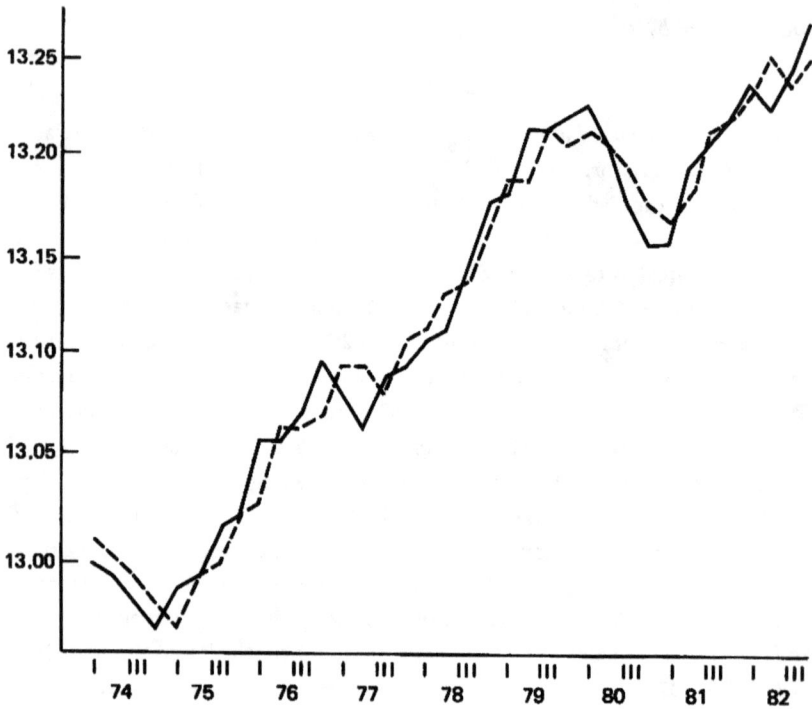

Figure 4.6
Actual (————) and predicted (—— —) values of logM1.

Table 4.6
Dynamic simulation of M1.

	Actual log M1	Predicted log M1
1980: II	13.212	13.241
III	13.183	13.251
IV	13.165	13.263
1981 I	13.165	13.276
II	13.203	13.288
III	13.216	13.297
IV	13.228	13.301
1982: I	13.246	13.307
II	13.235	13.318
III	13.251	13.326
IV	13.279	13.333

card" system is a device for checking on tax evasion that takes advantage of the tax-exemption clause on interest payments to small savers. However, such tax considerations do not fully explain the fact that it was demand deposits—whose interest rate is virtually zero—that the public abandoned.

The Supply Side of the Japanese Economy

In order to assess the effectiveness of Japan's demand-management policy, we need to review some of the features of aggregate supply in Japan. One important relationship is the Okun relationship between output and employment; another is the Phillips relationship between unemployment and increases in wages and prices.

Hamada and Kurosaka (1984) investigated Okun's law (the relationship between unemployment and the GNP gap) in Japan and found that 1 percent increase in the unemployment rate widens the GNP gap by roughly 28 percent. This contrasts with the Okun coefficient for the United States, where a 1 percent change in the unemployment rate is associated with a 3 percent change (more recently a smaller change) in the GNP gap. This high value of the Okun coefficient reflects in part the limited variability of unemployment statistics in Japan.[12] It probably also indicates that the adjustment behavior in the Japanese labor market is slower than in the United States. Changes in working hours as well as changes in the labor participation ratio result in apparently small changes in employment. It certainly indicates that the output loss due to business cycles is much larger than the low unemployment-rate statistics in Japan suggest.

Figure 4.7 depicts the Phillips relationship between wage and price increases and the unemployment rate in Japan. One can explain the Japanese Phillips relationship by appealing to the expectations-augmented Phillips curve advocated by Phelps (1967) and Friedman (1968). The original hyperbolic shape found by A. W. Phillips himself for British data was observable during the 1960s in Japan. However, during the 1950s and after 1970 one can see a vertical relationship between wages and unemployment.

After the Korean War and after the rapid inflation of the post–World War II reconstruction period, the Phillips relationship was vertical and also unfavorable to policy makers. There was still an excess supply of labor from rural areas. Then came a period of rapid growth and rapid technical progress. With more or less stable prices due to the monetary policy to keep the exchange rate constant, price expectations were stabilized. Thus, we can observe a downward-sloping hyperbolic Phillips curve. Then followed the period of "excess liquidity" and stagflation. The Phillips relationship shifted upward

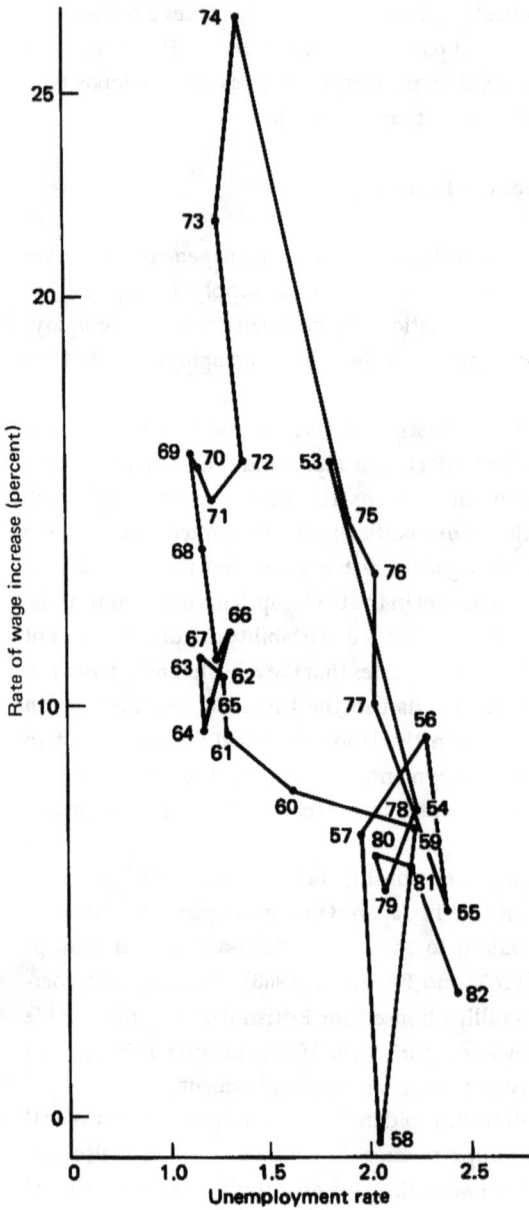

Figure 4.7
The Phillips relationship in Japan.

because of inflationary expectations. Whether the present situation (say, since 1980) can be regarded as a vertical segment of the Phillips curve, or as a situation where we can exploit the short-run tradeoff between inflation and unemployment, remains a question. We shall discuss this issue further in the next section.

Incidentally, the effect of inflationary expectations on the Phillips curve can examined by looking at the interwar period. Minami and Odaka (1972) have found that the regression coefficient of the inflation rate is much higher and more significant during the inflationary interwar period than during the period of rapid postwar economic growth.

In addition to the vertical shift of the Phillips curve shown in figure 4.7, we should consider its horizontal shift. The rigidity or inertia in the growth rate of real wage in the face of declining productivity growth and worsening terms of trade should shift the Phillips curve horizontally to the right, according to the first postulate of classical economics.[13] In spite of declining productivity due to the first oil crisis, the Japanese labor negotiation process kept real wages constant or even increasing. Therefore, after 1974 the Phillips curve shifted to the right. This real shock was an unexpected one. It took time for both parties of labor negotiations to notice the adverse effect of a decline in the terms of trade.

After the second oil crisis, however, real wages moved rather flexibly. In fiscal 1980, real wages in the nonagricultural sector declined by 1.7 percent. The real wage per efficiency unit of labor declined in fiscal 1978 and 1979 as well. Labor union leaders seemed to have learned the lesson. Thus, the Phillips relationship did not shift to the right after the second oil crisis. Figure 4.8 shows the relationship between the rate of wage increase minus labor-productivity increase and the job applicants–offer ratio of the previous year. The upward-sloping relationship indicates that real wage responds rapidly to the state of excess demand in the labor market. Japanese wage determination still maintains real wage flexibility. Thus, the favorable performance of the Japanese supply-side relationship after the second oil crisis depends on real as well as nominal wage flexibility. The *Shunto* practice (the system of simultaneous wage settlements for all the leading sectors of the economy) allows firms to adjust wage rates annually for all workers and, if some unexpected changes in productivity occur during the year, to alter labor compensation through adjustments in semiannual bonuses.

Does Anticipated Money Matter?

The neutrality hypothesis (Barro 1977) that only unanticipated money has real effects has recently attracted widespread attention and controversy because of

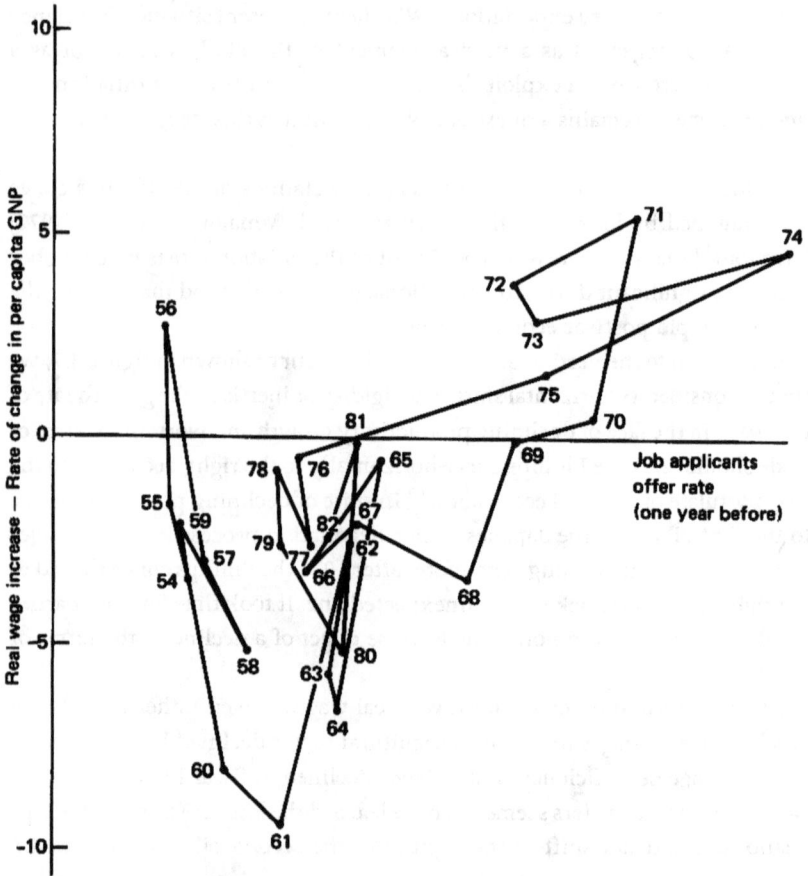

Figure 4.8
The relationship between the rate of wage increase minus the labor-productivity increase and the job applicants offer ratio.

its obvious policy implications. Formally, the hypothesis posits that the log of output at time t, y_t, can be decomposed into a time trend, a distributed lag of unanticipated money growth, and an exogenous error term u_t:

$$y_t = a_0 + a_1 t + b_0(DM_t - DM^e_{t-1}) + b_1(DM_{t-1} - DM^e_{t-1})$$
$$+ \cdots + b_n(DM_{t-n} - DM^e_{t-n-1}) + u_t, \tag{1}$$

where DM_t is the actual rate of growth of money from time $t-1$ to time t and DM^e_{t-1} is the anticipated MD_t conditional on information at time $t-1$. If the monetary authority follows the money-supply rule, then

$$DM_t = c'x_{t-1} + v_t, \tag{2}$$

where x_{t-1} is the vector of variables known at time $t-1$, c' is a row vector of coefficients, and v_t is an error term uncorrelated with x_{t-1}. If the public knows this money-supply rule, then DM^e_{t-1} is equal to $c'x_{t-1}$.

Recent empirical work by Mishkin (1982) using quarterly U.S. data does not support Barro's neutrality hypothesis; if the output equation (equation 1 above) is augmented to include on the right-hand side a distributed lag of anticipated money growth, then estimated coefficients for anticipated money are not only statistically significant but also quantitatively larger than those for unanticipated money. Pigott (1978) used quarterly Japanese data to arrive at the conclusion that unanticipated money does not matter at all.[14] However, research done at the Bank of Japan by Seo and Takahashi (1982), who used a different set of variables for the money-supply rule after carefully studying the past announcements made by the Bank of Japan at the times of changes in the official discount rate, shows that according to Japanese quarterly data unanticipated money is much more important in explaining the behavior of output, even though anticipated money is statistically significant. Roughly the same conclusion was obtained by Kato (1979) and Taniuchi (1982).[15] Thus, for Japan, anticipated money seems to matter, but its estimated quantitative significance depends on the specification of the money-supply rule, at least in the case of quarterly data. In this section we first present our own estimate of the augmented output equation, which includes anticipated as well as unanticipated money growth using Japanese monthly data from January 1965 to December 1982. We then reformulate the neutrality hypothesis in a manner more in line with Lucas's (1973) supply function and test it on the same monthly data.

Our first task is to specify the money-supply rule. From the above discussion of the Bank of Japan's monetary policy, and also from Seo and Takahashi 1982, it is reasonable to suppose that the growth rate of the money supply depends on the inflation rate, on changes in the Index of Industrial

Table 4.7
Right-hand-side variables, point estimates, and t values for money-supply equation.

R.H.S. variable	Point estimate	t	R.H.S. variable	Point estimate	t
DM_{t-1}	−0.0954	−1.27	DIP_{t-1}	−0.0475	−1.42
DM_{t-2}	−0.0416	−0.55	DIP_{t-2}	0.0294	0.86
DM_{t-3}	0.186	2.57	DIP_{t-3}	−0.000621	−0.02
DM_{t-4}	0.263	3.61	DIP_{t-4}	−0.0261	−0.75
DM_{t-5}	0.161	2.10	DIP_{t-5}	0.0335	0.96
DM_{t-6}	0.305	3.96	DIP_{t-6}	−0.115	−3.37
DM_{t-7}	0.0818	1.04	DIP_{t-7}	−0.0162	−0.49
DM_{t-8}	0.0748	0.98	DIP_{t-8}	−0.0126	−0.38
$DCPI_{t-1}$	0.0414	0.64	$RRSV_{t-1}$	0.00804	1.65
$DCPI_{t-2}$	−0.00845	−0.13	$RRSV_{t-2}$	−0.0106	−1.38
$DCPI_{t-3}$	0.0111	0.17	$RRSV_{t-3}$	0.00715	0.93
$DCPI_{t-4}$	−0.758	−1.15	$RRSV_{t-4}$	−0.00741	−0.96
$DCPI_{t-5}$	0.108	1.62	$RRSV_{t-5}$	−0.00285	−0.37
$DCPI_{t-6}$	−0.127	−1.93	$RRSV_{t-6}$	0.00517	0.68
$DCPI_{t-7}$	−0.00735	−0.11	$RRSV_{t-7}$	0.000623	0.08
$DCPI_{t-8}$	−0.193	−2.97	$RRSV_{t-8}$	−0.000999	−0.20
			Intercept	0.00408	2.75

$R^2 = 0.465$. Standard error of regression = 0.00496. Mean of dependent variable $(DM_t) = 0.0114$. Standard deviation of $DM_t = 0.00624$. Sample period: October 1965–December 1982. See text for definitions of variables.

Production, and on the stock of foreign currency reserves, so that the money-supply equation is

$$DM_t = c_0 + c_{11}DM_{t-1} + \cdots + c_{1m}DM_{t-m}$$

$$+ c_{21}DCPI_{t-1} + \cdots + c_{2m}DCPI_{t-m}$$

$$+ c_{31}DIP_{t-1} + \cdots + c_{3m}DIP_{t-m}$$

$$+ c_{41}RRSV_{t-1} + \cdots + c_{4m}RRSV_{t-m} + v_t, \tag{3}$$

where DM_t is the growth rate of M2 from time $t - 1$ to time t, $DCPI_t$ is the inflation rate measured in terms of the Consumer Price Index from time $t - 1$ to time t, DIP_t is the rate of change in the Index of Industrial Production (IP) from $t - 1$ to t, and $RRSV_t$ is the ratio of reserves (in millions of dollars) to the product of IP and the Wholesale Price Index.[16] The lag length m is taken to be 8 months. All the variables are seasonally adjusted by Census X11. Table 4.7

Table 4.8
Right-hand-side variables, point estimates, and t values for money-supply equation under fixed exchange rates.

R.H.S. variable	Point estimate	t	R.H.S. variable	Point estimate	t
DM_{t-1}	−0.319	−2.20	DIP_{t-1}	−0.0245	−0.45
DM_{t-2}	0.00872	0.06	DIP_{t-2}	−0.0330	−0.59
DM_{t-3}	0.0855	0.56	DIP_{t-3}	−0.000806	−0.02
DM_{t-4}	0.109	0.73	DIP_{t-4}	−0.100	−1.94
DM_{t-5}	−0.0100	−0.07	DIP_{t-5}	−0.116	−2.12
DM_{t-6}	0.215	1.47	DIP_{t-6}	−0.174	−3.24
DM_{t-7}	0.0187	0.13	DIP_{t-7}	0.0364	0.59
DM_{t-8}	−0.114	−0.88	DIP_{t-8}	0.108	1.74
$DCPI_{t-1}$	0.159	1.48	$RRSV_{t-1}$	0.000490	0.06
$DCPI_{t-2}$	0.0830	0.76	$RRSV_{t-2}$	−0.000458	−0.04
$DCPI_{t-3}$	−0.0121	−0.12	$RRSV_{t-3}$	0.0108	0.92
$DCPI_{t-4}$	0.0575	0.53	$RRSV_{t-4}$	−0.00348	−0.29
$DCPI_{t-5}$	0.137	1.20	$RRSV_{t-5}$	−0.0207	−1.73
$DCPI_{t-6}$	0.0132	0.12	$RRSV_{t-6}$	0.00794	0.74
$DCPI_{t-7}$	−0.0555	−0.50	$RRSV_{t-7}$	0.00412	0.04
$DCPI_{t-8}$	−0.0257	−0.24	$RRSV_{t-8}$	0.00885	1.20
			Intercept	0.0128	2.13

$R^2 = 0.565$. Standard error of regression = 0.00409. Mean of dependent variable $(DM_t) = 0.0144$. Standard deviation of $DM_t = 0.00493$. Sample period: October 1965–January 1973. See text for definitions of variables.

displays the estimated money-supply equation for the entire sample period, October 1965–December 1982.[17] It shows that an increase in $DCPI$, DIP, or $RRSV$ tends to depress the growth rate of M2. The $DCPI$ coefficient at the eighth lag is significant, suggesting that inflation has a long-lasting effect on the money supply.

We would not, however, expect the equation to be stable over the entire sample period. As noted above, the Bank of Japan appears to have paid much attention to the level of reserves in the 1960s and to the inflation rate in the period after the first oil shock. Furthermore, there was a clear regime change from fixed to floating exchange rates in February 1973. Thus, in order to locate parameter shifts, we try four breaking points (the end of December 1970, January 1973, December 1973, and December 1974) to split the sample and we perform the usual Chow test. Pertinent F statistics are 0.05, 1.56, 1.09, and 1.36, respectively. Only the January 1973 split shows a parameter shift that is significant at 5 percent. Table 4.8 reports the money-supply equation for the

Table 4.9
Right-hand-side variables, point estimates, and t values for money-supply equation.

R.H.S. variable	Point estimate	t	R.H.S. variable	Point estimate	t
DM_{t-1}	−0.153	−1.51	DIP_{t-1}	−0.0605	−1.29
DM_{t-2}	−0.203	−1.99	DIP_{t-2}	0.0328	0.69
DM_{t-3}	0.134	1.37	DIP_{t-3}	0.00339	0.07
DM_{t-4}	0.175	1.83	DIP_{t-4}	0.0270	0.55
DM_{t-5}	0.103	1.00	DIP_{t-5}	0.0962	1.96
DM_{t-6}	0.261	2.53	DIP_{t-6}	−0.109	−2.28
DM_{t-7}	0.0881	0.86	DIP_{t-7}	−0.0583	−1.33
DM_{t-8}	0.109	1.08	DIP_{t-8}	−0.0453	−1.04
$DCPI_{t-1}$	0.0714	0.78	$RRSV_{t-1}$	0.00805	1.10
$DCPI_{t-2}$	0.0609	0.66	$RRSV_{t-2}$	−0.00457	−0.40
$DCPI_{t-3}$	0.0499	0.52	$RRSV_{t-3}$	0.00585	0.51
$DCPI_{t-4}$	−0.0595	−0.63	$RRSV_{t-4}$	−0.00931	−0.83
$DCPI_{t-5}$	0.137	1.49	$RRSV_{t-5}$	0.00163	0.14
$DCPI_{t-6}$	−0.130	−1.36	$RRSV_{t-6}$	0.0000579	0.01
$DCPI_{t-7}$	0.132	1.38	$RRSV_{t-7}$	0.00350	0.31
$DCPI_{t-8}$	−0.256	−2.73	$RRSV_{t-8}$	−0.00397	−0.53
			Intercept	0.00268	1.05

$R^2 = 0.496$. Standard error of regression $= 0.00515$. Mean of dependent variable $(DM_t) = 0.00916$. Standard deviation of $DM_t = 0.00619$. Sample period: February 1973–December 1982. See text for definitions of variables.

sample period October 1965–January 1973, which shows a fairly significant response of money to $RRSV$. In contrast, the estimated-money-supply equation for the period of floating exchange rates (table 4.9) shows no such response. This is what we would expect from our discussion above. It is plausible that the Bank of Japan has shifted its attention from the level of reserves to the yen-dollar exchange rate, leaving the trade balance to be adjusted through changes in the exchange rates. To see if this is in fact the case, we estimate a money-supply equation that has six lags of the yen-dollar exchange rate in place of $RRSV$ for the period of floating exchange rates. The lag length for $DCPI$ is extended to 10 months to allow for the long-lasting effect of inflation on money supply. The yen-dollar exchange rate, denoted $EX¥\$$, is a monthly average of daily data. The parameter estimates appear in table 4.10, where the exchange rate has fairly significant coefficients.

The estimated-money-supply equation is then used to generate the unanticipated and the anticipated money that appear in the output equation. The

Table 4.10
Right-hand-side variables, point estimates, and t values for money-supply equation under flexible exchange rates.

R.H.S. variable	Point estimate	t	R.H.S. variable	Point estimate	t
DM_{t-1}	−0.122	−1.15	DIP_{t-1}	−0.101	−2.26
DM_{t-2}	−0.148	−1.39	DIP_{t-2}	0.0228	0.51
DM_{t-3}	0.135	1.38	DIP_{t-3}	0.0117	0.25
DM_{t-4}	0.136	1.43	DIP_{t-4}	0.0473	1.02
DM_{t-5}	0.0849	0.85	DIP_{t-5}	0.0902	1.98
DM_{t-6}	0.239	2.47	DIP_{t-6}	−0.111	−2.41
DM_{t-7}	0.0687	0.68	DIP_{t-7}	−0.0524	−1.14
DM_{t-8}	0.0667	0.69	DIP_{t-8}	−0.0187	−0.41
$DCPI_{t-1}$	0.0144	0.17	$EX\Psi S_{t-1}$	0.0000827	0.99
$DCPI_{t-2}$	0.0254	0.29	$EX\Psi S_{t-2}$	−0.000175	−1.30
$DCPI_{t-3}$	0.00984	0.11	$EX\Psi S_{t-3}$	−0.0000538	−0.39
$DCPI_{t-4}$	−0.0846	−0.91	$EX\Psi S_{t-4}$	0.000216	1.56
$DCPI_{t-5}$	0.0543	0.59	$EX\Psi S_{t-5}$	−0.0000684	−0.49
$DCPI_{t-6}$	−0.141	−1.57	$EX\Psi S_{t-6}$	0.0000195	0.22
$DCPI_{t-7}$	0.127	1.40			
$DCPI_{t-8}$	−0.250	−2.76			
$DCPI_{t-9}$	0.0739	0.77			
$DCPI_{t-10}$	0.0191	0.20			

$R^2 = 0.518$. Standard error of regression $= 0.00503$. Sample period: February 1973–December 1982. See text for definitions of variables.

fitted value, called DMF_t, is our estimate of the anticipated growth rate of money (DM_{t-1}^e), and the residual $(DMR_t = DM_t - DMF_t)$ is our estimate of the unanticipated money growth $(DM_t - DM_{t-1}^e)$.[18] There is no novelty in our (augmented) output equation:

$$\log (P_t) = a_0 + a_1\,TIME + a_2 DOIL + a_3 DOIL*TIME$$
$$+ b_0 DMR_t + b_1 DMR_{t-1} + \cdots + b_n DMR_{t-n}$$
$$+ d_0 DMF_t + d_1 DMF_{t-1} + \cdots + d_n DMF_{t-n} + u_t. \qquad (4)$$

In this equation, $DOIL$ is the oil-shock dummy, which equals 1 from January 1974 and 0 otherwise. Thus, the first four terms on the right-hand side allow the intercept and the time trend to differ before and after the oil shock. In all the previous estimates of the output equation mentioned above, the error term u_t exhibits a strong serial correlation. Thus, the error term u_t here is assumed to

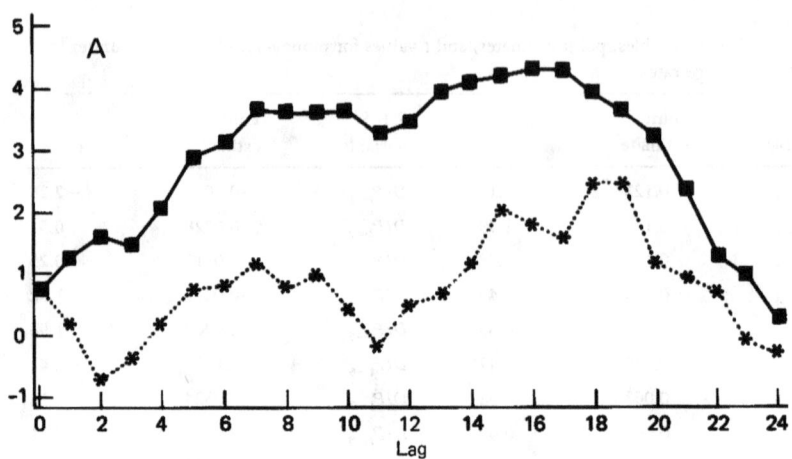

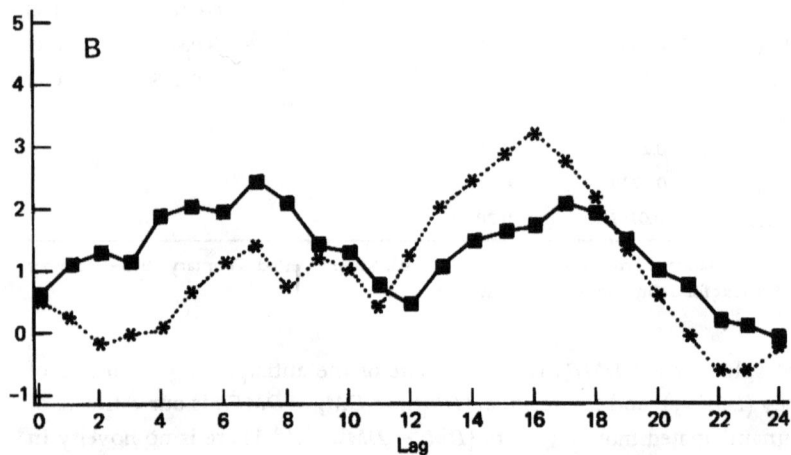

Figure 4.9
Lag distribution output equation. (———) Lag distribution for DMR; (· · ·) lag distribution
for DMF.

follow a fourth-order autoregressive process:

$$u_t = r_1 u_{t-1} + r_2 u_{t-2} + r_3 u_{t-3} + r_4 u_{t-4} + \text{white noise.} \tag{5}$$

The Barro neutrality hypothesis implies that the coefficients of anticipated money, $d_0, d_1, \ldots, d_m$, are all zero. Equation 4 is estimated by a two-step generalized least-squares method; the first step is to estimate the auto-regressive coefficients $r_1, \ldots, r_4$ from the OLS residuals, and the second step is to apply the OLS method to the data transformed by the variance-covariance matrix of the error term that is implied by the estimated autoregressive process. It turned out, somewhat surprisingly, that only the first autoregressive coefficient r_1 was significant and the other coefficients, r_2, r_3, and r_4, were very close to zero.

Figure 4.9 depicts the estimated lag distribution for unanticipated and anticipated money when the lag length n is 24 months. Panel A of figure 4.9 is based on the unanticipated and anticipated money series generated by the estimated-money-supply equation (which does not allow for a parameter shift) reported in table 4.7, and panel B is based on the money-supply equation reported in table 4.8 (for fixed exchange rates) and table 4.10 (for floating exchange rates). The majority of the coefficients of unanticipated money have t values exceeding 3. It is evident from figure 4.9 that the shape of the lag distribution for unanticipated money depends on which money series are used, although in either case almost all of the lag coefficients are positive and show a long-lasting effect of unanticipated money growth. The pertinent F statistics (which approximately have an F distribution with 25 and 129 degrees of freedom) for the Barro hypothesis $(d_0 = d_1 = \cdots = d_{24} = 0)$ is 2.78 for panel A and 3.87 for panel B, so in both cases anticipated money is statistically highly significant.[19] The sum of the estimated-anticipated-money coefficients $d_0, d_1, \ldots, d_{24}$ is about 19.5 for panel A and 24.1 for panel B, which implies that a permanent and anticipated increase in the growth rate of the money supply of one percentage point (annual rate) eventually shifts the time path of industrial production 1.6 percent to 2 percent above the original path. If the lag length n in equation 4 is 36 months, the lag distribution becomes longer and substantially larger, the neutrality hypothesis can be rejected at 1 percent, and the effect of a one-percentage-point permanent increase in the money growth rate (annual rate) is an increase in output of about 2.5–3.3 percent.

It is of some interest to speculate on the reasons for such a persistent and substantial effect of anticipated money. The Mundell-Tobin effect—that anticipated money affects the equilibrium capital stock through its effect on the real rate of return on money—could be one reason. However, taken alone, it does not explain the long-lasting (as opposed to instantaneous) effect of anticipated money. One could couple the fixed length of nominal wage contracts with the Mundell-Tobin effect. Yet, since wage contracts in Japan are not staggered, the Mundell-Tobin effect is not likely to last for more than a year, unless there is some important state variable (other than the capital stock) that affects output. Another possibility is the transmission mechanism running from money to investment and to consumption through Tobin's (1969) q ratio. As Yonezawa (1982) shows, a strong positive correlation exists in Japan between the q ratio and the ratio of M2 to the capital stock. But again, this does not really explain the persistence of anticipated money, because the correlation between q and M2 is largely contemporaneous and the effect of q on investment typically does not involve very long lags.

The augmented-output equation was estimated above under the assumption that the error term u_t is exogenous. This assumption, however, is dubious. One can easily think of other factors (such as government expenditure) that are likely to influence output and are correlated with money. For example, anticipated money can be significant in the augmented-output equation, not because it matters but because it is correlated with a distributed lag of unanticipated growth in government expenditure, which is part of the error term affecting output. Therefore, the exogeneity of the error term in Barro's output equation amounts to assuming that monetary factors influence output independent of other factors. Since this sounds implausible, we reformulate the neutrality hypothesis somewhat differently. Our formulation is more in line with those of Lucas (1973) and Sargent (1976). If we define the "cyclical" component of output as $y_{ct} = y_t - a_0 - a_1 t$, then equation 1 can be written as

$$y_{ct} = b(L)(DM_t - DM_{t-1}^e) + u_t, \tag{6}$$

where $b(L) = b_0 + b_1 L + b_2 L^2 + \cdots + b_n L^n$ and the lag operator L has the property that $L^k x_t = x_{t-k}$. Applying the inverse of $b(L)$ to both sides of this equation yields

$$B(L)^{-1} y_{ct} = (DM_t - DM_{t-1}^e) + b(L)^{-1} u_t, \tag{7}$$

which can be written as

$$y_{ct} = f_0(DM_t - DM_{t-1}^e) + f_1 y_{c,t-1}$$
$$+ f_2 y_{c,t-2} + \cdots + w_t. \tag{8}$$

If the filter $b(L)^{-1}$ happens to remove serial correlation in u_t, then w_t in equation 8 is not serially correlated. This last equation is precisely the Lucas supply function if we interpret the term $f_0(MD_t - DM_{t-1}^e) + w_t$ as the term

Table 4.11
Test of Granger causality.

| Lag length | F statistic for | | Sample period |
	DM coefficients are zero	DG coefficients are zero	
12 months	3.41[a]	1.40	Feb. 1966–Dec. 1982
24 months	2.46[a]	2.25[b]	Feb. 1967–Dec. 1982

a. Significant at 5 percent.
b. Significant at 1 percent.

representing the unanticipated change in the inflation rate.[20] Conversely, Barro's neutrality hypothesis can be thought of as a special case of the Lucas supply function where money is the only source of unanticipated inflation.

If the error term w_t is the part of unanticipated inflation that is not explained by unanticipated money, and if expectations are rational so that unanticipated changes are not correlated with the past, then equation 8 implies that nothing Granger-causes y_{ct}. In particular, the log of the money stock, m_t, should not Granger-cause y_{ct}. This, in turn, implies that the growth rate of IP, namely

$$y_t - y_{t-1} = y_{ct} - y_{c,t-1} + a_0,$$

should not be Granger-caused by the growth rate of the money stock, $m_t - m_{t-1}$, since Granger causality is invariant to linear filtering.[21] This is the implication of the reformulated neutrality hypothesis. We prefer to work with first differences rather than levels in order to incorporate a random-walk component in the log of output. This is important because, as Nelson and Plosser (1982) emphasize, it is by no means obvious that macroeconomic time series can be represented by a stationary process around a deterministic trend.

To test Granger causality from money and government expenditure to output, we regressed DIP (changes in the log of IP) on its own lags, lagged DM (changes in the log of M2), and lagged DG (changes in the log of government expenditure). The significance of the coefficients of lagged DM and DG is checked. For government expenditure we use expenditures on public works in the General Account of the National Budget, which is available on a monthly basis. As before, the data are seasonally adjusted by Census X11. Table 4.11 reports pertinent F statistics for two lag lengths. Government expenditure is significant when the lag length is 24 months and insignificant when the lag length is 12 months. In either case, money is significant at 1 percent. We conclude that the joint hypothesis of rationality and neutrality can be rejected.

Overall, then, our evidence based on Japanese monthly data strongly supports the idea that anticipated movements in the money stock have real effects. Two versions of the neutrality hypothesis have been formulated, and in both cases the hypothesis was decisively rejected. Although the estimate of the quantitative significance of anticipated money varies with the specification, it is uniformly substantial.

Concluding Remarks

The Japanese economy has been equipped with a high degree of wage-price flexibility. Real as well as nominal wage rates respond elastically to the state of excess demand in the labor market and to productivity changes. Accordingly, unemployment rates in Japan do not rise to very high levels, even if we take account of the bias toward low variability in the Japanese unemployment statistics.

Because of financial innovations Japan is experiencing now, and because of the shifts in the public's portfolio among bank deposits, postal savings deposits, and other saving instruments, the velocity of money has fluctuated and will continue to fluctuate to a considerable degree. In a country where the velocity of money could be volatile because of the forces mentioned above, concentrating on a single monetary aggregate would not be enough. Such policy may be valuable as a safety valve against severe inflation. However, any single monetary aggregate does not necessarily provide sufficient information to policy makers. Watching just a single monetary aggregate would be like piloting an aircraft by looking only at the altitude recorder: It may help prevent the airplane from crashing, but it is not a very wise way to fly. There are other indicators, such as interest rates, that the central bank can utilize to engineer suitable monetary policy. The relative success of Japanese demand management seems to stem from the following sources: First, the Bank of Japan paid attention to broader monetary aggregates, such as M2 and M3, rather than M1. Second, the Bank of Japan did not commit itself too mechanically to a single monetary aggregate. In general, the Bank considered other indicators—interest rates, liquidity conditions of firms, and so forth. The performance of the Japanese monetary policy will remain successful in the future if the Bank does not lose its balanced policy perspective.

In order to foster a more efficient and internationalized financial market in Japan, further deregulation of interest rates is inevitable as well as necessary. Deregulation is also desirable for the welfare of small savers, who for a long time earned only a minimal rate on time deposits. Because of the recent slowdown in the inflation rate, the process of financial innovation will be gradual.[22] Cautious innovation in Japan's financial system will be required so that the public's confidence in the solvency of the banking system will remain firm, but this cautious attitude must not be interpreted as approving the present excessive protection of financial institutions.

The unstable velocity of money is a reflection of the shifts in the demand for money documented above. The money-demand function for both M1 and M2 is highly unstable. Furthermore, it overpredicts recent M1. This provides another reason that policy makers should not commit mechanically to a single monetary aggregate.

In spite of the flexibility of real wages, the empirical results in the previous section suggest the effectiveness of anticipated money supply. More specifically, a permanent increase in the growth rate of money supply can increase output permanently. We do not take this result seriously enough to believe that the Japanese government can keep increasing output forever by continuously accelerating money growth. However, the emprical results do seem to suggest that discretionary monetary policy can be effective when output is chronically low.

Acknowledgments

We are indebted to Yoshio Kurosaka for helpful discussions and to Keiko Nosse for research assistance.

Notes

1. By the Bank of Japan Law, the Bank of Japan is under supervision of the Minister of Finance for its various activities. Monetary policy is determined by the Policy Board of the Bank of Japan, headed by the Governor of the Bank of Japan.

2. For excellent accounts of the Japanese monetary system and monetary policy in English, see OECD 1974 and Suzuki 1974.

3. Use of personal checks has not been popular in Japan. "Ordinary" deposits are not subject to drawing by checks, but are payable on demand at the bank counter or by use of a cash card at any branch of the bank. (In Japan major "city" banks have branches all over the country.) The Japanese financial system can be said to have shifted from a cash society directly to a cash card and credit card society without passing through the stage where checking accounts are important.

4. The *Kinri Chōsei Shingikai* consists of representatives of the Ministry of Finance, the Economic Planning Agency, the Bank of Japan, seven members from the commercial banking sector, three members from industry, and two members from the general public.

5. These members are requested not to sell newly issued government bonds in the open market for a prescribed period (currently months).

6. For a clear description as well as criticisms of the idea of interest-rate "system," see A. Kuroda 1982.

7. For a similar argument and many insightful observations, see Suzuki 1983.

8. The monthly money-stock series that are available at least from 1965 are the end-of-the-month values. (Monthly averages of daily money-stock data are available only from 1967.) The quarterly average of the monthly series is calculated as (the value at the end of the last month of the previous quarter)/6 + (the value at the end of the first month of the quarter)/3 + (the value at the end of the second month of the quarter)/3 + (the value at the end of the last month of the quarter)/6. The data on RCALL and RTD are quarterly averages of daily data.

9. Because of the presence of the lagged dependent variable in the money-demand function, our Chow test can be justified only asymptotically.

10. The correction for serial correlation was done using the AR1 option in TSP (Time Series Processor) version 3.5.

11. Ths same case of missing M1 was reported by Tsutsui and Hatanaka (1982). They used a similar money-demand function estimated on the sample period 1965: II–1978:IV.

12. According to Taira (1982), who estimated the Japanese unemployment rate according to the U.S. definition, the mean and the standard deviation of the unemployment rate almost double.

13. Friedman (1977) has stressed the upward-right shift of the Phillips curve under inflationary situations by a different reasoning.

14. The dependent variable in Pigott's output equation is *changes* in the log of industrial production or of real GNP.

15. In Taniuchi's quarterly model, the anticipated money that is relevant to the output equation is the expectation of money stock formed on the basis of information at the time of the annual *Shunto*. Thus, the neutrality hypothesis in Taniuchi's model allows anticipated money to influence output for just three quarters.

16. Both M2 and RRSV are the values at the beginning of the month (i.e., the end of the previous month). Monthly averages of daily values would be preferable, but such series do not go back to 1965. We also used simple averages of two successive end-of-the-month values to obtain results similar to the ones reported in this section.

17. Since the lag length is 8 months and since first differences are taken, the first nine observations are lost.

18. The use of estimated money series biases the *t* values for the estimated coefficients in the output equation. One way to avoid this is to estimate the money-supply equation and the output equation jointly with cross-equation restrictions. We decided not to do this, for in order to do it in our monthly model, with eight lags in the money-supply equation, 36 lags in the output equation, and four lags in the error term in the output

equation, we have to maximize a suitable objective function over more than 120 parameters. It is not clear in which direction the t values for the estimated money series are biased.

19. The F statistics that come out of our two-step generalized least-squares formulation (and the F statistics that will appear later in this section) do not have an exact F distribution, only an approximate one. The use of F statistics rather than χ^2 statistics makes rejection of a hypothesis less likely. In other words, if a hypothesis is rejected on the basis of an F statistic, then the same hypothesis can be rejected using the χ^2 statistic.

20. In Sargent's (1976) model, w_t includes unanticipated movements in government expenditures as well as in the error terms for the IS and LM equations.

21. See Pierce and Hough 1977.

22. The desirability of gradual but steady financial deregulation is stressed in Suzuki 1983.

References

Barro, Robert J. 1977. "Unanticipated Money Growth and Unemployment in the United States." *American Economic Review* 67, March, pp. 101–115.

Cagan, Phillip. 1965. *Determinants and Effects of Changes in the Stock of Money: 1875–1960* (National Bureau of Economic Research).

Eguchi, Hidekazu, and Koichi Hamada. 1977. "Banking Behavior under Constraints: Credit Rationing and Monetary Mechanism in Japan." *Japanese Economic Studies* 6, Winter, pp. 3–44.

Friedman, Benjamin M. 1980. "Postwar Changes in the American Financial Markets," in Martin Feldstein, ed., *American Economy in Transition* (University of Chicago Press).

Friedman, Milton. 1968. "The Role of Monetary Policy." *American Economic Review* 58, March pp. 1–17.

Friedman, Milton. 1977. "Nobel Lectures: Inflation and Unemployment." *Journal of Political Economy*, June, pp. 451–472.

Hamada, Koichi, and Yoshiro Kurosaka. 1984. "The Relationship between Output and Unemployment in Japan: Okun's Law in Comparative Perspective." *European Economic Review*, forthcoming.

Horiuchi, Akiyoshi. 1980. *Nohon no Kinyu Seisaku* [Monetary Policy in Japan] (Toyo Keizai Shinposha).

Ito, Takatoshi, and Kazuo Ueda. 1982. "Kashidashi Kinri no Kakakukino ni Tsuite: Shinki Kashidashi Shijo ni okeru Kinko Kasetsu no Kensho" [Test of the Equilibrium Hypothesis in the Japanese Business Loans Market]. *Economic Studies Quarterly* 33, pp. 25–37.

Iwata, Kazumasa, and Koichi Hamada. 1980. *Kinyu Seisaku to Ginko Kodo* [Monetary Policy and Banking Behavior in Japan] (Toyo Keizai Shinposha).

Jaffée, D., and F. Modigliani. 1969. "A Theory and Test of Credit Control." *American Economic Review* 59, December, pp. 850–872.

Kaizuka, Keimei. 1967. "Keizai Antei to Kinyu Seisaku" [Economic Stabilization and Monetary Policy], in K. Kinoshita, ed., *Keizai Antei to Zaisei Kinyu Seisaku* [Economic Stabilization and Fiscal and Monetary Polity] (Nihon Keizai Shinbun).

Kaizuka, K., and H. Onodera. 1974. "Shinyo Wariate ni Tsuite" [On Credit Rationing]. *Keizai Kenkyu* 25, pp. 13–23.

Kato, Hirotaka. 1979. "Keizai Riron ni Okeru Goriteki Kitaikeisei no Saikento" [Rational Expectations in Economic Theory]. *Kindai Keizaigaku* series, 49–54 (Toyo Keizai Shinposha).

Komiya, Ryutaro. 1976. "1973–74 Nen no Inflation no Gen-in" [The Causes of the 1973–74 Inflation]. *Keizaigaku Ronshu* 46, April, pp. 11–57.

Komiya, Ryutaro, and Yoshio Suzuki. 1977. "Inflation in Japan," in L. Krause and W. S. Salant, eds., *World-Wide Inflation* (Brookings Institution).

Kuroda, Akio. 1982. *Nihon no Kinri Kozo* [The Structure of Interest Rates in Japan] (Toyo Keizai Shinposha).

Kuroda, Iwao. 1979. Mechanism of Bank Loan Rates Determination in Japan. Discussion paper 3, Bank of Japan. (Translation of article in *Kinyu Kenkyu Shiryo*, no. 2.)

Lucas, Robert E., Jr. 1973 "Some International Evidence on Output-Inflation Tradeoff." *American Economic Review* 63, June, pp. 326–334.

Minami, R., and K. Odaka. 1972. *Chingin Hendo: Suryoteki Sekkin* [Wage Movements: A Quantitative Study] (Iwanami Shoten).

Mishkin, Frederic. 1982. "Does Anticipated Money Matter? An Econometric Investigation." *Journal of Political Economy* 90, February, pp. 27–51.

Modigliani, F., and L. D. Papademos. 1980 "The Structure of Financial Markets and the Monetary Mechanism," in Controlling Monetary Aggregates III, Federal Reserve Bank of Boston Conference Series no. 23.

Mundell, Robert A. 1971. *Monetary Theory: Inflation, Interest and Growth in the World Economy* (Goodyear Publishing Co.). See chapter 14.

Narikawa, Ryosuke. 1981. "Monetary Base Control no Yukosei ni Tsuite" [On the Effectiveness of the Control of the Monetary Base]. *Kinyu Kenkyu Shiryo*, no. 9, Bank of Japan.

Nelson, Charles R., and Charles I. Plosser. 1982. "Trends and Random Walks in Macroeconomic Time Series: Some Evidence and Implications." *Journal of Monetary Economics* 10, no. 2, pp. 139–162.

OECD. 1974. *Monetary Policy in Japan*.

Phelps, Edmund S. 1967. "Phillips Curve, Expectations of Inflation, and Optimal Unemployment Over Time." *Economica* 54, August, pp. 254–281.

Pierce, David A., and L. D. Haugh. 1977. "Causality in Temporal Systems." *Journal of Econometrics* 5, pp. 265–293.

Pigott, C. 1978. "Rational Expectations and Counter-Cyclical Monetary Policy: The Japanese Experience." *Federal Reserve Bank of San Fransisco Economic Review*, Summer.

Royama, Shoichi. 1982. *Nihon no Kinyu System* [Monetary System in Japan] (Toyo Keizai Shinposha).

Sargent, Thomas J. 1976. "A Classical Macroeconomic Model for the United States." *Journal of Political Economy* 84, June, pp. 631–640.

Seo, Jun-ichiro, and Wataru Takahashi. 1982. "Goriteki Kitai to Money Supply Seisaku" [Rational Expectations and the Money Supply Policy]. *Kinyu Kenkyu Shiryo* no. 11, Bank of Japan, February, pp. 37–70.

Suzuki, Yoshio. 1966. *Kinyu Seisaku no Koka* [Effectiveness of Monetary Policy] (Toyo Keizai Shinposha).

Suzuki, Yoshio. 1974. *Gendai Nihon Kinyu Ron* (Toyo Keizai). English translation: *Money and Banking in Contemporary Japan* (Yale University Press, 1980).

Suzuki, Yoshio. 1983. *Nihon Keizai Kinyu Ron* [Monetary Theory of the Japanese Economy] (Toyo Keizai Shinposha).

Taira, Koji. 1982. Labor Markets in Japan: How Unemployment is Minimized. BEBR discussion paper 916, University of Illinois (Champaign-Urbana).

Taniuchi, Mitsuru. 1982. *Atarashii Monetarism no Keizaigaku* [The New Economics of Monetarism] (Toyo Keizai Shinposha).

Tobin, James. 1969. "A General Equilibrium Approach to Monetary Theory." *Journal of Money, Credit and Banking* 1, February, pp. 15–29.

Tsutsui, Yoshiro. 1982. "Wagakuni Ginko Kashidashi Shijo no Fukinko Bunseki" [A Disequilibrium Analysis of the Loan Market in Japan]. *Economic Studies Quarterly* 33, pp. 38–54.

Tsutsui, Yoshiro, and Michio Hatanaka. 1982. "Nichibei Ryokoku ni Okeru Kaheijuyo Kansu no Anteisei ni Tsuite" [The Stability of the Money Demand Function in Japan and the United States]. *Gendai Keizai*, Autumn, pp. 124–135.

Ueda, Kazuo. 1982. Kashidashi Shijo to Kinyu Seisaku [The Loan Market and Monetary Policy]. Paper presented at a Bank of Japan research meeting on monetary policy.

Yonezawa, Hiroyasu. 1982. Tobin no *q*, Toshi Oyobi Shisanshijo [Tobin's *q*, Investment and Asset Markets]. Technical paper series no. 56, Japan Institute of Security Studies, August.

Comments

Stephen H. Axilrod

Both of the papers presented in this panel—not to mention the opening remarks of Messrs. Friedman and Tobin—raise very fundamental problems with respect to the formulation of monetary policy. Professor Gordon would, as he has explained, let monetary policy be guided by nominal final sales. (I will also use the term nominal GNP, which rolls off my tongue more naturally and which may fit my later comments more easily.) At the same time, though, Professor Gordon is not very clear—or at least not to me—about which financial lever the central bank should press, or which of several should be pressed with what degrees of pressure, to attain the desired nominal-GNP path.

Professors Hamada and Hayashi seek what they term a "balanced policy perspective," meaning that the central bank is guided by a variety of M's as well as other financial indicators such as interest rates. They do not explicitly say what would influence the relative importance as policy guides of the various financial indicators. Presumably, if pressed, they might be driven back to giving most weight to that indicator which this year is behaving most "normally" in relation to nominal GNP. If that is right, their view would seem to reduce to that of Professor Gordon, or his would reduce to theirs, and central bankers would be left with an approach to policy that amounts to no more (or no less) than exercising the best judgment they can.

However, Professor Gordon would add the complication that the central bank should announce a rather precise 10-year path for nominal final sales—and should also operate policy, somehow, on the basis of staff forecasts (kept secret according to him). There are two problems, at least, here. First, I would say that reliance on forecasts of the economy as the principal—and in Professor Gordon's case perhaps the only—guide to policy is rather too risky; forecasts are fallible, and even if they average out reasonably well they have a disturbing tendency to miss inflection points. I am not saying that forecasts should be ignored, of course. Second, it is naive to believe that the public or legislative bodies will look much beyond the first year or two of a 10-year nominal-final-sales path. Indeed, in the middle of a recession the public will urgently want to know not only the expected behavior of nominal GNP over the next year or two but also, and probably more important in such an environment, the behavior of real GNP—that is, they will want to know the anticipated speed of economic recovery.

In practice, the focus of a GNP target will inevitably shift away from the intermediate or longer run that Professor Gordon tends to stress to the short run, and real as well as nominal values will come into the issue. The whole process will, as a result, be greatly complicated by political considerations. Apart from the issue of whether it is appropriate for the central bank to set an objective for the nation's overall economic activity, there is the further question of whether it is generally practical to present as an objective a "realistic" nominal GNP for a year or two ahead—except possibly when economic conditions are generally stable and when there is in any event little pressure of public opinion on the central bank. There would also always be questions of conflict in the United States with Administration and Congressional Budget Office assumptions, projections, or objectives.

Because of practical problems in setting the objective and because it is not attainable with a reasonable degree of certainty, a nominal-GNP target would almost inevitably call the central bank's credibility into question. If misses from the target were sizable and persistent, the public would come to doubt the central bank's effectiveness, and destabilizing expectations—either inflationary or deflationary, depending on the situation—might well develop. Similar problems can, of course, develop with misses from any kind of target a central bank announces, including the money supply, but the odds on missing carefully chosen financial targets are probably less. In any event, financial targets, particularly for monetary aggregates, do not carry with them the promise that monetary policy alone is responsible for the nation's overall economic performance, with all the disappointment that lapses from such a promise may engender.

Furthermore, setting a nominal-GNP target is unlikely in practice to spare the central bank from taking a view on the mix between real activity and prices, as I mentioned earlier. As an objective, real GNP appeals to many because it would convey intentions about the pace of economic recovery from a recession and would also make the central bank indicate its attitude toward longer-term economic growth.

Among the problems with specifying real GNP would be the strong practical pressures that would work toward an upward bias in an announced real-GNP objective. It would almost always be difficult to make it understood that in a year ahead more real GNP is not necessarily better than less. So long as prices react to policy with a longer lag than real activity, a more expansionary target for activity would generally appear to be preferable in a policy horizon that includes a year or two ahead. This, of course, argues strongly for Professor Gordon's point of stating policy objectives insofar as they involve GNP over longer-term time horizons, in this case so that implications for future price pressures, and not merely current price effects, can be given due weight.

Over the longer term, however, real GNP and nominal GNP are even less conceptually satisfactory as objectives for monetary policy than they are over the short run. At least in the short run it can be argued that the central bank should make know how it intends to adjust its policy to affect the pace and timing of, say, an economic recovery. Economic growth over the long term depends fundamentally on factors (such as growth in the labor force, hours worked, and productivity) that are not controllable by the central bank.

I have thus far taken the discussant's liberty of being mainly critical or negative. That way lies a degree of safety, but it may not do much for advancing discussion. I tend to agree with the views in both papers that velocity is not always reasonably predictable, and that policy involves judgment. But I also believe that some sort of anchor is needed to help circumscribe judgment, minimize the chances of major policy errors, and inform the public of policy intentions so that private decisions can be made more effectively. I do not believe that announcement of a nominal-GNP objective or path for policy would be particularly helpful in those respects, for reasons given earlier. Over the long run, given the real factors that determine growth in output, the economic objective that monetary policy can influence is the average level of prices. In that sense, looked at over a sufficiently long run (and Professor Gordon's 10-year horizon seems quite long enough to me), the average level of prices (presumably stable prices) would be a more realistic economic objective for monetary policy than nominal or real GNP.

Unfortunately, the length of the run over which price performance is independent of real growth may be longer than is acceptable in relation to the public's concerns about the impact of policy. The stickiness of wages, the problems posed by exogenous price shocks (such as oil), and the speed and timing of an economic recovery from recession raise questions that cannot be easily avoided about the near-term impact on economic activity of a central bank's policy. If a central bank is to declare itself publicly in those respects, it should be in my view in the form of *projections* (not objectives) of economic activity (nominal and real) likely to evolve over the next several years consistent with a long-term objective of price stability.

The difference between projections and objectives is not just semantic. One would hope that use of projections would work to avoid public misunderstanding about the capacity of the central bank to control nominal or real GNP over the next year or two and would also enhance public understanding that fiscal policy and other public and private policies can have independent effects on GNP in addition to, or as an aspect of, the inherent degree of losseness in the relationship of money to GNP.

A central bank does nonetheless need some objective over the near term, for reasons of public accountability if for no others. Such an objective, it seems to me, is still, despite all the institutional difficulties, best expressed as some form of monetary aggregate (or aggregates), with ranges and frequent enough reevaluations needed so that clear and evident shifts in money demand (given income and interest rates) can be taken into account in the implementation of policy. A money guide or anchor is needed, among other reasons to help guard against the inevitable mistakes in economic forecasting by staffs and by policy makers themselves. In a sense, one must hope, if it is not too late to take measures to help ensure, that financial technology and market forces do not develop to the point where the money that bears some predictable relationship to, say, prices or GNP over a reasonable length of run does not simply become indeterminable in measurement.

Comments

Hermann-Josef Dudler

Professor Gordon's analysis of the role of monetary management in the United States and his recommendations for the future conduct of monetary policy by the Federal Reserve can be regarded as a serious, general challenge to the two-stage monetary-targeting framework on which major central banks have based their operating procedures since about the mid 1970s. If I interpret Professor Gordon's paper correctly, his key propositions do not necessarily depend on his specific empirical findings on the U.S. economy. (I leave it to specialists to judge the quantitative work presented by Professor Gordon, who seems to have made an attempt to refute "hard-core" monetarist propositions with the help of "hard-core" monetarist econometric tools.) Let me therefore turn directly to the policy and operational aspects of Professor Gordon's central suggestion, which is to guide monetary policy along a predetermined, longer-term nominal-GNP or "final-sales" path.

The longer-term financial-programming framework proposed by Professor Gordon as an alternative to money-stock targeting distinguishes his paper positively from familiar myopic "activist" monetary-policy prescriptions. At the same time, I sympathize with the skeptical position he takes on the usefulness of rigid monetary rules and on short-run operating procedures focusing on a "steady" expansion of the monetary base. Going a step further, I would enumerate some concrete areas where Professor Gordon's analysis and actual central-bank policy making seem to meet halfway:

● Many central banks—including the Bundesbank—associate their annual money-stock targets explicitly with nominal-GNP projections or "norms." The relevant price and output assumptions are either decided upon by governments or agreed between them and the central bank. They thus serve to coordinate monetary management and other branches of macroeconomic policy. Moreover, in a number of countries outside the United States official annual GNP projections are embedded in a medium-term financial-planning exercise.

• Central banks have fairly frequently established money-stock objectives that were clearly inconsistent with the rigid pursuit of medium-term monetary norms, and they have accepted, at times, a considerable "overshooting" or "undershooting" of their intermediate objectives. To use a term probably not acceptable to Professor Friedman but usefully employed by Professors Hamada and Hayashi, the perspective of central banks has often been "multiscoped" in an apparent effort to support the attainment of desirable ultimate policy objectives.

• It would seem to be obvious from these partly discretionary attitudes exhibited by central banks that they have not generally accepted "strong" policy-ineffectiveness propositions (as reflected in a Lucas-Sargent-Wallace "rational" expectations or extreme "adaptive" expectations model).

• Turning finally to the short-run operational end of Professor Gordon's policy prescriptions, I can at least state for our operating procedures in Germany that we *do* take account of "base drift" in deriving our annual monetary objectives, and that we attempt to map out a four-quarter interest rate and "borrowed reserve" path consistent with our four-quarter nominal-GNP and money-stock projections (we thus indulge, to some extent at least, in economic forecasting in the context of monetary targeting).

You may ask whether such a positive assessment of some of Professor Gordon's propositions must not logically lead to the conclusion that one should also accept his ultimate policy recommendation and abandon operating targets situated in the intermediate financial area altogether. Let me therefore raise a few—in no way exhaustive or elaborate—objections against his key proposals. These objections may help to explain why we can indeed only meet halfway, or, in other words, in what respects monetary policy has been influenced by "monetarism" beyond the use of new rhetoric.

• In countries where the derivation of GNP "norms" is a government responsibility or performs a coordination function for the main branches of policy, the behavior of fiscal and price/incomes policies cannot be visualized—as in the Gordon framework—merely as a monetary-policy "constraint"; at the same time, the specific contribution of the monetary authorities to the achievement of common policy objectives must be made transparent with the help of variables—other than GNP—reasonably under the control of central banks, if only to permit appropriate decisions on the "policy mix."

• Accountability of the central bank's behavior and public recognition of the likely thrust of monetary policy are even more necessary if monetary management is mainly assigned the task of preserving a reasonable degree of price stability. The specific, persuasive role that monetary-aggregates objectives can play in such a policy context tends to get lost in Professor Gordon's policy framework. He sketches out an optimal "final sales" policy on the basis of *given* or *predictable* aggregate "supply constraints," such as the short-run inflation-unemployment tradeoff and inflation "inertia"; central banks, on the other hand, have seen a need since the middle of the 1970s to *actively influence* these "constraint" elements and to change their parameters in a desired direction, because they had to cope with what they perceived to be volatile price and exchange-rate expectations.

● Even in the absence of shocks, I find it difficult to believe that our knowledge about the short-run and longer-run adjustment properties of our economies suffices to work out a credible long-term optimal path for nominal spending. Similarly, I am not sure whether we can directly link monetary instruments with ultimate goal variables in a way that permits predictable and controlled corrective action if nominal GNP deviates from its target path. If a "Gordonite" strategy were officially adopted today, the most likely outcome would probably be the following. We would see frequent "overreactions" by central banks, responding to actual or forecast departures of nominal spending from its projected trajectory. Public pressure to set nominal interest rates at levels deemed to be consistent with short-run output and employment maximization would intensify. In the end, a quite familiar destabilizing "policy rule" could reemerge, which goes like this: "Ease up" vigorously during the recession; "restrain," if at all, later (although in good time, where "in good time" has in practice often meant in the past) when consumer prices begin to rise at an unacceptable pace.

I realize, of course that Professor Gordon's recommendations are clearly not meant to pave the way to future "stop-and-go cycles." Nor have central banks succeeded in avoiding policy "overreactions" by pursuing their pragmatic monetary-targeting strategies. It is therefore clearly desirable to improve the existing policy concepts. But do we really need radical "new chic"? I do not believe that the policy options open to us are all that clear-cut. What we may yet have to learn is how to live in a world of uncertainties in which no simple, single "yardstick," "rule," or "strategy" is lying around to be picked up by intelligent and imaginative theoretical economists or central bankers.

Comments

Charles A. E. Goodhart

Professors Hamada and Hayashi have reported that the Bank of Japan is near its zenith. It is, indeed, a great pleasure to welcome the success of the Bank of Japan on the occasion of its centennial. Coming from a central bank that will be celebrating its own third centennial in about 10 years' time, I would like to reassure my hosts that it is not necessarily downhill all the way after the first hundredth birthday has been reached. Indeed, at the time of our own first centenary, in 1794, we were just recovering from a dispute with our American cousins on the incidence of our fiscal policy. Sam Adams had argued that if we taxed them less, they would grow faster—an early example of American concern with supply-side issues.

To return, however, to the present, I was struck by the similarity between the Bank of Japan's approach to monetary policy and that of the Bank of England. Consider, for example, the importance given to bank lending to the private sector as a crucial variable determining the pace of monetary growth and also acting as a major transmission link with the real economy; the appreciation that variations in the monetary base are a residual, endogenous, and essentially unimportant development, not a crucial mainspring of monetary growth; and the greater attention to broad, rather than narrow, monetary aggregates, with these also interpreted judgmentally in the context of other information variables. All such attitudes are closely reminiscent of the British position.

With respect to the set of variables that were described in the chapter as providing additional information to be taken into account in judging monetary conditions, I noticed one surprising omission: the level and rate of change of the exchange rate itself. Was that omission intentional, or an oversight?

Although the general approach to monetary policy adopted by the Bank of Japan has a lot in common with that of the Bank of England, the economic contexts these two central banks face are very different. Hamada and Hayashi note that "the Japanese economy has been equipped with a high degree of wage-price flexibility," whereas earlier in the chapter they record that the Japanese financial system is characterised by rigidities and in some respects remains underdeveloped. The contrast with the United Kingdom is only too obvious. Perhaps this suggests that the functioning of labor markets is much more crucial to economic success than the efficient functioning of financial markets. In this respect, however, I wondered how far the more contra-inflationary monetary policies of the Bank of Japan, in the course of the second oil shock, could take credit for the greater flexibility of labor markets that Hamada and Hayashi say occurred then, either directly (by monetary policy influencing labor expectations) or indirectly (simply by restricting the level of demand).

If the more flexible labor markets in Japan seem an unqualified blessing, what are we to make of the rather inflexible financial markets? First, some of us may wonder how the Japanese manage to retain such effective direct controls. Financial innovations over the last two decades have brought about a flexible world financial market. In the United Kingdom we believed that, once exchange controls over capital flows were removed, direct controls over domestic credit flows and interest rates would cease to be effective, for the company sector at least. But there is no reference in the chapter to the role of exchange controls in supporting "window guidance" and interest-rate con-trols at all. Perhaps it is partly a matter of the greater distance of Japan from the other financial centers. Indeed, a somewhat greater role in bringing about the current liberalization of the financial system is now attributed to the increase in the outstanding quantity of government bonds, issued to finance the fiscal deficit, than to the access of Japanese corporations to the world capital market.

In general, economic analysis of direct financial controls is condemnatory. Apart from causing financial intermediaries themselves to be less efficient and enterprising (and I noted in the chapter the statement that the "system of interest rates is usually determined in such a way as to secure normal profits for every financial intermediary"), it is normally argued that direct controls over interest rates and credit flows tend to lead to a reduction of savings and a serious misallocation of investment. When I read the chapter I wondered how the Bank of Japan itself now reckons up the balance sheet of the benefits and costs to the economy generally of direct controls over the financial system.

Overall, I found this chapter by Hamada and Hayashi, with a considerable intellectual assist from my friend Suzuki, lucid, informative, and sensible. My one reservation related to the section titled "Does Anticipated Money Matter?," where the work seemed rather hurried and not entirely convincing, either technically or economically. Why, for example, should an increase in foreign-exchange reserves be expected to reduce monetary growth? Nor can I see the supposed significance of reserves, adduced in the chapter, actually appearing in table 4.8. Perhaps it is the failure to estimate successfully a well-fitting monetary-reaction function that leads to the rather odd results from regressing output on anticipated and unanticipated monetary growth. It would appear that changes in anticipated as well as unanticipated monetary growth can lead to permanent increases in output. Could you then increase output indefinitely simply by larger and larger monetary injections? How do the findings in this section square with the evidence for a vertical Phillips curve presented earlier?

To conclude, I must say that I enjoyed the Japanese nomenclature for their savings deposits with deposit instruments called Big and Wide. Perhaps I may be allowed to use the same approach to describe this chapter as "Handsome."

Comments

Marie-Henriette Lambert

The comprehensive study conducted by Professors Hamada and Hayashi points to the relative success of Japanese adjustment policies over recent years. The inflation rate has been brought down with lesser cost in terms of unemployment than in other industrialized countries—although unemployment statistics do not accurately reflect the size of the output loss. The forces behind this successful macroeconomic performance of the Japanese economy are smooth money management and more flexible behavior of wages after the second oil shock. Smooth money management means that the policy of the central bank is not geared to the control of a single monetary aggregate. Indeed, the Bank of Japan watches a variety of indicators: levels of interest rates, price indices, liquidity conditions of firms, the retail sales index, and the general business outlook. Therefore, the conduct of monetary policy in Japan is not subject to narrow constraints set by fears of reviving inflationary expectations. Households and firms are not basing their price expectations on the behavior of one single financial variable, nor do the markets react to fluctuations in any single aggregate. The "credibility" of the monetary authorities is not at stake when there is a sudden increase in the level of money stock. Using Professor Tobin's words, I would say that the monetary authorities are not frightened by mass or market psychology.

Yet Japan has a large public-sector deficit, much larger than that in the United States. Private domestic saving, however, exceeds the financial requirements of the public sector, as implied by the large surpluses in the balance-of-payments current account, and measures of fiscal relaxation now being considered by the Japanese authorities are not adversely affecting price expectations or the course of interest rates. On top of this, I should add that Japanese households exhibit a large saving ratio but do not enjoy market-determined interest rates when they invest their savings in domestic financial assets. The coexistence of rigid regulated rates of interest on one side and market-determined interest rates on the other side amounts to a cross-subsidizing of the sectors in deficit—business and the government. The mixture of rigidities in the financial system and flexibility in the real economy contrasts with developments in most other industrialized countries where, as Tobin says in chapter 2 above, "prices and wages that are administrated or negotiated change less rapidly and readily than the prices of financial assets and commodities traded in auction markets." With wages reacting with less inertia than administered interest rates to a restrictive monetary policy, one can hope that price increases would slow down without important losses in terms of output. How those rigidities in the financial system can last in Japan while in most other industrial countries financial innovations have reduced conventional deposits in favor of instruments bearing market-related interest rates is a topic on which I had hoped to hear some comments by Hamada and Hayashi.

Broadly speaking, the Japanese economy, despite its openness in terms of goods and its dependence on imported energy, is relatively well sheltered from adverse external shocks. First, the downward flexibility of wages protects the business sector from shifts in factor shares due to a worsening in the terms of trade; so does the dual structure of interest rates, which smooths the impact on debtor rates of large rises in international money market rates. Second, there is no adverse effect on price expectations—and therefore no constraint on monetary policy—arising from changes in the anticipated government deficit or in any strategic financial variable. In these circumstances, the scope available to the authorities for encouraging an economic recovery is large. The absence of adverse supply shocks (i.e., forces that push up the inflation rate spontaneously without any required excess demand pressure) avoids for the authorities the extreme alternative of targeting real output or inflation. (See chapter 3.) They can accommodate the demand for liquidity without putting longer-term price stability at risk. Over a longer time span, the Japanese monetary authorities can concentrate their efforts on keeping an equilibrium between the domestic demand for goods and services and the amounts that can be supplied.

I am, however, struck by the limited array of instruments that the Japanese authorities are using in their monetary management, and by the narrowness of their financial coverage. Over past years, the main instrument used by the Bank of Japan has been the control of the amount of lending by commercial banks through moral suasion (window guidance).

Table 4.3 shows that bank lending accounts now for only one-third of total lending. I wonder whether, in a context in which lending to business and households would be expanding too much, the Bank of Japan could check this lending by controlling banks only. In Belgium, where disintermediation took place earlier than in the United States or Japan, it has been realized that this process implies that the control by the central bank will be extended to a wide range of financial instituions. An alternative to more comprehensive direct control of lending would be for the central bank to rely more heavily on interest-rate policy, but rises in interest rates could conflict with exchange-market objectives, while the dual-domestic-interest-rate system would deprive them of part of their influence on spending.

The answer to those contingent constraints in the choice of monetary policy objectives and instruments probably lies in the fact that, in Japan, monetary policy does not have to bear the whole burden of the struggle against inflation. Over recent years, the inflationary effects of the second oil shock were minimized through a successful mix of income-restraint, fiscal, and monetary policies. There is no reason to believe that in a context of demand-pull inflation monetary policy would have to bear more of the burden of restraint, posing to the authorities something of a "external versus domestic objectives" dilemma.

Comments

William E. Norton

I congratulate Professors Hamada and Hayashi on an interesting and provocative paper. My comments deal with the reasons given for the slowdown in economic growth in Japan and the suggestions for changes in policy. But first I note that for Japan the slowdown in economic growth has been relatively large. That is indicated by the accompanying table. According to Hamada and Hayashi, the main reason for this slowdown in the growth of production was a drop in profitability, or, as they put it, the gap that arose between the growth of real wages and the growth of productivity after correcting for the terms of trade. They go on to say that the leaders of the labor movement in Japan learned from the experience of 1974, when a jump in real wages, relative to productivity, was associated with a loss of jobs. As evidence of that learning, they refer to the experience in 1980, when, after the second oil crisis, there was no major cut in profitability.

Change in average rate of growth per year, 1974–1979 on 1960–1973

Gross domestic product		Industrial production	
Japan	−6.6	Japan	−10.7
Switzerland	−4.8	Switzerland	−6.2
Australia	−2.8	Sweden	−5.4
France	−2.6	Italy	−4.6
Italy	−2.6	Australia[a]	−4.4
West Germany	−2.3	West Germany	−4.4
Canada	−2.2	France	−4.2
Sweden	−2.2	Canada	−3.4
United Kingdom	−2.0	United Kingdom	−2.7
United States	−1.3	United States	−1.9

a. For Australia, data for the 1960s begin with 1964.

Unlike Hamada and Hayashi, I doubt that "the lesson of 1974" has had such a major effect on attitudes. Perhaps there was no major drop in profitability in 1980 for two reasons: Profitability, although higher than after the fall in 1974, was already low; and economic growth was still relatively moderate, as shown by figure 4.8. I suggest that a good deal of the slowdown in economic growth is still due to relatively low profitability. (See W. E. Norton, The Deterioration in Economic Performance, Reserve Bank of Australia Occasional Paper 9, September 1982.)

Hamada and Hayashi seem to accept that large budget deficits can, by reducing national savings and increasing real interest rates, lower economic growth. They also note that large deficits have added substantially to the ratio of government debt to gross domestic product and, with big maturities of debt in prospect, could soon undermine control over monetary conditions. Yet, after noting these problems from large budget deficits, they advocate a "more flexible budget policy"—a phrase that I assume implies even higher deficits. Why is this so? Will not larger deficits reduce economic growth by adding further to real rates of interest? Will not larger deficits increase inflation by making it harder to control monetary aggregates? A lower deficit, in contrast, would permit monetary policy to play a bigger part in promoting a return to higher levels of economic growth.

INTERNATIONAL ASPECTS
OF MONETARY POLICY

Monetary Policy in the Large Open Economy

Michael R. Darby

Economists are fond of downward-sloping demand curves and upward-sloping supply curves, except when describing a nation's international economic relations. In that case these curves are generally assumed to be either horizontal or vertical as required to describe a perfectly open or perfectly closed economy. The reason for this exceptional behavior on the part of economists is easy to see: Simple models can be used in either extreme case, but the analysis becomes rather complex in the intermediate case in which economies are open but far from perfectly so.[1] This chapter will first report on recent empirical research that rather conclusively rejects either extreme model for the major noncommunist industrial nations. The implications of imperfect openness for their central banks' monetary policies will then be analyzed. Finally, the role of capital flows in determining the long-run equilibrium values of the balance of trade and the real exchange rate will be discussed.

Goods and Assets as Imperfect Substitutes Internationally

Either or both of two major assumptions have been used to characterize perfectly open economies: that goods are perfect substitutes internationally or that securities are perfect substitutes internationally. This section reports on recent empirical work that decisively rejects both hypotheses. Most of the work summarized here was done as part of the NBER's International Transmission Project and is reported in Darby et al. 1983.

Goods Substitution

The "global monetarists," including Laffer (1975), argued that internationally traded goods are, for all practical purposes, perfect substitutes across borders, with prices rigidly linked by arbitrage.[2] Factor competition between tradable and nontradable goods was used to extend this arbitrage relation to the "law of one price level," which held that purchasing-power parity obtains continuously—not just in the long run, as in the Humean tradition.[3] Previous empirical research (Isard 1977; Kravis and Lipsey 1977, 1978; Richardson 1978) has concluded that goods are substitutable internationally, but far from perfectly so.

The International Transmission Project's results support that conclusion. In a medium-scale simultaneous-equations model of Canada, France, West Germany, Italy, Japan, the Netherlands, the United Kingdom, and the United States estimated for 1957–1976, the relative-price effects on the balance of trade implicit in export and import equations are small in the initial quarter, although they do increase over time (Darby et al. 1983, chapters 5 and 6). In bivariate Granger causality tests between domestic and foreign inflation for the same eight countries, lagged foreign inflation was generally insignificant. Furthermore, there was no evidence that price changes led money changes in nonreserve countries under pegged exchange rates, as suggested by analyses based on the law of one price level (Darby et al. 1983, chapter 4).[4] Only weak and far from universal foreign-price effects were found in reduced-form price equations estimated for the same eight countries (Darby et al. 1983, chapter 14). Thus our results confirm the previous conclusion: Goods are imperfect substitutes internationally.

Asset Substitution

A central bank's monetary policy may affect the balance of payments substantially and immediately through asset flows, even if the balance of trade responds only weakly at first. Indeed, in view of the previous empirical rejection of perfect good substitution, perfect asset substitution has become the usual defining characteristic of a perfectly open economy.[5] In this context, perfect asset substitution means that the domestic interest rate is equal to the foreign interest rate minus the expected appreciation (per annum) of the domestic currency over the term to maturity of the securities plus an exogenously given risk premium. In contrast, imperfect asset substitutability implies that there is a risk premium between the two interest rates that varies with the relative stocks of domestic and foreign assets and hence responds to international capital flows. Thus, lower domestic interest rates could induce finite capital outflows that would raise the risk premium on foreign assets enough that no further flows would be induced by the yields on domestic securities, which would be lower than the expected yields on foreign securities.[6]

The International Transmission Project approached this question in a number of ways. Cassese and Lothian found that lagged as well as current

American interest rates had significant effects on the other seven countries' interest rates during the pegged period; indeed, generally, the lagged effects were more important quantitatively, in contradiction to perfect short-run asset substitution (Darby et al. 1983, chapter 4). In the structural model the estimated interest-rate effects on capital flows were small; simulations confirmed that changes in monetary policy did not induce very large short-run balance-of-payments effects under pegged exchange rates (Darby et al. 1983, chapters 5–7).

An indirect approach provided strong evidence against perfect asset substitution for the seven nonreserve countries under pegged exchange rates. As is demonstrated in the following section, this condition is sufficient to render their domestic monetary policy impotent under pegged exchange rates. It was shown that domestic policy goals were in fact significant determinants of money-supply growth in these countries (Darby et al. 1983, chapter 10). Daniel Laskar estimated the fraction of a shift in the money-supply reaction function that would be reflected in the domestic money supply given the induced capital flows and the sterilization behavior of the central bank; for all seven nonreserve countries, under pegged exchange rates, this fraction significantly exceeded zero but did not significantly differ from unity (Darby et al. 1983, chapter 11). Thus, the actual exercise of short-run monetary control during the Bretton Woods era is inconsistent with the usefulness of the perfect-asset-substitution hypothesis.

Moreover, the International Transmission Project's strong results are consistent with the best recent empirical work reported in the literature. Using floating-exchange-rate data, Geweke and Feige (1979), Hansen and Hodrick (1980, 1982), Bilson (1981), and Cumby and Obstfeld (1981, 1983) all reject the hypothesis that the forward exchange rate is an unbiased predictor of the future spot rate as it would be under perfect asset substitution.[7] In contrast, Dooley and Isard (1979) and Frankel (1982) have reported an inability to relate risk premiums to outstanding bond supplies, but these results may well be explained by the rather low power of their tests.[8] Furthermore, these tests all examine the floating period in which assets should be relatively better substitutes than under pegged rates when capital controls and the risk of their imposition were more significant factors and when international financial markets were less well developed. The new evidence in Darby et al 1983 appears to virtually eliminate perfect asset substitution as a hypothesis.

Independent Monetary Policy under Pegged Exchange Rates

The fact that for large industrial countries such as Japan and West Germany neither goods nor assets are perfect substitutes internationally implies that changes in the central bank's reserves will permit it (within limits discussed below) to pursue monetary and exchange-rate goals simultaneously. Even under pegged exchange rates, independent monetary policy is, to an extent, feasible in the short run. Although the floating-rate regime is of most interest currently, it is helpful to consider first the simpler case of pegged exchange rates.[9]

In chapter 10 of Darby et al. 1983 I propose a simple graphical device for analyzing the simultaneous determination of the balance of payments and the nominal money supply in a large, imperfectly open economy maintaining a pegged exchange rate. The model combines the central bank's reaction function with the semi-reduced-form equation describing the economic environment within which the bank operates.

The central bank's reaction function provides a formal statement of the behavior of the monetary authorities working through the banking system. It may be written compactly as

$$\Delta \log M = \alpha \frac{B}{H} + X\beta + u, \tag{1}$$

where M is the nominal money supply, B/H is the current-period balance-of-payments surplus divided (or scaled) by nominal base (high-powered) money, X is a vector of all the other variables that systematically affect the central bank's behavior, and u is a random disturbance. Note particularly that lagged values of B/H or scaled reserves may appear in X. Here we are concerned with monetary independence within the short period, but the short-period curves may well shift in the next period in response to what happens in this period. The parameter α measures the extent to which the central bank sterilizes reserve flows within the period: If $\alpha = 1$, there is no sterilization; if $\alpha = 0$, sterilization is complete.[10] In other words, α represents the fraction of the current balance of payments that the central bank allows to be reflected in base money.[11]

Although this reaction function is stated in terms of base money, as is standard in the literature, it applies equally to other operating strategies of central banks. For example, monetary control managed through quantitative controls—manipulation of the money multiplier—can be expressed formally in this way. Then α measures the extent, if any, to which the controls are adjusted by the central bank in response to the contemporaneous balance of payments. An interest-rate target can similarly be represented by equation 1.

Although a complete structural model of the economy will not be offered here,[12] it is useful to define parity money growth $(\Delta \log M)_p$ as the change that is consistent with substituting in the money demand equation the exchange-rate-converted foreign price level and foreign interest rate:[13]

$$(\Delta \log M)_p = Z\delta + \varepsilon. \tag{2}$$

Money growth faster than $(\Delta \log M)_p$ will be associated with domestic interest rates lower and prices higher than their international parity values. Lower interest rates will induce capital outflows; higher prices will reduce the trade balance. Thus, money growth in excess of $(\Delta \log M)_p$ will reduce the balance-of-payments surplus. Formally, we can write the semi-reduced form for the scaled balance of payments as

$$\frac{B}{H} = \theta(\Delta \log M - Z\delta - \varepsilon) + S\lambda, \tag{3}$$

where S is a vector of all other factors affecting the balance of payments, such as those contained in the trade supply and demand equations. Specification of S is not of concern for the current analysis. Our primary concern is the function θ, which determines the derivative of the scaled balance of payments with respect to money-supply growth.

The scaled balance of payments is, by the accounting identities, the difference between the scaled trade balance (T/H) and the scaled net private capital outflows (C/H):[14]

$$\frac{B}{H} \equiv \frac{T}{H} - \frac{C}{H}. \tag{4}$$

Scaled net private capital outflows will be a function of the current covered interest differential (adjusted for expected exchange-rate changes) and other variables that may be taken as given for the current period:[15]

$$\frac{C}{H} = f(R - \rho - R^F), \tag{5}$$

where ρ is the expected depreciation of the exchange rate ($\rho < 0$ implies an expected appreciation, R^F is the given foreign interest rate, and so f' is negative. We find θ' by differentiating equation 4:

$$\theta' \equiv \frac{d(B/H)}{d\Delta \log M} - \frac{d(T/H)}{d\Delta \log M} - f' \frac{dR}{d\Delta \log M}$$

$$+ f' \frac{d\rho}{d(B/H)} \frac{d(B/H)}{d\Delta \log M}, \tag{6}$$

$$\theta' = \frac{1}{1 - \dfrac{d\rho}{d(B/H)}} \left(\frac{d(T/H)}{d\Delta \log M} - f' \frac{dR}{d\Delta \log M} \right). \tag{7}$$

The multiplier

$$1 \Big/ \left(1 - f' \frac{d\rho}{d(B/H)} \right)$$

states that if the expected depreciation ρ responds to the size of the balance of payments (as an indicator of the probability and size of a revaluation), then the direct trade and capital flow effects will be reinforced by induced "speculative" capital flows.[16] These induced speculative capital flows will be overwhelming unless

$$f' \frac{d\rho}{d(B/H)} < 1. \tag{8}$$

Thus, expected depreciation, which plays such an important role in recent analyses of floating exchange rates, is potentially important under pegged exchange rates also.

Solving equation 3 for money growth yields

$$\Delta \log M = \phi(B/H - S\lambda) + Z\delta + \varepsilon, \tag{9}$$

where ϕ is the inverse of the function θ.[17] That is, increases in the balance of payments relative to its parity value $S\lambda$ are associated with decreases in money growth relative to its parity value. Figure 5.1 plots equations 1 and 9 on the same graph to illustrate the simultaneous determination of the equilibrium money growth $(\Delta \log M)^{eq}$ and the balance of payments $(B/H)^{eq}$. The line for equation 1 would be vertical if the central bank completely sterilized the contemporaneous balance of payments; its positive slope here indicates partial sterilization. The line for equation 9 would be vertical if condition 8 was not met or under perfect international substitutability of goods or assets (see note 17); the line is drawn here as negatively sloping in the relevant region.[18] Unless the two lines happened to coincide, there would be no equilibrium if both lines were vertical. The intersection of the lines representing equations 1 and 9 gives the short-period equilibrium values of the scaled balance of payments and money growth.[19]

Suppose that economic conditions, characterized by X_1, include higher domestic unemployment than those in X_0 and that this increases the money growth desired by the central bank for any given value of the balance of payments $(X_1\beta > X_0\beta)$. As illustrated in figure 5.2, this shift in domestic policy goals induces an increase in money growth and a decrease in the balance of payments. The more open the economy, the steeper will be the downward-sloping line that represents the central bank's payments-balance/ money-growth tradeoff and the greater will be the balance-of-payments effect

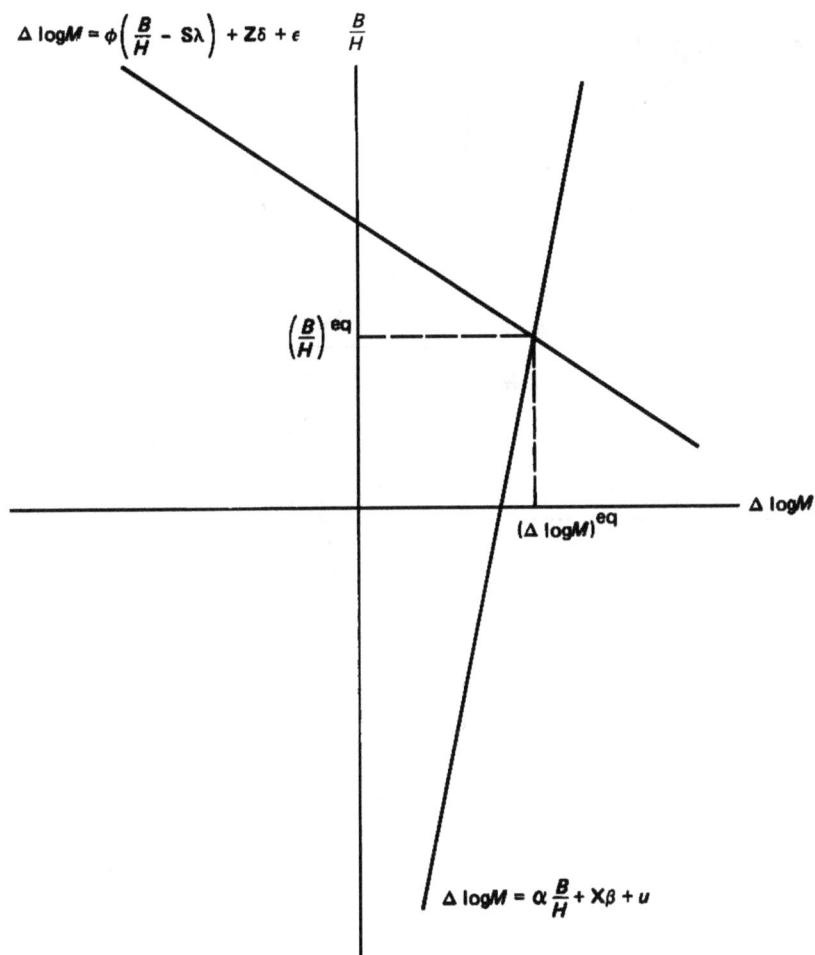

$$\Delta \log M = \phi\left(\frac{B}{H} - S\lambda\right) + Z\delta + \epsilon$$

$$\frac{B}{H}$$

$$\left(\frac{B}{H}\right)^{eq}$$

$$\Delta \log M$$

$$(\Delta \log M)^{eq}$$

$$\Delta \log M = \alpha\frac{B}{H} + X\beta + u$$

Figure 5.1
Simultaneous determination of balance of payments and nominal money under pegged exchange rates.

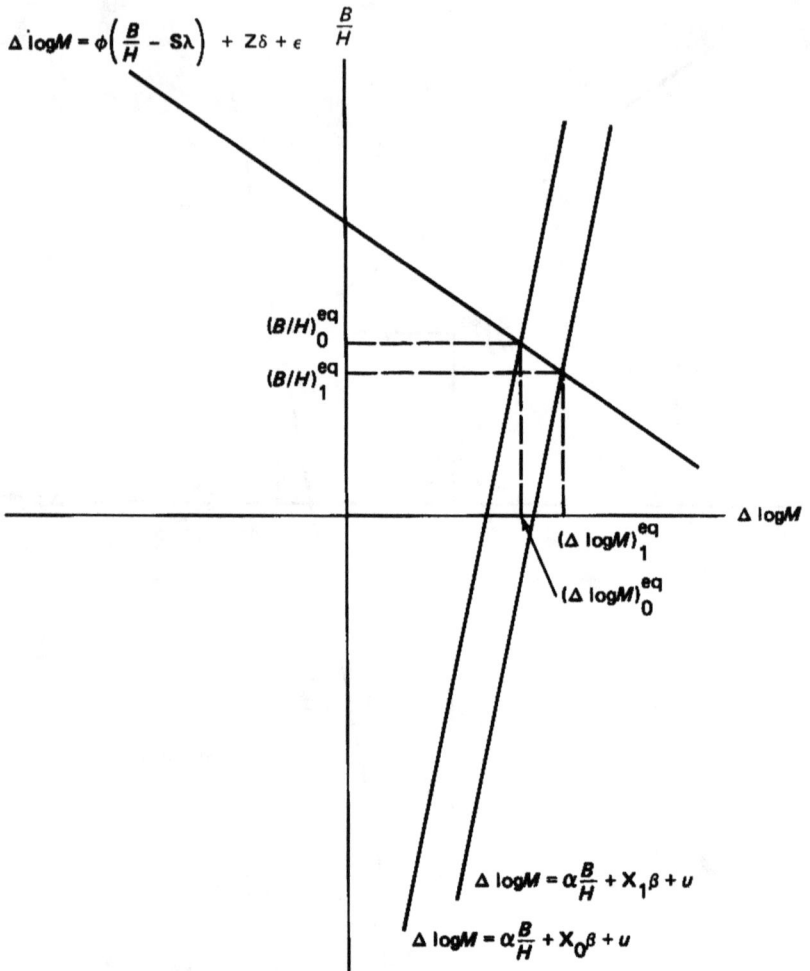

Figure 5.2
Effect of shift in domestic policy goals.

and the lesser the money-growth effect of any given shift in the central bank's reaction function.[20]

The graphical analysis did not take account of the possibility that both the probability and the size of a devaluation may increase with the absolute value of B/H or its deviation from its parity value $S\lambda$. If this is so, then $dp/d(B/H)$ will approach the critical value $1/f'$ for large absolute values of B/H and therefore the tradeoff will worsen, as in figure 5.3.[21] This possibility, as well as the implied effects on future tradeoffs, would limit the range within which the central bank would choose to operate. The size of this range remains unknown, but the evidence in Darby et al. 1983 suggests that a 10 percent deviation of the actual from the parity level of nominal money is near the limit of monetary independence for large open economies maintaining a pegged exchange rate. Furthermore, this deviation cannot be maintained indefinitely because of the cumulative effect on reserves of continuing large balance-of-payments deficits or surpluses. Ultimately either monetary policy or the exchange-rate peg must be adjusted.

Monetary Policy, Floating Exchange Rates, and the Trade Balance

The theoretical and empirical analysis of the effects of monetary policy under floating exchange rates has not progressed to the point that neat summary diagrams can be produced to illustrate major results. Indeed, we seem to know disappointingly little despite the expenditure of much talent and effort. If this section seems maddeningly tentative to policy makers, it must be recalled that false knowledge is far more dangerous than an awareness of ignorance.

Broadly speaking, economists' prior expectations of the results of widespread floating among major currencies have been confirmed in two major respects, but economists have been surprised in one important aspect. Economists were generally correct in their expectations of long-run neutrality and enhanced monetary independence but wrong in predicting that exchange rates would gradually move in reflection of relative inflation rates.

The long-run neutrality of the economy with respect to monetary policy is perhaps our most secure result. That is, an increase in the level of money will—in the long run and with other things equal—be reflected in an equal increase in prices and the nominal exchange rate with no effect on real output or the real exchange rate.[22] Superneutrality is rather less secure.[23] First, as in any closed economy, higher money growth and hence inflation may shift the aggregate production function downward, increase the investment-income ratio, and decrease labor input;[24] real output, the real interest rate, and the real exchange rate may be changed in either direction, depending upon the relative importance of the various effects and upon parameters describing the

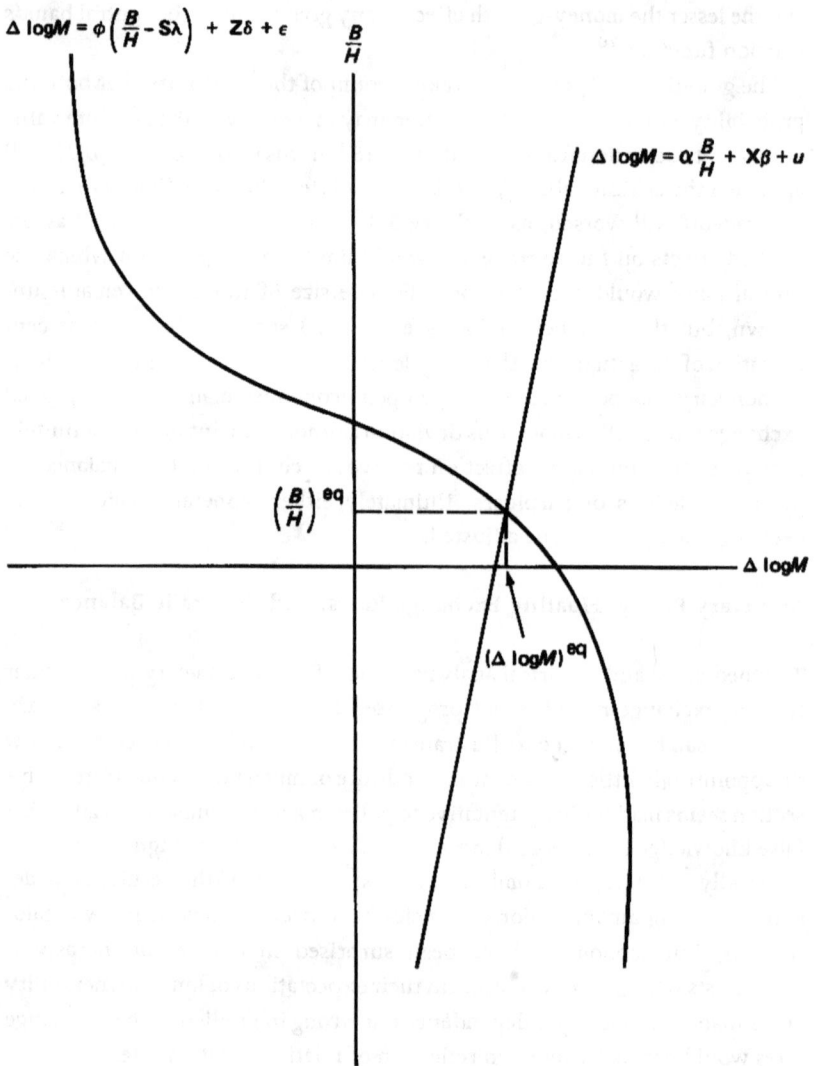

Figure 5.3
Simultaneous determination of balance of payments and money where potentially unstable speculation limits monetary control.

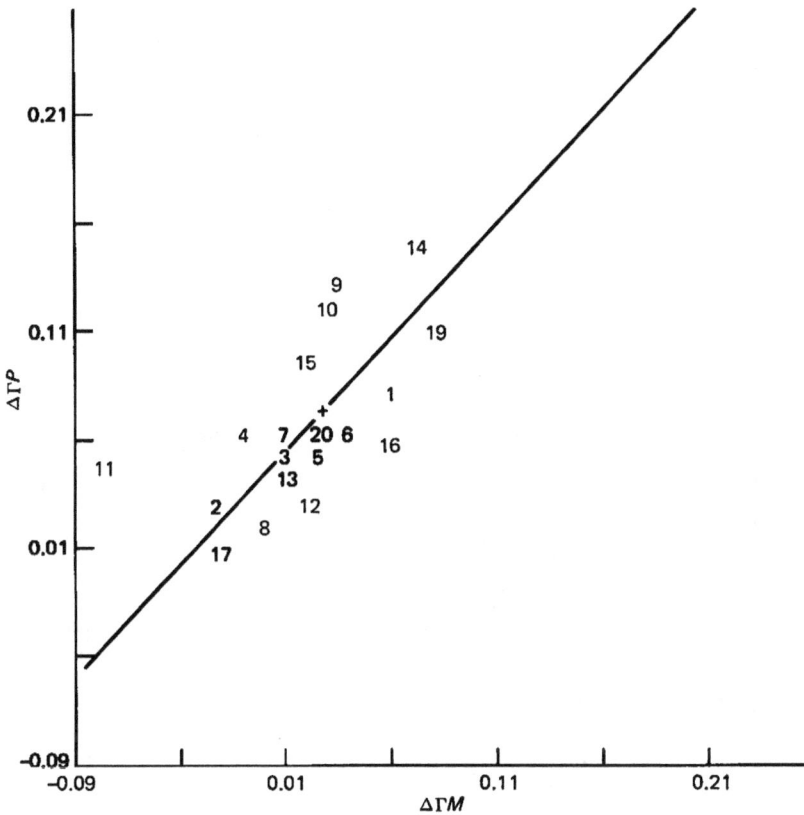

Figure 5.4
Growth shift in consumer prices versus growth shift in money for 20 OECD countries,
1956–1973 and 1974–1980. Source: Lothian 1983.

economy. Furthermore, if increased money growth is accomplished through
increased purchases of foreign reserves this will tend to depreciate the real
exchange rate.[25]

Lothian (1983) has recently made some calculations that demonstrate both
the strength of the neutrality results and the relative unimportance of any
deviations from superneutrality. In this work he analyzed for various variables the differences between their average growth rates for 1956–1973 and
1974–1980. Having obtained data on these "growth shifts" for 20 OECD
countries, Lothian showed that the growth shift in prices matched that in
money but found essentially no correlation between growth shifts in output
and those in money. Figures 5.4 and 5.5 illustrate these striking results.[26]
These results demonstrate that any shifts in levels of y and P due to failure of

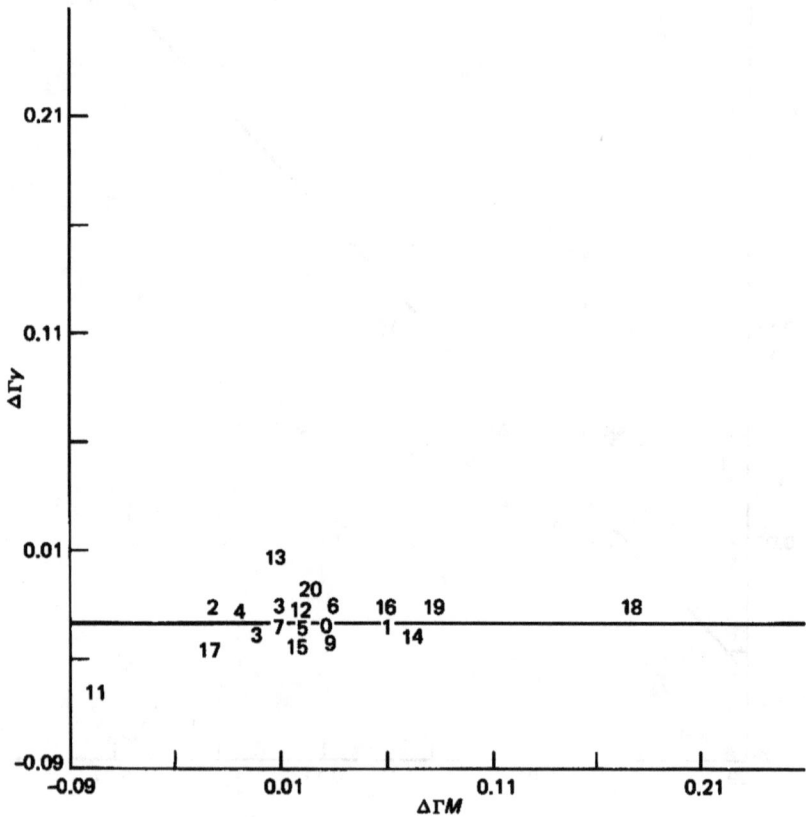

Figure 5.5
Growth shift in real output versus growth shift in money for 20 OECD countries, 1956–1973
and 1974–1980. Source: Lothian 1983.

superneutrality are negligible (when averaged over seven years) in comparison with random fluctuations in the growth rate of real output or with the
changes in the growth of prices induced by the growth shift in money.
Similarly, Lothian found that the growth shifts in either relative inflation or
relative money growth have an effect on the growth shift in the exchange rate,
which differs insignificantly from unity. Having thus noted that neutrality
and even superneutrality hold to an acceptable degree of approximation, we
can concentrate on the independence of monetary policy and the reasons why
its exercise might have a short-run impact on real output and the real
exchange rate even in the absence of any long-run effects.

Although they often react in the same way to international events, those
central banks that have not attempted to maintain pegs with other currencies
after the breakdown of the Bretton Woods system have certainly dem-

onstrated their ability to pursue independent monetary policies. (See Darby and Lothian 1983.) The primary impact on real exchange rates of unexpected changes in monetary policy has been associated with the liquidity (or real-interest-rate) effect of these monetary shocks.[27] The basic idea is a simple one: An unexpected change in the interest rate at home relative to that abroad will induce incipient capital flows. If a positive money shock lowers the domestic interest rate, for example, a capital outflow will be induced, with all other things equal. In order for this capital outflow to be stanched, the exchange rate must rise sufficiently that anticipations of later decreases in this variable reduce or eliminate the decrease in the interest-rate differential adjusted for expected depreciation. If assets were perfect substitutes internationally, the adjustment in expected depreciation would have to exactly offset the change in the interest rate. A smaller adjustment is required if assets are imperfectly substitutable internationally and some change in capital flows actually occurs because of either contemporaneous adjustment in the trade balance or changes in central banks' reserve purchases.

Suppose that increased money growth were perfectly anticipated so that equal contemporaneous changes occurred in the actual and expected inflation rate and growth rate of the nominal exchange rate. Then there would be no initial jump in the exchange rate along the lines just suggested. Thus, it is seen that the movements in the nominal and real exchange rates associated with unexpected changes in monetary policy are due to movements in the real interest rate.[28]

This impact effect of monetary policy on the real (and the nominal) exchange rate might be quite large. Goodhart and Temperton (1982) attribute nearly all of the 30 percent fluctuation in the British real exchange rate over 1979–1981 to monetary policy.[29] This exchange-rate impact adds a channel of influence for monetary policy that is not present under pegged exchange rates: Unexpected decreases in money growth immediately reduce the demand for traded goods and hence reduce the aggregate demand.[30] The immediate effect on the trade balance of these movements in the real exchange rate is estimated to be close to nil.[31] It is the lagged effects that apparently influence the adjustment process.

When we move from consideration of the initial impact of monetary shocks to the subsequent adjustment process, our empirical base becomes weak; however, some suggestive comments can be made. First, the initial movement of the real exchange rate is gradually eliminated over time, but whether this adjustment is smooth or involves overshooting depends on the adjustment path of the real interest rate. The trade balance increases over time in response to a positive monetary shock, but then the price advantage of an increased (depreciated) real exchange rate is eliminated over time. However, the temporarily increased trade balance implies private (or government) net accumulation of foreign securities in excess of what would otherwise be the case. Once this accumulation becomes important, it implies a lower domestic interest rate relative to the expected-depreciation-adjusted foreign interest rate. The implications of this asset accumulation are far from well understood, but apparently they depend in part on whether they are ultimately reversed, for reasons discussed below.[32]

Sterilized intervention in the foreign exchange market—a continuing central-bank exchange of foreign for domestic securities—can be used to moderate the required initial movement in the real exchange rate. This would be attractive if the otherwise disproportionate share of the costs borne by the traded-goods sector were to make an anti-inflationary policy politically unacceptable.[33] The same factors that permit a degree of independence to monetary policy under pegged exchange rates permit the simultaneous pursuit of monetary and exchange-rate goals under floating exchange rates; in each case the reserve movements must be accepted as the cost of the central bank's influence on the second variable. Again, the effect of these flows on the expectation that the operations will be abandoned and the exchange-rate change that would ensue would limit the central bank's freedom to pursue the secondary goal.

In summary, floating the exchange rate eliminates the short-run and long-run limits on monetary growth, but it also changes the impact of monetary policy by speeding and increasing the impact on the traded-goods sector. This difference can be ameliorated to some extent by sterilized intervention, but ultimately the choice of a pegged exchange rate is a decision to restrict monetary growth to a range—determined by the reserve country—within which the traded-goods sector can be protected by sterilized intervention. Abandonment of that complete protection is the cost of monetary independence.

Some Rational-Expectations Considerations

Thus far we have been concerned with the feasible set from which the central bank can select combinations of money growth, reserve flows, and exchange rates and with the results of that choice. Expectations have been left largely in the background, except for the expected rate of depreciation. But much recent macroeconomic research has demonstrated the importance of expectations in determining the point of departure relative to which we have been comparing the effects of unanticipated policy changes. This research cautions us that the short-run impacts of the policies considered depend crucially upon the un-expected nature of these policies. Therefore, the short-run impacts on the real economy would not exist if the central bank were to systematically attempt to exploit, say, the beneficent effects of accelerated money growth on the traded-goods sector under a floating-exchange-rate system.

Some economists working in the strict rational-expectations tradition associated with Robert Lucas and Thomas Sargent have gone beyond these well-known cautions against attempts to exploit effects associated with policy innovations. In particular, they have attempted to analyze the variance of output implied by simple models under alternative exchange-rate/monetary-policy regimes. See, for example, Saidi 1980; Weber 1981; Flood and Marion 1982; Flood 1982; Kimbrough 1983. These authors show that an optimal portfolio of foreign disturbances may reduce the variance of output and thus stabilize the economy relative to a policy regime that more effectively insulates the economy from foreign disturbances. Some authors emphasize the private sector's adjustment in the output-inflation tradeoff as the regime changes; others emphasize the potential informational content of exchange-rate movements.

The rational-expectations models remain very simple and cannot yet provide any practical guidance to policy makers. However, they do raise the issue of whether the relevant questions concern the feasibility and effect of a particular money growth under a particular exchange-rate regime or the stochastic structure of the economy that would result from alternative rules for choosing monetary growth.

Capital Flows, the Trade Balance, and the Real Exchange Rate in Long-Run Equilibrium

The discussion so far has treated the trade balance as predetermined, with capital flows and depreciation-adjusted interest rates adjusting to maintain equilibrium. The concept of an autonomous trade balance has little appeal once we move beyond the initial short period. Indeed, the long-run equilibrium is better characterized by autonomous net capital outflows and passively adjusting trade balance and real exchange rate. This is seen most easily by noting that only one real exchange rate is consistent with a given trade balance in long-run equilibrium.[34] Therefore, expected real depreciation is inconsistent with long-run equilibrium, and capital flows must be responding to actual differences in real interest rates. Suppose Japan has a high saving/income ratio relative to the rest of the world and the United States a relatively low one. If both economies always maintained zero trade balances and capital flows, the real interest rate would become low in capital-rich Japan and high in the United States.[35] Instead, capital outflows and trade surpluses for Japan and capital inflows and trade deficits for the United States have achieved a more efficient world distribution of the capital stock. However, these flows will not continue forever. As Japan's wealth rises, its growth rate (saving/wealth) will fall until it converges to the growth rate of output in the world economy.[36] Eventually, if this growth rate is less than the real return on capital, Japan's foreign-investment income will exceed its net foreign investments and the difference will finance (indeed force) a trade deficit. Throughout the adjustment process and in very long-run equilibrium, the excess saving in Japan (or the saving shortage in the United States) determines the equilibrium net capital outflows and hence the trade balance and the real exchange rate. Commercial policy can only alter the composition of the trade balance by affecting the relative delivered prices and hence the apparent comparative advantage.[37]

If, then, we adopt the view that in the long run national capital stocks and wealth will not be affected by unexpected money growth, we must conclude (as suggested above) that adjustment to monetary shocks cannot be smooth. The abnormal capital flows induced by initial movements in the real exchange rate must ultimately be undone by offsetting movements. It will be some time before a full understanding of the intermediate effects of monetary shocks is achieved.[38]

Conclusions

The Bretton Woods system afforded the major nonreserve central banks a range for independent monetary policy that was neither negligible nor unlimited. The banks' resistance to accelerating American inflation in the late 1960s ultimately broke down, and the resulting burst of inflation in the early 1970s led to the collapse of the Bretton Woods system.[39] The ensuing decade of generalized floating among major currencies (or currency blocs) has presented some surprises and so engendered much theoretical and empirical research.

The work to date suggests that the major source of instability in real exchange rates has been instability in monetary policy. The U.S. Federal Reserve system has long been infamous for accelerating money growth to reduce unemployment and then causing a recession to control the resultant inflation.[40] The high-inflation legacy of the Bretton Woods system has left the other major central banks with a similar dilemma and similar results. The impact of the exercise of independent monetary policy on the traded-goods sector is both quicker and stronger than that associated with the sorts of unexpected money growth that could occur under the Bretton Woods system.

The unstable U.S. monetary policy confronts other nations with a most unpleasant choice: Peg exchange rates and follow a similarly unstable monetary policy, or let exchange rates and the tradeables industries fluctuate with the vagaries of American monetary policy. As the potential reserve bank, the Federal Reserve should not guide its policy by international considerations lest we have n central banks determining $n - 1$ independent exchange rates. Rather, purely for reasons of domestic self-interest, the United States should begin to pursue a stable monetary policy. Only then can other central banks hope to achieve stable monetary policy and real exchange rates simultaneously.

Acknowledgments

The author acknowledges helpful comments from Sebastian Edwards, Maxwell Fry, James Lothian, Maurice Obstfeld, James Tobin, and members of the UCLA Workshop in Monetary Economics. The research reported here was supported partially by the National Science Foundation and is part of the NBER's research program in international studies.

Notes

1. Microeconomists are accustomed to choosing either the competitive or the monopolistic model according to the problem at hand; they thus generally avoid the numbing complexity and inconclusiveness of the various oligopolistic models. Unfortunately, such a choice between the extreme macroeconomic models would—as I attempt to demonstrate below—preclude serious analysis of monetary policy in the major industrial countries. Fortunately, the complexity of the intermediate model appears less severe than in the case of oligopoly.

2. The term in quotation marks was introduced in Whitman's (1975) survey article. In the relevant sense, price arbitrage requires that domestic prices be strictly proportional (not necessarily equal) to the exchange-rate-converted foreign prices. This implicitly assumes proportional shipping costs and tariffs and that each good is always shipped in the same direction.

3. Fausten (1979) persuasively distinguished the Humean tradition from the law of one price level.

4. The tests were run for periods ending in 1971, 1973, and 1976.

5. *Asset substitution* is used here to refer to various national interest-bearing securities; there is little if any evidence for the large industrial nations of direct substitution in demand of the national moneys ("currency substitution"). See also Cuddington 1983.

6. Imperfect asset substitution results in the portfolio-balance models pioneered by Branson (1968, 1970) and discussed at length below.

7. Covered interest arbitrage imposes the condition that the domestic and foreign interest rates will differ only by the discount or premium implicit in the forward rate. Under imperfect asset substitution, the forward rate will differ from the expected future spot rate by a risk premium that varies as capital flows change the outstanding holdings of bonds. This risk premium is normally related to the role of exchange-rate risk in the modern theory of finance (Solnik 1973), but Dooley and Isard (1980) argue that the political risk of capital controls varies with the stock of outstanding debt. This factor may well be the more important.

8. Michael Melvin, in chapter 13 of Darby et al. 1983, was rather more successful in applying Solnik's (1973) international asset pricing model to explaining international capital flows.

9. It could well be argued that a number of major European nations are, *de facto*, pursuing pegged exchange rates with the German mark, which in turn floats relative to the U.S. dollar, the yen, and other major currencies. The model would apply directly to these countries.

10. Independent estimates reported in chapters 6 and 11 of Darby et al. 1983 place α between 0 and 0.2 or 0.3 for all seven nonreserve countries; only for Germany and perhaps Japan and the Netherlands does α significantly exceed 0 for quarterly observations. Generally lagged adjustments are found to be substantial, however. Other authors who report evidence of substantial short-run sterilization are Herring and Marston (1977), Hilliard (1979), Connolly and Taylor (1979), and Obstfeld (1980, 1982). Laney and Willett (1982) present a tabular survey of estimated sterilization coefficients reported through 1980.

11. Some authors prefer to cast the central bank's reaction function in terms of the scaled change in domestic credit:

$$\frac{\Delta D}{H} = (\alpha - 1)\frac{B}{H} + \mathbf{X}\beta + u.$$

However, in the presence of even partial sterilization ($\alpha < 1$) domestic credit has no substantive role in either theoretical or empirical analysis and is accordingly dropped. Its computation is straightforward for the interested reader. Note that if $\alpha = 1$, scaled growth in domestic credit is $\mathbf{x}\beta + u$.

12. See chapters 5 and 6 of Darby et al. 1983.

13. A minor complication arises if the nominal money supply has a contemporaneous effect on real income. A considerable complication of the analysis arises if we consider the following (second-order) effect, which arises when assets are imperfect substitutes: A change in central bank reserve holdings moves the equilibrium domestic interest rate relative to the foreign interest rate. Then monetary policy can affect the money stock and output without affecting prices. This point, which is due to Maurice Obstfeld, suggests a way in which monetary policy would not be entirely impotent (given imperfect asset substitution) even if goods were perfect substitues. I assume here

that the money-demand effects of the balance of payments through both the interest-rate and output channels are negligible in the short period being analyzed.

14. The variable C/H is here defined as minus the net cash flow from international investment—that is, as net foreign investment less net securities income. However, we neglect within the short period the second-order effect of lower domestic interest rates increasing net securities income and hence lowering C/H; portfolio adjustments are assumed to overwhelm this effect.

15. Among these other variables is, of course, the lagged covered interest differential, since changes in the differential will cause portfolio revisions and hence net capital flows. These other variables are predetermined within the period and so implicit in the function $f(\cdot)$. As discussed in note 13, the balance of payments will have a direct effect on the parity value of the domestic interest rate under imperfect asset substitution, so we might prefer $C/H = f(R + \gamma[B/H] - \rho - R^F)$. However, this merely requires substitution of $[(d\rho/d(B/H)) - \gamma]$ for $d\rho/d(B/H)$ in equation 7. Since either term is definitely negative, none of the qualitative results are affected whether we think of the balance-of-payments effect on domestic interest rates as reflecting only an expected depreciation factor or also a portfolio-balance factor.

16. Given the (predetermined) lagged value of scaled reserves, B/H tells us the value of current scaled reserves, which Bilson (1979) and Harberger and Edwards (1982) argue is an important indicator of the probability of devaluation. Bilson also proposes a monetary indicator, which can be interpreted as the integral of $\Delta \log M - Z\delta - \varepsilon$; this is subsumed in the total derivative $d\rho/d(B/H)$.

17. If goods are perfect substitutes internationally (and $[d \log P/d(\Delta \log M)] > 0$), or if assets are (and $[d \log R/d(\Delta \log M)] < 0$), or both, then θ would reduce to a constant coefficient $-\infty$ so that ϕ would be the constant 0 and $\Delta \log M = Z\delta + \varepsilon$, which is the standard "monetary approach" result.

18. The multiplier of equation 7 is positive with condition 8 holding while $-\infty < [d(T/H)/d(\Delta \log M)] < 0$ and $\infty > [f'dR/d(\Delta \log M)] > 0$ under imperfect substitution. Therefore, $-\infty < \theta' < 0$, which implies $-\infty < \phi' < 0$.

19. If this also corresponds to a long-period equilibrium, it should be along a line from the origin with slope < 1. In that case, money growth derives from growth in both reserves and domestic credit.

20. However, in choosing α and β the central bank is aware of the (expected) tradeoff it faces, so generally alternatively shaped tradeoffs would induce alternative reaction functions. Lucas's (1976) critique implies that the shape of the tradeoff surface may also depend upon the central bank's choice of α and β. Furthermore, a government pursuing a nationalistic monetary policy may offset the balance-of-payments effects of the policy by changes in, say, commercial policy that affect $S\lambda$ so as to shift the line for equation 9 upward.

21. This analysis provides a rather simpler explanation of when balance-of-payments crises occur than that suggested by Krugman (1979). As the central bank moves money growth further from the parity value, the stability condition (equation 8) is finally violated and speculative capital flows become overwhelming. In the medium-scale

model reported in Darby et al. 1983, $d\rho/d(B/H)$ does increase in absolute value with $|(B/H)|$, but the stability condition appears to hold except at the time of actual balance-of-payments crises.

22. The nominal exchange rate is measured as domestic currency units per unit of foreign currency. The real exchange rate (also known as the purchasing-power ratio) is the nominal exchange rate times the ratio of the foreign to the domestic price level.

23. Superneutrality implies that the real variables in the economy (e.g., real output and the real exchange rate) are unaffected in long-run equilibrium by changes in the trend growth rate of nominal money.

24. The aggregate production function shifts are discussed in the traditional literature on the costs of inflation. Tobin (1965) initiated consideration of possible capital deepening, and Friedman (1977) introduced the possibility that higher unemployment is caused by higher inflation rates.

25. The argument is that increased government flow demand for foreign securities will increase equilibrium net exports, which can only be accomplished (under imperfect long-run goods substitutability) at a higher real exchange rate. Recent discussions of central banks' demand for foreign reserves under floating exchange rates include Heller and Khan 1978 and von Furstenberg 1982. A full steady-state analysis requires consideration of the service-account effects of the government purchases (which would ultimately reduce net exports) discussed by Obstfeld (1981). Further, long-run price elasticities may be much larger than the short-run elasticities, so long-run perfect goods substitutability may be a close approximation to the truth.

26. The lines are drawn through the sample means with the theoretical slopes (under neutrality and superneutrality) of 1 and 0, respectively. Lothian's regression analysis indicates that we cannot reject at the 5% significance level either that the coefficient of $\Delta\Gamma M$ is 0 in a linear regression explaining $\Delta\Gamma y$ or 1 in a similar regression for $\Delta\Gamma P$, where $\Delta\Gamma$ means "the growth shift in" and where y, M, and P are real GNP (or GDP), narrow money, and consumer prices, respectively. He also ran U.S. dollar exchange-rate (E) equations of the forms

$$\Delta\Gamma E = a + b(\Delta\Gamma M - \Delta\Gamma M_{\text{U.S.}}),$$

$$\Delta\Gamma E = a + b(\Delta\Gamma M - \Delta\Gamma M_{\text{U.S.}}) + c(\Delta\Gamma y - \Delta\Gamma y_{\text{U.S.}}),$$

and $\Delta\Gamma E = a + b(\Delta\Gamma P - \Delta\Gamma P_{\text{U.S.}})$;

as reported in the text, in each case b differed from 1 insignificantly at the 5% level.

27. A vast listerature has blossomed from Dornbusch's seminal 1976 contribution, but see also Dornbusch 1980, 1982. Horne (1983) reviews the empirical research to date and concludes that "the evidence of the 1970s supports the portfolio-balance model" (presented here).

28. If assets were perfect substitutes internationally, the home nominal (real) interest rate would equal the foreign nominal (real) interest rate plus the growth rate of the nominal (real) exchange rate. Thus, a policy that caused the domestic real interest rate to fall relative to the foreign real interest rate by an average of 3% per annum for 3

years would induce an immediate 9% real depreciation, so the real exchange rate could be expected to decrease (i.e., appreciate) by 3 percent per annum for the next 3 years. Isard (1982) in particular has argued that the long-run value of the real exchange rate is fixed by trade-balance considerations; Dooley and Isard (1981) extend the argument to apply qualitatively in an imperfect-substitution or portfolio-balance model.

29. Movements in the oil price (the prime alternative explanation) were found to have had a negligible impact.

30. Under pegged exchange rates, prices of traded and nontraded goods move much more synchronously in the absence of a revaluation.

31. That is, within the current quarter the changes in the quantities of exports and imports are approximately offset by the changes in their domestic-currency prices.

32. However, see Henderson 1980.

33. I am unaware of any attempt to compare the relative costs of sterilized intervention with direct subsidies to traded-goods producers.

34. If goods are perfect substitutes internationally, an infinity of trade balances will be associated with the single equilibrium real exchange rate. If goods are imperfect substitutes internationally even in the long run, then higher (more depreciated) real exchange rates will be associated with higher trade balances. In a growing economy, the trade balance is best measured as a ratio to GNP.

35. To the extent that Japan specializes in highly capital-intensive goods and the United States in less capital-intensive goods, this tendency is ameliorated. An alternative, complementary basis for net capital inflows to the United States is the political security of private investments there.

36. Japanese wealth was abnormally low in the early postwar period, both because of wartime devastation and because of the rapid growth in Japanese human capital. It is assumed in the text that the growth rate of Japanese labor measured in efficiency units will converge to a uniform world growth rate.

37. It is curious that U.S. labor unions would focus on the "jobs lost" due to the excess of imports over exports rather than the corresponding gain in employment and real wages due to the capital inflows financed by the trade deficit.

38. An exploratory effort integrating trade and capital flows in a full adjustment analysis is reported in chapter 12 of Darby et al. 1983.

39. A detailed discussion is provided in chapter 17 of Darby et al. 1983.

40. Whether this reflects a defect in the Federal Reserve system or in the American political system is not addressed here.

References

Bilson, John F. O. 1979. "Leading Indicators of Currency Devaluation." *Columbia Journal of World Business*, Winter, pp. 62–76.

Bilson, John F. O. 1981. "The Speculative Efficiency Hypothesis." *Journal of Business*, vol. 54, July, pp. 435–452.

Branson, William H. 1968. *Financial Capital Flows in the U.S. Balance of Payments* (Amsterdam: North-Holland).

Branson, William H. 1970. "Monetary Policy and the New View of International Capital Movements." *Brookings Papers on Economic Activity*, no. 2, pp. 235–262.

Connolly, Michael, and Dean Taylor. 1979. "Exchange Rate Changes and Neutralization: A Test of the Monetary Approach Applied to Developed and Developing Countries." *Economica*, vol. 46, August, pp. 281–294.

Cuddington, John T. 1983. "Currency Substitution, Capital Mobility, and Money Demand." *Journal of International Money and Finance*, vol. 2, August, pp. 111–133.

Cumby, Robert E., and Maurice Obstfeld. 1981. "A Note on Exchange-Rate Expectations and Nominal Interest Differentials: A Test of the Fisher Hypothesis." *Journal of Finance*, vol. 36, June, pp. 697–703.

Cumby, Robert E., and Maurice Obstfeld. 1983. "International Interest-Rate and Price-Level Linkages under Flexible Exchange Rates: A Review of Recent Evidence," in J. F. O. Bilson and R. C. Marston, eds., *Exchange Rates: Theory and Practice* (University of Chicago Press).

Darby, Michael R., and James R. Lothian. 1983. "British Economic Policy under Margaret Thatcher: A Midterm Examination." *Carnegie-Rochester Conference Series on Public Policy*, vol. 18, spring, pp. 157–207.

Darby, Michael R., James R. Lothian, Arthur E. Gandolfi, Anna J. Schwartz, and Alan C. Stockman. 1983. *The International Transmission of Inflation* (University of Chicago Press).

Dooley, Michael P., and Peter Isard. 1979. The Porfolio-Balance Model of Exchange Rates. International Finance Discussion Paper 141, Board of Governors of the Federal Reserve System.

Dooley, Michael P., and Peter Isard. 1980. "Capital Controls, Political Risk, and Deviations from Interest-Rate Parity." *Journal of Political Economy*, vol. 88, April, pp. 370–384.

Dornbusch, Rudiger. 1976. "Expectations and Exchange Rate Dynamics." *Journal of Political Economy*, vol. 84, December, pp. 1161–1176.

Dornbusch, Rudiger. 1980. *Open Economy Macroeconomics* (New York: Basic Books).

Dornbusch, Rudiger. 1982. Flexible Exchange Rates and Interdependence. National Bureau of Economic Research Working Paper 1035.

Fausten, Dietrich K. 1979. "The Humean Origin of the Contemporary Monetary Approach to the Balance of Payments." *Quarterly Journal of Economics*, vol. 93, November, pp. 655–673.

Flood, Robert P. 1982. "Activist Policy in the Open Economy." *American Economic Review, Papers and Proceedings*, vol. 72, May, pp. 51–55.

Flood, Robert P., and Nancy Peregrim Marion. 1982. "The Transmission of Disturbances under Alternative Exchange-Rate Regimes with Optimal Indexing." *Quarterly Journal of Economics*, vol. 97, February, pp. 43–66.

Frankel, Jeffrey A. 1982. "In Search of the Exchange Risk Premium: A Six-Currency Test Assuming Mean-Variance Optimization." *Journal of International Money and Finance*, vol. 1, December, pp. 255–274.

Friedman, Milton. 1977. "Nobel Lecture: Inflation and Unemployment." *Journal of Political Economy*, vol. 84, June, pp. 451–472.

Geweke, John, and Edgar Feige. 1979. "Some Joint Tests of the Efficiency of Markets for Forward Foreign Exchange." *Review of Economics and Statistics*, vol. 61, August, pp. 334–341.

Goodhart, C. A. E., and P. V. Temperton. 1982. The U.K. Exchange Rate, 1979–81: A Test of the Overshooting Hypothesis?," Bank of England report.

Hansen, Lars Peter, and Robert J. Hodrick. 1980. "Forward Exchange Rates as Optimal Predictors of Future Spot Rates: An Econometric Analysis." *Journal of Political Economy*, vol. 88, October, pp. 829–853.

Hansen, Lars Peter, and Robert J. Hodrick. 1982. "Risk Averse Speculation in the Forward Foreign Exchange Market: An Econometric Analysis of Linear Models," in J. Frenkel, ed., *Exchange Rates and International Macroeconomics* (University of Chicago Press).

Harberger, Arnold C., and Sebastian Edwards. 1982. "Lessons of Experience under Fixed Exchange Rates," in M. Gersovitz, C. Díaz-Alejandro, G. Ranis, and M. R. Rosenzweig, eds., *The Theory and Experience of Economic Development: Essays in Honor of Sir W. Arthur Lewis* (London: Allen and Unwin).

Heller, H. R., and M. S. Khan. 1978. "The Demand for International Reserves under Fixed and Floating Exchange Rates." *International Monetary Fund Staff Papers*, vol. 25, December, pp. 623–649.

Henderson, Dale W. 1980. "The Dynamic Effects of Exchange Market Intervention Policy," in H. Frisch and G. Schwodiauer, eds., *The Economics of Flexible Exchange Rates* (supplement to *Kredit und Kapital*).

Herring, Richard J., and Richard C. Marston. 1977. *National Monetary Policies and International Financial Markets* (Amsterdam: North-Holland).

Hilliard, Brian C. 1979. Exchange Flows and the Gilt-Edged Security Market: A Causality Study. Bank of England Discussion Paper 2.

Horne, Jocelyn. 1983. "The Asset Market Model of the Balance of Payments and the Exchange Rate: A Survey of Empirical Evidence." *Journal of International Money and Finance*, vol. 2, August, pp. 89–109.

Isard, Peter. 1977. "How Far Can We Push the 'Law of One Price?'" *American Economic Review*, vol. 67, December, pp. 942–948.

Isard, Peter. 1982. An Accounting Framework and Some Issues for Modelling How

Exchange Rates Respond to the News. International Finance Discussion Paper 200, Board of Governors of the Federal Reserve System.

Kimbrough, Kent P. 1983. "The Information Content of the Exchange Rate and the Stability of the Real Output under Alternative Exchange-Rate Regimes." *Journal of International Money and Finance*, vol. 2, April, pp. 27–38.

Kravis, Irving B., and Robert E. Lipsey. 1977. "Export Prices and the Transmission of Inflation." *American Economic Review*, vol. 67, February, pp. 155–163.

Kravis, Irving B., and Robert E. Lipsey. 1978. "Price Behavior in the Light of Balance of Payments Theories." *Journal of International Economics*, vol. 8, May, pp. 193–246.

Krugman, Paul. 1979. "A Model of Balance-of-Payments Crises." *Journal of Money, Credit, and Banking*, vol. 11, August, pp. 311–325.

Laffer, Arthur B. 1975. "The Phenomenon of Worldwide Inflation: A Study in International Market Integration," in David I. Meiselman and Arthur B. Laffer, eds., *The Phenomenon of Worldwide Inflation* (Washington: American Enterprise Institute for Public Policy Research).

Laney, Leroy O., and Thomas D. Willett. 1982. "The International Liquidity Explosion and Worldwide Inflation: The Evidence from Sterilization Coefficient Estimates." *Journal of International Money and Finance*, vol. 1, August, pp. 141–152.

Lothian, James R. 1983. Equilibrium Relationships between Money and Other Economic Variables: An Application to Long-Term Forecasting. Paper presented at Third International Symposium on Forecasting, Philadelphia.

Lucas, Robert E., Jr. 1976. "Econometric Policy Evaluation: A Critique." *Carnegie-Rochester Conference Series on Public Policy*, vol. 1, pp. 19–46.

Obstfeld, Maurice. 1980. Sterilization and the Offsetting Capital Movements: Evidence from West Germany, 1960–1970. National Bureau of Economic Research Working Paper 494.

Obstfeld, Maurice. 1981. "Macroeconomic Policy, Exchange-Rate Dynamics, and Optimal Asset Accumulation." *Journal of Political Economy*, vol. 89, December, pp. 1142–1161.

Obstfeld, Maurice. 1982. "Can We Sterilize? Theory and Evidence." *American Economic Review, Papers and Proceedings*, vol. 72, May, pp. 45–50.

Richardson, J. David. 1978. "Some Empirical Evidence on Commodity Arbitrage and the Law of One Price." *Journal of International Economics*, vol. 8, May, pp. 341–351.

Saidi, Nasser H. 1980. "Fluctuating Exchange Rates and the International Transmission of Economic Disturbances." *Journal of Money, Credit, and Banking*, vol. 12, November, pp. 575–591.

Solnik, Bruno H. 1973. *European Capital Markets: Towards a General Theory of International Investment* (Lexington, Mass.: Lexington Books).

Tobin, James. 1965. "Money and Economic Growth." *Econometrica*, vol. 33, October, pp. 671–684.

von Furstenberg, George M. 1982. "New Estimates of the Demand for Non-Gold Reserves under Floating Exchange Rates." *Journal of International Money and Finance*, vol. 1, April, pp. 81–95.

Weber, Warren E. 1981. "Output Variability under Monetary Policy and Exchange Rate Rules." *Journal of Political Economy*, vol. 89, August, pp. 733–751.

Whitman, Marina von Neumann. 1975. "Global Monetarism and the Monetary Approach to the Balance of Payments." *Brookings Papers on Economic Activity*, vol. 3, pp. 491–536.

6

Alternative Approaches
to Exchange-Rate
Determination and Some
Implications of the
Structural Balance-of-
Payments Approach
for International
Macroeconomic
Interdependence

Akihiro Amano

The degree of freedom and the effectiveness of monetary policy under the floating-exchange-rate system and increasing capital mobility depend, obviously, on the way in which one understands the process of exchange-rate determination. Therefore, this chapter considers first the mechanism by which exchange rates are determined, and especially the role of monetary policy. In the past 10 years there has been a tremendous surge of theoretical and empirical literature on exchange-rate determination, but we still seem to lack a firm foundation for establishing macroeconometric models under the flexible-exchange-rate regime that can be utilized by governments and international agencies to analyze current economic problems and policy issues.

In this chapter, a review of some basic lines of thought since 1973 regarding how to incorporate important factors affecting exchange rates in empirical studies[1] is followed by a discussion of earlier studies of asset-market approaches; then a few critical problems that were not adequately treated in simple asset-market approaches are examined.

An earlier version of the monetary approach based on twin assumptions of instantaneous purchasing-power parity and perfect price flexibility is inconsistent with most macroeconometric models, because these models usually incorporate rather low short-run price elasticities in trade equations and sluggish adjustments in wages and prices. An earlier version of the portfolio-balance approach was also unsatisfactory in that it did not pay due attention to the role of expectations and the mechanisms of asset supplies.

Later developments, reviewed below, have suggested the importance of the following factors:

● Under high international capital mobility the open-interest-parity condition plays an important role, connecting the current spot rate with the expected future spot rate and with nominal-interest-rate differentials. If assets denominated in various national currencies are perfect substitutes, then the open-interest-parity condition can completely characterize the exchange-rate-determination process. The problem of exchange-rate modeling then boils down to formulating exchange-rate expectations and nominal interest rates.

• However, if assets are not perfect substitutes internationally, as has been postulated in the portfolio-balance approaches, or if adjustments to desired portfolios take time, then the open-interest-parity condition cannot by itself determine the current spot rate, and other factors such as relative supplies of various assets and the discrepancies between desired and actual portfolios will have additional influences on exchange rates.

• When one is concerned with exchange-rate fluctuations over a longer time rather than with day-to-day fluctuations, it is essential to consider the inter-actions between stock and flow variables to account for changes in asset supplies.

These considerations have made it clear that the exchange-rate-determination process in macroeconometric models must take into account the conditions in both goods and assets markets, and their dynamic interactions.

The survey given below indicates that there are at least three alternative approaches along the lines incorporating these considerations: the extended monetary approach, the extended portfolio-balance approach, and the structural balance-of-payments approach. Extended monetary approaches are based on the open-interest-parity condition augmented by nonzero risk premia. A variety of formulations are possible, depending on how exchange-rate expectations and risk premia are determined. Cumulated current account balances often fill two roles: one as a determinant of expected future exchange rates and the other as a determinant of risk premia. However, the determinations of the size and the composition of net foreign assets in the countries concerned are left open. The extended portfolio-balance approaches are more explicit about asset demand functions, so it is much easier to incorporate them in macroeconometric models. In fact, one variant has been used in the Multi-Country Model of the Federal Reserve Board. The structural balance-of-payments approach, on the other hand, is often contrasted with asset-market approaches, with the criticism that the former approach is based on flow asset demand functions rather than stock demand functions. This criticism is misplaced, however, when international capital transactions in this approach are based on portfolio-selection theory. Rather, the main feature of this approach lies in the fact that no equation is normalized on the current spot exchange rate but the entire system is solved iteratively to find the level of the exchange rate that satisfies the equilibrium conditions of the system. Indeed, if structural equations in the capital-account sector were estimated with extremely high sensitivities with respect to expected international yield differentials, then exchange rates would be determined by the same set of factors as in asset-market approaches based on the open-interest-parity condition.

My preference lies with this last approach for three reasons. First, each balance-of-payments item is estimated from a structural equation, so that the danger of imposing wrong *a priori* conditions on the parameter values (such as the price elasticities of commodity arbitrage and the interest-rate sensitivities of international capital transactions) can be avoided. Second, it is sometimes found in the actual estimation of a single reduced-form exchange-rate equation that variables of theoretical importance are omitted—say, because of multi-collinearities. The structural balance-of-payments approach does not share this undesirable aspect. Finally, various forms of institutional constraints imposed on the movements of spot exchange rates can easily be incorporated in this approach at the stage of finding equilibrium solutions for exchange rates. An obvious example is the modeling of the European Monetary System.

The latter part of this chapter examines the properties of an open macroeconomy and the international transmission of real and monetary disturbances. The discussions in the section on the KYQ-FLEX model are based on a quarterly macroeconometric model of the Japanese economy, whereas those in the next section draw freely from the results obtained from the World Economic Model developed at the Economic Planning Agency.

It is not an easy task to summarize all the implications of simulation results, but let me indicate here some of the major findings related to the characteristics of the international macroeconomic system under exchange-rate flexibility.

In the first place, when a country is disturbed by an increased domestic real demand, economic activity in the country concerned as well as in other countries will generally increase. There are some variations as to the additional effects of exchange-rate fluctuations, but the general picture is not much different from that under the fixed-rate system. An expansion in one country is more or less propagated to other countries. The transmission pattern of demand-induced price inflation is somewhat different, however. An expansion in one country tends to propagate less inflationary impact to other countries when the exchange rates of the transmitting country depreciate, and vice versa. The latter case holds when increases in U.S. interest rates tend to depreciate other countries' floating currencies and propagate inflationary impacts to those countries.

Next, the effects of monetary disturbances put in a different appearance under exchange-rate flexibility. A tight money policy in one country will depress its domestic economy, and exchange appreciation caused by improvements in current and capital accounts will enhance the deflationary impact at home. The effectiveness of monetary policy is, therefore, generally increased by exchange flexibility. At the same time, it complicates the pattern of international transmission of economic activity. A tight money policy in one country may propagate an expansionary effect to some other countries. Usually two factors are at work to reduce economic activity in other countries: a decline in exports from other countries, and exchange-rate appreciation in the transmitting country that propagates price-inflationary impacts to other countries which tend to discourage private consumption in those countries. On the other hand, there may be some countries that can expand their shares of the export market in the face of exchange-rate appreciation in the transmitting country. A country that is less dependent upon the U.S. market and more competitive with U.S. exports will experience an increase in economic activity as a result of tight U.S. monetary policy.

As to the effects on prices, exchange flexibility again increases the effectiveness of monetary policy at home, because exchange appreciation contributes to domestic price stability. At the same time, it tends to raise domestic export prices in terms of foreign currency units. Therefore, as a general rule, it is correct to say that a tight money policy in one country has a tendency to export inflationary pressures abroad. Our simulation experiments clearly show that a high-interest-rate policy in the United States tends to depress economic activities in most other countries, and at the same time transmits price-inflationary effects to countries other than Canada, Australia, and Korea.

The broad implications of exchange-rate flexibility in an interdependent international economy suggested by our simulation experiments may be summarized as follows. First, exchange-rate flexibility among major countries has brought about some autonomy in national macroeconomic management. The bottling-up or insulation effects are far from perfect, but the pattern of international transmission of economic fluctuations from one country to another is not as straightforward or uniform as in the fixed-exchange-rate system. In particular, floating exchange rates can shelter the domestic economy from purely nominal changes occurring abroad in the medium run. These aspects should not be underrated in situations where economic policies in the leading countries are subject to marked changes after alternations in administrations. Second, it is also true that exchange-rate flexibility has strengthened international economic interdependence in some other respects—particularly when major shocks have taken the form of changes in monetary conditions. In the fixed-exchange-rate regime of the 1960s, the effects of changes in monetary conditions abroad could be absorbed by changes in official external reserves, provided that the domestic monetary implications of these reserve changes could be neutralized. Under the present conditions of high international mobility of capital coupled with divergent monetary-policy stances of major countries, however, it does not seem practical to regain national autonomy simply by moderating exchange-rate flexibility. A more important condition for world economic stability would be that monetary authorities in large countries have more international perspectives in formulating national monetary policies by taking into account their effects upon and repercussions from the world economy. A much more careful monitoring system, examining international consequences of national economic policies, appears to be called for.

Simple Asset-Market Approaches

Asset-market approaches to exchange-rate determination view exchange rates as determined in asset markets. They include monetary approaches (in a narrow sense) that give primary importance to the money market, and portfolio-balance approaches that take greater account of equilibrium in a broader range of asset markets.

A typical earlier formulation of the monetary approach can be seen in papers by Frenkel (1976, 1980) and Bilson (1978, 1979b), whose starting point is the presumption that the purchasing-power-parity relation holds in any short period of time.

Let the price of foreign currency in terms of domestic currency be S, and let the general price levels of home and foreign countries be P and P^*, respectively. (In what follows the natural logarithm of a variable is indicated by a lower-case letter.[2]) Then, the PPP relation dictates that

$$s = p - p^*. \tag{1}$$

It is also assumed that the equilibrium condition of the money market can be expressed as $M/P = KY^\eta \exp(-\varepsilon i)$, where M denotes the supply of money, Y denotes real output, i denotes the nominal interest rate, and K, η, and ε are parameters. Then, we have

$$p = m - k - \eta y + \varepsilon i; \quad p^* = m^* - k^* - \eta^* y^* + \varepsilon^* i^*. \tag{2}$$

Substituting equation 2 into equation 1 yields the exchange-rate equation:[3]

$$s = (m - m^*) - (k - k^*) - (\eta y - \eta^* y^*) + (\varepsilon i - \varepsilon^* i^*). \tag{3}$$

In this type of monetary approach, it is claimed that an increase in domestic real output or a reduction in the domestic nominal interest rate will, other things being equal, appreciate the domestic currency, because these factors will raise the domestic demand for money and must lead to reduced domestic prices with a given stock of money. However, the validity of this conclusion hinges crucially upon the assumption of perfect price flexibility and the PPP relation in the short run, both of which have been cast into doubt by empirical evidence (Hacche and Townend 1981).

One variation of the Frenkel-Bilson-type monetary approach, proposed by Girton and Roper (1977), is called the exchange-market-pressure approach. Their starting point is also the purchasing-power-parity theory, but they allow for the possibility that real exchange rates are affected by the money-supply policies of the home country and the foreign country (Canada and the United States, respectively). In other words, it is assumed that changes in the real exchange rate can be expressed as

$$\frac{\Delta S}{S} - \left(\frac{\Delta P}{P} - \frac{\Delta P^*}{P} \right) = \theta_1 \frac{\Delta D}{H} - \theta_2 \frac{\Delta H^*}{H^*}, \qquad \theta_1, \theta_2 \geqq 0 \tag{4}$$

where H is the supply of reserve money and D is the part of the reserve money supply that is issued against domestic assets. If we express the equilibrium condition of the money market in terms of reserve money as $H/P = KY^\eta \times \exp(-\varepsilon i)$ and note the relation $\Delta H = \Delta D + S\Delta R$ (where R denotes official external reserves), then we can write

$$\frac{\Delta P}{P} = \frac{\Delta D}{H} + S\frac{\Delta R}{H} - \eta\frac{\Delta Y}{Y} + \varepsilon\Delta i, \tag{5}$$

$$\frac{\Delta P^*}{P^*} = \frac{\Delta H^*}{H^*} - \eta^*\frac{\Delta Y^*}{Y^*} + \varepsilon^*\Delta i^*. \tag{6}$$

Substituting equations 5 and 6 into equation 4 yields

$$\frac{\Delta S}{S} - S\frac{\Delta R}{H} = (1 + \theta_1)\frac{\Delta D}{H} - (1 + \theta_2)\frac{\Delta H^*}{H^*} - \eta\frac{\Delta Y}{Y}$$

$$+ \eta^*\frac{\Delta Y^*}{Y} + \varepsilon\Delta i - \varepsilon^*\Delta i^*, \tag{7}$$

where the left-hand-side expression is called the exchange-market pressure. That is, a part of the exchange-market pressure that leads to the depreciation of the domestic currency (a positive value of the right-hand side) can be absorbed by a reduction in official external reserves.

This approach has one peculiar feature. As Hacche and Townend (1981, p. 215) pointed out, the expression on the left-hand side of equation 7 measuring the exchange-market pressure needs no estimation of behavioral parameters, and the pressure leading to a 1 percent depreciation can be absorbed exactly by an equivalent percentage reduction in official external reserves (measured by $S\Delta R/H$). The reason such a correspondence arises can easily be seen from equation 5. A 1 percent reduction of $S\Delta R/H$ implies, other things being equal, a 1 percent reduction in the money supply, which in turn reduces the domestic price level by 1 percent and appreciates the domestic currency by the same percentage through the PPP relationship.

The term "exchange-market pressure" usually connotes the extent of *ex ante* disequilibrium in the foreign exchange market, but a set of strong assumptions of perfect price flexibility and purchasing-power parity makes it possible to measure it from *ex post* data alone.

Next, Branson and his associates (Branson 1975; Branson and Halttunen 1979; Branson, Halttunen, and Masson 1979) took the initiative of empirical application of the portfolio-balance approach. Their basic model can be summarized as follows:

$$M = \tilde{M}\overset{(-)\ (-)}{(i, i^* + x)}\, W, \tag{8}$$

$$B = \tilde{B}\overset{(+)\ (-)}{(i, i^* + x)}\, W, \tag{9}$$

$$S \cdot F = \tilde{F}\overset{(-)\ (+)}{(i, i^* + x)}\, W, \tag{10}$$

$$W = M + B + S \cdot F, \tag{11}$$

where M, B, and F represent, respectively, the stocks of domestic money, domestic bond, and foreign bond, which are all given, W represents the financial net wealth of the domestic private sector, and x represents the expected rate of change rate. Equation 11 defines W, and the right-hand-side expressions of equations 8–10 are demand functions for various assets based on portfolio choice. The signs of the partial derivatives are indicated above the arguments. Because of the wealth constraint (equation 11), one of the equations 8–10 is not independent, and $\tilde{M} + \tilde{B} + \tilde{F} = 1$. Thus, denoting the partial derivative of M with respect to the jth argument by $\tilde{M}_j$, we must have

$$\tilde{M}_j + \tilde{B}_j + \tilde{F}_j = 0, \qquad j = 1, 2.$$

Therefore, three independent equations in 8–11 can determine W, i, and S, given M, B, F, and $i^* + x$.

Differentiating equations 9–11 totally, and arranging terms, we have

$$\begin{bmatrix} \tilde{B} & W\tilde{B}_1 \\ 1 - \tilde{F} & -W\tilde{F}_1 \end{bmatrix} \begin{bmatrix} d(S \cdot F) \\ di \end{bmatrix}$$

$$= \begin{bmatrix} -\tilde{B} \\ \tilde{F} \end{bmatrix} dM + \begin{bmatrix} 1 - \tilde{B} \\ \tilde{F} \end{bmatrix} dB + \begin{bmatrix} -W\tilde{B}_2 \\ W\tilde{F}_2 \end{bmatrix} d(i^* + x); \qquad (12)$$

this implies

$$\frac{d(S \cdot F)}{dM} = (W/Z)(\tilde{B}\tilde{F}_1 - \tilde{F}\tilde{B}_1) > 0,$$

$$\frac{d(S \cdot F)}{dB} - (W/Z)[(1 - \tilde{B})\tilde{F}_1 + \tilde{F}\tilde{B}_1] \gtrless 0, \qquad (13)$$

$$\frac{d(S \cdot F)}{d(i^* + x)} = (W^2/Z)(\tilde{B}_1\tilde{M}_2 - \tilde{B}_2\tilde{M}_1) > 0,$$

where

$$Z = -W\tilde{B}\tilde{F}_1 - W(1 - \tilde{F})\tilde{B}_1 = -B\tilde{F}_1 - (M + B)\tilde{B}_1 = -M\tilde{B}_1 + B\tilde{M}_1 < 0. \qquad (14)$$

We can thus express the exchange-rate equation as

$$\overset{(+)(\pm)\quad(+)}{S \cdot F = f(M, B, i^* + x)} \qquad (15)$$

or

$$\overset{(+)(\pm)(-)\quad(+)}{S = S(M, B, F, i^* + x).} \qquad (15')$$

In empirical studies, Branson and others assumed static exchange-rate expectations (i.e., $x = 0$) and extended the model to two countries, dropping the variables B and B^* because of data limitations. They estimated bilateral exchange-rate equations of the following specification for major currencies:

$$\overset{(+)(-)(-)\quad(+)}{S = S(M, F, M^*, F^*).} \qquad (16)$$

A similar approach was adopted in the OECD without much success (Martin and Masson 1979).

Reflections on Simple Asset-Market Views

As experience with the managed floating system has accumulated, it has become apparent that simple asset-market approaches cannot explain the actual movements of exchange rates in a satisfactory way. In the first place, changes in nominal exchange rates are often accompanied by changes in real exchange rates in the same direction so that the PPP relation does not appear to hold (at least in the short run). Second, it has been recognized that prices in asset markets are formed particularly on the basis of expected future returns, but simple asset-market approaches do not pay enough attention to the formation of exchange-rate expectations. Third, the role of the current-account balance of payments appears to be almost totally neglected in these approaches, but the variations of major currency values in the late 1970s demonstrated that movements of exchange rates (especially real exchange rates) in the medium run must have some association with underlying changes in the current-account balance. In this section I shall briefly summarize three important building blocks that have played important roles in later developments: international interest arbitrage, expectation formation, and the stock-flow interaction.

The importance of the first two elements was shown clearly by Dornbusch (1976). His model can be summarized by the following five equations:

$$i = i^* + x, \tag{17}$$

$$x = \theta(\bar{s} - s), \tag{18}$$

$$m - p = \eta y - \varepsilon i, \tag{19}$$

$$d = \delta(s + p^* - p) + \gamma y - \sigma i + u, \tag{20}$$

$$\dot{p} = \pi(d - y). \tag{21}$$

Equation 17 expresses the assumption that international open (speculative) interest arbitrage is perfect, so that expected returns on interest-bearing assets are completely equalized internationally. Equation 18 represents the assumption that exchange-rate expectations are formed regressively. Here, $\bar{s}$ denotes the long-run-equilibrium exchange rate of the present model to be obtained by imposing the long-run equilibrium conditions $s = \bar{s}$ and $\dot{p} = 0$ (where a dot over a variable designates a time derivative).[4] Equation 19 is the money-market equilibrium condition, but here perfect price flexibility is not assumed. Rather, prices are assumed to respond gradually to the conditions in goods markets as represented in equation 21, where demand for domestic output, d, is determined by real exchange rates, real domestic output, the domestic interest rate, and an autonomous factor, u, as in equation 20.

Eliminating x from equations 17 and 18, we have

$$s = \bar{s} + (1/\theta)(i^* - i), \tag{22}$$

which tells us that speculative interest arbitrage and expectations are the central elements in exchange-rate determination. Next, we find the long-run-equilibrium exchange rate from equations 17, 18, 20, and 21 together with the long-run equilibrium conditions as

$$\bar{s} = \bar{p} - \bar{p}^* + (1/\delta)[\sigma\bar{i}^* + (1 - \gamma)\bar{y} - \bar{u}], \tag{23}$$

where a bar indicates a long-run equilibrium value.[5] It is clear that the PPP relation is not assumed even in the long run in this model.[6] Similarly, from equation 18 we have

$$\bar{p} = \overline{m} - \eta\bar{y} + \varepsilon\bar{i}^*, \tag{24}$$

so that the long-run-equilibrium exchange rate can be rewritten as

$$\bar{s} = \overline{m} - \bar{p}^* + (\varepsilon + \sigma/\delta)\bar{i}^* - [\eta + (\gamma - 1)/\delta]\bar{y} - (1/\delta)\bar{u}. \tag{23'}$$

On the other hand, i can be solved for from equation 19 as

$$i = (1/\varepsilon)[\eta y - (m - p)]. \tag{25}$$

Finally, substituting equations 23' and 25 into equation 22, we obtain the exchange-rate equation

$$s = \{(\overline{m} - \bar{p}^*) + (\varepsilon + \sigma/\delta)\bar{i}^* - [\eta + (\gamma - 1)/\delta]\bar{y} - (1/\delta)\bar{u}\}$$
$$+ \{(1/\theta)\bar{i}^* - (1/\varepsilon\theta)[\eta y - (m - p)]\}. \tag{26}$$

On the right-hand side of equation 26, the terms in the first pair of braces represent the long-run effects; those in the second pair of braces represent the additional, transitory effects. If we add an assumption $\eta + (\gamma - 1)/\delta > 0$—i.e., that the direct and indirect effects of an increase in domestic real output will reduce the price of domestic output—then we can rewrite equation 26 as

$$s = s(\overset{(+)}{\overline{m}}, \overset{(-)}{\bar{p}^*}, \overset{(-)(-)}{\bar{y}}, \overset{(+)}{\bar{u}}, \overset{(+)}{\bar{i}^*}; \overset{(+)}{(m - p)}, \overset{(-)}{y}, \overset{(+)}{\bar{i}^*}). \tag{26'}$$

Since p is assumed sticky in the short run, it is obvious from the above expression that changes in m, y, and i^* (but not in p^* and u) cause exchange-rate overshooting; that is, their long-run and short-run coefficients are of the same sign.

Next, let us consider stock-flow interaction and the role of the current account. The importance of these elements in the process of exchange-rate determination was first taken up by Niehans (1977) and was then recapitulated and extended most succinctly by Rodriguez (1980).

Here it is assumed, for simplicity of exposition, that domestic residents hold only two types of assets, domestic money (M) and foreign money (F). Portfolio selection among these assets is represented by

$$m - s - f^d = a - \frac{1}{b}x, \tag{27}$$

$$\dot{f} = \lambda(f^d - f). \tag{28}$$

The left-hand side of equation 27 is the logarithm of $M/(S \cdot F^d)$, where F^d denotes the desired stock of foreign money; the right-hand side expresses it as a linear function of the expected rate of depreciation of the domestic currency. Equation 28 represents an assumption that the portfolio adjustment may take time (Niehans 1977).[7]

By the balance-of-payments constraint, accumulation of foreign money by domestic residents must be confined to the current-account surplus (C); thus, $\dot{f} = \dot{F}/F = C/F$, which may be approximated linearly as

$$\dot{f} = C_0 - \phi f. \tag{29}$$

Finally, the exchange-rate expectation is assumed to be formed in such a way that

$$x = \theta(\bar{s} - s). \tag{30}$$

Then equations 27–30 can determine the time paths of s, f^d, f, and x for given values of m and C_0.

If exogenous variables are fixed, we have the long-run equilibrium solution

$$\bar{f} = C_0/\phi, \quad \bar{s} = m - a - C_0/\phi. \tag{31}$$

The exchange-rate equation now becomes[8]

$$s = (m - a - C_0/\phi) + \frac{b}{b + \theta}\left(\frac{1}{\phi} - \frac{1}{\lambda}\right)(C_0 - \phi f). \tag{32}$$

This equation shows that an exogenous change in the current-account balance (say, an increase in C_0) will affect the exchange rate in the short run through three different channels: First, it will increase the long-run supply of foreign money, which will appreciate the domestic currency through expected appreciation of the long-run equilibrium rate. Second, it has a short-run impact that tends to depreciate the domestic currency, because the demand for foreign money is reduced by an expected long-run appreciation of domestic money. (This effect, however, cannot outweigh the first effect.) Third, when portfolio adjustment is not instantaneous, an increase in the current-account surplus will raise the relative supply of foreign money and hence appreciate the domestic currency directly. The first two effects exist in an instantaneous stock-equilibrium analysis and reflect the correct expectation that there will be an increase in the long-run supply of foreign money. The third effect can only arise in flow-equilibrium analysis, where an actual increase in the supply of foreign money occurs in the current period. The distinction may be important as long as one is concerned with a very short term in which stocks are fixed and expectations predominate the market, but when one is interested in the interaction of stocks and flows in an intermediate run it becomes a matter of degree rather than a matter of essence, since the expected supply of foreign money will have to come about sooner or later.

Extensions of Monetary Approaches

Since the validity of the short-run PPP relation was put in doubt, some form of speculative interest-arbitrage condition (equation 22 above) has come to the fore in the monetary approaches. A variety of alternative formulations are possible, however, depending on whether one assumes perfectly elastic open interest arbitrage (i.e., that domestic and foreign assets are perfect substitutes) or whether one endorses the validity of strict long-run PPP relationship (i.e., that there is no change in the long-run real exchange rate).

Let q be the (logarithm of the) real exchange rate:

$$s = q + (p - p^*). \tag{33}$$

Then one can write

$$x = E(\dot{s}) = E(\dot{q}) + (\pi - \pi^*), \tag{34}$$

where π denotes the expected rate of inflation and E is an expectation operator. Next, let ρ be the differential risk premium that speculators demand in holding foreign assets rather than domestic assets. Then the condition for speculative interest arbitrage may be written as

$$i - i^* + \rho = x, \tag{35}$$

or, in view of equation 34,

$$E(\dot{q}) = (i - \pi) - (i^* - \pi^*) + \rho. \tag{36}$$

Thus, the specification problem boils down to the choice one makes about how to formulate $E(\dot{q})$ and ρ.

Frankel (1979) assumes $\rho = 0$ and

$$E(\dot{q}) = \theta(\bar{s} - s).\tag{37a}$$

In other words, variations in real exchange rates are assumed to arise only from deviations of nominal rates from the long-run equilibrium rate.[9] Then from equation 36 we obtain

$$s = \bar{s} - \frac{1}{\theta}[(i - \pi) - (i^* - \pi^*)].\tag{38a}$$

If it is assumed that equation 3 holds in the long run, and that $k = k^* = 0$, $\eta = \eta^*$, and $\varepsilon = \varepsilon^*$, the long-run-equilibrium exchange rate is determined by

$$\bar{s} = (\bar{m} - \bar{m}^*) - \eta(\bar{y} - \bar{y}^*) + \varepsilon(\bar{i} - \bar{i}^*).\tag{39}$$

Frankel replaces $(\bar{i} - \bar{i}^*)$ by $(\pi - \pi^*)$ on the ground that real interest rates will be equalized internationally in the long run. Thus, equation 38a becomes

$$s = (\bar{m} - \bar{m}^*) - \eta(\bar{y} - \bar{y}^*) - \frac{1}{\theta}(i - i^*) + \left(\frac{1}{\theta} + \varepsilon\right)(\pi - \pi^*),\tag{40}$$

which is the basic equation used in estimation.[10]

Hooper and Morton (1982) also assume equation 37a, but they introduce a risk premium:

$$s = \bar{s} - \frac{1}{\theta}[(i - \pi) - (i^* - \pi^*) + \rho].\tag{38b}$$

Although expression 37a is formally the same, the variable $\bar{s}$ in the Hooper-Morton model involves variations in real exchange rates that are expected to arise in the adjustment of the current-account balance toward its long-run level. Let $\bar{s}_0$ and $\bar{q}_0$ designate nominal and real exchange rates, respectively, when the current-account balance attains its long-run equilibrium level, and let χ designate the deviation of the "intermediate-run" real exchange rate, $\bar{q}$, from its long-run level, $\bar{q}_0$. Then $\bar{s}$ in the Hooper-Morton model is expressed as

$$\bar{s} = \bar{q}_0 + \chi + (\bar{p} - \bar{p}^*), \qquad \bar{s}_0 = \bar{q}_0 + (\bar{p} - \bar{p}^*).\tag{41}$$

Therefore, nominal exchange rates are affected by transitory changes in expected "equilibrium" real exchange rates in the adjustment process.

Now, ρ and χ are related to the current-account balance in the following way. First, ρ is assumed to be determined by

$$\rho = \rho_0 + \rho_1 \sum C'; \quad \rho_0, \rho_1 > 0 \tag{42}$$

where $\sum C'$ is the cumulated current-account surplus adjusted for net acquisition of foreign assets by the monetary authorities. In other words, it is assumed that the accumulation of net foreign assets in the private sector will raise the differential risk premium on holdings of foreign assets.

Next, it is assumed that the intermediate-run real exchange rate in period t, $\bar{q}_t$, is expected to change so as to adjust that portion of the unexpected change in the current-account balance in the current period that is considered permanent, at a certain speed:

$$\bar{q}_t - \bar{q}_{t-1} = -\mu(1-c)\,[C_t - E_{t-1}(C_t)], \tag{43}$$

where C_t is the current-account balance at time t, $E_{t-1}(C_t)$ is the expected current account at time t which was formed at time $t-1$, c is the proportion of unexpected change in the current-account balance that is considered transitory, and μ is the adjustment coefficient. It is also assumed that the current-account balance is expected to converge to its long-run level, $\bar{C}$, at a certain speed $(1/\lambda)$:

$$E_{t-1}(C_t) = C_{t-1} + \lambda(\bar{C} - C_{t-1}). \tag{44}$$

$$\bar{q}_t = \bar{q}_0 + \lambda\mu(1-c)\bar{C}\cdot t - \mu(1-c)\sum_{j=0}^{t-1}[C_{t-j} - (1-\lambda)C_{t-j-1}]. \tag{45}$$

The last two terms on the right-hand side represent χ.

Finally, substituting equations 45, 41, and 42 into equation 38b, and assuming that $(\bar{p} - \bar{p}^*)$ is determined by the right-hand side of equation 39, we can rewrite equation 38b as

$$s = (\bar{m} - \bar{m}^*) - \eta(\bar{y} - \bar{y}^*) + \varepsilon(\pi - \pi^*) + \bar{q}_0 + \lambda\mu(1-c)\bar{C}\cdot t$$

$$- \mu(1-c)\sum_{j=0}^{t-1}[C_{t-j} - (1-\lambda)C_{t-j-1}]$$

$$- \frac{1}{\theta}[(i-\pi) - (i^* - \pi^*)] - \frac{\rho_0}{\theta} - \frac{\rho_1}{\theta}\sum C^t. \tag{40b}$$

This gives the specification used in Hooper and Morton 1982.

A variant of the extended monetary approaches that takes an intermediate position between Frankel and Hooper-Morton has been given by Fukao (1982), who assumes that the left-hand side of equation 36 is determined by

$$E(\dot{q}) = \theta(\bar{q} - q), \tag{37c}$$

where $\bar{q}$ is a constant. Fukao's estimation equation is therefore given by

$$q = \bar{q} - \frac{1}{\theta}[(i - \pi) - (i^* - \pi^*) + \rho]. \tag{40c}$$

An interesting feature of Fukao's work is that the risk premium ρ is assumed to depend not only on the cumulated current-account surplus of the country concerned but also on the weighted sum of the cumulated current-account surpluses of the third countries (weights being taken from the covariance matrix of real exchange rates). (See Chapter 4 of Fukao 1981.)

Another variant, provided by Kohsaka (1982), assumes that $\rho = 0$ and

$$E(\dot{q}) = \theta(\bar{q} - q), \qquad E(\dot{p} - \dot{p}^*) = E(p - p^*) - (p - p^*). \tag{37d}$$

Thus, Kohsaka's point of departure is

$$s = \bar{q} + (p - p^*) - \frac{1}{\theta}[(i - i^*) - E(p - p^*) + (p - p^*)]. \tag{38d}$$

In specifying $\bar{q}$, Kohsaka follows equation 45 with $\bar{C} = 0$; regarding $E(p - p^*)$, he assumes an adaptive expectation formation:

$$E_t(p - p^*) = c_0 + \sum_{j=0}^{\infty} \delta_j(p - p^*)_{t-j}. \tag{46}$$

Therefore, Kohsaka's basic specification is given by

$$s = \left(\bar{q}_0 + \frac{c_0}{\theta}\right) - \mu(1 - c) \sum_{j=0}^{t-1} [C_{t-j} - (1 - \lambda)C_{t-j-1}]$$

$$- \frac{1}{\theta}(i - i^*) + [1 + (\gamma_0 - 1)/\theta](p - p^*)$$

$$+ \frac{1}{\theta}\sum_{j=1}^{\infty} \delta_j(p - p^*)_{t-j}.$$

Hacche and Townend (1981) and Driskill (1981) attempted to estimate the Dornbusch exchange-rate equation (equation 26 or 26' above) directly. In the former attempt, however, the estimation results are not quite satisfactory; in the latter, $\bar{s}$ in equation 18 (and hence in equation 22) is replaced by m so that a reservation is necessary to call it a Dornbusch equation.

Extensions of Portfolio-Balance Approaches

The portfolio-balance approach considered above is based on a short-run model in which asset stocks are all fixed. However, the existence of a stock-flow interaction, which is caused by the current-account imbalance that leads to a change in net foreign assets and hence to dynamic changes in exchange rates, was recognized from the outset (Branson and Halttunen 1979).

Let us now dynamize the system of equations 8–11 above by adding the following two equations:

$$\overset{(+)\ \ (+)}{\dot{F} = T(S \cdot P^*/P, V) + i^*F,} \tag{47}$$

$$x = 0(\bar{S}/S - 1), \tag{48}$$

where T represents a function explaining the trade balance, V is an exogenous variable whose increase improves the trade balance of the home country, and $\bar{S}$ is the long-run-equilibrium exchange rate (Branson 1981).

Consider, first, the determinants of the long-run-equilibrium exchange rate in this model. Let $\dot{F} = x = 0$ and differentiate equations 15 and 47 totally to obtain

$$\begin{bmatrix} \bar{P}^*/\bar{P} \cdot T_1 & \bar{i}^* \\ \bar{F} & \bar{S} \end{bmatrix} \begin{bmatrix} d\bar{S} \\ d\bar{F} \end{bmatrix} = \begin{bmatrix} 0 \\ f_1 \end{bmatrix} d\bar{M} + \begin{bmatrix} 0 \\ f_2 \end{bmatrix} d\bar{B} + \begin{bmatrix} -\bar{F} \\ f_3 \end{bmatrix} d\bar{i}^*$$
$$+ \begin{bmatrix} -\bar{S} \cdot T_1 \\ 0 \end{bmatrix} d(\bar{P}^*/\bar{P}) + \begin{bmatrix} -T_2 \\ 0 \end{bmatrix} d\bar{V}. \tag{49}$$

Solving equation 49 for $d\bar{S}$, we obtain

$$\frac{d\bar{S}}{d\bar{M}} = -(1/Z')\bar{i}^*f_1 < 0,$$

$$\frac{d\bar{S}}{d\bar{B}} = -(1/Z')\bar{i}^*f_2 \gtreqless 0,$$

$$\frac{d\bar{S}}{d\bar{i}^*} = -(1/Z')(\bar{S} \cdot \bar{F} + \bar{i}^*f_3) < 0, \tag{50}$$

$$\frac{d\bar{S}}{d(\bar{P}^*/\bar{P})} = -(1/Z')\bar{S}^2 T_1 < 0,$$

$$\frac{d\bar{S}}{d\bar{V}} = -(1/Z')\bar{S}T_2 < 0,$$

where it is assumed that $Z' = (\bar{S} \cdot \bar{P}^*/\bar{P}) \cdot T_1 - \bar{i}^*\bar{F} > 0$. Thus, we can express the long-run-equilibrium exchange rate as

$$\overset{(-)\ (\pm)\,(-)\ \ (-)\ \ (-)}{\bar{S} = \bar{S}(\bar{M},\ \bar{B},\ \bar{i}^*,\ \bar{P}^*/\bar{P}, \bar{V}).} \tag{51}$$

An increase in the domestic supply of money and an increase in the foreign interest rate will appreciate rather than depreciate the domestic currency here, because they both raise $\bar{F}$, and hence a reduction in T is required to reestablish long-run equilibrium.

Next, substituting equation 51 into equation 48, and then substituting the result into equation 15, we can write the short-run exchange-rate equation as

$$\bar{S} = S(\overset{(+)}{\bar{M}}, \overset{(\pm)}{\bar{B}}, \overset{(-)}{F}, \overset{(+)}{\bar{i}^*}; \overset{(-)}{\bar{M}}, \overset{(\pm)}{\bar{B}}, \overset{(-)}{\bar{i}^*}, \overset{(-)}{\bar{P}^*/\bar{P}}, \overset{(-)}{\bar{V}}). \tag{52}$$

As we have seen above, endogenous explanation of exchange-rate expectations makes it clear that the determinants of such flow variables as the current-account balance can influence exchange rates in the short run, and that changes in M and i^* also have additional impacts through their effects upon expectations. (Changes in M and i^* now cause "undershooting.")

The theoretical literature abounds in dynamic portfolio-balance models with various disaggregations in goods and financial assets as well as sectors. But as the analytical framework incorporates a more and more general-equilibrium flavor with higher-order dynamics, it becomes more difficult to obtain a single reduced-form exchange-rate equation and estimate it. Hooper, Haas, and Symansky (1983) avoid this difficulty by concentrating on the aspect of international portfolio selection. They base their reduced-form equation on the following equilibrium conditions concerning the external asset and liability positions of the home country:

$$
\begin{aligned}
S \cdot F &= \tilde{F}(\overset{(+)}{i^* + x} - i)W, \\
B^* &= \tilde{B}^*(\overset{(-)}{i^* + x} - i)W^*,
\end{aligned}
\tag{53}
$$

where B^* and W^* denote the stock of domestic bonds held by foreign residents and the net wealth of foreigners, respectively (both expressed in foreign currency units). Or, if we assume that the elasticities of functions $\tilde{F}$ and $\tilde{B}^*$ with respect to their arguments are constant, we can rewrite equation 53 in the log form as

$$
\begin{aligned}
f &= \alpha_0 + \alpha_1(i^* + x - i) + w - s, & \alpha_1 > 0 \\
b^* &= \alpha_0^* - \alpha_1^*(i^* + x - i) + w^*, & \alpha_1^* > 0.
\end{aligned}
\tag{53'}
$$

Thus, we have

$$s = (\alpha_0 - \alpha^*_0) + (\alpha_1 + \alpha_1^*)(i^* + x - i) + (w - w^* + b^* - f). \tag{54}$$

The following equations describe how exchange-rate expectations are formed:

$$x = \theta(\bar{s} - s) + (\pi - \pi^*),$$

$$\bar{s} = \bar{q} + (\bar{p} - \bar{p}^*),$$ (55)

$$\bar{q} = \zeta_0 - \zeta_1 \sum C, \qquad \zeta_1 > 0.$$

The first two of these equations are derived from equations 33, 34, and 37a; the last one is a simplified version of equation 45.

Finally, substituting equation 55 into equation 54 and arranging terms, we obtain

$$
\begin{aligned}
s = \frac{1}{1 + \theta(\alpha_1 + \alpha_1^*)} \\
\times \{\alpha_0 - \alpha_0^* + \theta\zeta_0(\alpha_1 + \alpha_1^*)\left[(i^* - \pi^*) - (i - \pi)\right] \\
+ \theta(\alpha_1 + \alpha_1^*)(\bar{p} - \bar{p}^*) \\
- \theta(\alpha_1 + \alpha_1^*)\zeta_1 \sum C \\
+ (w - w^* + b^* - f)\}.
\end{aligned}
$$ (56)

Structural Balance-of-Payments Approaches

In the traditional balance-of-payments theory, the balance-of-payments constraint has been treated as an equilibrium condition that determines the changes in official external reserves under the fixed-exchange-rate regime and the changes in exchange rates under the flexible-exchange-rate regime. A natural question is: How can we relate this traditional view to the asset-market approaches reviewed above?

Table 6.1 summarizes various transactions of the residents of home and foreign countries in a general-equilibrium framework. This table is constructed in such a way that, for each row, the sum of the elements multiplied by the corresponding prices shown in the last row must be equal to zero by the budget constraint.[11] Also, setting the column sum equal to zero, we obtain an equilibrium condition for each market. Therefore, there are four budget equations and six market-equilibrium conditions embedded in table 6.1, but we have only nine independent equations because one market-equilibrium condition is not independent by Walras's law.

If G, Tx, ΔM_g, and ΔR (see table 6.1) are policy-determined variables, then the government budget constraint determines ΔB_g. Also, when A, Im, and

Table 6.1
A simple general-equilibrium tableau of sectoral transactions.

	Home goods	Foreign goods	Home bonds	Foreign bonds	Home money	Foreign money	Taxes
Home Country							
Private sector		Im	ΔB	ΔF	ΔM		Tx
Government sector	G	—	$-\Delta B_g$		ΔM_g	ΔR	$-$Tx
Foreign Country							
Private sector	Im*	$A^* - Y^*$	ΔB^*	ΔF^*		ΔM^*	Tx*
Government sector	—	G^*		$-\Delta F_g^*$		$-\Delta M_g^*$	$-$Tx*
Prices in home currency units	P	$S \cdot P^*$	1	S	1	S	1 or S

A = Private demand for goods produced in each country; Y = supply of goods produced in each country. Im = Import demand. G = Government demand for goods. B = Private demand for domestic bonds. B_g = Government supply of domestic bonds. F = Private demand for foreign bonds. F_g = Government supply of foreign bonds, M = Demand for money; M_g = its supply. R = Official external reserves. T_x = Taxes. P = Price of goods. S = exchange rate. Asterisk indicates foreign variables. Dash shows that transaction is assumed away.

any two of the financial variables ΔB, ΔF, and ΔM are determined by behavioral equations of the private sector, then the private budget constraint determines the remaining financial variable.[12]

Next, we may consider that the goods-markets equilibrium conditions determine either (P, P^*) or (Y, Y^*). For example, under perfect price flexibility they determine (P, P^*) for exogenously given supply of (Y, Y^*); under sticky prices they determine (Y, Y^*) and prices will be determined by behavioral equations. Therefore, the remaining endogenous variables, S, i, and i^*, are determined by the remaining three independent market-clearing conditions.

The balance-of-payments constraint for a country is nothing but the consolidated budget equations of private and government sectors. Take the home country, for instance. From table 6.1 the balance-of-payments constraint is

$$P(A + G - Y) + SP^*Im + (\Delta B - \Delta B_g) + S\Delta F$$
$$+ (\Delta M - \Delta M_g) + S\Delta R = 0, \tag{57}$$

and it does not add an independent equation by itself. It is in this sense that the balance-of-payments constraint is said to be a mere *ex post* identity. However, when we construct a model in which market equilibrium conditions for home goods, home bonds, and home money are shown explicitly, we have

$$P(A + G - Y) = -P\text{Im}^*,$$

$$B - \Delta B_g = -\Delta B^*, \tag{58}$$

$$\Delta M = \Delta M_g,$$

so equation 57 can be rewritten as

$$[(P/S)\text{Im}^* - P^*\text{Im}] - [(1/S)\Delta B^* - \Delta F] = \Delta R. \tag{59}$$

Thus, when one uses equation 59 to complete the model in place of either the market-clearing condition for foreign bonds or that for foreign money, the balance-of-payments equation is actually used as one of the equilibrium conditions. In other words, one may well say that S, i, and i^* are determined by three equilibrium conditions for domestic bonds, domestic money, and the balance of payments, which is equivalent to saying that these variables are determined by three independent equilibrium conditions out of four financial-market-clearing conditions. The difference is simply due to the way the model equations are expressed.[13]

In passing, if one interprets the difference operator in table 6.1 as representing a differential operator with respect to time, then the table shows a dynamic model with stock-flow interactions.[14] In either model we cannot "purge" flow variables from the exchange-rate-determination process unless we are concerned only with a very short period of time or a partial-equilibrium approach, which is rather inappropriate in exchange-rate analysis (Lindbeck 1976).

The variables in table 6.1 are largely endogenized in ordinary macro-econometric models. It is therefore natural, though not necessary, that the balance-of-payments condition is used as an equilibrium condition to determine, together with all other equilibrium conditions, the exchange rate. Since various balance-of-payments items that are not exogenously given must be determined by structural equations, this approach is sometimes called the structural balance-of-payments approach.

Helliwell and Maxwell (1972, 1974) offered the earliest application of this approach, but they applied it to the fixed-exchange-rate regime. It was applied to flexible-exchange-rate regimes by Sawyer et al. (1976), Berner et al. (1976, 1977), Urdang (1978), and Amano (1979). This approach has also been used in many-country models in the EPA World Economic Model project (see, e.g., Amano, Sadahiro, and Sasaki 1981 and Amano, Maruyama, and Yoshitomi 1982).

The following features of the structural balance-of-payments approach may be worth noting:

• Each balance-of-payments item is estimated from a structural equation in this approach, so that the danger of imposing wrong *a priori* conditions on the parameter values, such as the price elasticities of commodity arbitrage and the interest-rate sensitivities of international capital transactions, can be avoided. Furthermore, sufficient care can be taken for possible structural changes in the behavioral equations.

• It is sometimes found in estimating a single, reduced-form exchange-rate equation that variables of theoretical importance are omitted in actual estimation because of the existence of multi-collinearities or in order to avoid the loss of degrees of freedom. As a result, the model incorporating such an equation can be quite different from the one originally conceived. The present approach does not have this undesirable aspect.

• Various forms of institutional constraints imposed on the movements of spot exchange rates can easily be incorporated in this approach in the stage of finding equilibrium solutions for exchange rates. One may take this advantage in analyzing a period including both fixed- and flexible-exchange-rate regimes or a multi-country exchange-rate arrangement such as the EMS.[15]

Macroeconomic Behavior under Exchange-Rate Flexibility: The KYQ-FLEX Model

When exchange rates are endogenized by the structural balance-of-payments Approach, they are affected by many factors determining the balance-of-payments items. Exchange-rate fluctuations, in turn, have profound influences on domestic economic activities, mainly through their effects on domestic-currency prices of goods and services. Moreover, changes in the balance-of-payments conditions that often accompany exchange-rate fluctuations also affect domestic economic activities through changes in money supplies and interest rates. Therefore, macroeconomic behavior under flexible exchange rates becomes considerably more complicated than that under fixed exchange rates, which requires careful attention to identify possible transmission channels that are created by the exchange-rate flexibility.

In this section I attempt to analyze the characteristics of an open macroeconomy under flexible exchange rates by means of simulation exercises using a macroeconometric model of Japan. I constructed the KYQ-FLEX model used here on the basis of a quarterly macroeconometric model developed by Chikashi Moriguchi and his associates, KYQ/MACRO81.[16]

In what follows we shall consider the following four variants of the KYQ-FLEX model. Model A is the standard version of the model, where exchange rates are endogenized and the official discount rate is treated as the main instrument of monetary policy, with the supply of reserve money endogenized by a reaction function.[17] The reserve money is supplied either against net foreign assets or against net domestic assets. The former is determined by an equation explaining changes in official external reserves; the latter by a reaction function explaining the accomodating supply of reserve money to satisfy the demand arising from increased nominal GNP and a higher inflation rate, on the one hand, and to neutralize the effect of exchange-market intervention, on the other hand. Model D endogenizes the official discount rate (together with the interest rate on time deposits), and takes exchange rates and the supply of reserve money as exogenous. In practice, the official discount rate has been used as a major policy instrument in Japanese monetary management, so it is not quite appropriate to determine it endogenously while taking the supply of reserve money as an instrument. However, just for the purpose of studying the behavior of the system with quantitative monetary control, I estimated an equation explaining the official discount rate by the level of inflation and constructed a model in which nominal interest rates react to changes in the inflation rate. Model B is the endogenous-exchange-rate version of model D, and model C is the exogenous-exchange-rate version of model A.

I have performed four simulation experiments with each model to examine the macroeconomic effects of domestic and foreign disturbances.[18] The cases examined were a sustained increase in government investment expenditure in real terms by 10 percent compared with the standard solution; a sustained increase in the official discount rate by 100 basis points, or a sustained increase in the supply of reserve money by 10 percent compared with the standard solution, depending on the monetary-control assumption; a sustained decrease in all foreign interest rates by 100 basis points; and sustained increases in all foreign prices and foreign nominal variables by 10 percent compared with the standard solution.

Table 6.2 summarizes the results of the first simulation, showing the effects of a domestic real shock. Real GNP increases in every model as a result of increased government expenditure. In models where exchange rates are exogenous the "elasticity multiplier" stabilizes after the third year around 1.5, but in endogenous-exchange-rate models it continues to rise because of the increased real current-account surplus caused by exchange depreciation. The primary reason for exchange depreciation is the worsening of the trade balance. Higher domestic interest rates induce some capital inflow in the first year, but they are not large enough to outweigh the deterioration of the current-account balance. After the second year, the long-term capital-account balance deteriorates rather than improves, because the effects of increased net

Table 6.2
Effects of sustained 10 percent increase in real government investment expenditure (dynamic elasticity multipliers).

Variable	Model	Year 1	2	3	4	5	6
Real GNP	A	1.1	1.3	1.8	2.3	2.8	3.1
	B	1.1	1.2	1.5	1.9	2.1	2.4
	C	1.1	1.1	1.2	1.5	1.6	1.4
	D	1.0	1.1	1.2	1.4	1.5	1.4
Wholesale	A	0.5	1.3	2.1	2.8	3.4	4.0
prices	B	0.5	1.0	1.5	1.9	2.2	2.9
	C	0.3	0.5	0.7	0.9	1.1	1.3
	D	0.3	0.5	0.7	0.9	1.1	1.2
Exchange rate	A	1.7	3.8	5.6	6.0	6.8	8.2
	B	1.3	2.1	2.9	3.1	3.6	6.8

private financial wealth, which pushes up the demand for foreign assets, are larger than those of higher domestic interest rates. Therefore, when exchange rates are flexible they depreciate throughout the period. Especially large elasticities of real GNP in model A are also due to an accommodating monetary management that attempts to keep domestic interest rates unaffected.

Prices tend to rise in every model, but the elasticities in endogenous-exchange-rate models are three times larger in the sixth year than those in exogenous-exchange-rate models. In other words, under exchange-rate flexibility the tradeoff relationship between lower unemployment and higher inflation becomes more severe with respect to an expansionary fiscal policy. However, a shift of monetary management from interest control to money-supply control may be able to moderate it slightly, because higher domestic interest rates tend to discourage both domestic expansion and exchange-rate depreciation.

Next, let us consider the effects of monetary policy. In table 6.3 the official discount rate is raised by 1 percent per annum, with accompanying increases in the time-deposit rate according to a reaction function. Higher interest rates discourage domestic fixed investments and hence reduce real GNP. Under exogenous exchange rates both trade and current-account balances improve. Improvements in the service-account balance are noticeable because of reduced foreign liabilities and because of increased interest receipts on foreign assets. The long-term capital-account balance also improves. The level of official external reserves thus increases. Prices tend to decline slightly. Under endogenous exchange rates, on the other hand, exchange rates appreciate,

Table 6.3
Effects of sustained increase in official discount rate by 100 Basis Points.

Variable	Model	Year					
		1	2	3	4	5	6
Real GNP	A	−0.2	−0.9	−1.6	−2.0	−2.3	−2.3
	C	−0.1	−0.3	−0.3	−0.2	−0.1	−0.3
Wholesale	A	−0.5	−2.0	−3.2	−3.6	−4.2	−3.8
prices	C	−0.0	−0.1	−0.2	−0.2	−0.2	−0.2
Exchange rate	A	−4.4	−9.2	−9.8	−9.4	−10.0	−4.5
Current-account	A	0.1	0.3	−1.3	−3.6	−3.3	−3.4
balance	C	0.2	0.7	0.9	1.4	2.7	4.7
Long-term	A	1.0	0.7	0.6	2.0	1.6	1.8
capital-account	C	1.2	1.3	1.2	2.8	2.7	2.0
balance							
Changes in	A	0.7	1.0	−0.1	−0.3	−0.5	−1.6
official external	C	1.0	1.6	2.2	4.3	4.5	4.2
reserves							

Elasticities are given for the first three variables, whereas differences (Disturbed—Control) are reported for the remaining variables.

mainly because of improvements in the long-term capital account balance. (Initially, there are also improvements in the current-account balance.) The exchange appreciation reduces real exports of goods and services, and increases real imports, which creates additional downward pressures on real GNP and prices. The exchange appreciation itself has, of course, a strong impact on domestic prices through direct price linkages. These changes clearly show the existence of a "bottling up" effect of flexible exchange rates. In models B and D, we increased the supply of reserve money, and the results were quite similar to those of table 6.3 except that the direction of change was opposite.

The simulation is concerned with how changes in foreign interest rates affect the domestic economy. In this simulation all foreign interest rates in the model were lowered by 1 percent per annum. The results are shown in table 6.4.[19]

Under exogenous exchange rates, domestic interest rates are not affected much. An increase in the net inflow of foreign capital (mainly long-term) and an improvement in the current-account balance due to a reduction in interest payments abroad result in an increase in official external reserves. If it is sterilized as in model D, changes in foreign interest rates affect the domestic

Table 6.4
Effects of sustained decrease in foreign interest rates by 100 basis points.

Variable	Model	Year					
		1	2	3	4	5	6
Real GNP	A	−0.4	−1.4	−2.6	−2.6	−1.3	0.0
	B	−0.4	−1.2	−1.9	−1.7	−1.2	−1.2
	C	0.1	0.1	0.1	0.1	0.2	0.3
	D	0.1	0.1	0.1	0.1	0.2	0.3
Wholesale	A	−1.7	−4.9	−5.9	−3.4	0.6	0.1
Prices	B	−1.6	−4.4	−4.1	−1.7	−1.3	−3.5
	C	−0.0	0.0	0.0	0.0	0.0	0.0
	D	−0.0	0.0	0.0	0.0	0.0	0.0
Exchange rate	A	−12.7	−19.5	−12.7	3.5	12.8	−5.6
	B	−12.3	−15.5	−5.3	2.5	−5.0	−13.4
Current-account	A	−0.0	−0.8	−5.3	−8.2	−3.8	4.5
balance	B	−0.0	−0.8	−5.0	−6.7	−1.2	3.5
	C	0.3	0.5	0.6	0.8	1.7	3.7
	D	0.3	0.5	0.7	0.9	1.6	3.4
Long-term	A	2.0	1.2	1.4	2.8	4.1	2.3
Capital-account	B	1.8	0.3	1.0	3.9	4.3	−0.2
balance	C	2.7	2.4	2.1	2.3	2.2	2.0
	D	2.7	2.4	2.1	2.2	2.2	2.1
Changes in	A	2.3	1.4	−2.6	−4.0	0.5	5.3
official external	B	2.1	0.4	−3.0	−1.8	3.1	2.5
reserves	C	3.0	3.1	2.7	2.8	3.0	3.8
	D	3.1	3.2	2.9	2.9	2.9	3.7

See note to table 6.3.

economy only a little; real GNP is affected only to the extent that the service-account balance improves.

Under endogenous exchange rates, however, increased net capital inflow appreciates the exchange rate. Real GNP and domestic prices are then pushed downward. That is, easy money policies abroad will transmit a deflationary pressure to the domestic economy under the flexible-exchange-rate regime. The fixed-exchange-rate regime more or less insulates the domestic economy from the direct effects of foreign monetary shocks, but the flexible-exchange-rate regime does not. However, when the monetary authorities at home adhere to money-supply control rather than interest-rate control, the transmission effects are mitigated because domestic interest rates tend to move in the same direction as foreign interest rates. The conflict between national objectives of macroeconomic management may become acute when the transmitting

Table 6.5
Effects of sustained increase in foreign prices and nominal variables by 10 percent.

Variable	Model	Year 1	2	3	4	5	6
Real GNP	A	−0.0	0.4	−0.8	−2.0	−1.6	0.1
	B	−0.1	0.2	−0.7	−1.4	−0.9	−0.3
	C	0.2	1.7	2.6	2.7	3.0	3.6
	D	0.2	1.6	2.3	2.5	2.8	3.5
Wholesale prices	A	1.6	−0.9	−4.1	−4.1	0.1	3.1
	B	1.5	−1.4	−3.8	−2.1	1.0	−0.1
	C	2.5	3.5	4.3	4.9	5.3	5.6
	D	2.5	3.5	4.2	4.8	5.2	5.5
Current-account	A	−0.9	3.6	1.8	−5.9	−8.6	−2.7
balance	B	−0.9	3.7	1.5	−6.1	−6.4	2.6
	C	−0.7	4.3	6.8	8.2	7.0	10.0
	D	−0.7	4.6	7.3	9.1	8.2	11.5
Long-term capital-	A	1.5	0.5	−0.9	−0.6	2.5	5.9
account balance	B	1.7	0.1	−2.3	−0.1	4.8	5.1
	C	2.0	2.1	1.3	1.0	1.0	4.4
	D	2.4	3.0	2.0	2.1	1.8	4.9
Changes in official	A	1.6	4.1	1.4	−4.8	−4.2	3.4
external reserves	B	1.8	3.7	−0.5	−4.6	−0.0	6.3
	C	2.1	5.8	7.1	7.4	5.3	10.7
	D	2.4	6.8	8.4	9.4	7.1	11.7

See note to table 6.3.

country adopts money-supply control and the transmitted country adheres to interest-rate control.

Finally, let us consider how general inflation abroad affects the domestic economy. In the simulation reported in table 6.5, we increased all foreign prices and foreign nominal variables by 10 percent. Foreign interest rates were kept unchanged, however, because the time pattern and magnitude of nominal-interest-rate responses in such a hypothetical situation are rather difficult to estimate. Under exogenous exchange rates, world inflation puts strong upward pressures on domestic prices through direct price linkages. Trade and current-account balances worsen initially because of the J-curve effect, but they soon improve and raise the real GNP.

Under endogenous exchange rates, on the other hand, exchange rates appreciate. Exchange-rate appreciation is especially strong in the second year, and domestic prices tend to decline. The deflationary effect of strong appreciation also starts to reduce real GNP in the third year. However, the direction of exchange-rate movements is reversed to that of depreciation in the fourth year. (Note that the elasticities in table 6.5 represent the extents of divergence of the disturbed solution path from that of the standard case.) Therefore, we can see that, in the medium run, exchange-rate variations tend to neutralize the effects of foreign inflation on real domestic activities and prices, though with some short-run fluctuations. In the present case, again, the fluctuations in domestic variables are somewhat milder when monetary policies are based on money-supply control.

Two general observations can be made from the foregoing simulation experiments. First, we found that neither the law of one price nor the assumption of perfect capital mobility is a workable hypothesis in studying stabilization policies. Price elasticities in trade equations are fairly small in the short run, and the sensitivities of international capital transactions to interest rates and expected exchange rates are modest. On the other hand, international capital mobility is sufficiently large to make monetary policies more effective in domestic macroeconomic management. At the same time, it is also large enough to transmit the effects of foreign monetary disturbances to the domestic economy. In this sense national economies have become more interdependent under the generalized floating regime. Monetary authorities must carefully evaluate the direct and indirect effects of their behavior on the domestic economy that are propagated through changes in interest rates and exchange rates.

Exchange-Rate Flexibility and International Macroeconomic Interdependence: The EPA World Economic Model

The international transmission of economic activities under the generalized floating-rate regime cannot be analyzed adequately by means of a single-country macroeconometric model with flexible exchange rates or a multi-country econometric model with exogenous exchange rates. The pattern of interdependence among economic variables changes considerably with a shift from a fixed- to a flexible-exchange-rate regime. Furthermore, a change in economic conditions in one country (say, Japan) can have an impact on another (say, Canada) through its effects on the second country's major trading partner (say, the United States). In order to identify possible channels of international transmission of real and monetary disturbances, we need a multi-country framework under the present exchange-rate regimes.

The EPA World Economic Model was developed at the Economic Research Institute of the Economic Planning Agency exactly for this purpose. It is a quarterly macroeconometric model with some 1,900 equations, involving nine individual-country models (seven "summit" countries plus Australia and Korea) and one regional trade model, which are linked together by a trade-linkage model and various direct linkages among national variables.[20] Exchange rates of major currencies are endogenized by the structural balance-of-payments approach, as in the KYQ-FLEX model discussed above.[21] Here I shall summarize the results of two simulation experiments obtained from this model.

Tables 6.6–6.8 show the effects of increased real government expenditures in each country in the row heading upon countries in the column heading. This case is taken as an example of a real shock occurring in one country, and the effects on real GNPs (or GDPs), absorption deflators, and exchange rates are reported. Official discount rates and net government positions at the central banks are all assumed to be unchanged. In these tables, and in tables 6.9–6.11 below, Fix and Flex designate, respectively, that the model system was solved with exogenous exchange rates in all country models and with endogenous exchange rates in all countries but Korea.

In the Fix system, an increase in real government expenditure in one country tends to raise real GNPs and prices in all countries except in a few cases.[22] Except for these exceptional instances, an expansion in one country propagates similar effects to other countries. In general, the magnitude of cross-effects are larger the larger the original impact and the higher the import dependence of the transmitting country on the transmitted country.

Let me briefly indicate here how various balances of international payments are affected in the Fix system, because this will make it easier to understand the direction of exchange-rate movements in the Flex system. The trade and current-account balances in the transmitting country deteriorate without exception. Interest rates in that country tend to rise in almost all cases, and the capital-account balances improve in many cases. Therefore, the direction of change in the sum of current-account and capital-account balances depends on the relative magnitudes of these opposing changes. In the United Kingdom, France, Italy, Canada, Australia, and Korea, the worsening of the current-account balance dominates so that the overall balance of payments deteriorates. In Germany and Japan, on the other hand, the overall balance of payments improves initially because of the stock-shift effect of the capital-account balance, but as time goes on it tends to deteriorate because the stock-shift effects disappear and the deterioration of the current-account balance continues.

Now, in the Flex system, an increase in real government expenditure in one country has expansionary impacts on that country as well as on others. In Germany and Japan increased interest rates tend to appreciate the domestic currency in the first year and hence lessen a rise in domestic activity to some extent, but in a greater number of cases the worsening current-account balance tends to depreciate the exchange rate and amplifies the initial impact on itself. (I shall discuss the U.S. model shortly.) That is to say, the bottling-up effect can also exist in the case of fiscal policy.

There are two types of cross-effects for countries other than the United States. The first is that the exchange depreciation in the transmitting country limits the expansion of exports from other countries. This is the other side of the bottling-up effect. The second type may be called the "price-stabilizing effect." The exchange depreciation in the transmitting country tends to lower its export prices in foreign-currency units, and contributes to lower inflation rates in other countries. This, in turn, tends to stimulate private consumption in those countries. In table 6.6 one can find many cases in which the elasticities of GNP in other countries are smaller than those in the Fix system because of the bottling-up effect, but there are also instances in which they are larger than those in the Fix system because of the price-stabilizing effects.

The United States is in a somewhat special position in our world economic model. An increase in expenditure in the United States raises her real GNP and increases her imports from abroad. At the same time, concomitant increases in U.S. interest rates tend to induce capital outflow from other countries. In table 6.8 we can see that exchange rates depreciate in most other countries after an increase in U.S. expenditure. The effective exchange rates for the United States thus appreciate, having two different effects: U.S. real exports are discouraged; and the world-trade prices in U.S. dollar terms are lowered, contributing to a lowering of the inflation rate in the United States. Therefore, the own effects of an increased expenditure in the United States are not much different from those in Fix system. Rather, they are slightly larger in the Flex system, indicating that the latter favorable effects are more important.

In considering the impacts on prices we must now take into account the direct effects arising from the normal supply constraints, the indirect effects through changes in exchange rates, and the third-country effects. As regards the own effects, the inflationary pressure is strengthened in countries whose exchange rates depreciate, and vice versa. As just mentioned, exchange rates depreciate in many countries other than the United States. In these countries, therefore, expansionary fiscal policy implies a tightening of the unemployment-inflation tradeoffs, although this conclusion does not apply to the German and Japanese models in the present case for the first two years. In the United States, the inflationary pressure is mitigated by exchange appreciation.

The cross-effects can now have opposite signs, for various reasons. For a

Table 6.6
Effects of sustained increases in real government expenditure on real GNP or GDP (percentages).

		To							
		US		UK		FR		GE	
From	Year	Fix	Flex	Fix	Flex	Fix	Flex	Fix	Flex
US	1	1.31	1.33	0.18	0.22	0.06	0.06	0.07	0.28
	2	2.12	2.21	0.46	0.55	0.22	0.21	0.20	0.82
	3	2.55	2.71	0.54	0.60	0.34	0.69	0.30	1.55
	4	2.59	2.94	0.63	0.86	0.37	1.17	0.36	2.29
UK	1	0.01	0.01	1.25	1.28	0.09	0.08	0.08	0.05
	2	0.02	0.01	0.76	1.05	0.29	0.21	0.22	0.07
	3	0.01	0.02	0.59	0.87	0.34	0.20	0.24	0.07
	4	0.02	0.06	0.80	0.74	0.26	0.11	0.20	0.10
FR	1	0.01	0.01	0.07	0.07	2.20	2.23	0.08	0.03
	2	0.02	0.06	0.25	0.23	3.60	3.90	0.26	0.10
	3	0.03	0.05	0.26	0.20	3.01	3.26	0.37	0.14
	4	0.02	0.04	0.16	0.10	1.53	1.68	0.22	0.07
GE	1	0.01	0.00	0.17	0.16	0.26	0.24	1.95	1.80
	2	0.02	−0.03	0.46	0.36	0.88	0.67	2.66	3.03
	3	−0.00	−0.01	0.43	0.41	1.10	0.85	2.31	3.06
	4	−0.02	0.05	0.27	0.53	0.63	0.49	1.30	3.23
IT	1	0.01	0.01	0.05	0.04	0.11	0.08	0.08	0.04
	2	0.01	0.01	0.09	0.07	0.26	0.16	0.18	0.06
	3	0.00	−0.00	0.10	0.07	0.31	0.18	0.20	0.07
	4	0.00	0.02	0.11	0.09	0.24	0.12	0.17	0.05
CA	1	0.02	0.02	0.02	0.01	0.01	0.01	0.01	0.01
	2	0.05	0.07	0.06	0.05	0.05	0.03	0.05	0.03
	3	0.08	0.08	0.07	0.05	0.10	0.06	0.09	0.06
	4	0.08	0.09	0.08	0.03	0.11	0.06	0.09	0.09
JA	1	0.02	0.01	0.05	0.05	0.02	0.02	0.04	0.03
	2	0.02	0.01	0.16	0.14	0.12	0.11	0.12	0.06
	3	0.03	−0.01	0.17	0.15	0.18	0.17	0.16	0.05
	4	0.04	−0.00	0.19	0.20	0.18	0.13	0.14	0.03
AL	1	0.00	0.00	0.01	0.01	0.00	0.00	0.00	0.00
	2	0.01	0.00	0.05	0.04	0.02	0.02	0.02	0.01
	3	0.00	−0.02	0.04	0.03	0.04	0.04	0.04	0.02
	4	0.00	−0.02	0.02	0.03	0.03	0.04	0.03	0.05
KR	1	0.00	0.00	0.00	0.00	0.00	0.00	0.00	0.00
	2	0.00	0.00	0.00	0.00	0.01	0.01	0.01	0.00
	3	0.00	0.00	0.00	0.00	0.01	0.01	0.01	0.01
	4	0.00	0.00	0.01	0.01	0.01	0.01	0.01	0.01

US = United States, UK = United Kingdom, FR = France, GE = Germany, IT = Italy, CA = Canada, JA = Japan, AL = Australia, KR = Korea.

Data in tables 6.6–6.8 represent percentage changes in relevant variables caused by a change in real government expenditure in one country only. The size of an increase in real government

IT		CA		JA		AL		KR	
Fix	Flex	Fix	Flex	Fix	Flex	Fix	Flex	Fix	Flex
0.05	0.06	0.38	0.32	0.09	0.09	0.03	0.02	0.12	0.16
0.16	0.27	0.68	0.60	0.27	0.26	0.08	0.08	0.29	0.38
0.26	0.35	1.09	0.88	0.41	0.36	0.15	0.16	0.38	0.56
0.35	0.48	1.04	1.06	0.51	0.46	0.22	0.32	0.45	0.77
0.05	0.06	0.04	0.04	0.03	0.03	0.02	0.02	0.02	0.02
0.15	0.14	0.11	0.08	0.09	0.06	0.05	0.04	0.06	0.07
0.20	0.18	0.14	0.03	0.13	0.06	0.04	0.07	0.07	0.11
0.22	0.24	0.14	0.03	0.16	0.07	0.05	0.13	0.08	0.08
0.07	0.05	0.01	0.01	0.01	0.01	0.01	0.00	0.01	0.02
0.23	0.22	0.06	0.04	0.06	0.04	0.03	0.03	0.05	0.07
0.34	0.30	0.10	0.08	0.12	0.08	0.05	0.06	0.07	0.06
0.30	0.20	0.10	0.07	0.13	0.06	0.05	0.04	0.07	0.06
0.19	0.21	0.05	0.06	0.05	0.05	0.03	0.03	0.05	0.03
0.56	0.54	0.16	0.14	0.19	0.15	0.08	0.07	0.15	0.13
0.73	0.84	0.24	0.17	0.31	0.19	0.09	0.09	0.18	0.23
0.64	0.90	0.22	0.15	0.33	0.17	0.07	0.13	0.17	0.33
0.69	0.78	0.02	0.02	0.01	0.01	0.01	0.01	0.01	0.01
0.84	1.02	0.05	0.04	0.05	0.03	0.02	0.02	0.03	0.03
0.98	1.15	0.07	0.04	0.07	0.04	0.03	0.02	0.03	0.04
1.05	1.32	0.08	0.04	0.09	0.04	0.03	0.03	0.04	0.05
0.01	0.01	1.35	1.39	0.01	0.01	0.01	0.00	0.01	0.01
0.04	0.03	1.74	1.93	0.05	0.03	0.02	0.02	0.05	0.03
0.06	0.05	1.56	2.06	0.09	0.04	0.03	0.02	0.07	0.04
0.08	0.04	1.12	1.95	0.11	0.05	0.03	0.01	0.08	0.04
0.02	0.03	0.05	0.05	1.55	1.53	0.07	0.08	0.11	0.11
0.08	0.08	0.13	0.12	2.30	2.33	0.18	0.19	0.26	0.27
0.11	0.11	0.18	0.13	2.38	2.58	0.20	0.19	0.31	0.32
0.13	0.11	0.17	0.08	2.32	2.78	0.22	0.17	0.35	0.37
0.00	0.00	0.00	0.00	0.01	0.01	0.72	0.72	0.00	0.00
0.02	0.02	0.02	0.02	0.04	0.04	1.07	1.08	0.02	0.02
0.03	0.02	0.03	0.02	0.07	0.05	1.21	1.20	0.02	0.02
0.03	0.03	0.02	0.04	0.06	0.04	1.35	1.31	0.02	0.02
0.00	0.00	0.00	0.00	0.01	0.01	0.00	0.00	0.88	0.88
0.00	0.00	0.00	0.01	0.03	0.02	0.01	0.01	0.97	0.97
0.00	0.01	0.01	0.01	0.03	0.03	0.01	0.01	0.90	0.90
0.01	0.01	0.01	0.01	0.03	0.02	0.01	0.01	0.82	0.82

expenditure for each country is as follows: 10 billion dollars for US, 1 billion pound for UK, 10 billion francs for FR, 10 billion DM for GE, 700 billion lira for IT, 1 billion Canadian dollars for CA, 1 trillion yen for JA, 600 million Australian dollars for AL, and 100 billion Won for KR. Source: Amano, Maruyama, and Yoshitomi 1982, vol. II, part I.

Table 6.7
Effects of sustained increases in real government expenditure on absorption deflator (percentages).

From	Year	To							
		US		UK		FR		GE	
		Fix	Flex	Fix	Flex	Fix	Flex	Fix	Flex
US	1	0.06	0.02	0.04	0.07	−0.00	0.02	0.00	0.02
	2	0.00	−0.08	0.26	0.43	−0.02	−0.00	0.03	0.21
	3	0.16	−0.09	0.58	0.68	−0.05	0.47	0.09	0.63
	4	0.59	0.09	0.94	0.29	−0.04	0.84	0.16	1.30
UK	1	0.01	0.02	0.36	0.35	−0.01	−0.03	0.00	0.00
	2	0.03	0.02	1.00	1.43	−0.04	−0.11	0.03	−0.00
	3	0.05	−0.02	1.16	3.47	−0.06	−0.10	0.08	−0.02
	4	0.07	0.00	1.57	6.32	−0.04	−0.04	0.12	−0.03
FR	1	0.00	−0.01	0.01	0.01	−0.29	−0.16	0.00	−0.00
	2	0.02	−0.01	0.11	0.02	−0.67	−0.30	0.03	−0.02
	3	0.04	0.03	0.28	0.04	−0.67	−0.49	0.09	−0.03
	4	0.05	0.04	0.39	−0.00	−0.36	−0.12	0.15	−0.03
GE	1	0.02	0.05	0.05	0.08	−0.02	−0.08	0.11	−0.08
	2	0.07	0.09	0.30	0.28	−0.11	−0.31	0.62	0.57
	3	0.13	0.11	0.64	0.15	−0.17	−0.34	1.16	1.42
	4	0.15	0.10	0.88	−0.31	−0.11	−0.30	1.42	2.33
IT	1	0.01	0.01	0.01	0.01	−0.01	−0.05	0.00	−0.00
	2	0.02	0.01	0.07	0.04	−0.04	−0.09	0.03	−0.01
	3	0.03	0.02	0.14	0.03	−0.05	−0.07	0.07	−0.02
	4	0.04	0.02	0.21	0.00	−0.04	−0.07	0.10	−0.03
CA	1	0.01	−0.01	0.01	0.00	0.00	−0.00	0.00	0.00
	2	0.04	0.00	0.05	0.02	0.00	−0.01	0.01	0.00
	3	0.08	0.02	0.12	0.07	−0.00	0.00	0.03	0.02
	4	0.10	0.01	0.20	0.07	−0.00	0.01	0.05	0.04
JA	1	0.01	0.02	0.01	0.02	0.00	−0.00	0.00	0.00
	2	0.05	0.06	0.10	0.14	−0.00	−0.02	0.02	0.01
	3	0.07	0.07	0.24	0.22	−0.01	−0.03	0.06	0.01
	4	0.08	0.03	0.35	0.09	−0.02	−0.05	0.09	0.01
AL	1	0.00	0.00	0.00	0.00	−0.00	−0.00	−0.00	−0.00
	2	0.00	0.01	0.02	0.02	−0.00	−0.00	0.00	0.00
	3	0.01	0.05	0.06	0.03	−0.00	−0.00	0.01	0.00
	4	0.01	0.10	0.08	0.03	−0.00	0.00	0.02	0.01
KR	1	0.00	0.00	0.00	0.00	−0.00	−0.00	−0.00	0.00
	2	0.00	0.00	0.00	0.01	−0.00	−0.00	0.00	0.00
	3	0.00	0.01	0.01	0.01	−0.00	−0.00	0.00	0.00
	4	0.00	0.01	0.01	0.01	−0.00	−0.00	0.00	0.00

See note to table 6.6.

IT		CA		JA		AL		KR	
Fix	Flex	Fix	Flex	Fix	Flex	Fix	Flex	Fix	Flex
0.02	0.07	0.09	0.02	0.01	0.05	0.01	−0.03	0.03	−0.07
0.05	0.61	0.34	0.17	0.03	0.20	0.06	−0.12	0.07	−0.21
0.08	1.30	0.67	0.46	0.08	0.42	0.17	−0.40	0.13	−0.57
0.13	2.48	0.98	0.70	0.11	0.87	0.32	−0.89	0.27	−1.05
0.01	0.03	0.01	0.01	0.01	−0.00	0.01	0.01	0.01	0.03
0.04	0.02	0.06	0.02	0.02	−0.07	0.05	0.00	0.07	0.05
0.05	0.04	0.12	0.02	0.05	−0.19	0.14	−0.15	0.11	−0.05
0.06	0.31	0.16	0.02	0.06	−0.24	0.19	−0.22	0.13	−0.02
−0.00	−0.04	0.00	0.01	0.00	−0.01	0.00	−0.00	0.00	−0.02
0.00	−0.01	0.02	−0.01	0.01	−0.04	0.02	−0.03	0.03	−0.07
0.02	0.14	0.07	0.03	0.03	−0.06	0.08	0.02	0.06	0.03
0.02	0.05	0.11	0.05	0.04	−0.16	0.12	0.08	0.08	0.03
0.04	0.05	0.02	0.03	0.02	0.01	0.02	0.04	0.04	0.10
0.13	0.07	0.10	0.08	0.06	−0.13	0.11	0.15	0.17	0.23
0.18	0.46	0.22	0.12	0.11	−0.46	0.31	0.27	0.28	0.19
0.19	1.11	0.31	0.11	0.14	−0.86	0.43	0.20	0.32	0.03
0.05	0.43	0.01	0.00	0.01	−0.00	0.00	0.00	0.31	0.01
0.11	1.28	0.03	0.01	0.02	−0.03	0.03	0.02	0.04	0.03
0.19	2.04	0.06	0.02	0.03	−0.09	0.08	0.04	0.07	0.03
0.32	2.77	0.09	0.02	0.04	−0.16	0.11	0.05	0.08	0.03
0.00	0.00	0.36	0.47	0.00	−0.00	0.00	0.00	0.01	0.00
0.03	0.04	1.10	1.47	0.02	−0.01	0.03	0.02	0.05	0.03
0.05	0.09	1.49	2.41	0.04	−0.03	0.10	0.06	0.10	0.07
0.06	0.12	1.53	3.28	0.05	−0.07	0.16	0.09	0.12	0.07
0.01	0.02	0.01	0.01	0.09	−0.07	0.01	0.02	0.04	0.07
0.05	0.07	0.08	0.06	0.25	−0.09	0.11	0.14	0.16	0.19
0.07	0.04	0.16	0.11	0.12	0.61	0.29	0.33	0.21	0.15
0.06	0.02	0.20	0.11	−0.26	1.62	0.34	0.32	0.17	−0.08
0.00	0.00	0.00	0.00	0.00	−0.00	0.11	0.11	0.00	0.00
0.01	0.01	0.01	0.01	0.00	−0.03	0.35	0.39	0.01	0.02
0.01	0.01	0.02	0.02	0.01	−0.09	0.62	0.77	0.03	0.05
0.01	0.01	0.03	0.03	0.02	−0.16	0.75	1.04	0.03	0.06
0.00	0.00	0.00	0.00	−0.00	−0.01	0.00	0.00	−0.03	−0.02
0.00	0.00	0.00	0.00	0.00	−0.03	0.00	0.01	−0.02	−0.02
0.00	0.00	0.01	0.01	0.01	−0.06	0.01	0.02	0.02	0.02
0.00	0.01	0.01	0.01	0.01	−0.10	0.01	0.02	0.05	0.06

Table 6.8
Effects of sustained increases in real government expenditure on exchange rates (percentages).

From	Year	To US	UK	FR	GE	IT	CA	JA	AL
US	1	−0.64	0.78	0.74	2.14	0.82	−0.28	0.34	0.00
	2	−1.63	1.40	1.39	5.68	3.76	−0.34	0.96	0.04
	3	−4.36	0.64	9.84	12.13	8.06	1.05	2.06	0.02
	4	−6.68	−0.51	12.91	22.09	14.10	0.50	4.47	−0.22
UK	1	0.14	0.12	−0.36	−0.33	−0.03	−0.07	−0.07	−0.00
	2	−0.41	5.41	−0.52	−0.67	0.02	−0.12	−0.38	0.01
	3	−1.59	13.78	0.21	−0.14	0.62	−0.06	−0.70	−0.01
	4	−1.20	10.33	0.14	−0.16	1.30	−0.04	−0.72	−0.09
FR	1	−0.15	−0.00	1.82	−0.19	0.03	−0.03	−0.02	0.00
	2	−0.18	−0.43	3.24	−0.46	0.48	−0.04	−0.10	0.01
	3	0.30	−0.79	0.85	−0.90	0.47	−0.03	−0.32	0.00
	4	0.05	−0.55	1.97	−0.18	0.35	−0.02	−0.67	0.02
GE	1	0.44	0.01	−1.09	−1.19	−0.30	−0.07	−0.15	−0.01
	2	−0.05	−0.88	−1.72	3.07	−0.10	−0.19	−0.94	0.01
	3	−0.78	−2.69	−0.44	8.33	2.36	−0.20	−2.13	0.08
	4	−1.67	−2.10	0.16	13.13	5.44	−0.25	−2.98	0.13
IT	1	0.13	−0.03	−0.37	−0.29	1.66	−0.03	−0.03	0.00
	2	0.24	−0.15	−0.31	−0.57	4.61	−0.05	−0.17	0.01
	3	0.25	−0.34	0.00	−0.49	6.25	−0.04	−0.39	0.02
	4	0.32	−0.22	−0.20	−0.52	7.69	−0.06	−0.60	0.03
CA	1	−0.29	0.00	−0.01	0.01	0.01	0.84	−0.01	−0.00
	2	−0.66	0.00	−0.04	0.02	0.13	1.98	−0.07	0.00
	3	−1.20	−0.04	0.11	0.12	0.27	3.67	−0.22	0.01
	4	−2.04	−0.11	0.23	0.46	0.41	6.02	−0.32	0.03
JA	1	0.22	0.07	−0.10	−0.18	0.00	−0.08	−0.67	−0.00
	2	0.29	−0.06	−0.35	−0.59	−0.09	−0.15	−0.26	0.01
	3	−0.36	−0.70	−0.19	−0.40	−0.19	−0.12	2.81	0.10
	4	−1.62	−0.89	−0.02	0.33	0.05	−0.14	8.12	0.20
AL	1	0.01	−0.01	−0.01	−0.02	0.00	−0.01	−0.01	0.02
	2	0.09	−0.08	−0.06	−0.12	−0.02	−0.02	−0.16	0.16
	3	0.16	−0.17	−0.04	−0.14	−0.08	−0.01	−0.43	0.40
	4	0.13	−0.05	0.04	0.08	0.01	−0.03	−0.62	0.63
KR	1	0.01	0.00	−0.01	−0.01	−0.00	−0.00	−0.03	−0.00
	2	0.04	−0.00	−0.01	−0.03	−0.01	−0.00	−0.13	0.00
	3	0.06	−0.01	−0.00	−0.04	−0.01	−0.00	−0.24	0.00
	4	0.09	−0.01	−0.01	−0.04	−0.00	−0.01	−0.34	0.01

See note to table 6.6. Exchange rates are the price of the U.S. dollar in local currency units in countries other than the United States, and the index of the price of foreign currency basket in U.S. dollars for the United States.

large number of cases in table 6.7, an expansionary policy in one country propagates price inflation to other countries, as in the Fix system. When the transmitted countries experience exchange appreciation, however, prices in those countries may receive downward pressure. In table 6.7 these cases are from UK to GE and JA, from IT to GE and JA, and from CA and AL to JA. Finally, prices in the transmitted countries may receive downward pressure from declining export prices (expressed in foreign currencies) of their major trading partners. The effects from UK to AL and KR are due mainly to a reduction in UK export prices in dollar terms; those from US to AL and KR are caused by reductions in export prices of European countries and Japan.

It is now clear that under exchange-rate flexibility the direction of international transmission of price inflation accompanying an expansion in domestic demand in one country cannot be identified uniquely, as it can in the Fix system. Exchange-rate appreciation in the transmitted country may contribute to a lowering of the inflationary tendency in that country, and if exchange rates depreciate in the transmitting country at a rate higher than that at which prices increase then price-deflationary rather than inflationary pressures will be exported from that country.

Let us now turn to the effects of monetary policies. Since financial systems are rather different in different countries, an international comparison of monetary policies is not a straightforward matter. The results reported in tables 6.9–6.11 were obtained from simulations in which monetary-policy instruments in each country were shocked so as to produce roughly the same impacts on financial markets as would be produced by a 2 percent per annum increase in the official discount rate. (See note to table 6.9.)

In the Fix system, a tight money policy in one country reduces that country's own real GNP (or GDP), with only one exception.[23] The cross-effects are mostly deflationary, but there is one interesting exception: the effects of policies in other countries on the United States. As interest rates in these countries rise, receipts of investment income by U.S. residents increase, and so does U.S. real GNP. The U.S. service-account balance tends to improve as a result of tight money policies in the United Kingdom, France, West Germany, Canada, and Japan, because the foreign-interest-rate variable used in the U.S. investment-income-receipt equation includes only interest rates of these countries. The tight money policy in the United Kingdom has slight expansionary impacts on Canada and Korea; these are the results of an increase in the U.S. GNP.

As to the own effects on prices, a tight money policy exerts downward pressure in almost all cases.[24] Therefore, the cross-effects are also negative in

Table 6.9
Effects of tight money policies on real GNP or GDP (percentages).

		To							
		US		UK		FR		GE	
From	Year	Fix	Flex	Fix	Flex	Fix	Flex	Fix	Flex
US	1	−0.77	−0.72	−0.12	−0.02	−0.01	−0.04	−0.04	0.43
	2	−1.49	−1.32	−0.37	−0.29	−0.17	−0.21	−0.14	0.43
	3	−1.19	−1.02	−0.34	−0.34	−0.25	−0.07	−0.21	0.11
	4	−0.40	−0.27	−0.18	−0.11	−0.21	−0.23	−0.19	−0.30
UK	1	0.02	0.01	−0.11	−0.27	−0.00	0.02	−0.00	0.03
	2	0.04	0.00	−0.08	−0.16	−0.03	0.04	−0.02	0.02
	3	0.06	0.01	0.05	0.15	−0.02	0.09	−0.01	0.03
	4	0.06	0.06	−0.05	−0.14	−0.00	0.10	0.00	0.04
FR	1	0.01	−0.00	−0.01	−0.01	−0.32	−0.42	−0.01	0.02
	2	0.02	−0.01	−0.04	−0.05	−0.82	−0.96	−0.05	−0.02
	3	0.04	−0.02	−0.07	−0.05	−1.04	−1.33	−0.10	0.01
	4	0.04	0.00	−0.07	−0.05	−0.87	−1.03	−0.10	−0.01
GE	1	0.02	−0.00	−0.05	−0.06	−0.22	−0.21	−0.54	−1.07
	2	0.04	−0.05	−0.32	−0.41	−0.94	−0.84	−1.62	−2.57
	3	0.08	−0.07	−0.49	−0.60	−1.55	−1.54	−2.27	−4.01
	4	0.10	−0.10	−0.53	−0.79	−1.52	−1.41	−2.27	−4.61
IT	1	−0.00	−0.01	−0.01	−0.00	−0.02	0.01	−0.01	0.01
	2	−0.00	−0.05	−0.04	−0.04	−0.09	0.05	−0.07	−0.00
	3	−0.00	−0.09	−0.06	−0.05	−0.16	0.08	−0.11	−0.03
	4	−0.00	−0.10	−0.06	−0.03	−0.16	0.06	−0.12	−0.03
CA	1	—	—	—	—	—	—	—	—
	2	0.00	0.01	−0.00	0.00	−0.00	0.00	−0.00	0.01
	3	0.01	−0.00	−0.02	0.02	−0.01	0.02	−0.01	0.03
	4	0.01	0.01	−0.04	−0.01	−0.04	0.02	−0.03	0.04
JA	1	0.02	0.01	−0.00	−0.01	−0.00	0.00	−0.00	0.02
	2	0.03	0.01	−0.01	−0.01	−0.01	0.04	−0.01	0.03
	3	0.04	0.01	−0.02	−0.01	−0.02	0.06	−0.02	0.05
	4	0.04	0.04	−0.03	−0.00	−0.02	0.11	−0.02	0.07
AL	1	−0.00	−0.00	−0.00	−0.00	−0.00	−0.00	−0.00	−0.00
	2	−0.00	−0.00	−0.02	−0.02	−0.01	−0.01	−0.01	−0.01
	3	−0.00	−0.00	−0.03	−0.02	−0.02	−0.02	−0.02	−0.01
	4	−0.00	0.00	−0.02	−0.02	−0.02	−0.02	−0.02	−0.01
KR	1	−0.00	−0.00	−0.00	−0.00	−0.00	0.00	0.00	−0.00
	2	0.00	0.00	−0.00	0.00	−0.00	0.00	−0.00	−0.00
	3	−0.00	−0.00	−0.00	0.00	−0.00	−0.00	−0.00	−0.00
	4	−0.00	−0.00	−0.00	0.00	−0.00	0.00	−0.00	0.00

Data in tables 6.9–6.11 represent percentage changes in relevant variables caused by a change in monetary policy in one country only. Monetary shocks are all sustained and were given as follows: a 2 percent p.a. increase in the official discount rate for US, GE, and JA; a 2 percent p.a. increase in the minimum lending rate for UK; a 2 percent p.a. increase in the constant term of the short-term-interest-rate equation for FR and IT; a 6 percentage point p.a. increase in the M1 target growth rate for CA; a 2 percent p.a. increase in interest rates on Savings Bank Deposits, permanent

IT		CA		JA		AL		KR	
Fix	Flex	Fix	Flex	Fix	Flex	Fix	Flex	Fix	Flex
−0.03	−0.01	−0.18	−0.25	−0.06	−0.06	−0.03	−0.05	−0.08	−0.01
−0.12	−0.00	−0.79	−0.76	−0.21	−0.19	−0.06	−0.05	−0.21	−0.10
−0.18	−0.28	−0.73	−0.86	−0.31	−0.27	−0.04	−0.01	−0.23	−0.17
−0.19	−0.41	−0.66	−0.79	−0.33	−0.25	−0.00	0.02	−0.21	−0.25
−0.00	0.05	0.00	0.02	0.00	0.01	−0.00	0.01	0.00	−0.01
−0.01	0.01	0.00	0.04	−0.00	0.02	−0.00	−0.01	−0.00	−0.03
−0.01	0.00	0.02	0.08	−0.00	0.03	0.00	−0.04	0.00	0.00
−0.00	0.06	0.03	0.07	0.00	0.02	0.00	−0.02	0.01	0.06
−0.01	0.01	0.00	0.01	−0.00	0.00	−0.00	0.00	−0.00	−0.02
−0.04	−0.04	−0.00	0.00	−0.01	−0.00	−0.01	−0.01	−0.00	−0.02
−0.08	−0.02	−0.01	0.02	−0.02	0.01	−0.01	−0.00	−0.01	−0.03
−0.10	−0.06	−0.01	0.02	−0.03	−0.01	−0.01	−0.02	−0.01	−0.01
−0.06	−0.04	−0.01	0.02	−0.01	0.00	−0.01	−0.00	−0.01	−0.05
−0.38	−0.44	−0.08	−0.06	−0.10	−0.08	−0.05	−0.07	−0.09	−0.17
−0.71	−0.84	−0.18	−0.13	−0.24	−0.18	−0.09	−0.14	−0.16	−0.27
−0.92	−1.21	−0.23	−0.16	−0.35	−0.22	−0.11	−0.22	−0.21	−0.41
−0.21	−0.31	−0.00	0.00	−0.00	0.00	−0.00	0.00	−0.00	−0.01
−0.36	−0.81	−0.02	0.01	−0.01	0.01	−0.01	−0.00	−0.01	−0.05
−0.47	−0.80	−0.03	0.02	−0.03	0.01	−0.01	−0.03	−0.02	−0.06
−0.28	−0.47	−0.04	0.03	−0.04	−0.01	−0.02	−0.05	−0.02	−0.04
—	—	—	—	—	—	—	—	—	—
0.00	0.01	−0.01	−0.09	0.00	0.00	−0.00	0.00	−0.00	0.00
−0.01	0.04	−0.90	−0.97	−0.01	0.02	−0.01	0.01	−0.01	0.03
−0.03	0.02	−0.70	−1.74	−0.03	0.01	−0.02	0.00	−0.03	0.02
−0.00	0.01	0.00	0.02	−0.07	−0.15	−0.00	0.01	−0.01	−0.02
−0.00	0.02	−0.00	0.04	−0.23	−0.39	−0.02	0.01	−0.02	−0.02
−0.01	0.03	−0.00	0.06	−0.37	−0.62	−0.03	0.00	−0.04	−0.04
−0.02	0.06	−0.01	0.09	−0.47	−0.77	−0.04	0.01	−0.05	−0.02
−0.00	−0.00	−0.00	−0.00	−0.00	−0.00	−0.26	−0.26	−0.00	−0.00
−0.01	−0.01	−0.01	−0.01	−0.02	−0.01	−0.63	−0.63	−0.01	−0.01
−0.01	−0.01	−0.01	−0.01	−0.03	−0.02	−0.88	−0.88	−0.01	−0.01
−0.02	−0.02	−0.02	−0.02	−0.04	−0.02	−1.05	−1.02	−0.01	−0.01
0.00	−0.00	−0.00	−0.00	−0.00	−0.00	−0.00	−0.00	−0.02	−0.02
−0.00	−0.00	−0.00	−0.00	−0.00	0.00	0.00	−0.00	−0.00	−0.00
0.00	0.00	0.00	−0.00	−0.00	0.00	0.00	0.00	−0.00	−0.00
0.00	0.00	−0.00	−0.00	−0.00	0.00	0.00	0.00	−0.00	−0.00

Building Society Deposits, and Saving Bank Mortgages and a 10 percent reduction of Savings Banks' Lending Guidlines for AL; and a 2 percent p.a. increase in interest rates on time deposits in deposit money banks and in banks' lending rate for KR. The simulation for Canada starts from the second year, because our standard solution begins from 1974 whereas the M1 target was adopted in 1975.

Source: Amano, Maruyama, and Yoshitomi 1982, vol. II, part I.

Table 6.10
Effects of tight money policies on absorption deflator (percentages).

From	Year	To US Fix	US Flex	UK Fix	UK Flex	FR Fix	FR Flex	GE Fix	GE Flex
US	1	−0.03	−0.15	−0.03	0.02	0.00	0.10	−0.00	0.07
	2	−0.09	−0.24	−0.19	0.11	0.02	0.08	−0.01	0.36
	3	−0.44	−0.61	−0.46	−0.18	0.02	0.36	−0.05	0.55
	4	−0.74	−0.93	−0.65	−0.58	−0.00	0.01	−0.11	0.51
UK	1	0.00	0.03	−0.02	−0.26	0.00	0.02	−0.00	0.00
	2	0.00	0.06	−0.10	−1.40	0.00	0.04	−0.00	0.01
	3	0.01	0.07	−0.08	−2.41	0.01	0.01	−0.01	0.02
	4	0.02	0.05	−0.08	−2.65	0.00	−0.01	−0.01	0.02
FR	1	0.00	0.02	−0.00	0.02	0.02	−0.18	−0.00	0.00
	2	−0.00	0.02	−0.02	0.06	0.09	−0.07	−0.00	0.01
	3	−0.00	0.06	−0.05	0.08	0.15	−0.21	−0.02	0.01
	4	−0.00	0.07	−0.09	0.14	0.13	−0.02	−0.04	0.02
GE	1	−0.00	0.05	−0.01	0.06	0.01	0.01	−0.04	−0.10
	2	−0.03	0.04	−0.14	0.10	0.10	0.23	−0.29	−0.67
	3	−0.09	0.06	−0.45	0.16	0.23	−0.36	−0.71	−1.57
	4	−0.12	0.12	−0.80	0.50	0.26	0.61	−1.10	−2.61
IT	1	−0.00	0.01	−0.00	0.01	0.00	0.02	−0.00	0.00
	2	−0.01	0.04	−0.02	0.07	0.01	0.05	−0.01	0.01
	3	−0.01	0.09	−0.05	0.15	0.03	0.03	−0.02	0.02
	4	−0.02	0.12	−0.10	0.16	0.03	0.03	−0.05	0.02
CA	1	—	—	—	—	—	—	—	—
	2	0.00	0.01	−0.00	0.00	0.00	0.00	0.00	0.00
	3	−0.01	0.07	−0.01	0.04	−0.00	−0.00	−0.00	0.00
	4	−0.02	0.06	−0.04	0.09	−0.00	0.00	−0.01	0.01
JA	1	−0.00	0.02	−0.00	0.01	−0.00	0.02	−0.00	0.00
	2	−0.00	0.04	−0.00	0.06	−0.00	0.01	−0.00	0.00
	3	0.00	0.06	−0.02	0.15	0.00	0.01	−0.00	−0.00
	4	0.01	0.08	−0.03	0.23	0.00	0.03	−0.01	−0.01
AL	1	−0.00	−0.00	−0.00	−0.00	0.00	0.00	−0.00	−0.00
	2	−0.00	−0.00	−0.01	−0.01	0.00	0.00	−0.00	−0.00
	3	−0.01	−0.01	−0.03	−0.02	0.00	0.00	−0.00	−0.00
	4	−0.01	−0.01	−0.05	−0.01	0.00	0.00	−0.01	−0.00
KR	1	0.00	0.00	0.00	−0.00	0.00	0.00	0.00	0.00
	2	−0.00	−0.00	0.00	−0.00	0.00	0.00	0.00	−0.00
	3	0.00	−0.00	−0.00	0.00	0.00	0.00	0.00	−0.00
	4	0.00	−0.00	−0.00	0.00	0.00	0.00	−0.00	−0.00

See note to table 6.9.

IT		CA		JA		AL		KR	
Fix	Flex	Fix	Flex	Fix	Flex	Fix	Flex	Fix	Flex
−0.01	0.24	−0.03	−0.04	−0.01	0.25	−0.01	−0.12	−0.02	−0.31
−0.04	1.10	−0.28	−0.32	−0.02	0.75	−0.05	−0.34	−0.06	−0.51
−0.10	1.07	−0.62	−0.74	−0.08	1.21	−0.16	−0.61	−0.19	−0.70
−0.15	0.78	−0.77	−0.96	−0.11	1.68	−0.29	−0.68	−0.32	−0.68
−0.00	0.15	0.00	0.02	0.00	0.02	0.00	0.04	−0.00	0.05
−0.00	0.23	0.00	0.05	−0.00	−0.00	−0.00	0.15	−0.00	0.14
−0.00	0.11	0.00	0.06	−0.00	−0.09	−0.01	0.25	−0.01	0.14
0.00	0.10	0.01	0.07	−0.00	−0.20	−0.01	0.20	0.00	0.08
−0.00	0.05	0.00	0.01	−0.00	0.02	−0.00	0.02	−0.00	0.05
−0.00	−0.05	−0.00	0.02	−0.00	−0.01	−0.00	0.04	−0.01	0.06
−0.01	0.00	−0.01	0.04	−0.01	−0.02	−0.01	0.06	−0.01	0.12
−0.01	−0.14	−0.01	0.05	−0.01	−0.08	−0.03	0.09	−0.02	0.09
−0.01	0.04	−0.00	0.03	−0.00	0.04	−0.00	0.05	−0.01	0.12
−0.07	−0.25	−0.04	0.04	−0.03	0.04	−0.05	0.08	−0.09	0.12
−0.14	−0.49	−0.13	0.01	−0.07	0.16	−0.22	0.06	−0.21	0.12
−0.17	−1.14	−0.24	−0.00	−0.12	0.45	−0.38	0.06	−0.31	0.18
−0.01	−0.72	−0.00	0.01	−0.00	0.02	−0.00	0.01	−0.00	0.03
−0.04	−2.52	−0.01	0.04	−0.00	0.03	−0.01	0.07	−0.01	0.12
−0.06	−3.78	−0.02	0.07	−0.01	−0.02	−0.03	0.21	−0.03	0.20
−0.08	−3.83	−0.04	0.08	−0.02	−0.13	−0.05	0.27	−0.04	0.20
—	—	—	—	—	—	—	—	—	—
0.00	0.02	0.01	−0.11	0.00	0.00	0.00	0.00	−0.00	0.00
−0.00	0.12	−0.19	−0.81	−0.00	−0.01	−0.00	0.03	−0.01	0.02
−0.02	0.12	−0.54	−1.91	−0.01	−0.05	−0.03	0.03	−0.03	0.01
−0.00	0.02	0.00	0.01	−0.01	−0.55	−0.00	0.02	−0.00	0.10
−0.00	0.03	−0.00	0.02	−0.04	−1.52	−0.01	0.07	−0.01	0.19
−0.01	0.01	−0.01	0.03	−0.06	−2.54	−0.03	0.15	−0.02	0.22
−0.01	0.00	−0.01	0.04	−0.08	−3.48	−0.04	0.21	−0.02	0.25
−0.00	−0.00	−0.00	−0.00	−0.00	0.00	−0.03	−0.03	−0.00	−0.00
−0.00	−0.00	−0.00	−0.00	−0.00	0.01	−0.18	−0.20	−0.00	−0.01
−0.01	−0.01	−0.01	−0.01	−0.00	0.04	−0.45	−0.52	−0.01	−0.02
−0.01	−0.00	−0.02	−0.01	−0.01	0.09	−0.63	−0.80	−0.02	−0.04
−0.00	−0.00	0.00	0.00	0.00	0.00	−0.00	−0.00	0.00	0.00
−0.00	−0.00	−0.00	0.00	−0.00	0.00	−0.00	−0.00	0.00	−0.00
=0.00	−0.00	−0.00	−0.00	0.00	0.00	−0.00	−0.00	0.00	−0.00
−0.00	−0.00	0.00	−0.00	0.00	0.00	−0.00	−0.00	0.00	−0.00

Table 6.11
Effects of tight money policies on exchange rates (percentages).

From	Year	To							
		US	UK	FR	GE	IT	CA	JA	AL
US	1	−2.05	1.70	2.20	5.26	2.50	0.38	1.49	0.03
	2	−2.15	1.63	1.26	4.97	5.59	0.06	3.26	−0.00
	3	−2.46	0.10	4.68	4.38	4.50	−0.11	4.75	−0.01
	4	−1.47	0.45	−1.37	1.88	1.68	−0.19	5.80	0.07
UK	1	0.54	−3.26	−0.02	−0.22	0.39	−0.01	−0.02	−0.01
	2	1.10	−6.23	−0.12	−0.44	0.24	−0.04	−0.21	−0.00
	3	1.07	−5.52	−0.24	−0.35	−0.25	−0.07	−0.54	0.06
	4	0.59	−2.56	0.07	−0.07	0.11	−0.09	−0.82	0.11
FR	1	0.30	0.04	−2.16	−0.20	−0.17	−0.00	−0.02	−0.01
	2	0.15	0.02	−0.91	−0.08	−0.44	−0.01	−0.11	−0.00
	3	0.51	0.21	−3.57	−0.32	−0.58	0.01	−0.23	−0.01
	4	0.05	0.15	−0.03	0.03	−0.63	0.03	−0.40	−0.00
GE	1	1.01	0.16	−0.72	−4.15	−0.57	−0.00	−0.03	−0.01
	2	1.20	0.75	0.77	−6.33	−1.60	0.11	0.02	−0.02
	3	2.02	2.56	−0.63	−10.67	−2.97	0.17	0.65	−0.04
	4	2.89	2.38	1.12	−15.58	−5.85	0.18	1.66	−0.10
IT	1	0.01	0.01	0.03	−0.08	−3.28	0.00	0.03	−0.00
	2	0.10	0.06	−0.11	−0.37	−9.99	−0.00	−0.06	−0.01
	3	0.28	−0.02	−0.46	−0.60	−11.87	−0.02	−0.37	0.02
	4	0.36	−0.10	−0.19	−0.51	−9.97	−0.08	−0.81	0.07
CA	1	—	—	—	—	—	—	—	—
	2	0.35	−0.02	−0.01	0.01	0.09	−0.99	−0.00	−0.00
	3	1.49	0.16	−0.05	−0.02	0.39	−4.15	−0.11	−0.01
	4	1.71	0.06	0.07	0.15	0.36	−4.76	−0.25	−0.01
JA	1	0.55	0.06	0.05	−0.19	0.01	−0.01	−2.35	−0.00
	2	1.31	0.25	−0.11	−0.44	−0.09	−0.04	−5.41	−0.00
	3	1.94	0.39	−0.05	−0.60	−0.20	−0.03	−8.00	−0.03
	4	2.61	0.23	−0.06	−0.93	−0.30	−0.06	−10.18	0.07
AL	1	−0.00	0.00	0.00	0.00	−0.00	0.00	0.00	−0.01
	2	−0.03	0.03	0.02	0.04	0.01	0.01	0.05	0.07
	3	−0.09	0.10	0.03	0.10	0.03	0.01	0.19	0.24
	4	−0.13	0.09	0.04	0.12	0.05	0.01	0.37	−0.47
KR	1	−0.00	−0.00	0.00	−0.00	−0.00	−0.00	0.00	−0.00
	2	−0.00	−0.00	0.00	0.00	−0.00	−0.00	0.01	−0.00
	3	−0.00	0.00	−0.00	−0.00	0.00	−0.00	0.01	−0.00
	4	−0.00	0.00	0.00	0.00	−0.00	−0.00	0.01	−0.00

See notes to tables 6.8 and 6.9.

many cases, but there are some exceptions when there is an increase in U.S. real GNP, such as the effects from the United Kingdom to the United States and Canada and those from Japan to the United States.

In the Flex system the pattern of own effects on real GNP is the same as that in the Fix system, but in countries other than the United States exchange rates tend to appreciate because of improving current-account and capital-account balances. Therefore, the original deflationary pressure is strengthened in these countries. In the U.S. model, however, price-stabilizing effects are more important, as in the case of fiscal-policy simulation, and the elasticities of GNP become slightly smaller in absolute value than in the Fix system.

The pattern of cross-effects, on the other hand, is rather complicated in the present case. For example, West Germany's GDP increases in the first three years as a result of tight money policy in the United States. This arises because the extent of exchange depreciation caused by high U.S. interest rates is the largest in Germany, which helps expand Germany's exports even though total world trade is shrinking. With this exception, however, the U.S. tight money policy propagates deflationary impacts upon other countries. Similarly, tight money policies in West Germany and Australia have deflationary effects on the rest of the world.

On the other hand, the same policies in the United Kingdom, Canada, and Japan transmit, in many cases, upward pressures to real economic activities of other countries. France and Italy are in between. The reason the pattern of cross-effects is diverse in the Flex system is that there are several mutually opposing influences, including the following: (1) reduction in exports in the transmitted country due to a reduction in economic activity in the transmitting country, (2) reduction in consumption in various countries due to increased export prices in dollar terms in countries other than the United States, (3) expansion of exports from the transmitted country due to exchange-rate appreciation in the transmitting country, (4) expansion of exports from the United States caused by exchange-rate appreciation in other countries, and (5) increases in U.S. investment-income receipts resulting from increased interest rates. Items 1 and 2 will make the cross-effect negative, whereas items 3–5 will make it positive. The relative magnitudes of these opposing influences depend on the competitive/complementary relationships between the transmitted country, on the one hand, and the transmitting country and the United States on the other hand.

As regards the effects on prices, the own effects of price decline are much stronger than in the Fix system, because exchange rates appreciate in all countries. However, export prices in terms of foreign currencies tend to rise in the transmitting country. Therefore, the statement that a tight money policy in one country tends to export price inflation to the rest of the world is correct as a general tendency. In table 6.10 there are many cases in which the extent of price decline is smaller than in table 6.7, and some cross-elasticities are in fact positive. However, in some cases prices tend to decline more than in the Fix system. The effects from the United States to Canada, Australia, and Korea, from the United Kingdom to Japan, from West Germany to Italy, from Canada to Japan, and from Australia to Korea are the examples. This can arise in countries whose exchange-rate appreciation is particularly large, and it can also occur in countries whose import dependence on partner countries is high if those countries' export prices, expressed in terms of foreign currencies, decline substantially in response to tight domestic monetary policy.

Conclusion

The structural balance-of-payments approach to exchange-rate determination can provide a useful tool in short-to-medium-term macroeconomic analysis. In some country models, such as that for West Germany, exchange rates respond somewhat excessively to exogenous shocks in the medium run, indicating the need for further improvements; however, this approach can shed light on many important linkages in macroeconomic interdependence that have been brought forth by exchange-rate flexibility. Policy implications of the foregoing analyses have already been given in the opening section.

Notes

1. For a survey of theories of exchange-rate determination see Schadler 1977; Isard 1978; Mussa 1979; Helliwell 1979; Dornbusch 1979, 1980. The following papers also include a review of empirical studies based on asset-market approaches: Bilson 1979a; Murphy and Van Duyne 1980; Hacche and Townend 1981; Fukao 1982.

2. Here and in the next two sections I adopt this convention except for interest-rate variables, for which lower-case letters designate antilogarithms.

3. A variant of this approach assumes, instead of equation 1, that the PPP relation holds only with respect to tradable-goods prices, as in Clements and Frenkel 1980:

$$s = p_T - p_T^*, \tag{1'}$$

where P_T denotes the price level of tradables. If we further assume that the general price level, P, is determined by P_T and the nontradable-goods prices, P_N, so that $P = P_N^\beta \cdot P_T^{1-\beta}$, then we have

$$p_T = p + \beta(p_T - p_N), \quad p_T^* = p^* + \beta^*(p_T^* - p_N^*)$$

and upon substitution of equation 2 and the above expression into equation 1' we obtain

$$s = \beta(p_T - p_N) - \beta^*(p_r^* - p_N^*) + (m - m^*) - (k - k^*)$$
$$- (\eta y - \eta^* y^*) + (\varepsilon i - \varepsilon^* i^*).$$

An increase in the relative price of tradables tends to depreciate the domestic currency.

4. As was shown by Dornbusch (1976, p. 1167), if θ is determined such that the solution of the system of equations 17–21 satisfied $ds/dt = x$, then the expectation formation assumed in equation 18 is rational.

5. In the present model, m, y, u, i^*, and p^* are all assumed as exogenous and constant throughout the adjustment process. We distinguish their long-run values from the current values, however, because that makes it easier in later analysis to separate the effects of current changes from those arising from changes in expectations.

6. Except for the case where $\delta \rightarrow \infty$. That is, when international commodity arbitrage is perfectly elastic, the PPP relation holds for any short time period. See Amano 1983; Gylfason and Helliwell 1982.

7. This assumption is not necessary, since one can make λ infinite.

8. The regressive expectation becomes rational when $\theta = \phi$.

9. In the case where there are continuous inflations, s cannot stay constant unless $\pi = \pi^*$. Therefore, the long-run equilibrium does not imply a steady state as in the Dornbusch model in the previous section. In general, it is often the case that the concept of long-run equilibrium in empirical applications of monetary approaches is not well specified.

10. See Driskill and Sheffrin 1981, Haynes and Stone 1981, and Frankel 1981 for the controversy over the Frankel approach. Murphy and Van Duyne (1980) applied equations 16 and 38a to the DM-dollar rate and compared the explanatory powers, including a simple PPP equation.

11. Interest payments and receipts are neglected for simplicity of exposition.

12. Alternatively, we may consider that M, B, and F are subject to the wealth constraint $W = M + B + S \cdot F$. Then we have

$$\Delta W - F \cdot \Delta S = \Delta M + \Delta B + S \Delta F$$
$$= P \cdot Y - P \cdot A - S \cdot P^* \cdot \text{Im} - \text{Tx},$$

which determines the accumulation of wealth excluding capital gains from net foreign asset holdings.

13. See Stevens 1976 and Hooper et al. 1982. In a "one country" model where P^*, Y^*, and i^* are supposed exogenous, equilibrium conditions for foreign goods and foreign bonds are unnecessary. In this case the equilibrium condition for home goods determines either P or y, and either two independent equilibrium conditions out of those for domestic bonds, domestic money, and foreign money or two equilibrium conditions for domestic money and the balance of payments can determine S and i.

14. An example of interchanging difference and differential models can be found in Tobin and de Macedo 1980.

15. For an application of the EPA World Economic Model to the EMS see Amano et al. 1983.

16. See Moriguchi 1979 for the description of an earlier version of the KYQ model. The original KYQ/MACRO81 consists of 167 equations (with 76 estimated equations and 91 identities), but we aggregated some blocks and added domestic financial and exchange-rate blocks. The resulting KYQ-FLEX model involves 181 equations (with 86 estimated equations and 95 identities). For details of the KYQ-FLEX model see Amano 1982.

17. Interest rates on time deposits are often revised with a change in the official discount rate, so I introduce a reaction function relating the one-year deposit rate to the official discount rate.

18. The simulation experiment I conducted was an ordinary dynamic multiplier analysis. That is, each model was first run within a common sample period (the first quarter of 1975 to the first quarter of 1981) to produce the standard solution, and then one or a few exogenous variables were shocked.

19. Foreign-Activity variables have not been changed in this simulation. Therefore, we are examining partial effects of foreign interest-rate changes without taking into account the possible concomitant changes in foreign economic activities.

20. For the EPA World Economic Model see, e.g., Amano, Sadahiro, and Sasaki 1981 and Amano, Maruyama, and Yoshitomi 1982.

21. The weighted average exchange-rate index in the U.S. model is determined by an identity from the dollar exchange rates of Canada, Germany, Japan, France, and the U.K. Exchange rates in the Australian model are determined by an official reaction function, and those in the Korean model are treated as exogenous. For detail see Amano 1983.

22. The only case in which an expansion in one country reduces GNP in another country is found in the cross-effects from Germany to the United States in the third and fourth years. This arises because an expansion in Germany has an especially large impact on world commodity prices in our model, which raises U.S. import prices as well as consumer prices and depresses U.S. private consumption. Another exceptional case may be found in the behavior of the French absorption deflator. In the French model, the absorption deflator was explained by the unit labor cost, the import deflator, and the value-added-tax rate, and the estimation result itself appeared reasonable. But when there is an increase in domestic economic activity, total wage bills rise less sharply than real GDP, so a large decline in the unit labor cost is registered. Thus, expansion in real GDP tends to lower domestic prices. This part has been revised in the current version, and in what follows the third row and the third column of table 6.7 are omitted from the discussion.

23. The only exception is the third year in the U.K. model, where a decline in the consumption deflator stimulates private consumption.

24. Here, again, the row and column for France are omitted.

References

Amano, Akihiro. 1979. FLEX 1: A Quarterly Model of the Japanese Flexible Exchange Rates System. Annals of the School of Business Administration, Kobe University, no. 23.

Amano, Akihiro. 1982. A Structural Approach to Capital Flows and Exchange Rates. Discussion paper 179, Kyoto Institute of Economic Research, Kyoto University. An abridged version is published in L. R. Klein and W. E. Krelle, eds., Capital Flows and Exchange Rate Determination, *Zeitschrift für Nationalökonomie*, Suppl. 3 (1983).

Amano, Akihiro. 1983. "Exchange Rate Modelling in the EPA World Economic Model." In P. De Grauwe and T. Peters, eds., *Exchange Rates in Multicountry Econometric Models* (London: Macmillan).

Amano Akihiro, A. Sadahiro, and T. Sasaki. 1981. Structure and Application of the EPA World Economic Model. Discussion Paper 22, Economic Planning Agency.

Amano Akihiro, A. Maruyama, and M. Yoshitomi, eds. 1982. EPA World Economic Model, vols. I and II. EPA World Econometric Model Discussion Paper 11.

Amano Akihiro, N. Yasuhara, F. Hida, and M. Akaike. 1983. Exchange Rate Determination in the EMS: An Econometric Model. Discussion Paper 23, Economic Planning Agency.

Berner, Richard, Peter Clark, Howard Howe, Sung Kwack, and Guy Stevens. 1976. Modeling the International Influences on the U.S. Economy: A Multi-Country Approach. FRB International Finance Discussion Paper 93.

Berner, Richard, Peter Clark, Ernesto Hernández-Catá, Howard Howe, Sung Kwack, and Guy Stevens. 1977. A Multi-Country Model of the International Influences on the U.S. Economy: Preliminary Results. FRB International Finance Discussion Paper 115.

Bilson, John F. O. 1978. "The Monetary Approach to the Exchange Rate: Some Empirical Evidence." *IMF Staff Papers*, vol. 25, no. 1 (March), pp. 48–75.

Bilson, John F. O. 1979a. "Recent Developments in Monetary Models of Exchange Rate Determination." *IMF Staff Papers*, vol. 26, no. 2 (June), pp. 201–223.

Bilson, John F. O. 1979b. "The Deutsche Mark/Dollar Rate," in K. Brunner and A. H. Meltzer, eds., *Policies for Employment, Prices, and Exchange Rates* (Amsterdam: North-Holland).

Branson, William H. 1975. "Comment on M. v. N. Whitman: Global Monetarism and the Monetary Approach to the Balance of Payments." *Brookings Papers on Economic Activity*, vol. 6, no. 3, pp. 537–542.

Branson, William H. 1981. Macroeconomic Determinants of Real Exchange Rates. NBER Working Paper 801.

Branson, William H. and Hannu Halttunen. 1979. "Asset-Market Determination of Exchange Rates: Initial Empirical and Policy Results," in John P. Martin and Alasdair Smith, eds., *Trade and Payments Adjustment under Flexible Exchange Rates* (London: Trade Policy Research Center).

Branson, William H. Hannu Halttunen, and Paul Masson. 1979. "Exchange Rates in the Short-Run: Some Further Results." *European Economic Review*, vol. 12, no. 4 (October), pp. 395–402.

Clements, Kenneth W., and Jacob A. Frenkel. 1980. "Exchange Rates, Money, and Relative Prices: The Dollar-Pound in the 1920s." *Journal of International Economics*, vol. 10, no. 2 (May), pp. 249–262.

Dornbusch, Rudiger. 1976. "Expectations and Exchange Rate Dynamics." *Journal of Political Economy*, vol. 84, no. 6 (December), pp. 1161–1176.

Dornbusch, Rudiger. 1979. "Monetary Policy under Exchange Rate Flexibility," in *Managed Exchange Rate Flexibility* (Federal Reserve Bank of Boston). Reprinted in D. R. Lessard, ed., *International Financial Management: Theory and Application* (Boston: Warren, Gorhan and Lamont).

Dornbusch, Rudiger. 1980. "Exchange Rate Economics: Where Do We Stand?" *Brookings Papers on Economic Activity*, vol. 11, no. 1, pp. 143–185.

Driskill, Robert A. 1981. "Exchange-Rate Dynamics: An Empirical Investigation." *Journal of Political Economy*, vol 89, no. 2 (April), pp. 357–371.

Driskill, Robert A., and Steven M. Sheffrin. (1981). "On the Mark: Comment." *American Economic Review*, vol. 71, no. 5 (December), pp. 1068–1074.

Frankel, Jeffrey A. 1979. "On the Mark: A Theory of Floating Exchange Rates Based on Real Interest Differentials." *American Economic Review*, vol. 69, no. 4 (September), pp. 610–622.

Frankel, Jeffrey A. 1981. "On the Mark: Reply." *American Economic Review*, vol. 71, no. 5 (December), pp. 1075–1082.

Frenkel, Jacob A. 1976. "A Monetary Approach to the Exchange Rates: Doctrinal Aspects and Empirical Evidence." *Scandinavian Journal of Economics*, vol. 78, no. 2, pp. 200–224.

Frenkel, Jacob A. 1980. "Exchange Rate, Prices, and Money: Lessons from the 1920's." *American Economic Review*, vol. 70, no. 2 (May), pp. 235–242.

Fukao, Mitsuhiro. 1981. The Risk Premium in the Foreign Exchange Market. Ph. D. diss., University of Michigan.

Fukao, Mitsuhiro. 1982. The Risk Premium in the Foreign Exchange Market. Bank of Japan Discussion Paper 12. Published in L. R. Klein and W. E. Krelle, eds., Capital Flows and Exchange Rate Determination, *Zeitschrift für Nationalökonomie*, Suppl. 3 (1983).

Girton, Lance, and Don Roper. 1977. "A Monetary Model of Exchange Market Pressure Applied to the Postwar Canadian Experience." *American Economic Review*, vol. 76, no. 4 (September), pp. 537–548.

Gylfason, Thorvaldur, and John F. Helliwell. 1982. A Synthesis of Keynesian, Monetary and Portfolio Approaches to Flexible Exchange Rates. NBER Working Paper 949.

Hacche, Graham, and John Townend. 1981. "Exchange Rates and Monetary Policy:

Modelling Sterling's Effective Exchange Rate, 1972–80." *Oxford Economic Papers*, vol. 33, supplement (July), pp. 201–247.

Haynes, Stephen E., and Joe A. Stone. 1981. "On the Mark: Comment." *American Economic Review*, vol. 71, no. 5 (December).

Helliwell, John F. 1979. "Policy Modeling of Foreign Exchange Rates." *Journal of Policy Modeling*, vol. 1, no. 3 (September), pp. 425–444.

Helliwell, John F., and Tom Maxwell. 1972. "Short-term Capital Flows and the Foreign Exchange Market." *Canadian Journal of Economics*, vol. 5, no. 2 (May), pp. 199–214.

Helliwell, John F., and Tom Maxwell. 1974. "Monetary Interdependence of Canada and the United States under Alternative Exchange Rate Systems," in Robert Z. Aliber, ed., National Monetary Policies and the International Financial System (University of Chicago Press).

Hooper, Peter, and John Morton. 1982. "Fluctuations in the Dollar: A Model of Nominal and Real Exchange Rate Determination." *Journal of International Money and Finance*, vol. 1, no. 1, pp. 39–56.

Hooper, Peter, Richard D. Haas, and Steven A. Symansky. 1983. "Revision of Exchange Rate Determination in the MCM: A Progress Report." In P. De Grauwe and T. Peters, eds., *Exchange Rates in Multicountry Econometric Models* (London: Macmillan).

Hooper, Peter, Richard D. Haas, Steven A. Symansky, and Lois Stekler. 1982. Alternative Approaches to General Equilibrium Modeling of Exchange Rates and Capital Flows: The MCM Experience. Paper presented at 1982 LINK Meeting. Published in L. R. Klein and W. Krelle, eds., Capital Flows and Exchange Rate Determination, *Zeitschrift für Nationalökonomie*, Suppl. 3 (1983).

Isard, Peter. 1978. "Exchange-Rate Determination: A Survey of Popular Views and Recent Models." *Princeton Studies in International Finance*, no. 42 (May).

Kohsaka, Akira. 1982. The Quarterly Yen-Dollar Exchange Rate: 1973–1981. Paper presented at 1982 Annual Meeting of Japan Association of Economics and Econometrics.

Lindbeck, Assar. 1976. "Approaches to Exchange Rate Analysis—An Introduction." *Scandinavian Journal of Economics*, vol. 78, no. 2, pp. 133–145.

Martin, John P., and Paul R. Masson. 1979. Exchange Rates and Portfolio Balance. NBER Working Paper 377.

Moriguchi, Chikashi. 1979. "The Kyoto University Quarterly Model of the Japanese Economy," in S. Ichimura, ed., *Econometric Models of Asian Countries* (Center for Southeast Asian Studies, Kyoto University).

Murphy, Robert G., and Carl Van Duyne. 1980. "Asset Market Approaches to Exchange Rate Determination: A Comparative Analysis." *Weltwirtschaftliches Archiv*, vol. 116, no. 4, pp. 627–655.

Mussa, Michael. 1979. "Macroeconomic Interdependence and the Exchange Rate Regime," in R. Dornbusch and J. Frenkel, eds., *International Economic Policy: Theory and Evidence* (Baltimore: Johns Hopkins University Press).

Niehans, Jürg. 1977. "Exchange Rate Dynamics with Stock/Flow Interaction." *Journal of Political Economy*, vol. 85, no. 6 (December), pp. 1245–1257.

Rodriguez, Carlos Alfredo. 1980. "The Role of Trade Flows in Exchange Rate Determination: A Rational Expectations Approach." *Journal of Political Economy*, vol. 88, no. 6 (December). pp. 1148–1158.

Sawyer J. A., J. L. Carr, N. K. Choudhry, G. V. Jump, Y. R. Kotowitz, and J. W. L. Winder. 1976. "The TRACE Mark IIIR Annual Model of the Canadian Economy," in Jean L. Waelbroeck, ed., *The Models of Project LINK* (Amsterdam: North-Holland).

Schadler, Susan. 1977. "Sources of Exchange Rate Variability: Theory and Empirical Evidence." *IMF Staff Papers*, vol. 24, no. 2 (July), pp. 253–296.

Stevens, Guy V. G. 1976. Balance of Payments Equations and Exchange Rate Determination. FRB International Finance Discussion Paper 95.

Tobin, James, and Jorge B. de Macedo. 1980. "The Short-run Macroeconomics of Floating Exchange Rates: An Exposition," in John S. Chipman and Charles P. Kindleberger, eds., *Flexible Exchange Rates and the Balance of Payments* (Amsterdam: North-Holland).

Urdang, E. S. 1978. An International Flow of Funds Model with An Endogenous Exchange Rate. Mimeographed.

Comments

Charles Freedman

It is now about 10 years since the beginning of generalized floating and 13 years since the Canadian dollar was set free to float for the second time in the postwar period. They have been years of substantial volatility in the exchange markets, with rather long cycles in both nominal and real exchange rates. Partly in response to these developments, there has been a rapid development of the theoretical and empirical literature on exchange-rate determination, the role of exchange-rate movements in transmitting monetary impulses internationally, the insulation properties of flexible exchange rates (or the absence thereof) in response to different types of shocks, and the possible role of exchange rates as information variables or intermediate targets for monetary policy. Professor Amano, on whose paper I will concentrate my remarks, has presented a very interesting survey that focuses on the first three of these elements. The determination of exchange rates is treated theoretically while the role of the exchange rate in transmitting monetary impulses across borders and the insulation properties of flexible exchange rates are examined with the help of two empirical models: one of the Japanese economy, and a second which incorporates the principal trading countries of the world.

How can we characterize the decade of floating exchange rates? One important conclusion to be drawn from the experience is that in a floating-rate world the stability of nominal and real exchange rates depends on macroeconomic policies in the various countries being fairly similar in nature. In the face of the very divergent policy paths in different countries (themselves a result of a mix of different economic environments, institutional arrangements, and so on), we have seen at times long gradual cycles and at times dramatic shifts in the relative values of currencies. On some occasions the main driving force behind the movement in currency values has been changes in relative interest rates, on other occasions it has been changes in inflationary expectations and anticipations of future government policies, and on yet other occasions it appears to have been actual and anticipated current-account developments that have played the major role.

In response to these developments in the actual behavior of exchange rates there have been corresponding developments in the theoretical approaches to exchange-rate determination. As Professor Amano has very ably shown in his survey of models of exchange-rate determination, what began as sharply different views of the world have, with relaxation of some of the assumptions of the various models, tended to a rather marked convergence over time.

The earliest version of the monetary approach to exchange-rate determination was based on some very strong assumptions: complete price flexibility in the short run and instantaneous purchasing-power parity. The later Dornbusch version of exchange-rate determination relaxed these assumptions and yielded overshooting of exchange rates. One of the key building blocks in Dornbusch's own early treatment was that foreign and domestic securities are perfect substitutes. This assumption in turn has also been relaxed in a variety of models in which attention has been focused on risk premia, which are generally assumed to be related to the size of net domestic holdings of foreign assets.

Four other elements have played more or less important roles in various analyses. First, the modeling of the real exchange rate has grown more complex. Second, the treatment of expectations has grown increasingly sophisticated, especially in its analysis of "news." Third, there has been more attention paid to the horizon of analysis, particularly to stock-flow considerations and the dynamics of the movement from the instantaneous short-run equilibrium to the longer run in which changes in spending flows brought about by the initial exchange-rate movements play an important part. Fourth, over time there has been an increase in emphasis on the role of the current account. The latter has been introduced into the analysis of exchange rate determination in several ways: through its effect on the stock of wealth, through the flow of interest payments or receipts resulting from the change in debt, through the risk premium associated with the stock of outstanding debt, and through its role as a signal of changes in tastes, competitiveness, and so on that would necessitate a change in the real exchange rate in the longer run. The important point in these developments is that theory has been able to incorporate empirical insights, such that purchasing-power parity does not hold in the short run, that the current account does somehow play a role in exchange-rate determination, and that domestic and foreign assets are not perfect substitutes.

What is the current situation? We have a wide variety of theoretical models from which to choose, but the thrust to theoretical convergence is clear. Empirically, the various models of exchange-rate determination have been rather disappointing in their ability to explain the behavior of the 1970s, and attention has turned to the more technical and somewhat less interesting question of exchange-market efficiency. It appears from work done at the Bank of Canada that the joint hypothesis of market efficiency and no time-varying risk premium must be rejected. This leaves us with two possible conclusions: Either markets are not efficient or movements in the risk premium played an important role over the 1970s. Unfortunately there has been little success thus far in relating the risk premium to theoretically appropriate explanatory variables such as the stock of net foreign assets held by residents or the stock of net domestic assets held by foreigners. This is an important area for future research. Thus, despite convergence in theoretical models, the empirical work done so far has been somewhat disappointing, at least in terms of our ability to explain exchange-rate movements.

Before leaving the area of exchange-rate determination, I would like to mention Professor Amano's very clear exposition of the relationship between the balance-of-payments equation and the other equations in a fully identified structural model. Since the balance-of-payments equation is simply a transformation of the other equations in the model, it does not matter from a theoretical point of view, as he argues, whether we use that equation or, say, the demand for domestic bonds in the analysis of exchange-rate movements. Nor, in principle, does it matter empirically. However, in practice, I suspect it does make a difference empirically which equation is dropped and which is used, because the particular explanatory variables that researchers normally tend to use differ between equations and because the tendency to drop insignificant variables differs depending on the equation we started from.

With regard to the role of exchange-rate movements in transmitting monetary (and, for that matter, fiscal) policy impulses, I noted with interest that the exchange rate plays the key empirical role in the Japanese KYQ-FLEX model, just as it does in the Canadian models. That is, in comparing the four simulations Professor Amano has set out, it is evident that the difference in outcomes between worlds with fixed and flexible exchange rates is far greater than that between a world in which the monetary authority uses an interest-rate rule and one in which it uses a money rule. I suspect that the latter difference is understated by the nature of the model (e.g., the model may not have appropriate long-run properties, such as a long-run vertical Phillips curve). Nonetheless, the results are a striking indication that in a small or even a reasonably large open economy much of the effect of monetary policy works through the exchange rate. That this is true of even a large economy has been shown by the United States in the last couple of years. High real interest rates have resulted in a high real exchange rate, which in turn has had substantial effects on prices and on real output. Furthermore, the model points out that very large movements in exchange rates are possible when real interest rates change for any length of time. I was puzzled, however, by the particular numbers in some of the tables. For example, the cyclical movement over time in the exchange rate shown in table 6.6 (model B) seems rather odd.

Another aspect of these simulations that is of interest is the response of exchange rates to an expansionary fiscal shock with the money supply held constant. There are offsetting current-account effects (tendency to depreciation) and capital-account effects (tendency to appreciation). In Amano's simulations, the former dominate and we get a depreciation of the currency, particularly in the long run.

Returning to the monetary shock, I would suggest that Professor Amano add one more simulation to the series of shocked simulations of the EPA World Finance Model: a simulation showing the effects of a rise in interest rates in all countries. Whereas monetary policy can be substantially more powerful under flexible exchange rates than under fixed exchange rates for one country, for all countries together this cannot be the case, and the effect on world output and prices of a universal rise in interest rates should be very similar under flexible and under fixed rates. It would also be interesting to see whether there are differences in the distribution of effects across countries under the two regimes.

There has been much theoretical work over the last few years on the question of why the flexible exchange rate has not provided the insulating properties expected of it. The focus of the analysis has been on the various types of shocks, and a number of categorizations have been proposed: domestic versus external shocks, real versus nominal shocks, temporary versus permanent shocks, and supply versus demand shocks. The theoretical results, as illustrated by Professor Amano's simulations, are that flexible exchange rates do insulate against certain types of shocks but not against others and that the insulation properties may vary with length of horizon. For example, a domestic money-supply shock leads in the long run to corresponding increases in prices and in the exchange rate, but in the intermediate run there are effects on interest rates, output, and the real exchange rate.

A final and relatively recent focus of research in the exchange-rate area has been the possible role for exchange rates as information variables or intermediate targets of monetary policy. For example, during the debate in the United Kingdom in the late 1970s as to whether monetary policy was loose or tight, the behavior of the exchange rate was adduced as a major piece of evidence in favor of the latter interpretation. The formal treatment of this problem in the literature has built mainly on the Poole approach to the analysis of intermediate targets. It has typically involved the minimization of output variance under different exchange-rate and money-supply rules in the face of various shocks. Not surprisingly, the usual result has been that for certain shocks a money rule dominates and for certain shocks an exchange-rate rule dominates. In other versions of the model an intermediate policy, such as a controlled float, proves to be better than either a pure float or a fixed exchange rate.

Unfortunately, from a practical policy point of view, the literature developed thus far has not been overly helpful. One aspect of much of the literature that lessens its usefulness is the focus on minimization of the variance of output. In practice, the recent consideration of the role of the exchange rate as an intermediate target has derived principally from the potential effect on inflation of exchange-rate movements arising from shocks to the system at a time when policy was directed to slowing the rate of inflation. The type of model required to deal with this type of question is one in which shocks are superimposed on a disinflationary path and the analysis focuses on the effect of the shocks on the rate of inflation. More important, the Poole-type assumption made throughout this literature that the authorities have equally good knowledge of all sectors of the economy is precisely what is at issue in the policy discussion. If one assumes that there is "diffuse uncertainty" about most of the economy but the demand-for-money equation is believed to be stable, it is most unlikely that any policy will dominate the fixed-money-rule policy. However, it can be argued that there are certain types of shocks for which the authorities have a reasonably good ability to trace out the economic results, and hence that these shocks can be partially offset whereas the same assertion cannot be made for other types of shocks. In the case of the latter, a simple unchanged target for the monetary aggregate is probably the preferred policy. However, in the case of the former, one might be able to improve on the simple money rule by integrating the exchange rate into the policy process as part of a Poole-type combination policy. The challenge to research is to distinguish between the two types of shocks and to specify precisely how exchange rates can be used in the latter case.

Comments

Cesare Caranza

A main conclusion reached by both Professor Amano and Professor Darby is that exchange-rate flexibility has brought about greater autonomy in national macroeconomic management. In Professor Amano's words, "the bottling up or insulation effects of exchange-rate flexibility are far from perfect, but the pattern of international transmission of economic fluctuations from one country to another is not as straight or uniform as in the fixed-exchange-rate system," even if "exchange-rate flexibility has strengthened international economic interdependence in some other aspects, . . . particularly . . . when major shocks take the form of changes in monetary conditions."

It seems to me that they are right to be cautious in this respect, for in light of the experience of the past 10 years the hope that with floating exchange rates monetary policy could be almost exclusively oriented to domestic objectives has hardly been fulfilled.

Flexible exchange rates clearly facilitated the absorption of the oil and wage shocks of the 1970s. However, we have learned that any attempt at setting domestic monetary targets not consistent with those of the dominant world or regional economy can lead to excessive exchange-rate changes, on the basis of relative developments in economic fundamentals, with considerable costs in terms of resource misallocation and structural distortions.

If it is accepted that the exchange rate cannot be completely disregarded, then monetary policy in a medium-size open economy remains tightly constrained by external balance considerations. Take Italy as an example.

The Italian economy is highly open to international trade and, in particular, is heavily dependent on imports for the supply of crucial and highly price-inelastic inputs, such as energy. The relevance of this factor is enhanced by the existence of a highly responsive wage-indexation system. Furthermore, monetary management is complicated by the level of PSBR, whose ratio to GDP reached 16 percent in 1982. Thus, the external shocks of the 1970s came on top of serious domestic imbalances, leading to a sustained widening of the inflation differential with Italy's major trading partners.

Against this background, it has been an objective of Italy's exchange-rate policy to maintain the country's competitive position. However, in the pursuit of this objective the monetary authorities have been guided by the consideration that a relatively stable rate of exchange can represent a powerful restraint on domestic costs and prices. This has meant in practice that the central bank has not attempted to defend particular rates of parities that were no longer justified by the evolution of Italy's competitive position, but at the same time it has not made aggressive use of the exchange rate as an instrument of adjustment, both as a matter of principle and because of its negative repercussions on domestic inflation.

Italy's participation in the EMS since 1979 can in fact be viewed as a "strong currency option," even if the persistence of a wide inflation differential with other EEC countries has forced since then a number of exchange-rate adjustments. In my view the EMS experience has been useful in putting a rein on short-term movements of the exchange rate and as an indirect boundary to domestic cost and price pressures.

However, in order to stabilize the exchange rate within the EMS, Italy had to accept larger and more frequent interest-rate fluctuations—i.e., to adapt domestic monetary conditions to those prevailing abroad. The same was true for other EEC countries. To some extent this has been true for the Deutschmark vis à vis the dollar.

There is no sense of frustration in admitting that the monetary norm is set by the dominant economy, but it is important to be well aware of these international linkages among monetary policies, even in a world of flexible exchange rates, when monetary policies are designed in the leading industrial countries.

Comments

Georg Rich

The interesting and comprehensive chapters by Professors Amano and Darby are linked by a common theme. Both authors address the question how the shift from fixed to floating exchange rates has affected the ability of central banks to attain such internal policy objectives as price stability and a high level of employment. Moreover, they appear to reach very similar conclusions although their approaches are rather different.

Professor Amano presents two full-fledged macroeconometric models. The first one is confined to the Japanese economy, while the second one is designed to capture the economic linkages among nine major industrialized countries. These models are employed to simulate the impact on domestic prices, employment, and other endogenous variables of domestic monetary and fiscal policies, as well as of a variety of foreign disturbances. He concludes that exchange-rate flexibility has enhanced the potency of domestic monetary and fiscal policies but has also created new forms of international economic interdependence. In particular, he finds—somewhat surprisingly to a Swiss observer—that under fixed exchange rates the Japanese economy, at least in the short run, was more effectively insulated from foreign monetary disturbances than under the present system of floating.

Professor Darby focuses his attention on the effectiveness of monetary policy under the Bretton Woods system of fixed exchange rates. Examining the experience of eight medium-size and large industrial nations, he concludes that under the Bretton Woods system price arbitrage between national goods and assets markets was far from perfect, allowing the central banks, within limits, to pursue autonomous monetary policies. However, the degree of autonomy afforded to central banks was not as great as under the present system of floating.

Although I very much enjoyed reading the two chapters, I face a difficult task as a discussant. Both chapters summarize extensive empirical work but do not provide more than a cursory discussion of the underlying models and econometric techniques. For the derivation of the results, the reader is referred to unpublished papers and books that were not available to me. However, even if I had been able to scrutinize the quoted unpublished sources, I doubt that the organizers of this conference would have expected me to comment upon a book in press, an econometric model of Japan, and a 1,900-equation world model.

Considering these difficulties, I will only comment upon three issues, two minor ones and a major one. The first issue concerns Professor Darby's conclusion as to the imperfect substitutability of goods and assets under the Bretton Woods system. Although I do not wish to question the validity of that conclusion, I nonetheless wonder whether the evidence on substitutability, accumulated during the Bretton Woods era, would still be relevant if the industrial countries were to return to fixed exchange rates in the near future. Swiss experience—which I admit Professor Darby did not consider—suggests that the substitutability of domestic and foreign assets has increased noticeably since the 1960s. During the Bretton Woods era, domestic short-term interest rates were only loosely related to corresponding interest rates on Euro-Swiss-franc assets (that is, Swiss-franc loans and deposits granted or accepted by banks outside Switzerland). However, a very close link existed between Euro-Swiss-franc and Eurodollar rates. Evidently, asset substitutability was not sufficiently strong to equalize Swiss and foreign interest rates. In the early 1970s, these interest-rate patterns changed dramatically. Because of the transition to a floating Swiss franc, the link between Euro-Swiss-franc and Eurodollar rates was severed. However, domestic short-term interest rates became closely tied to Euro-Swiss-franc rates. This piece of evidence suggests that Euromarket growth has enhanced the substitutability of Swiss and foreign short-term assets, provided the latter are denominated in Swiss francs.

As to the second issue, I am intrigued by Professor Amano's finding that, in the short run, a foreign monetary disturbance such as a cut in foreign interest rates affects Japanese interest rates, real income, and prices more strongly under floating than under fixed exchange rates. Owing to substantial over-shooting, the floating yen, in the short run, tends to amplify the impact of the foreign monetary disturbance on the domestic economy. Moreover, Professor Amano's study suggests that Japanese monetary authorities, by intervening on the foreign exchange market, are able to moderate exchange-rate over-shooting significantly.

For a Swiss observer, these conclusions are interesting because they con-trast sharply with Swiss experience in two respects. First, although the Swiss economy is vulnerable to prolonged deviations in the Swiss franc exchange rate from purchasing-power parity, it does not seem to be very sensitive to exchange-rate overshooting in the short run. Real exports and imports, as well as real GDP, in particular, appear to respond to exchange-rate movements only with a very long time lag. Second, official intervention on the foreign exchange market does not strongly affect the Swiss franc exchange rate unless the Swiss National Bank (SNB) fixes a specific exchange-rate target. Such a target, however, poses an awkward dilemma for the SNB: The purchases and sales of foreign currencies required to reach the exchange-rate target may be so large that the SNB may not be able to neutralize the effect of the interventions on the domestic monetary base. Should the monetary base change, official intervention will be ineffective in shielding the Swiss economy from foreign monetary disturbances. The exchange rate will be stabilized, but the Swiss economy will now be exposed to the foreign monetary disturbances by way of increased fluctuations in the domestic monetary base.

My last and fundamental comment concerns the policy implications of Professor Darby's research. Even if arbitrage between national goods and asset markets were not to operate as perfectly as some economists seem to believe, I doubt that Darby's evidence would prompt a country such as Switzerland to return to fixed exchange rates. The degree to which goods and assets are substitutes internationally has little bearing on the question whether a country should opt for fixed or flexible exchange rates. Under a fixed-rate regime, a central bank such as the SNB is powerless in attaining its domestic objectives, no matter whether goods and assets are perfect or imperfect substitutes. The principal objective of Swiss monetary policy is price stability, a goal the SNB tries to attain by controlling tightly the growth in the monetary base. Without a floating exchange rate, this goal is beyond our reach unless prices are stable in the rest of the world. Under a fixed-rate regime, any attempt to keep prices in Switzerland stable while they rise elsewhere would result in mounting current-account and balance-of-payments surpluses. Clearly, these surpluses would emerge even if there were no capital flows between Switzerland and abroad and if the degree of substitutability between Swiss and foreign goods were modest. The SNB would not be able to sterilize the attendant increase in its foreign-exchange reserve forever; sooner or later it would be forced to expand the money stock in order to restore balance-of-payments equilibrium. The surge in the money stock, in turn, would cause domestic prices to rise in line with foreign inflation. Thus, Professor Darby's findings offer no comfort to a central bank striving simultaneously to maintain a fixed exchange rate and to insulate the home economy from foreign inflation.

Comments

H. H. van Wijk

The chapters by Professor Darby and Professor Amano contain an extensive theoretical survey, from both a national and an international standpoint, of the intricate external effects of domestic policy changes. Especially in the case of floating exchange rates the subject matter becomes very complicated, and Professor Darby is right when he apprehends that his analysis will seem maddeningly tentative to the policy maker. Consequently, the task of commenting on these chapters is not an easy one. It cannot be my ambition to enter into a theoretical discussion with the authors. Rather, I shall try to put forward the views held by the policy makers in the Netherlands on some of the issues raised. These views reflect the specific conditions of a small, extremely open economy, and do not necessarily fit in with those set out in the two chapters.

A first policy view determined by the nature of the Netherlands' economy concerns the relative importance to be assigned to monetary policy. The general opinion is that monetary policy should not play a predominant role. What is needed is a policy mix, made up of monetary, budgetary, and incomes policy. Monetary policy can be employed to counter demand-pull inflation and to prevent balance-of-payments disturbances ensuing from excess demand, which endanger the external value of the currency. But once an inflationary spiral has been set in motion, this spiral should be combated by a policy of voluntary or imposed wage restraint rather than by a restrictive monetary policy, which would unduly reduce economic activity. In fact, the favorable results achieved in recent years in the fight against inflation in the Netherlands are largely attributable to incomes policy.

Most economists agree that individual countries are more independent in the conduct of their economic policies under floating exchange rates than under fixed rates. Professor Darby and Professor Amano pay attention to this presumption, and I understand that they endorse it in the main. As small and relatively open economies naturally are less independent in their behavior than large and relatively closed economies, it might be expected that the Netherlands would be in favor of floating exchange rates. However, the opposite is true. Authorities and academics in my country have a clear preference for a regime of fixed rates. This preference, which also underlies the participation of the Netherlands in the successive European exchange-rate agreements, has various reasons. It is obvious that business people engaged in international trade benefit from the greatest possible elimination of uncertainty about exchange-rate movements. However, a more interesting consideration is that membership in a currency bloc imposes the discipline to pursue an economic policy that converges with that of the other members of the bloc. Since the beginning of the 1970s, it has particularly been the German economy that has served as an example for our policy makers. It can be concluded that the Netherlands has deliberately opted for a reduction of independence, because it is feared that the wider room for maneuvering inherent in floating rates might be abused by politicians.

In spite of the Netherlands' participation in the successive monetary agreements, the guilder has undergone an effective appreciation of about 25 percent since the collapse of the Bretton Woods system. In the first place, the guilder has gone up, together with the Deutsche mark, against most of the outside currencies. Moreover, the guilder and the Deutsche mark were revalued on several occasions against the currencies of other participants in the monetary agreements.

According to Professor Darby and Professor Amano, the prevailing view among theorists is that purchasing-power parity normally does not hold. In Netherlands practice, a distinction is made between the effects of an autonomous change in the relative rate of inflation and the effects of a change in the (nominal) exchange rate. In the case of a decrease in the inflation rate (relative to other countries), the authorities, as well as most theorists, presume that the consequent upward pressure on the exchange rate can be checked, so that a real depreciation of the country's own currency and a strengthening of its competitive position will ensue. This theory seems to be borne out by experience. For many years, attempts have been made in the Netherlands to reduce domestic costs, relative to other countries, with the aid of incomes policy. It turns out that these attempts have not been undone by the continuous nominal appreciation of the guilder. With respect to the currencies of the competitor countries as a group, the guilder has undergone a real depreciation of 13 percent since 1977.

In the case of an autonomous change in the exchange rate, opinions about the possible effects differ. There are two views. The proponents of the first argue that such a change will influence the real aggregates in the economy.

They therefore advocate a devaluation of the guilder so as to strengthen the competitive position of Netherlands industry, and they view with concern the continuing nominal appreciation of the guilder against most currencies other than the Deutsche mark since 1971. The advocates of the second view (among them the Netherlands Bank) do not deny that a nominal change in the exchange rate will influence the competitive position in the short term, but they point out that a devaluation will, in the longer run, lead to such an increase in domestic costs that the initial competitive advantage will be completely eliminated. In the reverse situation, a nominal appreciation of the guilder will, in the longer term, bring about a relative reduction in the domestic cost level. In this view, movements in the nominal exchange rate affect only the nominal aggregates in the economy and not the real aggregates.

Professor Darby inquires about the degree to which domestic monetary policy might be frustrated by compensatory capital flows. Related to this issue is the question of the extent to which domestic monetary policy and exchange-rate policy can be pursued independently. In both respects the experiences of the Netherlands monetary authorities are satisfying. Consequently, it might be worthwhile to examine more closely the method of monetary policy that has gradually developed in the Netherlands. It can be characterized as follows:

● The aim is not to bring about a specific interest-rate level but to control the monetary aggregate.

● The monetary aggregate is controlled not by means of a monetary base but by imposing direct limits on domestic money creation.

● Controlling the liquidity of the banks is an additional instrument that can be used for exchange-rate policy.

About the first characteristic I can be brief. Monetary policy is traditionally directed at keeping the national liquidity ratio (the monetary aggregate scaled by national income) at a level at which it does not cause undesired impulses to economic behavior. In periods of excess demand, a reduction of the ratio is aimed for. In periods marked by recession and current-account surpluses, the national liquidity ratio is permitted to go up a little. This goal is achieved by attuning money creation as finely as possible to the medium-term growth of national income in volume terms, augmented by price rises that have to be considered inevitable. A possible outflow of liquidity as a result of a deficit on the current account can contribute to the desired short-term monetary tightening.

The second characteristic of monetary policy in the Netherlands is more fundamental, as it implies that the interest-rate level is not an essential part of some transmission mechanism underlying the money supply. In times when a restrictive policy is considered necessary, the Netherlands Bank uses its statutory powers to impose a ceiling on the banks' domestic assets. Long-term funds raised or received by the banks may be used for lending without restriction. In other words, lending by the banking system is restricted to the extent that it is money-creating, and is not restricted to the extent that it is financed from long-term funds. The result is that any demand for credit over and above the volume allowable is shifted to the capital market, where it may push up long-term interest rates. Experience has shown that the inflow of foreign capital consequent on the rise in interest rates is not so extensive that the policy is defeated. On the contrary, some inflow is generally considered helpful because of its contribution to the restoration of balance-of-payments equilibrium and the defense of the exchange rate.

For a better understanding of the third characteristic mentioned, it must be noted that in the Netherlands there has always been a distinct boundary between the market for short-term money and that for long-term funds. Roughly speaking, paper traded in the money market has an original term to maturity of less than 2 years, whereas capital-market paper almost invariably has an average original term of 5 years or more. The system of redeeming long-term loans through drawings means that matured paper will not easily assume the function of money-market paper.

Given this boundary between the money market and the capital market, the Netherlands Bank controls the liquidity of the banking system in such a manner that short-term interest rates are in normal proportion to long-term rates, with due attention given to the exchange rate. In exceptional circumstances a tightening of money-market policy will cause short-term interest rates to rise temporarily to well above capital-market rates.

In the words of the former president of the Netherlands Bank, Dr. Zijlstra: "The basic monetary policy designed to control the money supply affects this control on a medium-term basis, influences long-term interest rates, and thus also, of course, contributes to achieving overall equilibrium on the balance of payments. The money-market policy is a short-term and complementary one; it avoids major fluctuations in short-term interest rates whenever possible and, hence, also tries to prevent exchange-rate movements which are not a reflection of the underlying position and development of the balance of payments." (Per Jacobsson lecture, 1981).

In order to strengthten confidence in the stability of the exchange rate, the Netherlands Bank mostly aims at keeping the guilder in a position that is either in the higher regions of the European Monetary System band or near the Deutsche mark.

POLICIES TO OVERCOME STAGFLATION

7   "Reaganomics" and Credibility

Thomas J. Sargent

Howard: Dandy, the Vikings had the momentum throughout the first half. Let's see if the momentum stays with the Vikes into the second half. Otherwise, it's going to be a long night for the Bears.

Dandy Don: Yes, Howard. It'll also be interesting to see if the Bears continue to be confused by the new formation that Bud Grant has installed for this game. We haven't seen the Vikings throw play-action passes as much as they have this evening, and this has surprised the Bears. If the Bears can figure out the Vikes' new strategy and adjust to it, it will be a new ball game.

Monday Night Football

An offensive football team is a collection of individuals with a common objective: to score a touchdown. This objective is attained by the cooperation of eleven players, each of whom is ultimately in control of his own actions. The effectiveness of any one player's actions depends intricately on the actions of his teammates. If the quarterback decides to throw the ball 30 yards downfield to the right side on a count of three, it is necessary for success that a receiver run a pass pattern that will place him in a position to catch the ball. If the quarterback calls a "keeper" and runs around the end, it is important that the end not run a pass pattern but that he block. Thus, the quarterback and the end, and all the other players, face a problem of coordination. It will not do to simply announce vague objectives in the huddle, such as "Let's score a touchdown." Instead, somehow each player must reach a precise understanding of what each of his colleagues is planning to do on the next play and of the "contingency plans" that each player will use as the play develops or breaks down. All football teams (except apparently one that I root for) accomplish this coordination task by giving one player, either the quarterback or a player just sent in by the coach, the authority to direct the actions of all the others by calling the play. A football team is an example of a system for which complete decentralization or "laissez faire" is not a good idea.

The example from football contains important lessons about making macroeconomic policy. Within a single country, the authorities who are charged with responsibility for making monetary and fiscal policy are very much in the position of the end and the quarterback, for their activities must be coordinated, one way or the other, and their objectives are presumably identical. In the world as a whole, the monetary and fiscal authorities of different countries have to somehow coordinate their policies, since one country's choices of monetary and fiscal strategies influence the options open to the others so long as there is some freedom to exchange goods and make loans across borders. However, despite the interrelated consequences of their actions upon a common system, fiscal and monetary authorities from different countries sometimes have differing and even opposing goals. (Sometimes the goals may even seem so opposed that the proper analogy is not to a quarterback and an end but to two opposing football teams—say the Cowboys and the Redskins.) Presumably, the example of the quarterback and the end rings truest for the coordination of monetary and fiscal policy within one country, for the assumption that the authorities share common objectives is better here than in the international case.

This chapter views the monetary and fiscal authorities of a single country as a "team" and judges their patterns of behavior against standards absorbed from the sports pages. This view provides a broad framework for summarizing classic doctrines and controversies in government finance, and also serves as a basis for criticizing the way in which monetary and fiscal policies have been coordinated *de facto* in the United States over the last several years.

I shall begin with a few formal definitions of concepts that will help to clarify the analogy between the quarterback-end problem and the monetary-fiscal problem.

Dynamic Games

A *game* consists of a collection of players and a set of rules specifying rewards and penalties. A *dynamic game* is one that requires time to complete and whose current score depends on past actions of the various players. In life, most games are dynamic.

Each player in a game is supposed to have a goal or objective that depends on the rewards and penalties specified in the rules of the game. This goal may be idiosyncratic (such as personal glory or personal profit) or altruistic (such as the success of one's team or country). A *team game* is one in which two or more players have a common objective. Football and soccer are team games. So, perhaps, is the game of managing a country's monetary and fiscal affairs, at least if those in charge have in mind a common objective.

Each player in a dynamic game tries to achieve his objective by choosing a *strategy*. A strategy is defined as a rule that describes how a player's actions during the game depend on the information he receives during the course of the game. Another term for a player's strategy is *contingency plan*. This term evokes the notion that each action taken by a player ought to depend on the situation as it is understood when that action is executed. A strategy relates a player's actions over time into a sensible pattern. Since time elapses during a dynamic game, whether a single action (or *move*) is a good one cannot be judged in isolation from past and subsequently planned moves.

In general, each player chooses his strategy given his perception of the strategies of other players and given his perception of the influence that his own choice of strategy has on the strategies chosen by other players. If player A correctly believes that he influences the choice of player B's strategy, then player A is said to be *dominant* relative to player B. To complete a description of a dynamic game, it is necessary to specify a structure of dominance across the players in the game. An *equilibrium* or *solution* of a dynamic game is a structure of dominance and a collection of strategies of all the agents in the game that maximize their respective objective functions, subject to each player's perception of the strategies of all the remaining agents. Evidently, a solution of a dynamic game requires that all agents' perceptions of the structure of dominance be consistent and that their chosen strategies be mutually feasible, in the sense of being consistent with the physical technologies in place and with the strategies being employed by the other agents.

Alternative structures of dominance give rise to different ways of playing a game, or really different games. For example, in a *Nash equilibrium* each agent in the game takes the strategies of the other agents as given and beyond his influence. Nash players interact in this way despite the fact that each player's choice of strategy influences the strategies chosen by all the other players. In a *Stackelberg* or *dominant-player* equilibrium, one player takes into account the influence that his choice of strategy has on the strategies of the remaining players; the remaining players act as followers and ignore the influence of their strategies on the dominant player's strategy. Usually, the dominant player is imagined to be large and powerful and the followers are imagined to be individually weak, numerous, and dispersed. If there is a small number of powerful players (say, two), then possibilities exist for a struggle between them for dominance. It can happen that each of two players wants to be dominant and wants the other player to act as a follower. If both sides try to implement their desired strategies, an impasse, or a state of *Stackelberg warfare* exists. Stackelberg warfare is not an equilibrium or a solution of the game, because the wishes and perceptions on which the two players are acting are not mutually consistent. Situations of Stackelberg warfare are pathologies and represent attempts to implement disorderly and infeasible coordination schemes. Below, I shall assert that recent American monetary and fiscal policy has been in a state of Stackelberg warfare.

A fundamental and general principle that emerges from the study of dynamic games is that agents' strategies are interdependent. Interdependence of strategies generally holds regardless of the structure of dominance, though the exact forms of dependence will hinge on it. In football, the principle of strategic interdependence is reflected in the need for a quarterback and an end to coordinate their strategies. It is also reflected in the coordination problem facing monetary and fiscal authorities.

The reader who is familiar with the game of football will be able to recognize how the categories defined above apply to football. From the viewpoint of a single football team, football is a dynamic team game in which each player's optimal strategy depends on the optimal strategies of the other players as well as on the strategy being used by the opposing team and the rules set by the league. The optimal strategy for a given team depends on the rules of the game and on the strategies chosen by the opposing team. Since my main purpose is to analyze the macroeconomy and not the National Football League, I will not pursue the analysis of football as a dynamic game any further here. Instead, I shall now describe aspects of the economy of a single country as a dynamic game.

An Economy as a Dynamic Game

The economy or game is imagined to consist of three players: the public, the monetary authority, and the fiscal authority. The public consists of people, who are organized into households, agencies of the government, and corporations and who are the ultimate beneficiaries of all economic activity. The public makes decisions about consumption, investment, and private employment and pays the taxes imposed on it by the fiscal authority. The public also sets the terms on which it will accumulate government debts of various forms. The fiscal authority makes decisions about public expenditures and about the rates at which taxes are to be collected from the public. By making these decisions, the fiscal authority determines the rate of government deficit—the amount by which government expenditures exceed tax collections.[1] The deficit is financed by the issuing of government debt, either in the interest-bearing form of government bonds or in the non-interest-bearing form of currency and bank reserves (often called "high-powered money"). The decision about the composition of the debt as between bonds of various maturities and currency or high-powered money is, at each point in time, under the control of the monetary authority. The monetary authority exercises this control through its authority to engage in open-market exchanges of one kind of public debt for another. Thus, while the fiscal authority influences the rate of addition to the public debt, the monetary authority determines its composition. *Debt management* is a term that is aptly used to describe what the monetary authority does.[2]

Macroeconomic analysis of the rational-expectations variety aims to study the interactions of these three classes of agents as a dynamic team game. Abstracting from distributional effects across members of the public (according to a long tradition in macroeconomics), the monetary and fiscal authorities are imagined to share common objectives with the public and with each other. These common objectives make it a team situation. The aspect that all three players are making decisions that affect the future state of the system makes it a dynamic game. Thus, the public chooses investment rates in physical and human capital and the terms on which it is willing to accumulate various amounts and types of government debt, the fiscal authority determines the current and the prospective state of total government indebtedness, and the monetary authority determines the composition of the debt.

I now put this structure of ideas to work by using it to analyze a classic issue of government finance that is important today: the inflationary consequences of government deficits and of alternative ways of financing them.

Government expenditures can be financed by alternative combinations of levying taxes, borrowing in interest-bearing form, and printing high-powered money. The consequences for the price-level path of alternative methods of financing a given stream of government expenditures can differ, and in ways that depend on how the strategies of the public and of the fiscal and monetary authorities are imagined to interact. To discuss these consequences, we need models of the decision strategies of each of our three groups of agents and of their interactions. We can describe some of the major issues with the aid of simple strategic models for each of our players.

In the tradition of Keynes, the public is assumed to be willing to hold interest-bearing government debt on the same terms on which it holds private evidences of indebtedness. This means that public borrowing is assumed to pay the same interest rate as private borrowings and that the total amount of government and private borrowing must be consistent with the public's limited capacity to accumulate wealth. Let us assume that all interest-bearing government debt is one period in maturity, and let us denote the one-period real pre-tax net rate of return on private securities between t and $t + 1$ as $r(t)$. We assume that $r(t)$ is an exogenous sequence and that $r(t)$ is greater than 0. For simplicity, we assume an economy that is not growing over time. We also abstract from uncertainty.

The public's willingness to accumulate real interest-bearing government debt, $B(t)$, is assumed to be limited. In particular, we assume that $B(t)$ is constrained by

$$B(t) \leq \bar{B}. \tag{1}$$

Equation 1 asserts that, like all private borrowers, the government is faced with an upper bound on the amount of debt that it can place. One upper bound on $B(t)$ is total wealth in a country. When all savings of a country have been absorbed in government debt, no more government debt can be placed. In practice, the actual upper bound $\bar{B}$ is far lower than the total wealth. In August 1982, $B(t)$ in Mexico appeared to have hit $\bar{B}$. In France, between 1924 and 1926, $B(t)$ appeared to have been close to $\bar{B}$, precipitating a continuing financial crisis and the "waltz of the portfolios" of the finance ministers of France.

The public's willingness to accumulate base money is assumed to be described by a demand function of the specific form[3]

$$\frac{M(t)}{p(t)} = a(1) - a(2)E_t[p(t + 1)/p(t)], \qquad a(1) > a(2) \geq 0 \tag{2}$$

where $M(t)$ is the stock of base money at time t, $p(t)$ is the price level at time t, and $E_t[\cdot]$ is the value of $[\cdot]$ expected to prevail by the public as of time t.

Equation 2 is a version of the demand function for money that Cagan (1956) used to study hyperinflation. It depicts the demand for real base money as a decreasing function of the expected gross rate of inflation $E_t[p(t + 1)/p(t)]$. A variety of theories imply a demand function for base money of this form. There is also ample empirical evidence that is consistent with the inverse dependence between real balances $M(t)/p(t)$ and expected inflation $E_t[p(t + 1)/p(t)]$ that is posited by equation 2. For example, in the year before August 1946 the price level in Hungary increased by a factor of about 4×10^{24}. It is reasonable to expect that people had caught on to the extraordinarily rapid ongoing inflation, so that $E_t[p(t + 1)/p(t)]$ was large by the middle of 1946. In August 1946, the real value of high-powered money $M(t)/p(t)$ in Hungary, measured in 1946 U.S. dollars, was less than $25,000.

The system that emerges from writing down the version of equation 2 that is appropriate for dates $t, t + 1, t + 2, \ldots$ can be solved to express $p(t)$ solely in terms of expected future values of $M(t)$:

$$p(t) = \frac{1}{a(1)} \sum_{j=0}^{\infty} \left(\frac{a(2)}{a(1)}\right)^j E_t M(t+j).$$ (3)

Equation 3 expresses the price level at t as a function of the supply of base money expected to prevail from now into the indefinite future. The logic underlying this equation is simple: Equation 2 implies that the price level at t varies directly with the money supply at t and with the price level expected to prevail at $t+1$. Equation 2 also implies that the price level at $t+1$ varies directly with the money supply at $t+1$ and with the price level expected to prevail at $t+2$, and so on. Upon the elimination of future expected price levels from this infinite sequence of relationships, equation 3 emerges. Notice that in the special case of $a(2) = 0$ equation 3 becomes a simple version of the quantity theory of money, stating that the price level at t is proportional to the supply of high-powered money at t.

Equation 3 shows how the price level at t is determined by the interaction of the public's preference for holding high-powered money, which is reflected in the parameters $a(1)$ and $a(2)$, with the expected path of high-powered money now and into the indefinite future. According to equation 3, if government deficits are to influence the price level, it can only be through their effects on the expected path of high-powered money. In this sense, equation 3 embodies the monetarist presumption that inflation is always a monetary phenomenon.

The government deficit and the level and rate of change of the stock of base money are not related in any necessary way at a particular point in time. The reason is that the government can (at least up to a point) borrow by issuing interest-bearing debt, and so need not issue base money to cover its deficit. More precisely, we can think of representing the government's budget constraint in the form[4]

$$G(t) - T(t) = \frac{M(t) - M(t-1)}{p(t)}$$
$$+ B(t) - [1 + r(t-1)]B(t-1),$$ (4)

where $G(t)$ is real government expenditures at t, $T(t)$ is real tax collections net of transfers (except for interest payments on the government debt), and $B(t)$ is the real value at t of one-period bonds issued at t, to be paid off at $t+1$ and to bear interest at net real rate $r(t)$. Equation 4 asserts that the real government deficit at t, $G(t) - T(t)$, can be financed by a combination of printing new high-powered money in the amount $M(t) - M(t-1)$, which raises $[M(t) - M(t-1)]/p(t)$ in real resources, and borrowing in interest-bearing form $B(t)$ in excess of the principle and interest on the debt that is maturing, $[1 + r(t - 1)]B(t - 1)$. Equation 4 must hold for all t. For simplicity, equation 4 assumes that all government interest-bearing debt is one period in maturity. It is important to point out that the formulation of equation 4 assumes in effect that government debt is indexed and constitutes a sure claim on given amounts of future goods. Either the debt is regarded as explicitly indexed, or else the bonds are nominal ones, with the nominal rate of interest imagined to adjust by the subsequently realized rate of inflation so that they turn out to bear real rate $r(t)$ in equilibrium. In a rational-expectations model in which there is no objective uncertainty—the kind of model we have in mind here— these two interpretations are equivalent. In either one of these interpre- tations, the government is imagined to honor its commitments to repay interest-bearing debt at the real interest rate that was anticipated at the time the debt was contracted. In reality, when part of the outstanding government debt is nominal the government has the option of "defaulting" on part of it by acting so as to inflate at a higher rate than had been expected when the debt was contracted. In the subsequent presentation, I shall begin by assuming that the government always abstains from defaulting on any of its interest- bearing debt.

Imagine that there is a fiscal authority that selects a time stream of $G(t)$ and $T(t)$. A consequence of the fiscal authority's choice is a stream of government deficits net of interest payments, $G(t) - T(t)$. There is also a monetary au- thority that determines the composition of the government debt in the hands of the public through open-market operations. The monetary authority's open-market operations at time t are subject to a constraint, which is derived by simply rearranging equation 4:

$$M(t) + p(t)B(t) = M(t - 1) + [1 + r(t - 1)]p(t)B(t - 1)$$
$$+ p(t)[G(t) - T(t)].$$

The monetary authority is free to choose $M(t)$ and $p(t)B(t)$ subject to the constraint that they add up to the total on the right-hand side of the preceding equation. In other words, at a point in time the monetary authority can exchange base money for bonds of equal value.

Are Government Deficits Inflationary?

Under the system formed by equations 3 and 4, the inflationary consequences of a government deficit at time t depend sensitively on the government's strategy for servicing the debt that it issues. This dependence can be illustrated by considering two polar regimes for servicing the debt and for coordinating monetary and fiscal policy.

Consider first a strict Ricardian regime in which government deficits have no effects on the rate of inflation. In this regime, the government always finances its entire deficit or surplus by issuing or retiring interest-bearing debt. Additional base money is never issued to finance a deficit. This regime can be characterized by either of the following two equations, which are equivalent in view of equations 4 and 1:

$$M(t) - M(t - 1) = 0 \text{ for all } t, \tag{5}$$

$$B(t) = E_t \sum_{j=0}^{\infty} R_{tj}^{-1} [T(t + j + 1) - G(t + j + 1)] \text{ for all } t, \tag{6}$$

where

$$R_{tj} = \prod_{i=0}^{j} [1 + r(t + i)].$$

Equation 5 states that the supply of base money is always a constant; equation 6 states that the real value of interest-bearing government debt at t equals the present value of prospective government surpluses. In this regime, a positive value of interest-bearing government debt signals a stream of future government budgets that is in surplus in the present-value sense of equation 6. Increases in government debt are necessarily temporary, in a sense made precise by equation 6.[5]

In the Ricardian regime, government deficits have no effects on the price path because they are permitted to have no effects on the path of base money. For the path of base money to be unaffected by government deficits, it is necessary that the government deficits be temporary and be expected to be accompanied by offsetting future government surpluses. In the Ricardian regime, the government behaves like a firm with respect to financing its deficit. To finance a given deficit, the government competes for funds from lenders on an equal footing with private borrowers. To attract funds, the government must offer lenders a prospective stream of net revenues sufficient to support the value that it presently proposes to borrow. The government's stream of net revenues is $T(t) - G(t)$. The present value of this stream forms the "backing" for the government's borrowing, just as the present value of a stream of prospective net revenues from a new machine might form the backing for a private loan. Furthermore, like any private borrower, the government can borrow in interest-bearing form only a limited amount, determined by the maximum present value of the prospective government surpluses that the economy can support. This is the limit $\bar{B}$ embodied in equation 1.

The Ricardian regime may seem remote as a description of recent behavior of the U.S. government and some major U.S. trading partners. It is worthwhile to recall that states and cities in the United States are constitutionally required to operate under a Ricardian rule, since they have no right to issue base money. In the nineteenth century, the Ricardian rule was followed, with temporary lapses, by Great Britain, the United States, and the more advanced European countries. (It is no coincidence that the economically advanced countries all adopted such a rule, and that they all abandoned it at about the same time, during and after World War I. There are irresistible forces impelling countries that trade with each other to coordinate their monetary and fiscal policies. These forces often cause countries to run similar fiscal policies. A country had to follow a Ricardian rule, or something close to it, in order to adhere to the international gold standard.)

There are alternatives to the Ricardian debt-servicing regime under which government deficits are inflationary. To take an example at the opposite pole from the Ricardian regime, let us consider a rule that was followed for a while during the great revolutions in France and Russia, was used during each of the great European hyperinflations of the twentieth century and was advocated in one version by Milton Friedman in 1948. This rule can be characterized by either of the two following equations:

$$B(t) = 0 \text{ for all } t, \tag{7}$$

$$G(t) - T(t) = [M(t) - M(t - 1)]/p(t) \text{ for all } t. \tag{8}$$

In view of the government budget constraint (equation 4), these two equations are equivalent characterizations of a rule in which the entire deficit is always immediately financed by the printing of additional base money. Interest-bearing debt is never issued. In this regime, the time path of government deficits affects the time path of both base money and the price level in a rigid and immediate way that is described by equation 8 and by our theory of the price level, equation 3. Under this debt-servicing regime, it is possible for the government budget to be persistently in deficit, within limits imposed by equation 8 and by the demand function for base money (equation 2) or its implied theory of the price level (equation 3). Deficits need not be temporary.

In this regime, the government finances a current deficit not by a promise to run surpluses in the future, as in the Ricardian regime, but instead by levying an immediate "inflation tax" on the present holders of base money. Whereas the Ricardian regime involves a commitment ultimately to abstain from any resort to an inflation tax, the polar alternative (Friedman 1948) involves a promise that any government deficit will be immediately and fully monetized. I shall return later to the question of why Milton Friedman, who has never been an advocate of monetary regimes leading to rampant inflation, would at one time have advocated full monetization of government deficits—the regime that has accompanied the worst inflations in history.

It is possible to imagine deficit-financing regimes that are intermediate between Ricardo's and Friedman's. Bryant and Wallace (1980) and Sargent and Wallace (1981) have described such regimes. In all versions of these regimes, interest-bearing government debt is issued, but it is eventually repaid at least partly by the issuing of additional base money. In the regime studied by Sargent and Wallace, the deficit path involves such a persistent stream of large deficits that eventually the inflation tax must be resorted to; increases in base money have to be used to finance the budget.

In all these intermediate deficit-financing regimes of the Bryant-Wallace variety, increases in interest-bearing government debt are typically inflationary, at least eventually, because they signal eventual increases in base money. Sooner or later, these prospective increases in base money will increase the price level; how soon depends on the coefficients $a(1)$ and $a(2)$ in equation 2. According to equation 3, the closer $a(2)/a(1)$ is to unity the bigger is the effect of a given future increase in base money on the price level today. This is true because, according to equation 2, the larger $a(2)$ is relative to $a(1)$ the more sensitive the current price level is to the expected future price level, and therefore also to expected future values of base money.

The preceding discussion indicates that the observed correlation between government deficits and the price level depends on the debt-repayment regime that was in place when the observations were generated. On the one hand, under a Ricardian regime, deficits and the price level would be uncorrelated, because government deficits would not cause movements in the stock of base money. On the other hand, under Friedman's regime, deficits would be highly correlated with the price level. It would therefore be a mistake to estimate the relationship between the deficit and the price path from time-series observations drawn from a period under which a Ricardian regime was in place and to assert that this same relationship will hold between the deficit and inflation under a regime like that described by Friedman or Bryant and Wallace. It would be a mistake because private agents' interpretations of observed deficits, and consequently the impact of observed deficits on the price level, depend on the debt-servicing regime that they imagine to be in place.

The Ricardian regime, Friedman's 1948 regime, and the intermediate Bryant-Wallace regimes each involve solutions of one kind or another to the problem of coordinating the actions of the monetary and fiscal authorities. The government budget constraint (equation 4) implies that coordination is necessary, for a monetary authority, by virtue of its control over the division of government debt in the hands of the public between interest-bearing debt and base money, controls the flow of revenues from the inflation tax that can be used to cover current and future deficits. In principle, the monetary authority has the power to force the system into the Ricardian regime by simply refusing to monetize any interest-bearing government debt. The fiscal authority would thereby be compelled to place its debt with private lenders, presumably by competing on an equal footing with other borrowers.

Under each of the debt-servicing regimes described so far, interest-bearing government debt has been assumed in effect to be indexed. As mentioned earlier, either the debt is regarded as explicitly indexed, or else the rationality of the public's price-level expectations and the fact that the government is imagined to adhere to policies or entire time paths of $G(t) - T(t)$, $M(t)$, and $B(t)$ mean that a system with nominal government debt behaves just like a system with indexed government bonds.[6]

Since we want to apply the results of our reasoning to recent U.S. experience in which government borrowing is in nominal terms, it is important to stress the aspect of the preceding regimes that government plans are adhered to. Though in some of the above regimes the government may resort to an inflation tax, it is known in advance that the government plans to do so. There is no element of fraud or deception in the inflation generated under such regimes.

However, when all or part of the government interest-bearing debt is in nominal form, at each point in time the government appears to have the option of defaulting on part of the debt by inflating at a rate greater than had initially been expected. In the context of the rational-expectations assumption that we are working with here, inflation at a greater rate than had initially been expected by the public is brought about when the government departs from an initial plan for $G(t) - T(t)$, $M(t)$, and $B(t)$ that was thought by the public to be in place and embarks on a plan implying a higher price level for the present period than had originally been anticipated. Resorting to this option is a form of default, because it gives holders of interest-bearing government debt and base money different real rates of return than they initially had bargained for on the basis of the originally planned time paths of $G(t) - T(t)$, $M(t)$, and $B(t)$. This default option can be represented by reformulating the government budget constraint (equation 4) in terms of the nominal interest rate on government interest-bearing debt. Let $r_n(t)$ be the nominal interest rate on one-period debt from period t to $t + 1$. Then the real rate of interest $r(t - 1)$ is related to $r_n(t - 1)$ as follows:

$$1 + r(t - 1) = [1 + r_n(t - 1)]\frac{p(t - 1)}{p(t)}.$$

This equation states that, with a previously fixed nominal rate of interest, the realized real rate of interest between $t - 1$ and t is lower the higher is the price level at t. We can use the above equation to write the government budget constraint as

$$G(t) - T(t) = \frac{M(t) - M(t - 1)}{p(t)} + B(t)$$

$$- B(t - 1)[1 + r_n(t - 1)]\frac{p(t - 1)}{p(t)}. \tag{9}$$

This equation shows how generating a higher price level than had previously been expected helps to finance a current deficit and to diminish the need to sell new government debt.

There are serious questions about whether, and under what circumstances, a government should resort to the option of defaulting that is present when part of the debt is in nominal terms. There is also a serious question of the scope that a government actually has for repeatedly resorting to the default option.[7] Presumably, a government that once reneges on its plans for $G(t) - T(t)$, $M(t)$, and $B(t)$ is less likely to be trusted the next time. The public can be expected to evaluate subsequent government plans and announcements against the background of the government's reputation for executing previous plans. Prospective lenders to a government and holders of its base money thus have some latitude to punish a government with a history of defaulting on its plans.

Reaganomics and Credibility

I have argued that the government budget constraint requires that monetary and fiscal policies be coordinated, and that a variety of coherent and default-tree schemes for coordinating them can be imagined, the Ricardian regime and Friedman's 1948 regime being polar examples. I have also indicated that when some of the government debt is in nominal form (and remember that base money itself is in such a nominal form) there lurks the possibility of defaulting on part of the debt by reneging on the original plan for time paths of monetary and fiscal variables. I shall now use these ideas as a basis for criticizing the program for coordinating monetary and fiscal policy that was implicit during the first year and a half or so of the Reagan administration.

The Reagan administration came into power encouraging a policy for the monetary authority that would be appropriate for the Ricardian regime but advocating plans for taxes and expenditures that could be feasible only, if at all, under some version of a Bryant-Wallace regime. The administration initially supported a commitment to a monetarist policy of $M(t) - M(t - 1) = 0$ forever. Simultaneously, however, in conjunction with the Congress, the administration adopted tax and expenditure plans that implied large positive values of $G(t) - T(t)$ into the indefinite future. As we have seen above, such monetary and fiscal policies are incompatible; it is simply not feasible to carry out both of them.

My colleague Neil Wallace has described the scheme for coordinating monetary and fiscal policies that was being utilized at the inception of the Reagan administration as coordination via resort to a "game of chicken." The monetary authority had promised to stick to a tight money policy of $M(t) - M(t - 1) = 0$ for all future t's, come hell or high water, but meanwhile the fiscal authority had set in place tax and expenditure plans that implied large values of $G(t) - T(t)$ into the indefinite future. On the one hand, if the monetary authority could successfully stick to its guns and forever refuse to monetize any government debt, then eventually the arithmetic of the government's budget constraint would compel the fiscal authority to back down and to swing its budget into balance. On the other hand, if the fiscal authority were to stick to its guns and simply refuse to reduce the stream of $G(t) - T(t)$, then eventually the arithmetic of the government budget constraint would compel the monetary authority to monetize large parts of the deficit. All that is clear is that in this situation one of the two parties to the conflict eventually has to give in. (The party to capitulate is called a "chicken.")

This situation can be likened to one in which the quarterback of a football team (the fiscal authority) announces that he is going to run the ball and wants the tight end to block, while simultaneously the tight end (the monetary authority) announces that he wants to catch a pass and will run a pass route on the next play. The quarterback and the tight end point out to one another that the other had better capitulate, or else the next play will go badly. About the only thing that is certain about this situation is that it cannot long endure.

Coordination of monetary and fiscal policy by use of such a game of chicken necessarily confronts private agents with uncertainty about subsequent taxes, rates of inflation, and rates of interest on government securities. Unlike uncertainty about the weather or about the success of a new technology or machine, the uncertainty injected into the economy over the outcome of a struggle between monetary and fiscal policies such as I have described is entirely avoidable and unnecessary. Private agents are forced to form opinions about when and how the conflict between government agencies will be resolved. Some of the observed market reactions to that situation can be interpreted in terms of the preponderance of public opinion about how the conflict would eventually be resolved. For example, the high long-term nominal interest rates that prevailed in 1981 and 1982 can be interpreted as reflecting the market's guess that large deficits would persist and eventually be monetized in large part, leading to high inflation rates in the future. In addition, the very injection of substantial extraneous uncertainty is capable of triggering contractions in output and expansions of unemployment due to the additional sheer confusion faced by agents.

In this interpretation, Reaganomics was not credible because it was not feasible. It was simply not feasible to simultaneously carry out both the fiscal and the monetary aspects of Reaganomics. Therefore, to rational observers, Reaganomics was incredible. This was paradoxical because, more than in any other recent administration, spokesmen for the Reagan administration initially placed substantial stress on "announcement effects" and the immediate benefits that would flow from adhering to a credible long-run strategy.

However, there may be another, more favorable interpretation of Reaganomics that involves a more complicated game of chicken against the background of the government budget constraint. This game of chicken involves not two but three players. Imagine that a first player sets a path for $T(t)$, a second player sets a path for $G(t)$, and a third player (via open-market operations) sets a path for $M(t) - M(t - 1)$. Suppose that the first and third parties wish to reduce the size of the government, as measured by the stream of $G(t)$. Although these two parties do not directly control $G(t)$, by acting together they can bring pressure upon it, for if the entire path of $T(t)$ is somehow reduced, and if the monetary authority maintains a policy of setting $M(t) - M(t - 1) = 0$ for all future t's, then the arithmetic of equation 4 and the implied need to finance current deficits by promising to run future surpluses will cause the second party to capitulate and to reduce $G(t)$.

Though oversimplified, this three-party game captures the motivation of some advocates of the Reagan administration's policies. The administration can be viewed as having implemented a strategy of moving quickly to reduce taxes before announcing or planning concrete expenditure reductions, while simultaneously encouraging tight monetary policy, and then opposing rescinding tax decreases in order to balance the large deficits that threatened to develop in the future. Viewed in this way, this game of chicken, fought against the backdrop of the arithmetic of equation 4, is a struggle over how large the government of the United States is to be. The particular strategy for reducing the size of the government that I have described is attractive, even for one who wants a smaller government, only if one is relatively confident that the uncertainties injected into monetary and fiscal arrangements by fighting the struggle in this way will not have an unduly adverse effect on the performance of national output and employment.

Conclusion

There are a variety of methods of coordinating monetary and fiscal policies that are superior to Wallace's game of chicken. For example, a case can be made that either the Ricardian regime or Friedman's 1948 regime dominates the game of chicken. The game of chicken that I have described amounts to a struggle for dominance between the fiscal and monetary authorities, in which each party promises to stick to a strategy that is feasible only if the other player acts as a follower. (Such a situation, in which each player seems to behave like a leader, is the case of Stackelberg warfare referred to above.) Under the Ricardian regime, the monetary authority in effect dominates the fiscal authority insofar as decisions about the present value of government deficit are concerned. Under Friedman's 1948 regime, it is the fiscal authority that dominates the monetary authority insofar as decisions about the rate of growth of base money are concerned. Each of these polar regimes has a well-defined structure of dominance, and each has relatively straightforward implications for the paths of government interest-bearing debt and base money, to which the public can be imagined to adjust readily. Furthermore, each of the polar regimes entails a relatively clear assignment of responsibility for inflation, insofar as government policy influences the rate of inflation. As I have portrayed the structure of the economy and characterized the conduct of policy under the Ricardian regime, inflation can emerge only if there occur changes in the preferences of the public, in the structure of legal regulations, or perhaps in the conduct of foreign governments that supply substitutes for base money and government debt, each of which would be reflected in a change in our parameters $a(1)$ and $a(2)$. Under Friedman's 1948 scheme, government deficits have direct and immediate inflationary consequences that everyone can see.

How is the question of coordination of monetary and fiscal policies to be resolved? Current legislation in the United States leaves the method of resolution open, so that in practice it is resolved by the successive interactions of a succession of personalities and administrations within our fiscal and monetary institutions. It can be argued that superior outcomes would be achieved if the responsibilities of the monetary and fiscal authorities were to be legislatively or constitutionally restricted so as to determine in advance which institutions are to lead and which are to follow.

Notes

1. Technically, this is the government deficit net of interest payments.

2. Since its decisions about the composition of the debt influence the interest payments that the government must make, the monetary authority helps determine the government deficit gross of interest payments, and thereby the rate at which total government debt changes.

3. When $a(2) = 0$, equation 2 becomes a simple version of the quantity theory of money.

4. Another way to write equation 4 is

$$G(t) - T(t) + r(t - 1)B(t - 1)$$

$$= \frac{M(t) - M(t - 1)}{p(t)} + B(t) - B(t - 1). \tag{3'}$$

The term $G(t) - T(t) + r(t - 1)B(t - 1)$ is often called the government deficit gross of interest payments, while $G(t) - T(t)$ is termed the government deficit net of interest payments. The monetary authority is assumed to control the ratio of $B(t)$ to $M(t)$ at each point in time. It thereby influences the subsequent rate of growth of total government indebtedness by influencing the interest expenses $r(t - 1)B(t - 1)$ that appear in equation 4.

5. One way to implement the regime given by equations 5 and 6 is simply to adjust current taxes $T(t)$ by an amount equal to any variations in interest payments $r(t - 1)B(t - 1)$ that are associated with variations in past government expenditures or taxes. This policy amounts always to levying current taxes sufficient to service the interest payments that are currently due. This is the way McCallum (1984) proceeds in one of his experiments.

6. This is one of the findings of the theoretical literature on indexed government bonds: that, under general circumstances, they make no difference to a rational-expectations equilibrium. See Liviatan 1983 or Peled 1980.

7. These questions are raised and discussed by Kydland and Prescott (1977) and Calvo (1978).

References

Bryant, John, and Neil Wallace. 1980. A Suggestion for Further Simplifying the Theory of Money. Research Department Staff Report 62, Federal Reserve Bank of Minneapolis.

Cagan, Phillip. 1956. "The Monetary Dynamics of Hyperinflation," in M. Friedman, ed., *Studies in the Quantity Theory of Money* (University of Chicago Press).

Calvo, Guillermo. 1978. "On the Time Consistency of Optimal Policy in a Monetary Economy." *Econometrica*, vol. 46, no. 6, pp. 1411–1428.

Friedman, Milton. 1948. "A Monetary and Fiscal Framework for Economic Stability." *American Economic Review*, vol. 38, June, pp. 245–264.

Friedman, Milton. 1960. *A Program for Monetary Stability* (New York: Fordham University Press).

Kydland, Finn E., and Edward C. Prescott. 1977. "Rules Rather than Discretion: The Inconsistency of Optimal Plans." *Journal of Political Economy*, vol. 85, no. 3, pp. 473–491.

Liviatan, Nissan. 1983. "On Equilibrium Wage Indexation and Neutrality of Indexation Policy," in P. A. Armella, R. Dornbusch, and M. Obstfeld, eds., *Financial Policies and the World Capital Market: The Problem of Latin American Countries* (University of Chicago Press).

McCallum, Bennett T. 1984. "Are Bond-financed Deficits Inflationary? A Ricardian Analysis." *Journal of Political Economy*, vol. 92, no. 1, pp. 123–135.

Peled, Dan. 1980. Government Index Bonds—Do They Improve Matters? Ph.D. diss., University of Minnesota.

Sargent, Thomas J., and Neil Wallace. 1981. "Some Unpleasant Monetarist Arithmetic." *Federal Reserve Bank of Minneapolis Quarterly Review*, vol. 5, no. 3, pp. 1–17.

8   Coordination of Monetary and Fiscal Policies

Albert Ando

The term *stagflation* was coined several years ago to characterize the performance of the economies of the industrialized countries after 1970, which was decidedly less satisfactory than it had been between the Second World War and 1970. A number of studies have been undertaken to determine the causes of this decline in the performance of these economies, and I believe that there is reasonable conscensus among specialists on some aspects of this history while there appears to be little agreement on others.[1]

I believe there is little disagreement among us that the history of the 1960s left the United States, the largest and dominant economy among OECD countries (certainly at the end of the 1960s if not at the beginning of the 1980s), the legacy of inflationary undertones at the beginning of the 1970s. Most economists would also say that the economies of the OECD countries suffered more severe, unexpected shocks more frequently in the 1970s than in the 1960s, and that an unusually large number of these shocks tended to be unfavorable to the performance of these economies.

Beyond these observations, it becomes much harder to find any consensus among economists of different persuasions. This is not surprising. To go beyond these observations, and to answer such questions as how these shocks affected the economies of OECD countries or how these shocks interacted with a particular set of economic policies pursued by some specific country, one must commit oneself to a specific description of how the economy works, and we have had innumerable controversies and disagreements on how to model economies from a macroeconomic point of view during the past 15 years.

In a short chapter such as this one, I will not be able to summarize, let alone evaluate, various subtle differences among contending theories, and to arrive at a set of carefully considered policy actions based on such an evaluation. I will, instead, propose my own list of policy actions that seem to me to be conducive to improving the prospect and the speed of a recovery. These suggestions are a result of my having followed developments of the 1970s and the 1980s with my own model, and therefore they depend on the particular theoretical framework that I have used in trying to understand the causal relationships in the economy. I have, however, tried to emphasize those propositions that are not dependent on detailed specifications of the model or on specific values of estimated parameters and that therefore are more likely to be acceptable to those who are inclined to look at these problems from different points of view.[2]

The dominance of the United States in the world economy has significantly declined since the 1960s. I believe, however, that the performance of the U.S. economy and the policies followed by the U.S. government and the Federal Reserve Authority are still the most important factor determining how the world economy will recover during the next several years. This is so partly because the United States is still the largest economy in the world, partly because financial markets in the world have become so closely tied together that the conditions in the New York financial market are rapidly reflected in the conditions of other financial centers, and most importantly because American economic policies are currently undergoing an exceptionally uncertain phase, and their eventual resolution will make major differences in how the U.S. economy and hence the world economy will perform during the next decade or so. For this reason, I will initially concentrate on the prospects for the U.S. economy and speculate only briefly on the repercussions in other countries of some alternative possibilities for the U.S. economy.

In order to briefly cover a fairly wide range of topics involved, in the first part of the chapter I outline my observations and propositions without attempting to provide theoretical or factual support for them. In the second part, I present some background material for these propositions.

Short-Run Issues

The Phillips Curve

The Phillips curve, the relationship between the rate of unemployment and the rate of change in nominal wages, has been a subject of analysis and controversy for three decades. It is often claimed that this relationship has not been at all stable, and that its instability was an important contribution to the perceived failure of macroeconomics as it was understood at the end of the 1960s.

In a recent paper (Ando and Kennickell 1983), I presented evidence on the performance of a representative form of this equation (as formulated in the

MPS macroeconometric model of the United States, with which I have been associated) when it is used together with other equations representing our hypothesis concerning the process of price formation given the nominal wage.[3] The evidence accumulated during the last 12 years or so shows that there is little indication for instability of this set of equations. This set of evidence does support the proposition, however, that in the long run the Phillips curve is vertical; that is, we can define the "natural" rate of unemployment at which there is no tendency for the rate of inflation to accelerate or decelerate. I wish at this point to emphasize that I do not attach any normative connotations to the concept of the natural rate, as I would to the notion of "full employment." For me, it is strictly a characterization of the dynamic equilibrating process in the labor market, and I will argue later that one of the important long-run policy issues is how to lower the level of the natural rate.

Natural Rate of Unemployment

Once we accept the notion of the natural rate, we must recognize it as a critical indicator of the conditions of the economy; indeed, it is one of the most plausible targets of countercyclical policy actions, because if the rate of unemployment is higher than the natural rate then output can be increased without risking the acceleration of inflation. The obvious questions, then, are how we can measure this concept and what its historical value has been. I describe below a particular procedure that we have followed in measuring it. The result suggests that the natural rate of unemployment may well have been considerably higher than was previously supposed. Our estimate is that it was between 5 percent and 6 percent from the late 1950s through the early 1970s, gradually rose to near or slightly above 7 percent toward the end of the 1970s, and has been declining slowly since the end of the 1970s. As I indicate below, details of my estimates may not be very reliable, but in view of the evidence presented in my paper with Kennickell I believe that the general order of magnitude and the long-range trend are believable.[4]

If we accept these estimates as within 1 percent of the true value, then we will have to conclude that the policy objective of attempting to achieve an unemployment rate of 4 percent was inconsistent with the maintenance of stable prices, and that the inflationary pressure that developed in the economy beginning in the late 1960s was a natural consequence of the policies followed in that period.[5] On the other hand, there is little doubt that the current rate of unemployment is substantially above the natural rate. This suggests that we can move monetary policy in a more stimulative direction without risking acceleration of the rate of inflation again. Before we can accept this proposition, however, we must ask another important question: Is it possible that the rate of money growth has some unspecified direct influence on the rate of inflation, given the unemployment rate?

The "Direct Effects" of the Money Supply on Prices

I share with older monetarists the belief that monetary policies are quite powerful in determining the course of the economy. In particular, given other factors (including fiscal policy), the money supply contributes importantly to the path followed by the unemployment rate over time. Since the movement of the rate of inflation depends critically on the unemployment rate, monetary policies have important effects on the movements of prices as well.

However, in the MPS model, monetary policy works its effects on all aspects of the economy through its ability to affect interest rates, and only through interest rates. Interest rates affect the demand and supply conditions in goods and labor markets, and only through the demand and supply conditions in goods and labor markets do they affect prices. In Ando and Kennickell 1983 I present additional evidence for the proposition that, given the conditions in labor and goods markets, as indicated by the rate of unemployment, movement of the supply of money by itself has no additional impact on prices in the economy.

The Case for a More Expansionary Monetary Policy

It is therefore my contention that the most important immediate condition for recovery is for the Federal Reserve's policies to be directed toward lowering market interest rates still further, since market rates of interest less any reasonable expected rate of inflation are exceptionally high by historical standards. There may be a period in which the rate of growth of the money supply will appear unusually high as a consequence, but in view of the evidence given in Ando and Kennickell 1983 and elsewhere there is little danger that a somewhat higher rate of growth of money will rekindle an acceleration of inflation so long as the rate of unemployment remains clearly above the natural rate, certainly when the rate of unemployment is above 8 percent.

Of course, as more expansionary monetary policies induce the unemployment rate to decline from the present level of above 9 percent to 8 percent or less, the deceleration of inflation will be slower than it would have been had the monetary policy been more restrictive and the rate of unemployment higher. There may even be some period in which the rate of inflation (especially when it is measured in terms of the final goods prices) appears to rise moderately as the prices of raw materials and agricultural goods stop declining and perhaps rise somewhat, because these prices appear to be somewhat too low relative to other prices at the moment. What is the justification, however, of refusing to consider a policy that is needed to reduce the rate of unemployment because doing so has some chance of reducing the rate of deceleration of inflation, when the rate of unemployment is above 9 percent and the inflation rate is already less than 5 percent and declining? It is as though policy makers, with the support of the majority of the public, have decided that inflation is so evil, whereas unemployment is basically costless, that the policy should always be directed solely toward the reduction of inflation, no matter what impact such a policy has on unemployment.

To be sure, the Federal Reserve authorities have brought down the nominal rate of interest substantially during the past year (1982) while letting the supply of money increase at a rate considerably higher than that announced earlier, thereby contributing to the economic recovery in the United States since the beginning of 1983. Recent developments in the money market suggest, however, that this pattern has reversed itself and the Federal Reserve authority is now prepared to let the nominal rate of interest rise moderately in order to reduce the rate of growth of the money supply. Since the rate of inflation will continue to fall slowly at the current rate of unemployment, such a policy will have the effect of increasing the real rate of interest, thus aborting the economic recovery.

In this connection, it should be remembered that the income velocity of money depends on the nominal, rather than the real, rate of interest. As the inflation rate falls, in order to keep the real interest rate constant the nominal rate must be continuously falling at the same pace as the inflation rate. This means that the income velocity of money must be falling in order to keep the real rate of interest constant when the inflation rate is falling. In other words, the money supply must be increasing faster than the rate of growth of nominal income, adjusted for the secular trend, when the inflation rate is falling. The order of magnitude of this discrepancy depends on the elasticity of the demand for money with respect to the rate of interest, and one must be prepared to encounter some instability in this elasticity and to proceed somewhat experimentally, but I believe that these are vital considerations in designing policies to ensure recovery for the immediate future.

Issues for the Intermediate Horizon: Consequences of Large Structural Deficits in the Federal Budget

Effects of Fiscal Policies on Interest Rates

The path of the market (real) rate of interest generated by a monetary policy aimed at moving the economy nearer to the equality of the actual unemployment rate and the natural rate of unemployment depends on the fiscal policy posture, among other things. In general, the more stimulative the fiscal policy is, the higher the market rate of interest such a monetary policy generates. In addition, policies designed to stimulate investment by reducing the real, after-tax cost of capital for firms and individuals for a given market rate of interest—such as investment tax credits and accelerated depreciation allowances—tend to raise the market rate of interest under the monetary policy envisaged here, especially if such provisions of tax law apply to wide categories of investment.[6]

A number of provisions in the tax law accumulated over the post war years have tended to increase the wedge between the market rate of interest and the after-tax cost of capital, and these provisions have to some extent contributed to the increased level of the market rate of interest over the years. The situation has become much more dramatic during the past 3–4 years. Since 1979, the Federal Reserve's policy has been directed more clearly toward maintaining the rate of unemployment at somewhat above the natural rate in order to reduce the rate of inflation. At the same time, since 1981, the economic program of the Reagan administration has in effect made the fiscal policies much more stimulative than they were earlier. The combination of these two policies has resulted in a market real rate of interest that is substantially higher than any we have seen for some time.

The Condition for Stability of National Debt

This combination of stimulative fiscal policies with sufficiently stringent monetary policy aimed at keeping the rate of unemployment high enough to place downward pressure on the rate of inflation has a number of grave consequences. In order to appreciate the problem, it is useful to recall a well-known proposition from the literature on simple growth models: When the market rate of interest on government securities is below the rate of growth of some measure of nominal domestic output of the economy (say net national product in current dollars), and if the government runs a deficit (defined as total expenditure, excluding interest payments less total revenue) that is on average a modest proportion of nominal output for the economy, then the total national debt will settle down as a fixed proportion of the national-output measure. However, if the market rate of interest on government securities is above the rate of growth of nominal domestic output of the economy, and if the government runs a fiscal policy that on average generates deficits rather than surpluses, then the national debt will grow without limit and will become larger and larger in proportion to the national output.

Throughout the entire postwar period, until 1979, the market rate of interest has been, on average, somewhat below the rate of growth of nominal output in the United States. Furthermore, the federal budget showed surpluses rather than deficits in the sense defined above most of the time, and even when it was in deficit the size of the deficit was very modest. Consequently, federal government debt as a proportion of national output was declining throughout the postwar era.

The policy package pursued by the Reagan administration reversed this situation. We now have a situation in which the market rate of interest on government securities is higher than the rate of growth in current dollars, and we have substantial deficits excluding government interest payments. The proposition stated here and elaborated below suggests that, under this set of conditions, the government debt will become larger and larger in proportion to the national output, eventually creating an unmanageable situation unless the condition is reversed.

Prospects for the U.S. Economy under Current Policies: Needed Adjustments

Of course, for an economy in the deepest depression since the 1930s, with an unemployment rate still above 9 percent, government deficits of substantial size are clearly justified and any immediate tightening of fiscal policy is a mistake unless the action is accompanied by changes in the monetary policy to overcompensate its effects. The easing of monetary policy since the summer of 1982 has permitted the beginning of a recovery in the United States, but in order that the recovery continue until the unemployment rate is lowered to a level near the natural rate it is necessary to pursue an expansionary monetary-policy posture for some time to come, even with fiscal policy remaining as it is. In all likelihood, further reduction in nominal rates of interest will be a necessary condition for continued recovery as the expected rate of inflation in the minds of economic agents adjusts to the lower rate of actual inflation. Since the level of national debt in the United States is now quite low, substantial deficits for 2 or 3 years will not do much harm.

Given the current configuration of fiscal policy, if monetary policy is sufficiently eased to ensure a satisfactory recovery, as the unemployment rate approaches the natural rate, it will become necessary either to make fiscal policy less expansive or to raise the market (real) rate of interest in order to keep the economy from going significantly past the natural rate of unemployment and creating a situation in which the rate of inflation will begin to accelerate. That is, in order to maintain stable prices, the market rate of interest consistent with the maintenance of the natural rate of unemployment, given the current fiscal policy posture, must be kept quite high, almost certainly higher than the rate of growth of nominal output.

Many analyses of current fiscal-policy plans—including those by the Congressional Budget Office (1983), those used in the administration's budget projections (Office of Management and Budget 1983), and my own—come to the conclusion that, even when the economy recovers to the point where the actual rate of unemployment is close to the natural rate, government deficits excluding the government interest payment will remain substantial. In other words, if and when we recover to the point where the actual rate of unemployment is close to the natural rate without any significant change in the administration's fiscal policies, we will face the situation in which the market rate of interest on government securities is higher than the rate of growth of nominal output, while the government is running significant deficits not as a cyclical anomaly but as the normal condition of the economy. Such deficits at "full employment" are very different from cyclical deficits. If such a condition is allowed to develop, government debt in proportion to national output will increase fairly quickly, and this will soon become very difficult to reverse.[7]

The rapid growth of the national debt in proportion to the national output has, of course, serious consequences domestically. Given the savings behavior in the economy (I do not believe that saving is very responsive to variations in the interest rate), the larger the share of national debt as a proportion of national output, the smaller the accumulation of productive capital in the economy will be. This would slow down the growth of output for the economy, something undesirable in itself. But the situation can be much worse than that. The reduction of the accumulation of productive capital will be brought about through higher and higher market rates of interest. The increasing market rate of interest and the progressively slower growth rate of output will in turn further aggravate the deficit problems of the federal government, thus accelerating the whole process further.

Eventually, the situation must become intolerable. At that point, unless the economy goes through a painful and costly structural reform, it faces the conditions of totally irresponsible financing of government expenditures identified by Sargent (1982) as the fundamental cause of hyperinflation in a number of countries between the two world wars. This is a type of situation that the American economy has not faced before. It did not appear plausible for the United States until the advent of the Reagan administration and its unconventional fiscal policies.

International Repercussions

The international financial market is still dominated by conditions in the U.S. financial market. In the absence of extraordinary measures (such as an interest-equalization tax on earnings from assets located abroad), interest rates on most financial centers in the world tend to equalize, adjusting for the expected rate of change of exchange rates. When the government and the central bank of another country (such as Japan, England, or West Germany) attempt to maintain a domestic interest rate different from the American rate, it has serious effects on the exchange rate for the currency of that country. It is, therefore, difficult for a country such as Japan to lower the rate of interest beyond certain limits defined by the high U.S. rate of interest, even though the Japanese government and the Bank of Japan may consider it desirable, from the viewpoint of domestic economic policy, to lower the domestic rate of interest.

Under the circumstances, in countries such as Japan and West Germany, where the rate of inflation is quite low and the rate of unemployment is fairly high, governments may wish to stimulate the economy if possible but find it difficult to achieve this objective because for external reasons they must maintain higher interest rates than they consider appropriate. If they attempt to lower interest rates, their currencies depreciate. Normally, this may stimulate exports and reduce imports, setting in motion the classical corrective process. But under current world economic conditions, such a course often runs into serious resistance in the form of trade friction and barriers. These conditions may then make it necessary for these countries to resort to one of two possible alternatives, neither of which is wholly attractive.

First, the governments of these countries can try to stimulate the economy through the standard fiscal measures, such as tax reduction or public investment. I believe that public investment, if it is chosen wisely and carried out efficiently, may be a quite attractive alternative. However, any measure to stimulate the economy with traditional fiscal policies while the market rate of interest remains high inevitably involves sizable deficits, and at worst any country can get itself into the serious predicament I have described above: A rate of interest substantially higher than the rate of growth, accompanied by government deficits incurred in order to keep unemployment manageable, results in growth of the national debt at a higher rate than the rate of growth of output. Of course, countries with higher prospective growth rates than that for the United States, such as Japan, have a little more room for maneuvering, but the danger cannot be ignored.

Second, these countries can increase their subsidies on capital investment, mainly through special provisions in their tax systems such as investment tax credits, an accelerated depreciation schedule, and deductibility of mortgage interest payments for tax purposes coupled with the exclusion of imputed rents on owner-occupied houses from income for tax purposes. These provisions reduce the after-tax real cost of capital given the market rate of interest, and in the United States significant increases in these provisions since the 1950s have widened the wedge between the market rate of interest and the real after-tax cost of capital. This in turn enabled the American monetary authorities to maintain the market rate of interest substantially higher than in early years after the Second World War without discouraging investment expenditures noticeably. Since this is an important reason why the U.S. rate of interest remains high, other countries can adopt similar provisions to maintain reasonably high levels of investment expenditures in the face of the high market rate of interest. Every country has in its tax structure some of these special provisions, in a variety of complex forms, and it is difficult to make precise comparisons among them, but it can be said that by increasing these provisions most OECD countries could stimulate investment further, thus contributing to higher level of economic activity at a given market rate of interest. Furthermore, some governments may find that some of these provisions are convenient devices for stimulating investment in specific areas where needs are most strongly felt—for instance, in Japan, for new and specific types of housing construction in order to make more efficient use of the extraordinarily expensive urban land. However, any program designed to intervene in the economy through these special provisions in taxes has an important and inherent weakness: It inevitably distorts the choices of economic agents and makes the allocation of resources in the economy less efficient.

From the viewpoint of the world economy, therefore, it is clearly better that U.S. fiscal policy be adjusted to reduce these special provisions, to be made less expansive as the economy recovers, allowing the market rate of interest in the United States to be lowered and to remain lower than it is. Other countries can then lower their market rates, setting the stage for more orderly and sounder recovery of the world economy. However, as there is little hope of a reform of

U.S. fiscal policy in the immediate future, it is probably more helpful on balance for other countries to adopt some of these specific provisions to stimulate investment expenditures (including investment by households in consumer durables) than not to.

Special Problems of Developing Countries

The advanced countries, while they may be harmed to some extent by the high U.S. interest rate, can nevertheless cope with the situation with manageable costs to themselves. The situation is much more disastrous for less developed countries, especially those that have borrowed to finance some of their development needs (for instance, the social overhead capital). Here, we can state a proposition concerning the controllability of such a country's external debt analogous to the one we have stated for the national debt of a government.

We assume that the foreign debt of a developing country and the interest payment on such a debt are denominated in an international reserve currency, say dollars. We also suppose that the critical ratio here is the ratio of external debt to domestic output, with both measured in the same currency. (If some other measure of the basic capacity of the country, such as export earnings, is more appropriate as the base to which the debt should be compared, it can be substituted for domestic output so long as the base is stated in terms of the international currency).

If the rate of interest in the dollar market is less than the rate of growth of the developing country's output measured in dollars, then the country can run the external trade deficit defined to exclude interest payments on the external debt up to a fixed proportion of the country's output measured in dollars. But if the rate of interest in the dollar market is more than the rate of growth of the developing country's output measured in dollars, then the developing country must run an external surplus large enough in proportion to its output measured in dollars to stabilize the external debt; otherwise, the external debt will grow without limit relative to the country's output. The condition for stabilizing the external debt is more severe the larger the external debt relative to the output of the country measured in dollars was to begin with.

For most of the more promising developing countries, such as Mexico and Brazil, the rate of growth of their output measured in dollars (that is, including movements of exchange rates and the inflation rate of the dollar itself) was generally larger than the short-term rate of interest in New York until 1978. They were thus able to borrow in the dollar market without serious danger that their external debts would suddenly get out of control so long as they took care to limit their external deficits to be, on average, less than some fixed proportion of the domestic output measured in dollars. However, in 1979 the U.S. rate of interest rose dramatically, going well above the rate of growth of output in these countries measured in dollars. Under this new and unfamiliar condition, these countries continued to run external deficits, or did not run large enough surpluses to cover interest payments on a current basis, and their external debts began to accumulate rapidly relative to their resources. When external debts begin to accumulate under these conditions, the interest payments by the country in question to external creditors become very large, and this causes the country's balance of payments to become unfavorable. This, in turn, forces the currency of the country to depreciate against the dollar and makes the country's output or resources (defined in dollars) smaller. The external debts then become a still larger proportion of the country's resources, and the vicious cycle continues.

During the years 1981 and 1982 enormous debts incurred by a number of developing countries and consequent difficulties faced by them, even the danger of their bankruptcy, have raised serious concern for officials everywhere. In a relatively small number of cases, the misguided policies of countries themselves may have been the main cause of their difficulties, but in many cases the countries had been moving along quite satisfactorily and no major policy change took place. It was simply that the rate of interest they faced rose sharply, and the crime of the governments of these countries was merely that they did not grasp the implications of this rise in the rate of interest quickly enough. It would be extremely difficult for these countries to recover under the circumstances, unless the real rate of interest in the world financial markets were to come down to a more normal level.

Some Tentative Conclusions

The foregoing discussion has outlined my reasoning for concluding that the current configuration of fiscal and monetary policies in the United States contains seeds for serious problems to come for the domestic U.S. economy itself, for the industrialized countries of the West, and for the developing countries. Earlier, I stated that, in the short run while the rate of unemployment remains unambiguously higher than the natural rate of unemployment, the monetary authority could act on its own to reduce the market rate of interest. But this is purely a temporary adjustment. As the lower interest rate stimulates aggregate demand and output, the structure of the current set of policies is such that, even at an actual rate of unemployment close to the natural rate, the expected deficits of the federal government remain very

Table 8.1
Effects of an increase in personal income tax and a corresponding reduction in federal fund rate to keep the unemployment rate approximately unchanged for 5 years.

Changes in	1983	1984	1985	1986	1987
GNP in 1972 dollars	−21	−23	−3	14	15
Personal consumption	−22	−33	−25	−14	−12
Rate of change of GNP deflator	0.5	−0.2	−0.5	−0.4	0.2
Unemployment rate	0.4	0.6	0.4	0	−0.2
Federal fund rate	−1.5	−2.0	−1.5	−0.9	−0.7
AAA corporate rate	−0.4	−0.6	−1.0	−1.1	−0.8
Personal taxes	62	84	85	85	82
Other taxes	−6	0	8	10	6
Interest payments		−16	−28	−38	−45
Surplus or deficit of federal government	60	99	121	133	133

large, and the rate of interest must be moved up enough to keep the economy from being stimulated beyond the point at which the rate of inflation will again accelerate. The market real rate of interest at that point is quite likely to be substantially above the rate of growth of output, and hence the deficit problem of the federal government will be difficult to solve and likely to deteriorate rapidly.

It is thus at least prudent to adjust the balance between the monetary and fiscal policies substantially, so that the market rate of interest can be lowered while the deficits in the federal budget will become smaller when the economy will recover enough and the actual unemployment rate is close to the natural rate. As I stressed earlier, the fiscal policy adjustments can be undertaken with some time lag so that they become effective, say, 12–15 months from now as the economy gradually recovers, since at this very moment high unemployment and low output are the overwhelming concerns.

Furthermore, the fiscal-policy adjustments do not have to be as large as supposed if the monetary policy is also adjusted in the more expansionary direction to counteract the contractionary effects of fiscal-policy adjustments. The conditions 3- 5 years hence appeared so alarming because of the cumulative effects of deficits and higher rates of interest to begin with. To illustrate the order of magnitude involved, I show in table 8.1 the effects of raising federal personal income taxes and reducing the federal fund rate to keep the level of unemployment roughly the same. These figures are differences between two otherwise identical 5-year simulations of the MPS model; the second differs from the first in that a sufficient surcharge was imposed on personal income tax to raise revenues by some $60 billion in 1983 and a little over $80 billion thereafter. The monetary policy is determined by a rule that reacts to this fiscal action and lowers the federal fund rate enough to keep the rate of unemployment not too different from the one traced by the first simulation.

I wish to emphasize that I did not make any serious effort to make the base simulation on which the computation of the differences is based into the most "reasonable" projection of economic conditions during the next 5 years, nor am I advocating this particular set of policy changes as especially desirable. Indeed, as I have stressed before, the primary policy issue of 1983 is to reduce unemployment and increase production. Increasing taxes starting in 1983 is at best questionable policy, even if it is accompanied by more expansionary monetary policy. The only point of table 8.1 is to exhibit the order of magnitude of the changes in the market rate of interest and the eventual changes in the size of federal budget deficits in response to an extremely simple change in fiscal policy. In particular, I think it is interesting that, for a relatively small change in the rate of interest, the reduction in the interest payments by 1987 is quite large, and it is more than 50 percent of the increase in the revenue resulting directly from the tax surcharge. This is because we are in the unstable region of the debt growth rate–interest rate relationship discussed earlier, and a small change in one of its components results in a large change within a few years. In order to put the system into the stable region, if we are to do so using only an income tax surcharge, a surcharge generating $120–130 billion in revenues rather than one generating $80 billion appears to be required. But this is probably not feasible or desirable, and other means of reducing the deficits should be considered—for instance, reducing the defense budget or increasing other taxes.

I presume that if U.S. policies are adjusted so that the market rate of interest is lowered in the United States by, say, 2 percentage points, other industrial countries will follow in the same direction, although not necessarily by the same amount. The benefits are obvious, and comments by the Japanese and some European policy makers suggests that they are waiting for the opportunity. In the example shown in table 8.1, I assumed that the elasticity of a weighted average of foreign interest rates with respect to the U.S. rate is 0.5 and let the exchange rates respond to this change in accordance with the model equations. I believe that this is probably on the conservative side under the circumstances. The benefits to developing countries with substantial external debts are also quite apparent.

Some Structural Policies for Improving Economic Performance

The term *stagflation*, as I said at the beginning, emphasizes the combination of the accelerating inflation with high unemployment and low output as the most important symptom of deteriorated performance of the economies of the industrialized countries. We can describe this condition analytically as resulting from the natural rate of unemployment, which rose appreciably in the 1970s relative to earlier periods, from the sluggish, unsatisfactory responses of these economies to a series of adverse supply shocks encountered in the 1970s, and from the interaction between these two factors. I have described some characteristics of macroeconomic policies that are detrimental to orderly recovery of the U.S. economy in particular and of the world economy in general. There are, however, more basic issues of what we can do to improve the performance of these economies: We need to search for actions of governments and central banks that should reduce the natural rate of unemployment, and to make the adjustments of economies to external shocks more efficient and less painful.

These policies are, I am afraid, not macroeconomic but structural, and their effects are more difficult to analyze and measure. Although even a fairly large-scale macroeconomic model cannot serve as an effective tool for analysis of this type of problem, a well-designed model can be quite suggestive in isolating those aspects of the economy that create especially severe inefficiencies under a certain set of conditions. Here we are concerned specifically with the question of the ability of an economy to adjust to large changes in relative prices, for instance in the prices of energy and food, and factors that tend to keep the natural rate of unemployment high. I would like to comment on some of these issues, concentrating on the role of government and types of actions that government can undertake to improve the performance of the economy, without paying any attention to the political feasibility of actions considered.

I believe it is also helpful at this point to remember that, while some rigidities in prices obviously interfere with efficient functioning of the economy, the complete flexibility of prices does not necessarily guarantee that the economy will be continuously as efficient as it can be, since with perfectly flexible prices and a reasonably realistic specification of dynamic adjustment processes the economy may be unstable. Some price rigidities may actually contribute to the stability. We know that some of the conditions under which the Walrasian general-equilibrium system has an efficient and stable equilibrium solution, especially the requirement for existence of complete contingent markets and of tatonement processes, cannot be duplicated in the real world.

We are thus looking for a number of marginal improvements in the ability of the economy to move more smoothly and directly toward efficient and full utilization of resources, but not completely.

Lucas (1972) emphasized the importance of the possibility that, under some conditions, economic agents may not be able to distinguish between movements of the relative prices and movements of the absolute price level by observing the market price available to them. Lucas's observation is accepted by most economists as an important insight into one of the basic causes of economic fluctuations, but I have thought that the implications of his insight have been too narrowly interpreted in the literature that has developed since the publication of his paper.

Consider, for example, the question of the definition of the absolute price level in an economy that is both open and has some nonreproducible resources. When the final goods prices rise relative to the factor prices in the economy because the foreign-produced goods become much scarcer relative to the domestic factor availability, it is clearly a relative price change, and this fact can be understood by those who are prepared to think the question through and interpret the available data correctly. However, experience suggests that most citizens do not understand it, and they think of the movement of some broad price index, especially the CPI, as the indicator of the movement of the absolute price level. They feel in some sense entitled to have their income adjusted to the movement of such an index. This is a form of confusion on the part of economic agents, and it occurs even though information is in some sense available.

Another example is related to the interaction between the tax-transfer payment structure of most countries and the varying rate of inflation. Since the tax structure is defined in nominal terms, real incidences of taxes change when the rate of inflation varies. Thus, the tax system has large, unintended effects on the economy whenever the rate of inflation changes significantly. In addition, since the effects of taxes depend upon the economic status of the agent, it is extremely difficult for economic agents to analyze the "relative price effects" of variations in the aboslute price level, and they find it impossible to interpret movements of prices observable to them.

The recent literature has analyzed implications of Lucas's insight in the context of equilibrium rational-expectations models, but the above illustrations suggest that confusions in interpreting observed price changes are very widespread. In a detailed econometric model, we can often see that some (but by no means all) of the consequences of this phenomenon result in serious deterioration of the performance of the economy.

Once this issue is clearly recognized, one can think of a series of government actions that would substantially alleviate the problem. To begin with, it would be extremely helpful to construct a carefully defined price index that represents an average price of domestic factor contributions to output. Though this is not the occasion to go into details, I believe that a fixed-weight version of the domestic, private, nonfarm, business deflator, adjusted to net out the effects of indirect business taxes and to exclude value of nonreproducible inputs as much as possible, is closest to what we need. Such an index has the property that, if there is no movement of relative prices at all in the economy, then all income earners in the economy except owners of nonreproducible resources can expect their incomes to move proportionately with this index without causing inconsistencies in the economic system. If, on the other hand, members of some group in the economy receive an increase in nominal income greater than the movement of this index without specific justification in terms of their productivity, then some redistribution of income among groups in the economy for reasons other than efficiency must have taken place.[8] By constructing such an index, publishing it frequently and regularly, and explaining its significance to the public thoroughly, the government can provide the public with a means of decomposing any change of the price of a specific commodity or of the wage rate of a particular group into the relative price change and the change in the absolute price level. Second, I would like to see some government securities (in the case of the United States, some Treasury Bills and possibly some longer-maturity issues) indexed to this basic price index. This would enable us to observe in the market the real rate of interest, and would thus provide major additional information for policy makers and for the public. Moreover, the simultaneous presence of indexed and non-indexed bills of the same maturity would enable us to observe the market's expectation of the inflation rate.

In order that the information generated by the proposed indexed bills could be interpreted correctly, the tax system of the country would have to be made as neutral to the rate of inflation as possible. Of course, as I stated earlier, the reform of the tax system is very important in its own right as well. Without going into details, I list below main reforms of the tax–transfer system in the United States that I believe would be helpful for making the economy more easily adaptable to changes.

● The most important item associated with the role of indexed bills and monetary policies is the treatment of interest payments. Only the real part of interest payments, defined in terms of the basic index discussed above, should be subject to tax and also deductible for tax purposes. As indicated in earlier sections, the inclusion of the remainder of interest payments for tax computations had a significant role in pushing up the nominal rate of interest higher than was otherwise necessary, causing serious distortions in financial markets. With this reform, in order to maintain a monetary policy posture similar to the present one, assuming an inflation rate of 5 percent and an average marginal tax rate of 40 percent, we should be able to bring down the market rate of interest before tax by approximately 2 percent without changing the after-tax real rate and without any appreciable effect on tax revenue. In addition to reducing the distortion of resource allocations domestically, this should contribute to the reduction of federal government deficits (through lower interest payments) and to the improvement of the debt problems of the less developed countries. The main problem from the economic rather than the political point of view is the arrangements for the transition period, especially for existing long term bonds. I do not have time to go into the discussion of these issues, but I do not believe it is unsurmountable.

• On the corporate side, I believe the most sensible reform is to allow corporations to deduct the purchase cost of capital goods immediately upon purchase, to allow them to choose the timing of deductions within very broad limits, so long as the present value of the deductions at the market rate of interest at the time of the purchase remains the same. Simultaneously, the investment tax credits and other special provisions should be largely eliminated. It is essential also to eliminate the deductibility of interest payments for tax purposes, since they are already covered by the deduction of the purchase cost of capital. A major problem is the treatment of firms that continually suffer losses for some time, so that they cannot take advantage of deductibility provisions, even given the maximum flexibility in timing of deductions. (I do not, nevertheless, believe that negative taxes for corporations are desirable.) Such a tax system will come close to meeting the so-called Samuelson neutrality condition for the corporate profit tax, and it is to a large extent a tax on oligopoly rents and not on factor costs. A fairly detailed study done earlier by some of my associates indicated that such a reform, provided that some of my associates indicated that such a reform, provided that some more important special concessions are eliminated from the system, can collect about as much revenue as was collected (1979–80) at a tax rate not very different from that then prevailing.

• On the personal side, in addition to the exclusion of the nominal part of interest payments and receipts from the definition of taxable income, I believe that three reforms will be especially helpful: the indexation of all concepts in terms of which taxes are defined, the adoption of the principle that all deduction must be against specific income for which the deduction in question can be shown to be an expense, and the gradual strengthening of the minimum tax provision. These propositions include, among other things, the inclusion of the net (of depreciation) rent of owner-occupied houses, or, alternatively, elimination of the deductibility of mortgage interest payments and real estate taxes from the personal income tax code. Eventually, it is desirable to move toward a comprehensive tax-transfer system that involves a substantial credit per person (with some allowance for the difference between the head of household and the remaining members and for older persons) and a flat-rate tax on a very comprehensive definition of income . Such a system should replace not only the personal income tax system but also the Social Security system and other components of transfer systems, with the exception of support for individuals affected by major disasters such as floods and major and prolonged illnesses. It is important that the definition of income be really comprehensive, and that the basic credit per person be quite large, say $2,000 in 1985. Otherwise, a system such as this can become a major redistribution of income in favor of the wealthy, and most proposals in this direction currently discussed in public suffer from this defect.

The basic purpose of the definition and construction of the value-added price index discussed earlier is to provide the public with information in terms of which the distinction between price-level movements and relative-price movements can be recognized. I have been discussing reforms of government activities, especially tax and transfer systems, so that they are all defined in real terms using this index. I also believe that government wages should be indexed to movements of this index, with an understanding that any movement of wages (both for individuals and for aggregates) that is not proportional to this index is a change in the relative wage of government workers. Although it is probably not desirable to do anything compulsory about wages in the private sector, the hope here is that a thorough educational program plus the government's reforms will convince the private sector of the wisdom of measuring everything in terms of this index, and that eventually more and more contracts will be formulated in terms of this index, including labor contracts.

As international capital movements have become easier and easier, it has become more and more difficult for any single country—especially an open, small country—to maintain a different level of the interest rate. It seems that this should be conducive to efficient allocation of capital over international borders, but this is often negated by the fact that different countries maintain different ways of taxing capital and income from capital, and the same market rate of interest means different internal rates of return. This problem is exacerbated by the fact that tax provisions are often obscure, and it is difficult for anyone to master all the subtleties of tax systems of all countries and then make appropriate comparisons. The tax reforms that I have outlined above, when they and similar changes are undertaken by a number of countries, should make international comparison of rates of return on capital easier, thus reducing the most serious distortions. Most significant, when undertaken by the United States these reforms should reduce the tendency for surplus countries (such as Saudi Arabia) to earn very high rates of return while deficit countries incur unreasonably high costs of borrowing.

It should be emphasized here that past experiences with indexation, especially in Belgium, Italy, and Israel, went badly not because indexation is inherently unworkable but because the schemes were badly designed and were tied to the wrong price index. Most careful studies of indexation indicate that indexation by itself is not inflationary. On the contrary, by providing economic agents with the means of decomposing total price changes into relative price changes and movements of the absolute level of prices, proper indexation should reduce the probability that a large relative price disturbance will be translated into inflationary tendencies and that the adjustment process will be accompanied by allocational and employment problems more serious than is necessary.[9]

Before I conclude this part of the chapter, I wish to comment on a very different point. Under the present conditions of the world economy, every country would like to increase its exports, thereby increasing its employment and output. Thus, every country is trying to impress on its trade partners that they should take measures to increase their imports while attempting to reduce or at least hold constant its own imports. I do not believe that any of this is very helpful, and to the extent that some of these attempts succeed they simply reallocate production and employment among countries without improving the overall conditions of the world economy. But a coordinated measure to reduce import barriers in all countries is quite another matter, and it would have a very powerful stimulative effect on the world economy. This is especially clear in the case of a simultaneous reduction of import duties by all countries. Since such a simultaneous reduction of import duties is basically equivalent to a reduction in the worldwide sales tax, it must stimulate the world economy and reduce the rate of inflation at the same time. To the extent that other forms of import barriers can be converted into equivalent import duties, the result would be the same. Thus, if political leaders could be persuaded to shift their arguments from "correcting bilateral imbalance in trade" to "eliminating import barriers everywhere," the world as a whole would benefit greatly.

I have listed above, with brief comments, a certain set of reforms that appear to me to be generally beneficial and that should strengthen the ability of the economy to respond to what have become known as "supply" shocks. I believe that if these reforms could be undertaken the design of macroeconomic policies in the future would also become a little more rational, because these reforms would make the functioning of the economy somewhat more transparent and our task of predicting effects of macroeconomic actions by government a little easier.

Of course, my list of reforms is by no means exhaustive, and others will undoubtedly find other sets of reforms more critical and especially more politically feasible. Perhaps my list will contribute to stimulate discussions of these important issues.

Background

The Phillips Curve and the Natural Rate of Unemployment

The paper by Ando and Kennickell (1983) covers the issue of the historical performance of the particular Phillips curve equation together with the equations explaining various components of output prices given the wage rate. Whether or not there is a "direct" effect of money supply on prices is also dealt with in that paper.

In order to compute the natural rate of unemployment, we begin with the estimate of the Phillips curve and the basic price equation given the wage rate:

$$\frac{\Delta W}{W_{-1}} = f^w(u) + \sum_{i=1}^{12} \beta_i \left(\frac{\Delta P^f}{P^f_{-1}}\right)_{t-i} + \gamma \frac{\Delta T}{W_{-1}}$$

$$+ \sum_{i=1}^{6} \alpha_i \left(\frac{B_i}{(1-\tau)W}\right)_{t-i} + \text{Constant}, \tag{1}$$

$$\ln P^v = f^v(u) + \sum_{i=1}^{6} b_i \ln W_{t-i} + \sum_{i=0}^{10} c_i \left(\ln \frac{X}{L}\right)_{t-i}$$

$$+ \text{(Terms for short-run responses to changes in raw-material prices)}$$

$$+ \text{constant}, \tag{2}$$

$$\sum_{i=1}^{12} \beta_i = 1.0, \quad \sum_{i=1}^{6} b_i = 1.0, \quad \sum_{i=0}^{10} c_i = 1.0$$

where W is total compensation per man-hour, P^f is the price index for final goods, P^v is the fixed-weight value-added price index net of indirect business taxes, u is the unemployment rate, T is the contribution to social insurance (both for unemployment insurance and OASI-related), B is unemployment insurance paid per hours lost by unemployment, τ is the average personal income-tax rate, X is value-added output in 1972 prices, and L is man-hours employed. (All variables, as far as possible, refer to the private, domestic, nonfarm, business sector, excluding oil extraction.)

Even if we take the rate of unemployment u and the rate of productivity X/L to be given from outside, we still need another relationship between P^f and P^v to complete the system. This last relationship between the final goods-price index and the fixed-weight value-added deflator is in fact a complex set of relationships involving definitional identities and some behavioral equations, and the results reported in Ando and Kennickell 1983 take these additional relationships as a part of the system. In order to make clear the nature of the relationship involved, we may summarize the relationship between P^f and P^v as

$$P^f = \frac{V}{F}P^v + \frac{R}{F}P^R$$

where F, V, and R represent, respectively, final goods, value added, and raw materials at the base-year prices, and P^R is the price index for raw materials. The above relationships and equations 1 and 2 make it clear that the behavior of prices and wages will be profoundly different depending on whether the distributed lag of the rate of change of prices in equation 1 is in terms of P^f, as the equation is written, or in terms of P^v. If it is in terms of P^v, the system is recursive and equations 1 and 2 are capable of generating P^v and W by themselves given the rate of unemployment, the current and past productivity, and T and B. P^f is determined by the definition given above, and it is affected by but does not affect P^v. That is, any variation in P^R affects P^f but not P^v or W. However, when the distributed lag term in equation 1 is defined in terms of P^f, the system is not recursive, and variations in P^R affect not only P^f but also P^v and W, thus creating the possibility that supply shocks such as the OPEC price increases may set an inflationary spiral going.

There is no theoretical basis for choosing P^v or P^f in equation 1. It is determined instead by the institutional setting in the labor market of a specific country. In the United States, it appears reasonably certain that the choice has to be P^f under present conditions; in Japan, it seems plausible to say that it was P^f before 1978 but has been P^v since 1978, and this change is the major cause of the difference in the responses of the Japanese economy to the 1973–74 oil-price increase and to the 1979–80 increase.

For the purposes of defining the natural rate of unemployment, however, it does not seem sensible to let the natural rate be affected by such things as the oil-price increase. When the price of oil is increased exogenously, if the distributed lag term in equation 1 is defined in terms of P^f, then not only P^f but also P^v and W will increase. In such a system, whenever exogenous shocks raising prices like the oil price increases of 1973–74 and 1979–80 occur, the natural rate of unemployment must rise. The same can be said of an increase in the rate of Social Security contributions, T. For the purposes of defining the natural rate, therefore, we have equated the coefficient γ in equation 1 to zero, replaced the sum $\sum \beta_i (\Delta P^f / P^f_{-1})_{t-i}$ in equation 1 by $\Delta P^v / P^v_{-1}$, replaced the sum $\sum b_i \ln W_{t-i}$ by W_t in equation 2, and replaced the sum $\sum c_i [\ln(X/L)]_{t-i}$ by X/L in equation 2.

After these replacement, if we take the derivative with respect to time of the simplified equation 2 and substitute the simplified result into equation 1, the term $\Delta W/W$ also drops out and the resulting equation becomes a relationship among u, $B/(1-\tau)W$, and $\Delta (X/L)/(X/L)$:

$$f^w(u) + \frac{\Delta f^v}{\Delta u}\frac{\Delta u}{\Delta t} + \frac{\Delta(X/L)}{X/L} + \sum_{i=1}^{6} \alpha_i \left(\frac{B}{(1-\tau)w}\right)_{t-i} + \text{Const} = 0. \qquad (3)$$

We cannot, however, use the historical value of the rate of change of productivity, $\Delta (X/L)/(X/L)$, directly in this equation, because the historical value contains a good deal of cyclical variations which we do not wish the natural rate of unemployment to reflect. For this purpose, then, we must refer to the equation explaining X/L in the MPS model. This equation takes the basic form

$$\ln(L/X) = g \text{ TIME} + \sum h_i \ln(\text{VPDA})_{t-i}$$

$$+ \sum k_i \ln(\text{EOA})_{t-i} + \sum l_i \ln\left(1 - \frac{\text{LE}}{\text{N16}}\right)_{t-i} + \text{Const}$$

$$\text{Terms representing cyclical variations,} \qquad (4)$$

where TIME is calendar time, VPDA is a complex distributed lag of the optimal capital output ratio (as a function of the after-tax real cost of capital) implied by the estimated investment function under the assumption of the putty-clay technology, EOA is the ratio of the energy price to the value-added price index, LE is employment, and N16 is population 16 years and over.

The rate of growth of output that should enter equation 3 for the purposes of generating our estimates of the natural unemployment rate should be the basic, secular pattern of the growth rate, free of cyclical components.

Therefore, we define

$$\ln(L/X)^* = g \text{ TIME} + \sum h_i \ln(\text{VPDA})_{t-i} + \sum k_i \ln(\text{EOA})_{t-i}$$

$$+ \sum l_i \ln\left(1 - \frac{\text{LE}}{\text{N16}}\right)_{t-i} + \text{Const}^*, \tag{4'}$$

where the constant term is adjusted so that the mean of $\ln(L/X)^*$ is equal to the mean of $\ln(L/X)$ over the sample. Equation 4' then generates the productivity growth that is needed in equation 3.

I wish to comment on what I consider to be relatively less reliable aspects of the three critical equations that we have utilized above for generating our estimates of the natural rate of unemployment.

In equation 1, the most controversial term is the distributed lag of the past rate of change of prices. This term, to my mind, represents both the expectation of the future rate of change of prices by participants in the labor market and the past movements of prices indicating the effort by participants in the labor market to adjust the wage rate to keep the wage in line with the cost-of-living changes of the recent past. To the extent that it represents the expectations of future rates of change of prices, the formulation of expectations is simply adaptive rather than conforming to the notion of the rational-expectations hypothesis. This point becomes especially critical when a fairly radical change in monetary policy is contemplated and we are interested in analyzing the effects of such a policy change. My defense of this formulation is basically empirical, and it hinges on two observations. The first is the good empirical performance of this equation, especially since 1979, when a fairly radical change in the monetary policy rule did take place, as reported in Ando and Kennickell 1983. The second is that formulations incorporating some version of the rational-expectations hypothesis have not performed well empirically. I do not know of a reasonably satisfactory estimate of this equation that is based on the rational-expectations hypothesis, and my own attempts at it have never been successful.

The second point about this term is the choice of a particular price index to construct the distributed lag term, which has already been discussed. It should be stressed again, however, that the choice of the specific index to form this distributed lag term reflects a particular institutional setting in a particular country at a specific time, and it can change over time as the Japanese example indicates.

The third important question concerning equation 1 is the absence of the term involving the rate of growth of productivity. I believe there is a reasonable ground for the inclusion of the rate of growth in this equation, when it is considered by itself. Moreover, I believe that the presence of the productivity term in equation 2 with the sum of the coefficients of unity (which, I believe, is essential for equation 2 to make sense) combined with the absence of the rate of productivity growth term in equation 1 makes the natural rate of unemployment respond too strongly to the rate of growth of productivity, and I am uncomfortable with the situation. Thus, I would have preferred to have included the productivity growth term in equation 1. The reason for its absence is strictly empirical. We have never been able to find the significance for this term in equation 1. Moreover, when we tried to force it in, the fit and the characteristics of the equation deteriorated significantly.

The final question about equation 1 concerns the definition of the unemployment rate. There is some evidence presented in the literature that it should be defined as the unemployment rate of the primary workers or some restricted class of workers who may be considered as in some sense "regular" workers, or that it should be a fixed-weight average of unemployment rates of various classes of workers. I believe that the theory can be worked out in any number of ways, and hence the issue is empirical. We did not get much improvement in the performance of this equation by moving away from the normal definition of unemployment, and we have retained this simple formulation.

Equation 2 can be derived fairly formally as the equation representing the price-wage frontier for firms operating in a specific type of oligopoly market and where the output price is determined by a mark-up on the minimized average cost. This is an equation which has had very little trouble over the years, and I feel quite confident in its stability and reliability.

Equation 4 originally had a simpler form, consisting of the terms in TIME, VPDA, and terms representing cyclical variations. The terms in TIME and VPDA are implications of the putty-clay technology estimated in the investment function; the terms representing cyclical variations have been formulated following the work of Holt, Modigliani, Muth, and Simon on linear decision rules for inventory, for production schedules, and for work force. These specifications, I believe, are on a reasonably firm foundation, and they have withstood performance tests quite well since the early days of the MPS model in the early 1970s. Terms in EOA and $(1 - LE/N16)$ are added for the late 1970s, when energy-price variations and structural changes in labor force became significant. These two terms, in my view, are not as carefully thought out as the others, and they have been operating only during the past 5 years or so. Thus, I have somewhat less confidence in our estimates of the coefficients of these two terms than in the remaining parameter estimates in equation 4.

The Relationship among the Rate of Interest, the Rate of Growth of Output, and the National Debt

The discussion in the text is an application of very simple identities which are well known to most economists but whose implications on the relationship between the government finance and the monetary policy does not seem to have been widely realized.

Let us focus our attention on a simplified balance sheet of the government. We have an accounting identity:

$$\dot{D} = g\text{PX} + r\text{D} - \tau\text{PX} - \tau'r\text{D}, \tag{5}$$

where D is total net national debt outstanding in current dollars, PX is a measure of output (e.g., net domestic product) in current dollars, P is the price index for PX, r is the nominal market interest rate for government securities, g is the ratio of government expenditures on goods and services to PX, τ is the ratio of total net revenues of government excluding taxes on interest payments on government securities (revenues from all taxes excluding tax on interest payment on government securities less all transfer payments) to PX, and τ' is the net tax rate on interest payments on government securities. We also define the ratio of national debt to output, d, by

$$D \equiv d\text{PX}. \tag{6}$$

We therefore have

$$\dot{D} = \dot{d}\text{PX} + d\dot{\text{P}}\text{X} + d\text{P}\dot{\text{X}}. \tag{6'}$$

From equations 5 and 6', we have

$$\dot{d}\text{PX} + d\dot{\text{P}}\text{X} + d\text{P}\dot{\text{X}} = g\text{PX} + r\text{D} - \tau\text{PX} - \tau'r\text{D}.$$

Dividing both sides of the above expression by PX and rearranging terms, we have[10]

$$\dot{d} = d\left[r(1 - \tau') - \left(\frac{\dot{P}}{P} + \frac{\dot{X}}{X}\right)\right] + (g - \tau). \tag{7}$$

It is obvious that equation 7 is a differential equation of first order in d, and its stability requires that the coefficient of d be negative. The expression in brackets is the difference between the nominal, after-tax market rate of interest on government securities and the rate of growth of nominal income. The "nonhomogeneous" part of the equation, $(g - \tau)$, is the ratio of deficits of the government to PX, in which the deficit is defined as excluding interest payments and taxes collected on interest payments. The trouble with these concepts is that, for most countries, it is almost impossible to know the numerical value of the tax rate on government interest payments, since such a rate obviously depends on who owns the government securities in question and on complex economic conditions of the owners. Therefore, it is useful to rearrange equation 7 into another form:

$$\dot{d} = d\left[r - \left(\frac{\dot{P}}{P} + \frac{\dot{X}}{X}\right)\right] + (g - \tau - \tau'rd). \tag{7'}$$

In this form, the expression inside the brackets is equal to the difference between the market rate of interest on government securities and the rate of growth of nominal output, the quantity that can be readily observed. The second term on the right-hand side is equal to the deficit defined as total expenditure excluding interest payments minus total net taxes, also a quantity that is relatively easy to observe.

In equation 7', d appears in the second term, and the equation is less convenient mathematically to work with than equation 7; however, given that 7' involves only observable quantities, we can carry out numerical analysis more easily using it. For analytical purposes, however, let us focus on equation 7, and to make our discussion concise let us define

$$A \equiv r(1 - \tau') - \left(\frac{\dot{P}}{P} + \frac{\dot{X}}{X}\right)$$

and

$$B \equiv g - \tau.$$

If A is positive, equation 7 is fundamentally unstable. When d is positive and A is also positive, B can be made sufficiently negative most of the time so that $\dot{d}$ is kept continuously negative. That is, it is theoretically possible that, even when A is positive, a government can run large enough surpluses most of the time to keep moving the ratio of national debt to PX toward zero. But d will become zero eventually, and then negative. Once d becomes negative (that is, once government eliminates its debt and begins to accumulate net assets), then the continuation of surpluses in its budget will make the net assets of government as a proportion of PX larger and larger without limit. This, of course, is highly unlikely. In a more likely case, starting with a situation in which d is positive, when A is positive and B is also positive, $\dot{d}$ must remain positive and become larger over time. That is, if A is positive and the government runs any deficit (defined as excluding interest payments on national debt), then the ratio of national debt to PX must increase over time at an increasing rate. I believe this is the situation that we now face in the United

States since the 1982–83 period, even when we define government deficits as excluding the part that is due largely to the recession.

If A is negative, on the other hand, equation 7 is stable and the value of d will stabilize at $-(B/A)$. Since A is negative, the sign of d is the same as that of B; that is, if the government runs deficits as a rule, then the ratio of national debt to PX will settle down to some finite value. On the other hand, if the government runs surpluses as a rule, then the ratio of government ownership of assets relative to PX will settle down to some finite value.

In practice, some of government deficits will be absorbed as reserves against currency, for which the national treasury does not pay interest. It is easy to modify our formulation for this additional complication.

Between 1947 and 1980, except for cyclical movements, the United States had the situation in which A was continuously negative, although I believe the absolute value of A was quite small. Furthermore, the federal government has continuously run surpluses as defined above (excluding interest payments) with the exception of two severe recession years, although the surpluses were very small. Since the value of d was very large at the end of the Second World War, this meant that the value of d was positive and falling very slowly throughout those years.

It is fairly obvious that there is a close parallel between the problems of national debt discussed above and the problems associated with external debt of a country, and I can be very brief in the discussion of the latter. We are concerned here with the real asset-liability position of a country, not with the liquidity problem. The real asset-liability position of a country can change only with a surplus or a deficit in the trade balance, and we can write

$$\dot{B} = (\text{IM} - \text{EX}) + rB, \tag{8}$$

$$B \equiv qbX, \tag{9}$$

where B is net external borrowing (gross liabilities less assets) measured in dollars, IM is imports excluding interest payments for external debt (gross) measured in dollars, EX is exports excluding interest payments on external assets (gross) measured in dollars, r is the interest rate in the dollar market, q is the exchange rate of the dollar in terms of the local currency, X is the output of the country in terms of the local currency, and b is the ratio of B to qX defined by equation 9. Taking the derivative with respect to time of both sides of equation 9 and combining the resulting equation with equation 8, we have

$$\dot{q}bX + q\dot{b}X + qb\dot{X} = (\text{IM} - \text{EX}) + rB.$$

Dividing the above expression through by qX, we finally have

$$\frac{\dot{q}}{q}b + \dot{b} + b\frac{\dot{X}}{X} = \frac{IM}{qX} - \frac{EX}{qX} + rb,$$

$$\dot{b} = b\left[r - \left(\frac{\dot{q}}{q} + \frac{\dot{X}}{X}\right)\right] + \left(\frac{IM}{qX} - \frac{EX}{qX}\right). \tag{10}$$

Equation 10 is identical in its form to equation 7, so the same line of analysis applies. We note that $(\dot{q}/q + \dot{X}/X)$ is the rate of growth of the country's output in terms of dollars, and that equation 10 is simpler than equation 7 because a tax system does not intervene.

It may be useful at this point to provide some orders of magnitudes for the quantities involved. Figures 8.1 and 8.2 show a set of estimates of real rates of interest. For Treasury bills and corporate AAA bonds, the expectation of inflation is assumed to be adaptive. In the case of bills it is based on actual inflation in the previous two quarters; in the case of bonds a weighted average of the inflation rate for the previous 12 quarters was used. The real rate on equities was measured as profits (adjusted for inventory valuation, capital consumption, and for capital gains in debts) divided by the value of equities.

Since market expectations of the inflation rate are not directly observed in these cases, the time patterns of real rates on the Treasury bills and the corporate bonds will depend on the assumption chosen as the expectation formation, and what I have plotted can be disputed.[11] I do not feel that we are in the position to settle the question of exactly how the expectations of the inflation rate looked, because of the lack of direct observations on this critical variable, but I think the qualitative features of the time pattern of the real rate remain invariant with respect to the choice of the assumption on the expectation formation. Market rates on Treasury bills and bonds rose mildly from the mid 1950s to the mid 1970s, fell noticeably in the second half of the 1970s, and then rose dramatically after 1980. On the other hand, the return on equity rose unmistakably in the mid 1970s and has remained high ever since. The recovery of the stock market has reduced this rate somewhat since the summer of 1982, but this reduction is almost insignificant in size relative to the rise since 1974.

This difference is further accentuated by the fact that, for corporations, interest payments on debts are deductible for tax purposes while dividend payments on equity are not. It is a little hard to pin down exactly how much this deductibility is worth to American corporations in general because it depends on what the marginal tax rate happens to be for each corporation before interest payments are deducted. The marginal rate is surely, on average, less than the statutory rate of 46 percent, but it is hard to believe that it is as low as 20 percent. Figure 8.2 illustrates these two limiting cases for the

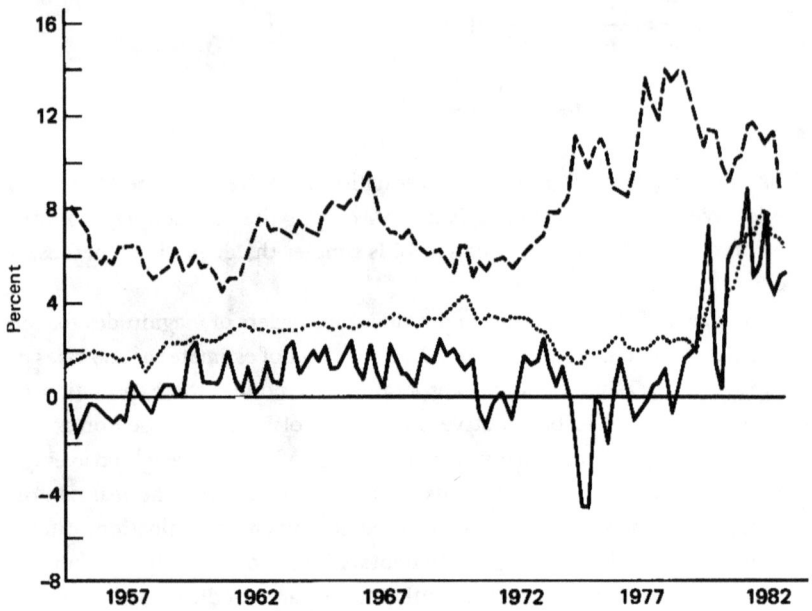

Figure 8.1
Estimates of real rates of return. (———) Treasury bills; (·····) corporate bonds; (-
nonfinancial corporate equities.

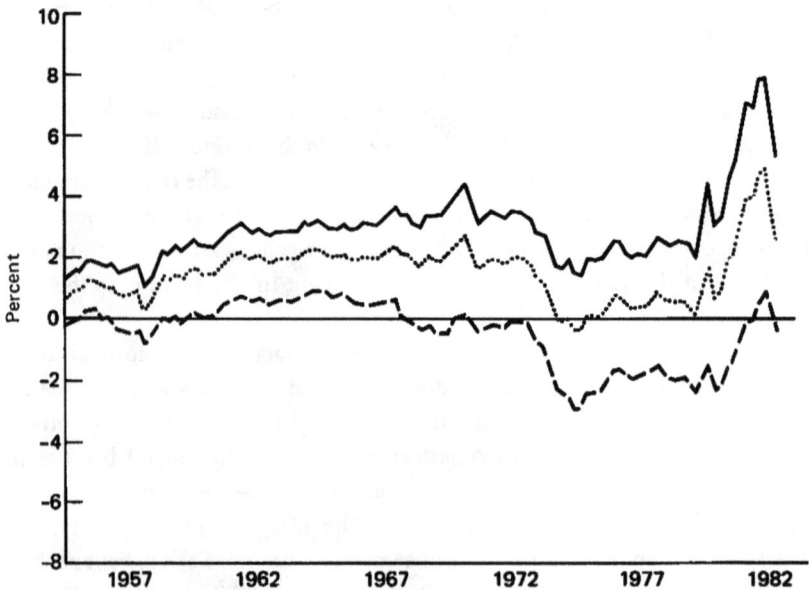

Figure 8.2
After-tax real interest rates on corporate AAA bonds. (———) Tax rate = 0; (·····) tax
rate = 0.2; (————) federal corporate income tax marginal rate.

AAA corporate bond rate. Since the American tax laws are defined strictly in nominal terms, the higher the rate of inflation and the higher the nominal rate of interest to reflect it the more valuable the deductibility of interest payments for tax purposes will be. This is clearly reflected in the comparison of figures 8.1 and 8.2. Therefore, since the mid 1970s the required return on equity has been unusually high while the real required return after tax on bonds has been very low (perhaps negative, at least in some years). Even for the period since 1980, in which the market real rate of interest before tax has become very high, it is not clear that the real rate on bonds after tax is so high. Under the circumstances, there is an unusual amount of uncertainty as to what the time pattern of the total required rate for corporations has been, since it depends critically on how we average the rate of return on equity and the rate of return on bonds.

In table 8.2 I present the factor by which the cost capital must be multiplied in order to give the internal required rate. This ratio becomes unity when the present value of the depreciation allowance for tax purposes at the time of the purchase of a machine is equal to the purchase cost of the machine and there are no other special tax provisions, such as the investment tax credit. This is the numerical counterpart of the well-known proposition of P. A. Samuelson on the conditions under which the corporate profit tax is neutral in decisions by corporations on the capital/labor ratio. Since this condition is not satisfied in reality, the ratio reported on table 8.2 is not unity but varies from 1.4 in 1955 to 1.03 in the first quarter of 1983. Over the years, the introduction of the investment tax credit, the gradual broadening of its applicability, and the increase in its rate, and also the liberalization of the depreciation allowance, have reduced this ratio, bringing it down almost to unity by 1983. Thus, the corporate profit tax is almost neutral under the present law, except for the deductibility of interest payments on debts. Thus, under the current law, what is being taxed is mainly oligopoly profits, accompanied by subsidies for those who finance their investment by debts. Of course, this is the nationwide average, and conditions vary a great deal from one industry to another, from profitable companies to loss-making ones, and from fast-growing companies to stationary ones. The resulting taxes and subsidies affect the allocation of resources in a variety of directions surely unintended by a generation of policy makers responsible for these provisions.

An important consequence of this situation is that the elasticity of the real, after-tax, net cost of capital with respect to the market rate of interest is quite small, and therefore, in order to have significant impact on investments, the monetary authority must move the nominal market rate of interest by a very large amount. This is one of the reasons why the market rate of interest has

Table 8.2
Factor by which market real rate (after tax for debts) is multiplied to yield required internal rate of return on investment, net of depreciation.

1955	1.43
1956	1.42
1957	1.46
1958	1.46
1959	1.36
1960	1.33
1961	1.27
1962	1.19
1963	1.19
1964	1.11
1965	1.11
1966	1.11
1967	1.09
1968	1.19
1969	1.21
1970	1.31
1971	1.26
1972	1.14
1973	1.11
1974	1.13
1975	1.13
1976	1.11
1977	1.12
1978	1.13
1979	1.09
1980	1.12
1981	1.07
1982	1.08
1983:I	1.03

Table 8.3
Ratio of net federal government debt to GNP.

1952	0.56
1953	0.54
1954	0.57
1955	0.52
1956	0.48
1957	0.45
1958	0.46
1959	0.43
1960	0.42
1961	0.41
1962	0.39
1963	0.38
1964	0.36
1965	0.33
1966	0.31
1967	0.30
1968	0.29
1969	0.26
1970	0.25
1971	0.25
1972	0.25
1973	0.24
1974	0.22
1975	0.23
1976	0.24
1977	0.25
1978	0.25
1979	0.23
1980	0.23
1981	0.23
1982	0.26
1983	0.31[a]
1984	0.34[a]
1985	0.36[a]
1986	0.39[a]
1987	0.42[a]
1988	0.44[a]

a. Based on Congressional Budget Office predictions.

become so high since 1980, when the Federal Reserve authority moved decisively in the direction of reducing the aggregate demand in order to create downward pressure on the rate of inflation.

In table 8.3 I present the time series of the ratio of the net debt position of the federal government to the gross national product. These figures are net of federal debts held by the federal agencies (except for Federal Reserve hold-ings) and also net of financial liabilities of the private sector held by the federal government. As is generally known, this ratio has been declining ever since the end of the Second World War, quite rapidly through 1968 and more slowly thereafter until 1980. In 1982 it began to rise, and if we take the projections of the Congressional Budget Office seriously it has risen drama-tically since then. This is the situation that was discussed in a more abstract manner in the earlier part of this section.

Notes

1. See, for instance, Blinder 1979; Eckstein 1978; Feldstein 1980.

2. At the meeting, Mr. K. Shigehara of the Bank of Japan, the coordinator of these sessions, distributed tables giving the monetary and fiscal multipliers of the MPS model and its two variants.

When the specifications of a model are changed, multipliers, of course, must change, and whether these changes are reasonable cannot be judged unless all the details of the specification changes are known. Since Mr. Shigehara did not provide us with any information on what changes he introduced into the MPS model in order to generate these different sets of multipliers, the numerical details of his tables *per se* mean very little, and Mr. Shigehara must have known this. His points, therefore, must be that multipliers are sensitive to detailed specifications of the model, that, we cannot say with any degree of confidence which one of several plausible specifications is the best approximation to reality, and that therefore we cannot rely on these models to tell us how the economy will respond to any changes in monetary and fiscal policies. Mr. Shigehara must feel very strongly about this, because he apparently considered that it warranted the extraordinary step of using his chair as the coordinator to make this point at length. Under the circumstances, I feel compelled to respond to his point.

Multipliers depend not only on specifications of the model but also on the initial conditions and on the assumptions concerning responses of policy variables as con-ditions of the economy unfold over time. It is quite possible that, when some specifi-cations of the model are changed, multipliers appear to change substantially under one condition and not under others. For instance, fiscal multipliers may change substan-tially in response to changes in the specifications of some equation for a component of the aggregate demand when the assumed monetary policy is to keep the pattern of the money supply the same when fiscal policy is changed, but they may not change substantially when the assumed monetary policy is to follow some reasonable stabiliza-tion rule. Furthermore, those specification changes that induce substantial changes in multipliers are likely to be critical specifications of the model, and in the case of these critical specifications it is not true that any alternative is equally reasonable. The issue is not whether multipliers change in response to specification changes, as Mr. Shigehara seems to suggest, but whether Mr. Shigehara's way of computing the multiplier is at all sensible, and if it is, then which of the three models he used (and therefore the multipliers associated with it) is the most believable. For this purpose, however, Mr. Shigehara would have had to present his revisions of the model and the conditions under which he computed multipliers in complete detail, and the conference was not a suitable forum for such a discussion.

The uncertainties associated with these choices may be considered quite excruciating, but the only alternative—to rely on more qualitative and less explicit analysis—is no solution. Any "law" in economics, however abstract and general, can never be true unconditionally; it can hold only approximately and under some specific circumstances. When one attempts to specify the circumstances under which a particular "law" holds and its degree of approximation sufficiently explicitly so that it is usable for a policy analysis, one will find that detailed choices of specifications are necessary to the same degree no matter what the style of the initial formulation may be. To pretend that one can make policy recommendations without facing these choices is irresponsible.

3. For an example of tests of a similar point by others, see Gordon 1982.

4. There is certain arbitrariness in the practical definition of the natural rate. It arises in the choice of in what sense the tendency of the rate of inflation to rise or fall should be absent. Should the temporary increases in the inflation rate due to causes that are external to the system (for instance, the rise in the price of oil) be excluded from the definition of the natural rate, or not? I have chosen to calculate the figures quoted in the text using the definition in which externally induced increases in inflation automatically raise the level of the natural rate. I have done so against my own inclination because I sense that the public in general prefers to counter external shocks in this way. See also my discussion in the second part of this chapter.

5. It should be remembered that the fiscal policies of the late 1960s were pursued against the advice of the government's economic experts, who knew that they were overly expansionary. On the other hand, it should also be recognized that some substantial improvements resulted from the somewhat overheated economy, especially in the employment conditions of otherwise poor and unskilled segments of the labor force. The number of families below the poverty line declined more during this period than in any other period in recent history.

6. In the MPS model there exists a rule for monetary policy decision using the federal fund rate as the instrument that, when given a proper setting of parameters, is capable of pushing the economy steadily toward a path on which the actual unemployment rate is close to the natural rate and returning the economy to such a path quite effectively after a variety of shocks. Given this setup, we can numerically compare market rates of interest that emerge under alternative fiscal-policy configurations, and we can be much more specific about the proposition stated in the text. Some readers may not find any evidence that comes out of a model such as the MPS model especially persuasive, since they do not find the model itself an acceptable representation of reality. However, I believe that the above proposition is consistent with a variety of models, and I invite the reader to consider the proposition in terms of the model most congenial to him.

7. This is not always true. If the private savings rate in the economy is so high that, at full employment, the government can run significant deficits while maintaining a market rate of interest clearly lower than the rate of growth of nominal output without risking acceleration of inflation, the situation can be tolerated indefinitely.

8. If this point is well understood and accepted by the public, in terms of behavioral equations in most econometric models, it will have, among other things, the effect of replacing the current and past rates of change of the consumer price index now appearing in the Phillips-curve equation by the price index defined above. This means that, whereas under the current formulation the nominal wage rate rises to compensate for the increase in such external supply shocks as the oil-price increases, with the reform proposed here the nominal wage rate will not respond to these supply shocks directly. This makes a profound difference in the economy's susceptibility to inflation.

9. For a recent analysis of indexation along these lines, see Marston 1983.

10. This expression is not independent of the rate of inflation. This feature is the result of the formulation of equation 5, in which the tax of government interest payments is made proportional to the total nominal interest payments—that is, the real capital gain that the government makes on its nominal debts has no implications on real tax revenues. This is, of course, a concession to the tax system in the real world. If, on the other hand, it is assumed that only "real" interest payments are taxed, so that the tax revenue in question is equal to $\tau'(r - \dot{P}/P)D$ in equation 5, then equation 7 becomes

$$\dot{d} = d\left[\left(r - \frac{\dot{P}}{P}\right)(1 - \tau') - \frac{\dot{X}}{X}\right] + (g - \tau).$$

This form is independent of the rate of inflation.

11. In particular, on the basis of indirect observations it may be argued that the expected rate of inflation in the period 1974–1978 was considerably lower than the values used here, since economic agents failed to adjust to the rapidly rising rate of inflation; since 1982 it has been somewhat higher than the assumption here implies because economic agents are again failing to adjust to the rapidly falling rate of inflation. On the other hand, on the basis of a strict version of the rational-expectations hypothesis, the opposite argument could be mounted.

References

Ando, A., and A. Kennickell. 1983. "Failure" of Keynesian Economics and "Direct" Effects of Money Supply: A Fact or a Fiction? Unpublished manuscript.

Blinder, A. S. 1979 *Economic Policy and the Great Stagflation* (New York: Academic).

Blinder, A. S. 1982. Issues in the Coordination of Monetary and Fiscal Policy. Paper presented at conference on "Monetary Policy Issues in the 1980s," Jackson Lake Lodge, Wyoming.

Blinder, A. S. 1983. Reaganomics and Growth: The Message in the Models. Paper presented at Urban Institute Conference on the Reagan Economic Program and Long Term Growth.

Congressional Budget Office. 1983. *Baseline Budget Projections for Fiscal Years 1974–78* (Washington: Superintendent of Documents).

Eckstein, O. 1978. *The Great Recession* (Amsterdam: North-Holland).

Feldstein, Martin, ed. 1980. *The American Economy in Transition* (University of Chicago Press).

Gordon, R. J. 1982. "Inflation, Flexible Exchange Rates, and the Natural Rate of Unemployment," in Martin N. Baily, ed., *Workers, Jobs and Inflation* (Washington: Brookings Institution).

Lucas, R. E. 1972. "Expectations and Neutrality of Money." *Journal of Economic Theory*, vol. 4, no. 2, pp. 103–124.

Marston, R. C. 1983. Real Wages and the Terms of Trade: Alternative Indexation Rules for an Open Economy. NBER Working Paper 1046.

Office of Management and Budget. 1983. *Budget of the United States, Fiscal Year 1984* (Washington: Superintendent of Documents).

Sargent, T. J. 1982. "The Ends of Four Big Inflations," in R. Hall, ed. *Inflation: Causes and Effects* (University of Chicago Press).

Tobin, J. 1980. "Stabilization Policy Ten Years After." *Brookings Papers on Economic Activity*, I.

Comments

Sylvia Ostry

These two chapters are in one respect a resounding refutation of George Bernard Shaw's dictum that if you laid all the economists in the world end to end they would not reach a conclusion. Professors Sargent and Ando—two economists of widely divergent views of how economies work—arrive, from quite different premises, at a common conclusion on a crucial point: The prospective U.S. budget deficits are inconsistent with noninflationary growth. Indeed, if I follow the logic of the papers, the proposition could be strengthened: If current spending and/or tax schedules are not substantially modified, the present situation is untenable and can only deteriorate seriously. This conclusion is very familiar to anyone who has attended OECD meetings, where it is regularly repeated, in suitably diplomatic language, by all member countries.

However, the fact that there are economists—including some at this meeting, and perhaps more important some at elevated levels in the U.S. administration—who would strongly disagree suggests that George Bernard Shaw can rest peacefully in his grave. Perhaps some of the dissenters will "prove" to us that the inflation-adjusted out-year structural deficit of the United States is a mirage.

The big analytical difference between Sargent and Ando is in the transmission of monetary restraint to the real economy. Ando can explain what happened through a process of adaptive expectations and transmission which goes from short-term to long-term rates. Sargent has more "rational" or forward-looking expectations and transmission from monetary aggregates and inflation expectations to long-term rates. The policy differences that follow from the two approaches are well known. Ando emphasizes the sticky expectations and poor returns to keeping unemployment well above the natural rate; for him the Fed tightened too much and the recession need not have been as bad as it was. Had it not been for the old-fashioned demand impact of fiscal policy, the recession would presumably have been worse.

Sargent claims that fiscal policy adversely affected inflationary expectations so that they did not adapt to stated policy goals. Uncertainty (generated by the three-way game of "chicken") induces a supply response, which causes a decline in output and a rise in unemployment. If I understand what Professor Sargent is saying, had it not been for the tax cuts etc. the recession would have been less severe. So the authors imply different signs on the impact of recent U.S. fiscal changes, though, as I said, they agree on the necessity to cut the out-year structural deficit. What is not clear to me is whether in Professor Sargent's view the decline in output and the rise in unemployment are mainly or even entirely due to the uncertainty stemming from the game of "chicken." Was some of this due to the fact that Fed policy was unintentionally tight at the end of 1981 and during 1982 until the summer? Or—in the terminological spirit of his chapter—did the name of the game change from "chicken" to "cold turkey"? By August—or September—would Wallace have declared the Fed chicken? How will we know when the game is over? And, most important, who is the coach?

Professor Ando makes clear that looser monetary policy lowers interest rates and stimulates demand. Expectations play no role in this, yet it is difficult to reject the view that policy makers believe that expectations matter and that this belief is a powerful constraint on their room to maneuver.

It sometimes appears to me that market expectations are not formed by policy announcements but that policy announcements are formed by market expectations. Parenthetically, it is not clear to me what explanation Professor Ando would provide for the present level of short rates. Since the Fed has eased, rates fell until the beginning of this year and then plateaued or rose. Long rates are explicable in his model given short but why are the latter where they are now?

Professor Sargent's chapter deals mainly with the "flation" part of the stagflation problem and only with the U.S. policy mix. Ando refers to the international consequences of the U.S. policy mix and in particular points to the serious implications for the highly indebted developing countries. For the latter the conditions for debt stabilization spelled out by Ando are similar to those described in a number of recent analyses by international institutions and private researchers. He does not, however, include any reference to factors other than LDC growth and interest rates such as OECD growth rates, commodity and oil prices, and exchange rates. Are his conditions both necessary and sufficient?

One issue missing from both chapters is the importance of international linkage in the present world economic situation. After OPEC II (partly because of the unhappy experience of divergent policy responses to the mid-decade shock, which left the underlying rate of inflation in 1979 at 9 percent for the area as a whole), the OECD countries adopted a synchronized tightening of monetary and fiscal policy designed to contain the exogenous price pulse. The consequences of synchronized policies—given the strong linkages within the OECD and the growing interdependence between the OECD and the non-OECD countries—were significantly different from those expected by each country individually.

At the first session of the conference we discussed the difficulties of calibrating domestic monetary policy. The far greater difficulty of calibrating synchronized or convergent policies in an interdependent world has not been confronted, except in the fleeting exchange on the futility of seeking inter-national coordination. Still, the problem will not go away even if the solution eludes us. In Sargent's game-strategy terms, will the resolution be centralized or decentralized? Is the most likely outcome that of one player but several coaches?

Finally, in the second part of Professor Ando's chapter, which we received on arrival at the conference, he presents some ideas on structural reform. Rightly focusing on the need to adjust to change, he selects two examples—changes in relative prices and the impact of inflation on the tax-transfer system—and proposes structural reforms in the U.S. context (though the proposals likely have wider applicability).

The problems of rigidity in the European economies are not—understandably—treated in either paper. The structural component of un-employment appears to be, from our analysis, far greater in Europe than in North America and certainly far greater than in Japan, and it by no means stems from a single source. The greater rigidity of real wages and especially of nonwage labor costs in Europe is another problem requiring structural rather than macro policy treatment. The underlying dynamism of the United States and its greater flexibility and responsiveness can be illustrated in many ways, but one striking manifestation was the record of job creation over the 1970s: U.S. employment increased by over 20 percent, compared with a 2 percent or 3 percent growth in Europe. The far greater rate of births and deaths of small firms provides another significant contrast, as does the greater mobility of the labor force in every dimension—geographic, industrial, and occupational. The European concern with actual as opposed to structural budget deficits, which has led a number of European countries to what can only be described as procyclical gross tuning with results akin to running up the down escalator, marks yet another difference with the United States. I do not suggest we should discuss all these issues. I raise them for two reasons: First, the current problem for many of the low-inflation countries of the OECD, which have restored their inflation rates to the level of the 1960s, is probably not well described by the word stag*flation*. Second, just to redress the balance, it is very misleading to suggest that all the economic problems in Europe or elsewhere bear the stamp "Made in the U.S.A."

Comments

Richard G. Davis

Of the two chapters under discussion, the Sargent chapter deals exclusively with the relationship between fiscal and monetary policy; the Ando chapter covers a wide range of topics, but a substantial part of it is also devoted to the fiscal/monetary nexus. My comments will concentrate on this issue.

In tracing the connections between the U.S. fiscal outlook and its potential problems for monetary policy, both chapters go well beyond current journalistic and market discussions. Both suggest that the current fiscal outlook poses not merely problems, but truly alarming risks for monetary and price stability.

Professor Sargent argues that "it is simply not feasible" to carry out both a policy of noninflationary monetary growth rates and the prospective pattern of fiscal deficits. That large deficits represent at least a problem for monetary policy is of course a commonplace. We all know that uncontrolled deficits and the need to finance them at the central bank have been a very frequent cause of major inflation. In the United States, however, we generally tend to believe that the market for government securities is sufficiently broad that deficits can always be financed without recourse to the central bank. And because of the way in which monetary policy is normally conducted, we usually assume that there need be no necessary connection between deficits and monetary policy.

Professor Sargent, however, does introduce such a necessary connection. He does this by positing an absolute limit on the debt that may be sold in the market. If such a limit exists, then, given a path for the deficits, a tight money policy now simply hastens the day when the central bank will be forced to monetize further deficits. The reason is that a tighter money policy means fewer purchases of government debt by the central bank and thus more purchases by the public. Hence, a tighter money policy now also means a more rapid rise now in the public's holdings of debt. Thus, it hastens the day when the posited absolute limit on such holdings is reached. It therefore also hastens the day when the central bank must purchase most or all increases in the public debt. Such monetization, in turn, brings on inflation. It does so in the future, at least, and will do so even in the present if price expectations are formed "rationally" and if the demand for base money is negatively related to expected future inflation rates.

With these assumptions, restrictive monetary policy will be, as Professor Sargent says, literally infeasible given deficits that stretch out indefinitely into the future and given a real interest rate in excess of the real growth rate.

The general logic of Professor Sargent's argument is clear enough. However, I really do not understand why he makes its centerpiece an absolute limit to the willingness of the public to take on government debt. It would seem to me far more natural simply to assume (as Professor Ando does) that, over the relevant range of values, the public will take on increasing amounts of public debt, provided the real rates of interest on this debt rise absolutely and/or in relation to the real yields on alternative assets. In this case, the problem of conflict between large deficits and monetary restraint becomes less dramatic but, I think, more relevant to the actual situation.

I do not think market participants, or anyone else, are really worried about the technical ability of the U.S. government to sell its bonds without recourse to the central bank. However, the market may well be worried about the implications of large current and prospective deficits for real interest rates, and this worry may extend further to the willingness (not the ability) of the central bank to persist in noninflationary monetary growth rates in the face of high real interest rates.

As I understand it, the usual argument is that high real interest rates brought on by large deficits will ultimately produce political pressures to accelerate money growth. Moreover, worry about the inflationary implications of this scenario adds to the inflation premium the market puts on nominal interest rates.

Whatever its precise quantitative importance, this line of argument seems plausible to me. For this reason alone, it seems clear that large current and prospective deficits create problems for conducting an anti-inflationary monetary policy, even in the United States. However, in the United States at least, these problems do not seem to me to be primarily the technically determined problems that Professor Sargent describes. Instead, they may be more in the nature of "political economy" problems that the market translates into currently higher nominal and real interest rates. As the market sees it, the higher are the deficits the greater may be the risks that monetary policy will not be allowed to continue on a noninflationary course. But the problem is not primarily one of arithmetic. No one can say for sure what level of prospective deficits would make noninflationary monetary policy literally infeasible. The answer to the question may depend as much on one's analysis of the priorities of the electorate as it does on purely economic considerations.

Professor Ando's very interesting chapter also looks at (among other things) the relationships among interest rates, real growth, deficits, and the government debt ratio and the implications of the latter for the feasibility of a noninflationary monetary policy. The result is a rather chilling scenario of how deficits under current conditions may represent a threat to the ultimate feasibility of such a policy. First, Professor Ando suggests that, because of current and prospective U.S. deficits, the real rate of interest that would be associated with the natural rate of unemployment exceeds the growth rate of the economy. He then notes some arithmetic also cited by Professor Sargent: If the rate of interest exceeds the growth rate of the economy, in the absence of surpluses, the ratio of debt to GNP will rise, and at an increasing rate. Professor Ando goes on to note that such a rise will require a progressive rise in the real (and the nominal) interest rate on the debt. This rise in interest rates, in turn, will exacerbate the problem, first by accelerating the rise in the debt and second by slowing down the growth in output. In principle, the outcome is an unsustainable, explosive rise in the debt ratio and thus in interest rates. Ando believes that current and prospective fiscal policies and the associated interest rates satisfy the conditions for such an outcome.

I find Ando's argument of considerable interest, but before knowing how heavily it should be weighted as a practical matter I would want to know the answer to several questions: Is the real interest rate associated with the natural rate of unemployment in the United States in fact greater than the economy's potential growth rate? If it is, can feasible fiscal policies reduce it enough to eliminate the problem? Perhaps most important, just how rapidly would rises in the debt ratio push up the real interest rate associated with an economy running at the natural rate of unemployment? The answers to these questions are needed to determine whether the mechanism described by Professor Ando is powerful enough to add significantly to the problems we already know are created by large prospective deficits.

Professor Ando notes that the ratio of the debt in private hands to the GNP is now actually much lower than it was earlier in the postwar period. However, his calculations, with which I generally agree, suggest that under the so-called current services budget this ratio could rise sharply over the next several years, reaching roughly 45 percent in the late 1980s (a level last approached in the late 1950s). In other words, by the late 1980s we would still be at debt levels by no means unprecedented in the United States or in other countries experiencing reasonably satisfactory economic conditions. Nevertheless, the sharp rise projected for this ratio without action on the fiscal front is clearly a sobering calculation, and I think it deserves more widespread attention.

I am persuaded that in the long run deficits, if not brought under control, represent a threat to the ultimate viability of noninflationary monetary policy. An understanding of the interconnections is improved by these two chapters in their focus on portfolio considerations. I do not doubt the urgency, from many points of view, of getting the deficit under control. However, without trying to draw any conclusion, I would like to note that either the market does not understand the mechanisms described in these papers, or it does not think them empirically important, or it thinks the fiscal problem will be resolved before major damage is done. At the moment, the U.S. yield curve is roughly normally sloped for this point in the business cycle. This suggests to me that the market expects no explosive rise over any horizon in either real or nominal rates or in the rate of inflation. Let us hope this reflects a rational expectation that the Ando scenario will not materialize.

Comments

Erik L. Karlsson

Professor Sargent has shown that there are risks involved in having a big government budget deficit and that there also are risks involved in having big government expenditures. Large expenditures and big deficits imply that important goals for economic policy will not be reached. Price stability is unlikely to be maintained. The credibility of the anti-inflationary policy is at stake. He is referring to a big country, in particular the United States, but what he says is also true for small countries. Sweden is one of them, and like other central bankers I wish to refer particularly to my own country.

In Sweden government expenditures have increased enormously in the last few years. In the early 1970s, before the first oil crisis, total public expenditures amounted to about 45 percent of GDP. Now they are 70 percent, half of them consisting of transfers to various sectors. We have got this increase as a result of the policy pursued after the oil-price shocks, a policy involving among other things subsidies to enterprises. The government budget deficit has increased from 2–3 percent to 13–14 percent of GDP.

In the meantime we have learned a few things:

• We have recognized that the increase in public-sector expenditures must be stopped, having reached such a high level. There is a risk that further increases cannot be covered by increased tax rates. Increases in tax rates now tend to lead to lower economic activity, and through that to a lower tax base and finally to lower tax revenues.

• The structure of the tax system has to be taken into consideration. The high marginal income tax rate must be reduced. Value-added taxes seem to function better. The tax system should not dampen the interest sensitivity of household spending; to achieve this end, interest costs should not be deductible from taxable income.

• Subsidizing of enterprises should be avoided. Sargent points out that tax relief and other subsidies to enterprises lead to bigger government deficits, higher interest rates, and a worsened situation for enterprises. To that can be added that subsidies also negatively affect the behavior of enterprises. Enterprises become more interested in getting further government support than in pursuing normal business activity.

• Increasing government budget deficits have a clearly and strongly negative impact on the current account of the balance of payments. Sharply falling public-sector financial savings are not normally balanced by a similar increase in private-sector savings. Instead they lead to a weaker current account of the balance of payments and a fast-rising foreign debt.

• The interest trap is observed too late. During the first few years of big government budget deficits, the interest service on the debt is small. Suddenly the interest costs amount to a large proportion of the total deficit. In 1976 interest payments on the government debt were less than 5 percent of total government expenditures, which were then rather low. In 1983 they are 18 percent of government expenditures, which are now much larger. Before the first oil crisis, Sweden's net interest payments on foreign debt were zero. Now they are close to 10 percent of total earnings on exports of goods and services.

• Big government deficits are difficult to finance tightly enough. Even if interest rates on government securities are raised substantially, it is not possible to sell the necessary amounts of the securities outside the banking system. Investors become fed up with government bonds and bills. The resistance against government securities increases fast when the outstanding amount reaches high levels.

Here I enter the field of monetary economics and monetary policy.

In Sweden, monetary growth arises primarily from the government budget deficit and from the way it is financed. Bank lending is not excessive and is a comparatively small factor. Like other small open economies, Sweden has occasionally experienced private foreign-exchange outflows, which have resulted in residual changes in the money stock. Because of this effect, domestic credit expansion is a more meaningful aggregate than the money supply, which has little meaning as a target for this type of economy.

We do not target the monetary base, either. The banks are normally in a debt position with respect to the central bank, and short-term interest rates are mainly governed by the interest rate that is charged for bank borrowing in the central bank. This method differs from the methods used in countries that target monetary aggregates. However, I wonder if the realities are so very different. Interest rates are the main factor in the field of monetary policy. As Professor Ando correctly points out, when monetary policy is linked to monetary aggregates its effects are transmitted to the economy via interest rates.

In the implementation of interest-rate policy, Sweden does not focus exclusively on the government budget deficit and the way it is financed. The central bank also takes into account the interest costs for enterprises and the effect of these costs on real investment. Here there is a dilemma. Higher interest rates help the government to raise revenues in the private markets, but at the same time they hamper real investment and business activities (i.e., real growth). Big government budget deficits crowd out industry via high interest rates.

Growing profitability and low real investment have led to a high level of liquidity within the Swedish business sector. Increasing economic activity could easily be accompanied by high wage increases. In the prevailing situation, price increases are due not to demand pull but to cost push; total demand is now low. To keep back the cost push factor and to avoid a demand pull in the future, an improved incomes policy would be an advantage.

It should not be taken for granted that a very high interest rate is always the best way to counteract the negative impacts of big government spending. At least in countries where an incomes policy is possible, adherence to high interest rates as the only means should be avoided. In Sweden, an incomes policy would undoubtedly reduce inflation and aid business enterprises in the task of expansion.

In Sweden, public-sector expenditures, the government budget deficit, and the structure of government borrowing would by themselves create a problem of credibility. Looking at these phenomena, no one would believe that inflation will be reduced further, yet there is still a belief that inflation can be brought down further. The prerequisite for such a development, however, is not thought to be still higher interest rates. The prevailing rates of 4 percent real interest for government borrowing and 5 percent for business-sector borrowing are looked upon as high enough. The belief in a further lowering of inflation is based on the way wage agreements are arrived at. Sweden has nationwide trade unions, which offer possibilities of reaching wage agreements that can lead to low wage increases. A strengthening of fiscal policy, a continuation of an interest-rate policy with modestly high interest rates, and an improved incomes policy could, I believe, keep inflation back and create an economic environment in which the business sector could get a fair chance to expand.

Comments

Yoshio Suzuki

The world economy seems to be in the middle of its long struggle to overcome the stagflation from which it has suffered during the last decade. Concerted disinflationary policies implemented by major industrial countries since 1979 seem to have succeeded in dampening the inflation that originated in the late 1960s. However, high rates of unemployment caused by severe restraining policies still remain in these countries. Under these circumstances, the next steps that we should take are to get out of this synchronized worldwide recession and to achieve sustainable growth without rekindling inflation. Without finishing these tasks, we cannot say that we have overcome stagflation.

It seems to me, and maybe to most participants in this conference, that the world economy has begun to recover gradually since the beginning of this year (1983). However, the character of this recovery is not yet clear. Is this recovery led by the policies taken by industrial countries' governments, or is it caused by the market mechanism reacting to declining inflation rates? The idea of a policy-led recovery is that the government sector, an engine of expansion, absorbs most of the domestic private savings by issuing a large amount of government bonds accommodated by monetary policy and disburses these funds through public expenditures, tax cuts, and interest subsidies to the private sector. In this case, the economy would continue to expand in spite of the persistence of high real interest rates. In contrast, spontaneous recovery, in my definition, means that the private sector becomes the autonomous engine of the recovery; that is, deceleration of the inflation rate cuts wage increases, interest rates, and oil prices, eliminates inflationary expectations and future uncertainty, and increases real money balances. All these effects will improve the profit condition of business corporations, pick up their investment, and finally boost individual consumption and housing construction. The critical point of this spontaneous process is the decline of interest rates in the early stage of recovery. Without a decline of interest rates, this type of recovery will not be sustained.

Actually, the present recovery of the world economy seems to me a mixture of policy-led and spontaneous recovery, and the weights of these two aspects are different from country to country. The recovery of the United States seems to me the typical policy-led recovery. Professor Tobin pointed out the active role of accommodative monetary policy taken by the Federal Reserve since the autumn of 1982, and Professors Ando and Sargent referred to the effects of expansionary fiscal policy being implemented by the U.S. government. I understand that some spontaneous aspects are observed in the present U.S. economic recovery; however, those autonomous aspects are much stronger in West Germany, the United Kingdom, and Japan.

Then what are the appropriate policy responses to each of these aspects of the recovery? With respect to the policy-led recovery in the United States, Professor Tobin proposed more expansionary monetary policy. On the contrary, Professor Sargent pointed out that this recovery will not be able to continue without changing the present policy mix. Sargent's argument is that a policy mix of disinflationary monetary control and fiscal expansion with a large public-sector deficit is inconsistent, so that either of the two policies should be abandoned.

Not all government deficits are necessarily inflationary or harmful to the economy. In growing economies in which the growth rate is higher than the interest rate, a substantial amount of the public-sector deficit can be financed by both noninflationary base money and bonds without creating instability or inconsistency. Professor Sargent's assertion is, however, correct when the government is running deficits while the total output for the economy is not growing, or when, even though the economy is growing, the government deficit is so large that it is by itself greater than the total saving in the economy (at full employment). In such situations, an accommodative monetary policy would surely induce inflation, and if it were followed by tighter monetary policy, stagflation would follow. If my understanding is correct, Sargent's implicit answer for such a situation is that expansionary fiscal policy with large public-sector deficits should be eliminated by some kind of policy coordination.

Professor Ando insisted that the present policy mix should be changed and that a tax increase and an easier monetary policy are needed. His recommendation of these policy changes is based on three facts. First, the U.S. supply side has deteriorated because of the persistence of high real interest rates. These high rates reflect the expected crowding-out caused by an accumulation of government debt. Second, industrial countries other than the United States have been suffering as a result of the policy constraints imposed by the high-interest-rate policy of the United States. Third, the accumulation of external

debts by developing countries has been one of the main reasons for the instability of the international financial system. I agree with Professor Ando's
reasoning. The present policy-led recovery in the United States will not necessarily lead to sustainable worldwide growth unless the interest rate is lowered
below the growth rate.

The next point we have to discuss is appropriate policy responses to the
spontaneous recovery. Judging from the papers presented to this conference
and the discussions so far, most of participants seem to accept the following
two hypotheses: that the long-run Phillips curve is vertical and that the
formation of inflationary expectations in the shorter run is not rational in the
strong form. As for the long-run Phillips curve, Professors Ando, Gordon,
Hamada, and Hayashi use the natural-rate-of-unemployment hypothesis in
their chapters. Under this hypothesis, the economy, once having received a
shock, will reach an equilibrium on a vertical Phillips curve sooner or later
without any demand stimulus, if the rate of inflation is low and stable, and if
no additional shocks occur. As for the formation of inflationary expectation,
Professor Ando uses not rational but adaptive price expectation, Professors
Hamada and Hayashi point out that the macro rational-expectation hypothesis
in the strong form is not supported empirically, and Professors Tobin and
Gordon seem negative to it. If expectations are adaptive, then it always takes
some time for the economy to return to an equilibrium on the vertical Phillips
curve.

There arises one big question: Should we wait until the economy automatically reaches equilibrium on the vertical long-run Phillips curve, or should we
stimulate the economy and control the path to equilibrium on the curve
through discretionary policy shocks? When Professors Tobin and Gordon
discussed [at the conference] how to control the path of nominal GNP or
nominal final sales, they preferred discretionary policies. Professor Ando also
seems to prefer demand stimuli. Professor Hamada said that he prefers the
combination of a more flexible budget and easier money for the present
Japanese economic situation. He also pointed out that some demand stimuli
are necessary. However, such a policy change should cause depreciation of the
real exchange rate of the yen because of the expected divergence of interest
rates between Japan and the United States. Depreciation of the yen would
surely cause price increases and a decline in output because of deterioration in
the terms of trade. In contrast, if the present policy is maintained, with a 7–8
percent rate of growth in M2 + CD, Japan's economy will recover and Japan
will be able to wait until idle capacities and resources are utilized, because
Japanese nominal and real prices and wages are very flexible and the adjustment to equilibrium on the long-run Phillips curve after an external shock will

be rather quick. If the present high interest rates in the United States decline because of decreased public-sector deficits, the yen will be appreciated. This will remove Japan's policy constraint, accelerate the present spontaneous recovery by improving the terms of trade, lead to a further decline in the inflation rate, and increase real income.

In conclusion, I suggest that the character of the present economic recovery and the appropriate policy responses are at the core of policy issues related to the overcoming of stagflation.

SUMMARIES

Summing Up

Yoichi Shinkai

I understand that my assignment is to extract a small number of common themes from chapters 3–8 and the discussions about them. This is a difficult task because the six papers are fairly voluminous and deal with many topics of interest. Whatever I may do, I will have done injustice to the authors and discussants. Anyway, I have taken the liberty of choosing only three common themes: the international monetary linkage, proposals for domestic monetary policies, and the monetary consequences of fiscal policy.

International Monetary Linkage

Let me first take up the topic of international monetary linkage, or the problem of interest-rate synchronization, as I will name it. I take up this topic first because I am most interested in it, but also because it seems to me to have been the most important topic of the conference.

Two of the chapters are concerned with the problem: Professor Darby's and Professor Amano's. I do not intend to summarize or discuss each chapter; this was left to our able discussants. Rather, I shall spend a minute mentioning the parts of the chapters I will not discuss. Both papers are well researched, and each contains many sections that I reluctantly have to ignore. Darby's chapter has a section on the finding that goods and securities are imperfect substitutes internationally. This finding will surprise no one, but it is reassuring to learn that the fact has been proved rigorously. I have to skip his long section on the analysis of monetary policy under fixed exchange rates, without implying of course that it is unimportant or uninteresting. Amano's chapter has fairly long sections on the evolution of exchange-rate econometrics. I am afraid I will have to skip this part, too, with the same apology.

I will thus be concerned primarily with monetary policy under flexible exchange rates. Comparisons with the fixed-rate regime may be interesting, but I will not discuss this aspect. As Lucas has argued, macro coefficients will be different under alternative regimes, and the comparison will be of limited applicability, though I have no intention of claiming that it is useless. For instance, Darby provides two interesting graphs (figures 5.4 and 5.5) showing that, over the two regimes, money has been almost neutral in the long run.

Now I turn to my main concern. Professor Darby is of the opinion that central banks "have certainly demonstrated their ability to pursue independent monetary policies." This assertion is based on his view of the role of the exchange rate as a shock absorber, as well as on the long-run neutrality of money. To quote him, "The basic idea is a simple one: An unexpected change in the interest rate at home relative to that abroad will induce incipient capital flows. ... In order for this capital outflow to be stanched, the exchange rate must rise [depreciate] sufficiently [so] that anticipations of later decreases [appreciations] in this variable reduce or eliminate the decrease in the interest-rate differential adjusted for expected depreciation."

Darby has qualifications, such as that this is only an impact effect and the subsequent adjustment process is not understood too well, but his main message is clear: The real-interest-rate differential is adjusted for by a (probably large) change in the exchange rate; capital flow is only incipient and no large capital flow will be realized. Though he does not say so explicitly, interest rates need not be equalized between the two countries. Hence his assertion that monetary policy can be autonomous under floating exchange rates.

Darby has some more things to say on this topic. He correctly notes that the exchange-rate adjustment will have a potentially severe impact on the trade sector. To remedy it, official intervention may be used at the cost of abandoning some of the autonomy of monetary policy. These are topics that should be discussed further, but I cannot pursue them here.

That under flexible exchange rates real interest rates need not move together between two countries is Darby's main point, if I am not mistaken. But is this the commonly held view? Professors Hamada and Hayashi assert otherwise, and one of Amano's main points is that there is an interest-rate linkage (though he does not distinguish between nominal and real rates).

The last two sections of Amano's chapter are concerned with monetary linkage (among other things). His method of analysis is that of dynamic simulations by means of two macroeconometric models, and the most useful pieces of information he reports concern the adjustment process of a monetary shock. Some of the pertinent findings (all for the float version) are that a cut in the foreign interest rate (easy money policy abroad) results in an appreciated exchange rate, a decrease in real GNP, and a decrease in the domestic interest rate (for the first three years); that inflation abroad can be broadly neutralized by exchange-rate appreciations; and that in the world model an increase in the U.S. interest rate results in a depreciation of the yen and a decrease in real GNP in Japan. Of these findings (there are many other findings, of course), the second is in agreement with the Darby paper and I find it reassuring. One may find a minor inconsistency between Amano's other two findings in that in the first a lower interest rate abroad decreases Japanese real GNP whereas in the third a higher U.S. interest rate has the same effect. This inconsistency is a minor one, I think, because I presume that in the simulation that leads to the first finding only the foreign interest rate is changed, but correctly the foreign activity variable should have been changed simultaneously. Anyway, I need not pursue this point further.

In my opinion, Amano's most noteworthy result is the interest-rate synchronization found in the case of a cut in the foreign interest rate. A change in foreign interest is partly absorbed by exchange-rate changes, as in the Darby paper. (This is confirmed by both the first and the third finding mentioned above.) However, the capital flow is not stanched. In the case of a sustained decrease in the foreign interest rate, table 6.5 shows that the long-term capital inflow (see case B) is substantial in the first year, in the sense that it affects the domestic interest rate. Hence the interest-rate synchronization and Professor Amano's conclusion that international capital mobility is "large enough to transmit the effects of foreign monetary disturbances to the domestic economy."

Does this result indicate that we cannot ignore the adjustment period after a foreign monetary shock? On impact the exchange rate may absorb the shock, but as time goes by do capital flows become significant? Since Professor Darby concedes that his clear-cut analysis is concerned with impact effects, I will have to conclude that subsequent adjustments are such that interest rates are, after all, linked internationally. Having said this, I am tempted to make one point about Professor Amano's result.

Table 6.5 indicates that when long-term capital flows in official reserves are increased by roughly the same amount in the first two years. In other words, as the foreign interest rate is reduced and the yen tends to appreciate, the monetary authority intervenes by "leaning against the wind." Why does it intervene? The answer will be that the Japanese authority has always behaved in this manner and the simulation merely traces this behavior. This I can agree to, but just for the sake of argument suppose the authority does not intervene. The yen will appreciate more than is indicated. Will the yen appreciate enough to stanch the capital inflow? I do not know, but I suspect that the inflow will be smaller and the interest-rate synchronization less pronounced.

Proposals for Domestic Monetary Policies

I have argued above that there is room for domestic monetary policies in countries other than the United States. Interest linkage may be present, but I venture to say that it is less strong than is commonly perceived if the authority is prepared to allow exchange rates to be fully flexible. Of course, exchange-rate changes will have effects on the traded-goods sector, as Professor Darby notes, and Professor Gordon counts it as one of the constraints on domestic monetary policies. This reminds me also of Professor Amano's emphasis on the effect of exchange-rate changes on domestic prices. The extent to which exchange rates constrain domestic monetary policy should be discussed further.

We have two chapters on domestic monetary policy, one by Professor Gordon and the other by Professors Hamada and Hayashi. The former is, like all Gordon's papers, highly readable. Moreover, the message is simple and forcefully presented (therefore it is all the more controversial), so that I hardly need to summarize it.

Professor Gordon has two policy recommendations: that monetary policy should be used to offset cyclical movements by targeting stable rates of increase in nominal GNP (or net final sales), and that, when the initial situation is one of severe recession, policy should aim at a soft landing to full employment (or to the natural rate of unemployment) through high rates of nominal GNP growth at first and slower rates later. These recommendations are based on his diagnosis of U.S. macro variables, which is that changes in M1 or the monetary base have not contributed much to the explanation of changes in nominal GNP and that inflation inertia has been strong and has not become weak recently.

Taken together, Professor Gordon's arguments are persuasive. Since I am no expert on the U.S. economy, and since I believe that Gordon's chapter will provoke lively discussions, let me raise just two points that come to my mind. One is concerned with the inertia of inflation. Professor Gordon argues plausibly that the inertia has not lessened recently. But is there no chance of the U.S. economy shifting toward greater price flexibility? When I ask this question, I have the United Kingdom in mind. As I recall a few studies of its wage-price scene, notably by W. Nordhaus, we were told that inflation in the U.K. is cost-push par excellence, with no demand role whatever. Then came Mrs. Thatcher, and we are told now that inflation there is much lower because of her restrictive monetary policy. If the extreme inertia of the U.K. can change, so may the American inertia. The other point is concerned with the effect of supply shocks. If my reading is correct, Professor Gordon's supply-shock variable is event-specific. Therefore, there is no way of assessing the numerical effect of a new supply shock. When a new supply shock occurs, is he, or are Federal Reserve economists, in a position to calculate an optimal GNP path that should be pursued?

I turn next to the contribution of Professors Hamada and Hayashi. It is the largest chapter, and very rich in descriptive and statistical material on the Japanese monetary scene. This material will be very useful to interested economists, especially non-Japanese ones. The chapter also has two technical sections, on the money demand and the short-run neutrality of money. It is difficult in summarizing to do justice to all the aspects of the chapter. I have to be very selective, as I had to be with the other chapters.

One interesting finding of Hamada and Hayashi (table 4.4) is that the monetary base has not necessarily contributed to the explanation of M2, and that lending by banks seems to explain M2. The former may be contrasted with Gordon's finding; the latter is consistent with the often-made assertion that Japanese monetary institutions are well represented by the credit paradigm.

I was interested in the short-run neutrality tests. Though I have no time to go into the details, I cannot help making two observations on the tests. Of the two tests, the authors seem to prefer the latter, the results of which are summarized in table 4.11. This test rejects the neutrality hypothesis, the hypothesis that only unanticipated money affects real output. The results are plausible and will no doult please central bankers. However, this is not equivalent to the effectiveness of anticipated money. An equivalent statement must be that something other than unanticipated money affects output.

The first test used by Hamada and Hayashi does reject the hypothesis that anticipated money has no influence on output. But does it really show that anticipated money affects real activity? Though I must confess I am not compctent enough to appreciate the technical method used, it seems to me that the test only shows that real output is correlated with its past values and/or past reserves (or exchange rates). However, since similar methods have been employed by other prominent economists, perhaps I should not press my point too hard.

The two observations above are meant to call into question the conclusion drawn by Hamada and Hayashi that the empirical results "suggcst the effectiveness of anticipated money." [Note: Since the phrase originally quoted here by Shinkai was eliminated by Hamada and Hayashi in a revision, we have substituted an alternative quote that, in our opinion, serves the same purpose.—Eds.] I have just suggested that the conclusion is not proved rigorously, but this is not an important point. My more important question is this: Since the authors emphasize that Japanese wages and prices are flexible, why is discretionary monetary policy justified? I recall that Professor Gordon based his discretionary policy on the inflation inertia in the U.S. economy.

As specific policy recommendations for the present Japanese economy, Hamada and Hayashi suggest that fiscal policy should not be tightened (though they do not favor an easier budget) and that monetary policy should aim at lower interest rates, given the recommended fiscal stance. Since Japan is not out of recession yet, their recommendation may be likened to that of Professor Gordon, in spirit if not in specifics. I presume many people will agree with the Hamada-Hayashi policy mix. It implies a large budget deficit, though. The long-term interest rate will stay high unless easier monetary policy is implemented. To reduce the long-term interest rate, do they recommend an open-market purchase by the Bank of Japan of outstanding treasury bills? They are not specific on this point, but if this is the course they have in mind we are confronted with the possibility of the monetization of large government deficits. This topic is discussed by Professor Sargent. I now turn to it.

Monetary Consequences of Fiscal Policy

I would like to summarize the Sargent and Ando papers under this heading. What I have in mind is, of course, the possible effects of large budget deficits on interest rates and inflation.

Professor Sargent's chapter addresses this topic almost exclusively, though he has little to say on interest rates. His paper is unusually readable (not least because of its moderate length), and his message is clear, so my summary can be brief. (This does not mean that there is no complaint. His analogies to American football are all Greek to non-Americans. A large number of definitions of game-theory jargon may be counterproductive. But after the third section the going is smooth.)

Sargent is concerned with the problem of whether budget deficits lead to inflation. In the Ricardian regime where all deficits are financed by the floating of treasury bills there is no threat of inflation, but in this regime the maximum amount of outstanding public debt is given. As Sargent says, it is given by "the prospective government surpluses that the economy can support." Such surpluses will presumably be small, given political realities, and may even be nonexistent. Then the Ricardian regime cannot be sustained. When it is the case, there may ensue a battle of wills between the treasury and the central bank. The former is faced with political realities and wants to raise the "inflation tax" by having the latter monetize at least part of the deficits;

the latter is concerned about inflation and wants to have the treasury decrease the deficits. This aspect of the coordination of fiscal and monetary policies, Professor Sargent argues, is unstable (a game of "chicken") and produces uncertainties that may keep the interest rate high.

Professor Ando seems to have much the same perception of the problem. His chapter is also concerned with other topics—the estimation of the natural rate of unemployment and the proposals for short-run monetary policy are very interesting examples—but I will skip those and focus on his discussion of the effects of prospective budget deficits.

After invoking the Domar theorem on the relation between GNP and debt growth, Ando writes: "As the lower interest rate stimulates aggregate demand and output, the structure of the current set of policies is such that, even at an actual rate of unemployment close to the natural rate, the expected deficits of the federal government remain very large, and the rate of interest must be moved up enough to keep the economy from being stimulated beyond the point at which the rate of inflation will again accelerate. The market real rate of interest at that point is quite likely to be substantially above the rate of growth of output, and hence the deficit problem of the federal government will be difficult to solve and likely to deteriorate rapidly."

Professor Ando is also concerned with the effects of the high U.S. interest rate on other industrial countries, and most notably their effect on the external-debt problem of less developed countries. This is related to the problem of international interest linkage discussed above. Another important point he raises is that the high interest rate discourages productive investments. Though he does not mention it explicitly, there can be one way out of the situation. A substantial capital inflow (every year) from Japan to the United States will lead to a lowering of the U.S. interest rate and may reduce the Japanese budget deficit. However, this implies a substantial Japanese trade surplus with the United States, and it will not be sustainable politically.

Both Sargent and Ando have the U.S. economy in mind. As a Japanese, I cannot help applying their framework to the Japanese fiscal-monetary scene. The Japanese budget deficit is of the order of 5 percent of GNP. A recent EPA calculation indicates that the full-employment deficit is of the order of 3–4 percent of GNP. And there is no prospect of substantially closing the deficit in the near future. Does this mean that the Ricardian regime we are now in will be in trouble? At least there is a good chance of observing a game of "chicken" between the Bank of Japan and the Japanese treasury.

As I mentioned above, Professors Hamada and Hayashi do not seem to be worried about the outcome. They assert that the Bank of Japan has attained its autonomy. I for one am very happy to find the two experts confident on this matter. In the future battle of wills it may be the treasury that chickens out, but there are quite a few persons who are worried that the outcome may be the other way round. This is going to be a grave issue not only in United States but also in Japan and in other countries.

Discussions on the Three Themes

This section summarizes the discussions at the conference on the three themes I have extracted from the six chapters I have discussed.

The first topic is concerned with the autonomy of national monetary policy under floating exchange rates. If the U.S. real rate of interest is high, does this prevent the monetary authority of Japan, say, from pursuing a low-interest-rate policy? There was lively discussion on this topic, and it seems to me that two separate issues emerged.

One was whether the Japanese monetary authority can lower Japan's interest rate if it allows the exchange rate to be fully flexible. I call this issue "private-sector linkage." Professor Darby seems to be of the opinion that Japan can accomplish this, and I summarized his view above. I think some of us are of the same opinion. Mr. Axilrod argued that this should be the case. Mr. Rich told us that the experience of his country, Switzerland, testifies to the same view.

On the other hand, Professor Amano's simulation results indicate that when the U.S. interest rate is raised the Japanese rate will rise also. When I wrote my summary on international monetary linkage (above), I misunderstood the transmission mechanism of his model. I thought, incorrectly, that capital flow and official intervention have to do with interest-rate linkage. Professor Amano told us in his reply to a discussant that the main route is through an exchange-rate-depreciation-induced inflation that brings about a rise in the Japanese interest rate. Now it seems to me that if the yen were to depreciate fully, the interest rate would rise more than in the case of intervention. I may be mistaken again, but his model seems to indicate that "private-sector linkage" does exist. I recall that some participants were of the same opinion. So I submit that there is as yet no agreement on this issue.

The second issue is this: Even if there is no private-sector linkage, there can be interest-rate linkage through the action of the monetary authority. It may intervene to prevent exchange-rate depreciation, or it may keep the interest rate high to prevent depreciation. Why does it do this—to create interest-rate linkage, so to speak? Professor Darby mentioned a consideration of the burden on the traded-goods sector. Other discussants, Mr. Caranza for example, mentioned the fear of imported inflation. I am not sure that this issue was discussed fully. Take the case of Japan again. Is the threat of imported inflation serious? It seems to me that our experience after the second oil crisis testifies against this notion. Mr. Freedman mentioned the case of France. After hearing Mr. Raymond's comment, however, I wonder whether France could have succeeded in expanding her economy without inflation if the U.S. interest rate had been lower. My remarks are meant to stimulate further discussions in which I hope that private-sector linkage and linkage through policy actions will be distinguished.

Let me turn to the topic of domestic policy proposals. On this topic, two issues that I think can profitably be pursued further are inflation inertia (to borrow Professor Gordon's words) and the state of our economic knowledge.

If I am not mistaken, Professor Gordon based his proposal for discretionary policy (soft landing) on U.S. inflation inertia. I presume that even if he were content with a monetary target, he would still propose some discretion on this ground. On the other hand, Professors Hamada and Hayashi say that Japanese inflation inertia is much less pronounced now. They nevertheless propose a discretionary policy mix for Japan. I wonder what are the opinions of the participants as to the relation between inflation inertia and the exercise of discretion on the part of policy makers.

The issue of the state of our economic knowledge is puzzling to me. If I am not mistaken, quite a few discussants criticized the Gordon proposal on the ground that we do not know enough about our economy to calculate the optimal path over 10 years. Mr. Axilrod, Mr. Dudler, and Professor Darby are among them. Professor Gordon seems to be moderately optimistic on this point, and he writes also that some errors will be of little consequence given the inertia. I presume on the other hand that some participants are of the opinion that our knowledge provides us with enough information. A third position is that of Professor Friedman, if I understood him correctly. He argued that the incentives of the policy makers are more important than the state of knowledge in proposing a policy rule. So where do we stand? What is the state of our economic knowledge, and what is its relation to the macro policy proposals? I would like to learn more on this issue.

My third topic is the monetary consequences of fiscal deficits. In his discussion of the Hamada-Hayashi paper, Mr. Norton raised this issue and wondered if the Hamada proposal of a flexible budget policy might not lead to large deficits and higher interest rates. And of course Professors Sargent and Ando, whose views were summarized above, addressed the issue directly. There were objections to their views. Some participants felt that, given the proper growth policy, fiscal deficits can be reduced and/or the interest rate can be brought down relative to the growth rate. So this is an unsettled issue, and I am curious whether the point raised by Professors Sargent and Ando is relevant to the United States, Japan, and other countries. If the answer is yes, then there comes the question of what to do about it. There were arguments that for the foreseeable future government debt can be absorbed by the financial markets. To this Professor Sargent countered that this also depends on the future prospect of deficits. But the main issue here is the coordination of fiscal and monetary policies. Some fundamental points were raised by Professor Friedman and others. This is also related to the international coordination of national macro policies. Some representatives of the developing countries had something to say on this issue from their perspective, which was very useful. It seems to me, then, that there is room for further discussion on this topic.

Concluding Comments

Alexandre Lamfalussy

Let me begin by thanking the Bank of Japan for organizing this meeting. A dialogue between central banks and academic economists on current monetary-policy issues could not have come at a more opportune time—a time when, as I shall argue in a moment, an unusual combination of circumstances presents a major challenge to both policy makers and academics.

On a more personal note, I have particularly appreciated this opportunity to meet a number of central-bank economists from the Pacific area. For someone who has just taken a crash course (in more than one sense) on Latin America, this was a healthy reminder that neither the developing world as a whole nor the newly industrialized countries form a homogeneous lot.

My co-rapporteur has bravely and generously agreed to perform the difficult job of summing up our discussions properly, thus leaving to me the lighter task of presenting a few themes in my concluding discussion. These themes naturally reflect my own thoughts, biases, and prejudices (but, one hopes, also my experience) on the subject matter of our conference, which is monetary policy *in our times*.

The main point I should like to elaborate on and then to illustrate is that we find ourselves today in a situation for which there is no meaningful historical precedent. We are, therefore, navigating in uncharted waters, faced with the dilemma of choosing between two courses of action: on the one hand, "adhocry" (*"naviguer à vue,"* as it was expressed some years ago by a prominent French statesman), which may seem to some of you intellectually unsatisfactory as well as risky in its longer-term consequences, and, on the other hand, the rigid application of theoretical constructions derived from observations in times and places that, in the eyes of some others gathered in this meeting, bear no recognizable resemblance to current circumstances.

When I speak about the lack of meaningful historical precedent, I am not saying, of course, that there are no historical precedents for many of the current characteristics of the world economic scene. Inflation is not a new thing; neither is recession. There have been many instances in the past of domestic and even international financial fragility. What seems radically new to me is the simultaneous emergence of all these (and some other) problem areas in a world that has reached an unprecedented degree of "real" and financial integration at a time of considerable political instability. The result is a highly unstable and potentially explosive mixture. Let me spell this out in a few words.

As regards the "real" economy, the most obvious problem in the OECD countries is stagflation. Restrictive monetary policy has led to a sharp decrease of inflation rates in a number of countries, but who would dare to claim, with inflation inertia being what it is, that the war against inflation has been won? Recovery is underway in the United States and perhaps also in some European countries, but who can disregard the facts that the OECD countries' growth trend has been disappointing for almost a decade (and we do not really know why), that capital formation has fallen to levels that threaten to undermine our future growth potential, and that prospects for reducing unemployment are slim? One needs a solid dose of optimism to believe that further restraining the growth of monetary aggregates will quickly overcome inflation inertia and that at the same time the normal working of market forces will somehow push our economies back onto a more satisfactory growth path. Unless you believe both these things, you are bound to raise some questions about the proper stance of monetary policy in these circumstances, especially in countries with high structural public-sector deficits.

The industrial countries' stagflation problems have to be set against developments in the rest of the world economy and, in particular, in the less developed countries. As a result of a growing interlinkage between all parts of the world through trade flows, developments in the industrial world and the LDCs are interacting. The good news of the last 10–15 years has been the takeoff into diversified industrial growth of a number of LDCs, notably in Latin America and in the Pacific area, but this has added a "structural" dimension to the problems faced by the industrial countries. Conversely, the anti-inflationary policies undertaken by the latter have played a significant role in bringing LDC growth to an abrupt halt.

On the monetary-financial scene within the industrial countries the accelerating pace of financial innovations has not made it easier, to say the least, for the monetary authorities to implement monetary policy effectively. We do not know with any degree of precision what are the driving forces behind these innovations: the use of particular techniques of monetary control (such as non-interest-bearing reserve requirements)? deregulation? the high and variable rates of inflation? interest-rate volatility? other forms of uncertainty? Whatever the reasons, financial innovations create two kinds of interconnected problems for monetary management: first, an identification problem (which is particularly severe in those countries that rely on the short-term targeting of a single monetary aggregate); second, the problem of assessing the impact of new financial techniques on the transmission mechanism (for instance, the implications of floating-rate lending). With both these problems on your hands, you will have a difficult time in deciding whether a marked shift in velocity is reversible or whether it is once for all. You may even wonder whether, in any meaningful sense, velocity has changed.

The international financial scene has been dominated by increasing integration, perhaps even more so than the field of trade. Two manifestations of this integration deserve to be pointed out. First, as a result of the high degree of freedom permitted to capital flows between the main financial centers, monetary impulses emanating from one of the countries (and in particular from the largest of them) are quickly transmitted to the others via interest-rate and/or exchange-rate developments. Contrary to earlier expectations, floating exchange rates do not seem to ensure freedom of action for domestic monetary management, since monetary authorities cannot disregard the cost-push inflationary impact of currency depreciation; one should bear in mind the German dilemma in 1981–82, which seems now to be reappearing. Second, since 1973 Western commercial banks have come to play a decisive role in balance-of-payments financing, in particular vis-à-vis the LDCs. As a result of this development, the LDCs' external debt has acquired a maturity profile strongly biased toward the short end, their interest charges tend to vary dramatically with the fluctuation of short-term interest rates, and their ability to finance future current-account deficits depends critically on the banks' readiness to pursue international lending. For the banks, the consequence is that their international exposure has reached an unprecedentedly high level. This is true irrespective of the way international exposure is measured: in the share of external claims in total assets, in claims on individual countries in comparison with equity; and, for the non-U.S. banks, in the share of assets and liabilities denominated in foreign currency in the total balance sheet. On top of this, a number of banks have become dependent on the interbank market for the provision of loanable funds.

The fact that we live today in a multi-polar world plagued by a succession of political tensions has a major bearing on monetary policy, both domestic and international. Bretton Woods worked as long as the United States remained unquestionably the dominant economy and the power center of the non-communist world. This is not true any longer; hence the difficulty of coordinating monetary policies (whatever this may mean) and, *a fortiori*, of seeking to establish a new world monetary order (whatever this, too, may mean). International tensions or conflicts have become numerous: East-West, North-South, intra-West, intra-East, intra-South. The Yom Kippur war, events in Iran, and the Iran-Iraq war (by triggering or entertaining the oil-price explosions), and the Polish crisis and the Falklands conflict (by sharpening the banks' awareness that country risks are not negligible), have all had major impacts on the world economy and on international finance. All these events were "exogenous" shocks that could not be disregarded by policy makers.

It was in this environment that, around 1979, the largest Western industrial countries embarked upon a policy of disinflation, mainly by applying restrictive monetary policy. Therefore, the question they have faced over the last year or so and are still facing today is not whether and how to start fighting inflation. Nor is it how to keep their economies on a steady, noninflationary growth path—we are far from this happy state. Most Western countries find themselves at present right in the middle of a process of disinflation; the question their monetary policy makers are facing is how to get them from here to there—in other words, how to pursue this process without exposing their countries, en route, to the risk of some nasty accident.

The accident one has in mind is, of course, a financial crisis. Signs of domestic financial fragility appeared in some countries in 1981–82. I will not dwell on this, but will say something on the international aspects of financial fragility and its implications for the monetary policy conducted by the major industrial countries.

The story is by now sufficiently well known to allow me to be sketchy. From around the mid 1970s on, some of the Eastern European countries and a number of LDCs (mainly the NICs) started accumulating an external debt (to a notable extent vis-à-vis Western banks) at a rate that in many instances would have become unsustainable even in a relatively favorable economic environment. You can call this overborrowing or overlending according to your particular standpoint; at any rate, I leave it to historians to tell us who bears the "responsibility." There is no doubt, however, that the disinflationary process of the OECD countries, through its sharp and strong impact on the debtor countries' export volumes, terms of trade, and interest charges, has brought forward dramatically "the moment of truth." Just one example: For the three largest Latin American debtor countries (Argentina, Brazil, and Mexico) the ratio of net external interest payments to the value of their exports shot up from 28 percent in 1980 to 51 percent in 1982.

At the same time the lending commercial banks were affected by the "regionalization syndrome," under the influence of the Polish crisis with regard to Eastern Europe and (to some extent) under the influence of the Falklands conflict and the Mexican election campaign with regard to Latin America. As a result, they stopped lending altogether to these groups of countries. Thus, a "stock problem" was added to a prospectively even more difficult "flow problem." The international exposure of the banks being what it is, the potential backlash of this whole process on the health of the banking industry can be easily visualized.

Some of you might, perhaps, wonder why monetary authorities should feel concerned by this chain of events. Why not let market forces take their course? I see at least three reasons for not sharing this view. First, there is the simple question of size: You cannot apply the same reasoning to the debt-servicing problems experienced by a whole continent as to the difficulties of a single (even a large) corporate borrower. There is no world government that could take care of the wider domino effects. Second, who can know with any degree of certainty which of the debtor countries experience "merely" liquidity problems, as opposed to long-run inability to service debt? Finally, a sovereign country is not a private corporation: Banks cannot get part of their claims back by cutting it into pieces, as they can with a private corporation. The technical advantages of a bankruptcy are, to say the least, doubtful.

It is against this background that the authorities of the Western countries have had—and still have—to conduct their monetary policy. Faced at the same time with a marked slowdown of velocity, the interpretation of which was rendered more difficult by the financial innovations referred to a moment ago, they had to choose between two courses of action: to bring their monetary aggregates back into their target ranges, which would imply a corresponding increase in short-term interest rates, or to allow them to continue to overshoot, thus running the risk of reviving inflationary expectations. I cannot blame them for having adopted an intermediate course.

Let me suggest, by way of a conclusion, that policy makers and those academic economists who criticize their decisions enter into a pact of mutual understanding. Practitioners should recognize that "ad-hocry" can have dangerous results (as it has in the past), that credibility does matter, and therefore that rules can be useful. In exchange, academics could perhaps acknowledge that the combined features of the present world economic situation present a challenge—not only a practical one to the decision makers but also an intellectual one to themselves.

Program of the Conference

Institute for Monetary and Economic Studies
Bank of Japan

First International Conference
"Monetary Policy in Our Times"

June 22–24, 1983
International Conference Hall, Keidanren Kaikan,
1-9-4, Otemachi, Chiyoda-ku, Tokyo, Japan

Program Committee

Ryuichiro Tachi, University of Tokyo (Chairman)
Koichi Hamada, University of Tokyo
Yoichi Shinkai, Osaka University
Hidekazu Eguchi, Bank of Japan
Yoshio Suzuki, Bank of Japan

Overseas Special Advisers

Milton Friedman, Hoover Institution
Franco Modigliani, Massachusetts Institute of Technology
James Tobin, Yale University

Purpose of the Conference

Since early 1970s, major industrial countries have been suffering from stagflation, i.e. the persistently high rate of inflation coupled with the stagnation
of economic activity. In addition, accumulation of fiscal deficits, the higher
interdependence of individual economies, the external/internal dilemma, and

ongoing financial innovation have become main factors complicating the implementation of economic policies in those countries.

Under these circumstances, policy makers and economists in industrial countries have been confronted with the following issues: (a) what kind of policy response would be desirable to overcome stagflation; (b) what role should monetary policy play among various economic policy instruments.

The purpose of the conference is to analyze and discuss problems concerning Monetary Policy in Our Times and to shed light on the key issues. It is envisaged to bring together leading academics at home and abroad and prominent economists of central banks as well as international organizations. Conference papers to be prepared by academics will be policy-oriented, covering some empirical analysis related to various experiences of major industrial countries in recent years, and designed to stimulate dialogue on broad policy issues between theorists and practitioners of monetary policy in various countries.

Wednesday, June 22

Session I (morning)

Chairman
Hidekazu Eguchi (Bank of Japan)

Opening Address
Haruo Mayekawa (Governor, Bank of Japan)

Keynote Speeches
Milton Friedman (Hoover Institution), "Monetarism in Rhetoric and in Practice"
James Tobin (Yale University), "Monetary Policy in an Uncertain World"

Session II (afternoon)

"The Domestic Aspects of Monetary Policy"

Chairmen
Robert Raymond (Banque de France)
Ahn Seung-Chul (Bank of Korea)

Coordinator
Kumiharu Shigehara (Bank of Japan)*

Papers:
Robert Gordon (Northwestern University), "The Conduct of Domestic Monetary Policy"
Koichi Hamada (University of Tokyo) and Fumio Hayashi (University of Tsukuba), "Monetary Policy in Postwar Japan"

Comments:
Stephen Axilrod (Federal Reserve Board)
Herman-Josef Dudler (Deutsche Bundesbank)
Charles Goodhart (Bank of England)
Marie-H. Lambert (National Bank of Belgium)
W. E. Norton (Reserve Bank of Australia)

Free discussion

*Coordinator also for Sessions III–V.

Thursday, June 23

Session III (morning)

"The International Aspects of Monetary Policy"

Chairmen
Rudolf Rhomberg (IMF)
Edgardo Zialcita (Central Bank of the Philippines)

Papers:
Michael Darby (University of California, Los Angeles), "Monetary Policy in the Large Open Economy"
Akihiro Amano (Kobe University), "Approach to Exchange Rate Determination"

Comments:
Charles Freedman (Bank of Canada)
Cesare Caranza (Bank of Italy)
Georg Rich (Swiss National Bank)
H. H. van Wijk (Bank of Netherlands)

Free discussion

Friday, June 24

Session IV (morning)

"Policies to Overcome Stagflation"

Chairmen
P. W. E. Nicholl (Reserve Bank of New Zealand)
Lin See Yan (Bank Negara Malaysia)

Papers:
Thomas Sargent (University of Minnesota), "Reaganomics and Credibility"
Albert Ando (University of Pennsylvania), "Coordination of Monetary and Fiscal Policies"

Comments:
Sylvia Ostry (OECD)
Richard Davis (Federal Reserve Bank of New York)

Erik Karlsson (Sveriges Riksbank)
Yoshio Suzuki (Bank of Japan)

Free discussion

Session V (afternoon)

Summing-up and General Discussion

Chairmen
Frank E. Morris (Federal Reserve Bank of Boston)
Ryuichiro Tachi (University of Tokyo)

Summing-up:
Alexandre Lamfalussy (BIS)
Yoichi Shinkai (Osaka University)

Free discussion

Participants

Ahn Seung-Chul
Bank of Korea

Akihiro Amano
Kobe University

Albert Ando
University of Pennsylvania

Stephen H. Axilrod
Board of Governors, Federal Reserve
System

Cesare Caranza
Banca d'Italia

Michael R. Darby
University of California, Los Angeles

Richard G. Davis
Federal Reserve Bank of New York

Hermann-Josef Dudler
Deutsche Bundesbank

Hidekazu Eguchi
Bank of Japan

Charles Freedman
Bank of Canada

Milton Friedman
Hoover Institution and University of
Chicago

Charles A. E. Goodhart
Bank of England

Robert J. Gordon
Northwestern University

Koichi Hamada
University of Tokyo

Fumio Hayashi
Tsukuba University

Erik L. Karlsson
Sveriges Riksbank

Ryutaro Komiya
University of Tokyo

Marie-H. Lambert
National Bank of Belgium

Alexandre Lamfalussy
Bank for International Settlements

Lin See Yan
Bank Negara Malaysia

Frank E. Morris
Federal Reserve Bank of Boston

Peter W. E. Nicholl
Reserve Bank of New Zealand

Chiaki Nishiyama
Rikkyo University

William E. Norton
Reserve Bank of Australia

Sylvia Ostry
Organization for Economic
Cooperation and Development

Robert Raymond
Banque de France

Rudolf R. Rhomberg
International Monetary Fund

Georg Rich
Swiss National Bank

Thomas J. Sargent
University of Minnesota

Yoichi Shinkai
University of Osaka

Kumiharu Shigehara
Bank of Japan

Slangor
Bank Indonesia

Yoshio Suzuki
Bank of Japan

Ryuichiro Tachi
University of Tokyo

Teh Kok Peng
Monetary Authority of Singapore

James Tobin
Yale University

Hirobumi Uzawa
University of Tokyo

H. H. van Wijk
Nederlandsche Bank

Chaiyawat Wibulswasdi
Bank of Thailand

Yu Guantao
People's Bank of China

Edgardo P. Zialcita
Central Bank of the Phillipines

Name Index